Motives for Language Change

This specially commissioned volume considers the processes involved in language change and the issues of how they can be modelled and studied. The way languages change offers an insight into the nature of language itself, its internal organisation, and how it is acquired and used. Accordingly, the phenomenon of language change has been approached from a variety of perspectives by linguists of many different orientations. This book brings together an international team of leading figures from different areas of linguistics to re-examine some of the central issues in this field and also to discuss new proposals. The volume is arranged in six parts, focusing on the phenomenon of language change, linguistic models, grammaticalisation, the social context, contact-based explanations and the typological perspective. It seeks to cover the subject as a whole, bearing in mind its relevance for the general analysis of language, and will appeal to a broad international readership.

RAYMOND HICKEY is Professor of Linguistics at the Department of English, Essen University, Germany. His main research interests are computer corpus processing, extraterritorial varieties of English (especially Irish English) and general questions of language change. In the first area he has published extensively and in the latter his most recent publications are *A source book for Irish English* (2002), and *Collecting views on language change* (special issue of *Language Sciences*, 2002).

Motives for Language Change

Edited by

Raymond Hickey

Essen University, Germany

CAMBRIDGE
UNIVERSITY PRESS

CAMBRIDGE UNIVERSITY PRESS
Cambridge, New York, Melbourne, Madrid, Cape Town, Singapore,
São Paulo, Delhi, Dubai, Tokyo

Cambridge University Press
The Edinburgh Building, Cambridge CB2 8RU, UK

Published in the United States of America by Cambridge University Press, New York

www.cambridge.org
Information on this title: www.cambridge.org/9780521135245

First published 2003
Third printing 2004
This digitally printed version 2010

A catalogue record for this publication is available from the British Library

Library of Congress Cataloguing in Publication data

Motives for language change / Raymond Hickey (editor).
  p. cm.
Includes bibliographical references and index.
ISBN 0 521 79303 3 (hardback)
1. Linguistic change. 2. Linguistic models. 3. Languages in contact.
I. Hickey, Raymond, 1954–
P142 .M68 2002
417´.7 – dc21 2002067362

ISBN 978-0-521-79303-2 Hardback
ISBN 978-0-521-13524-5 Paperback

Contents

Notes on the contributors

JEAN AITCHISON is Rupert Murdoch Professor of Linguistics at the University of Oxford. She is known for her many books on language change and on semantics, the mental lexicon and cognition. Of late she has published on the origin of language.

BERNARD COMRIE is Professor at the Max-Planck-Institute for Evolutionary Anthropology, Leipzig. He is a foremost authority on language typology and linguistic relationships. He is the author of a large number of books, including some on the description of verbal systems.

DAVID DENISON is Professor of English Language at the English Department of the University of Manchester. He has specialised in the diachronic development of the verbal system of English and from there concerned himself with questions of language change in general.

MARKKU FILPPULA is Professor of English Language at the University of Joensuu, Finland. He is known for his original research into questions of language contact (in the context of Irish and Scottish English) and into the role of dialect input in varieties of English.

RAYMOND HICKEY is Professor of Linguistics at the University of Essen, Germany. His main areas of research are Irish English (with regard to questions of language contact, shift and possible creolisation), socially motivated language change (in present-day Dublin) and typological change in Irish.

RICHARD HOGG is Professor of English Language at the English Department of the University of Manchester. He is known for his ground-breaking work in the analysis of Old English, particularly phonology, and is the editor-in-chief of the *Cambridge History of the English Language*.

GREGORY K. IVERSON is Professor of Linguistics at the University of Wisconsin-Milwaukee. He has done much detailed research into the phonological interpretation of well-known changes, offering new insights into these. His work covers a wide range of languages from German to Korean.

DAVID LIGHTFOOT is Professor of Linguistics at Georgetown University, Washington, DC. He is renowned for original work on diachronic syntax within the framework of generative grammar and has re-formed much of linguistic thinking on the manner in which language change is carried from one generation to the next.

PETER MATTHEWS is Emeritus Professor of Linguistics at the University of Cambridge, England. His work on Latin and his synthetical work on morphology and syntax along with his assessments of modern grammatical theory have given him an international reputation. He is also concerned with questions of language change.

APRIL MCMAHON is Professor of Linguistics at the University of Sheffield. She has produced acclaimed synthetical work on language change and contributed original research in the field of phonology, especially within the framework of lexical phonology.

JAMES MILROY is Emeritus Professor of English Language at the University of Sheffield. The pioneering work on social networks which he carried out in Belfast (with Lesley Milroy) established his reputation as one of the foremost sociolinguists today. Of recent years he has been concerned with language variation and change and with concealed notions of standardness in language.

FREDERICK J. NEWMEYER is Professsor of Linguistics at the University of Washington, Seattle. He is known for his acclaimed surveys of linguistics and linguistic theory, especially the development of generative grammar over the past few decades. He has also written assessments of different basic approaches to language analysis.

MALCOLM ROSS is Professor of Linguistics at the Australian National University, Canberra. He has devoted his linguistic research time to investigating languages in the south-west Pacific and has specialised in language contact as a factor in change.

JOSEPH C. SALMONS is Professor of Linguistics at the University of Wisconsin-Madison. He is known for original research into changes in early (Indo-)Germanic in northern Europe (particularly in accentual systems). Together with Gregory Iverson he has furthermore done research into the Nostratic question.

ELIZABETH CLOSS TRAUGOTT is Professor of English Linguistics at the University of Stanford, California. Her name has been, in recent years, primarily associated with grammaticalisation as a type of language change. Apart from much original research in this area she is known for work on English diachronic syntax and theories of semantics/pragmatics.

Acknowledgements

This book began as a volume intended to celebrate the scholar Roger Lass on the occasion of his sixty-fifth birthday in 2002. The response to an initial invitation to contribute was considerable and it soon became apparent that not all the projected papers could be accommodated within a single book. For this reason the editor, in consultation with Cambridge University Press, decided that the best way forward was to divide the group of contributions into a more general and a more specific set. Those contributions of a more general nature, which treated the theme of language change from a broader perspective, have been collected in the present volume. The other contributions, which touch on many issues of concern to Roger Lass in the course of his long and productive career, have appeared as a dedicated volume of the journal *Language Sciences*, entitled *Collecting views on language change* (2002, ed. Raymond Hickey). Readers interested in the questions presented in the present volume may consider consulting the special issue of the journal for other studies in a similar vein, dealing in particular, but by no means exclusively, with the history of English.

During the entire project the editor enjoyed considerable support from Cambridge University Press and it is his pleasure to acknowledge in particular the great help and practical advice which he received from the linguistics editor Dr Kate Brett. The criticism and suggestions of a number of anonymous readers were also welcome and have hopefully contributed to the linguistic content and orientation of the volume as a whole. A word of thanks goes as well to the linguistics team at the English Department of Essen University who provided much practical assistance with corrections of various kinds.

RAYMOND HICKEY
September 2002

The publisher has used its best endeavours to ensure that the URLs for external websites referred to in this book are correct and active at the time of going to press. However, the publisher has no responsibility for the websites and can make no guarantee that a site will remain live or that the content is or will remain appropriate.

Introduction

Raymond Hickey

A cursory glance at recently published books on linguistics shows that the theme of language change is as much an object of interest among linguists as it has ever been. In the history of the discipline the main concern has been with language reconstruction, in the classical Neogrammarian sense, and this achieved its clearest theoretical statement in Herman Paul (1975 [1880]). The nineteenth-century concern with the gradual and wholesale mutation of sound systems was to lead to dissatisfaction at the beginning of the twentieth century. With the establishment of the structuralist paradigm, first in Europe and then in America, the synchronic perspective dominated. The structuralist paradigm of the first half of the twentieth century was important in that it led to a shift in focus from phonology and morphology, typical of Indo-European studies, to encompass other levels of language. However, despite the theoretical reorientation introduced by Chomsky in the late 1950s, the majority of linguistic discussions were based on data from present-day languages. In the late 1960s the application of generative grammar to concerns in historical linguistics was heralded by Robert King's 1969 monograph on the subject. In the 1970s much activity arose in connection with diachronic syntax (Li 1975, 1977; Lightfoot 1979; see also Fischer, van Kemenade, Koopman and van der Wurff 2000 as well as Pintzuk, Tsoulas and Warner 2001). While disagreement was quickly evident, the main thrust of the research became immediately obvious: the concern was primarily with the principles of language change and only secondarily with language reconstruction (for a recent interpretation, see Durie and Ross 1996). This interest in the way languages change was engendered by works such as Lass 1980, *On explaining language change*. The title reflects the concern then and now: the illumination of the principles which determine the dynamic nature of language. This interest among scholars has continued over the past two decades.

The investigation of language change has taken place within certain theoretical frameworks. Two others should be mentioned here. The first is language typology, which with the project under Joseph Greenberg at Stanford University in the 1970s (see Greenberg 1978), experienced a great expansion of interest in the details of typology far beyond simple language classification. This interest

1

was soon to develop a diachronic dimension and since then studies in this field have been explicitly concerned with typological shifts. Among the more recent works broadly in this vein are Nichols (1992), Campbell (1998) and Croft (2000).

Some recent developments in linguistics are by their very nature diachronic. Perhaps the most salient of these is grammaticalisation theory which seeks to account for shifts in the formal status of linguistic elements throughout history, and in particular to make generalisations from data to typical pathways of language change (Hopper and Traugott 1993; Pagliuca 1994).

The second theoretical framework concerned with language change is of course that of sociolinguistics. From its beginning as an independent field within linguistics, established by the seminal work of William Labov in the 1960s, the issue of change resulting from the inherent variation in the social use of language was a central concern. As sociolinguistics was concerned with minute variation in present-day varieties of language, its attention was naturally drawn to linguists who were also concerned with small but observable change, that is with the Neogrammarians of the nineteenth century (Labov 1981, 1994, 2001).

The significance of sociolinguistics for the study of language change can hardly be overestimated. It led to the locus of change being established firmly with speakers (and not with a language system which of course can only be an abstraction of the knowledge of speakers). Sociolinguistics also established new standards in the methodology of data collection and data evaluation. Apart from extrapolating from present-day varieties to historical ones, there also arose a specific direction of historical sociolinguistics (Romaine 1982), a line of research which has been characterised by particular activity in the past two decades.

The rise of other new directions in linguistics led to their being applied to language change. This has been the case, for instance, with various developments in theoretical phonology. It is probably fair to say that every model of phonology, which has been developed in the past forty years, has been applied to various sets of intractable data from the history of English.

The chapters of the present volume are intended to reflect the areas of language and approaches to language change which are currently topical. The initial chapters are concerned with theoretical issues, such as the chapter by Peter Matthews on Chomsky's distinction between I and E language. Frederick Newmeyer deals in his chapter with a recurring issue in studies of language change, formal and functional motivation. The contribution by Jean Aitchison looks at metaphorical language and David Denison examines the progress of language change and its representation in S-curves. Richard Hogg looks at suppletion, especially with regard to established changes in the history of English.

There are two phonological studies on two central concerns in the history of Germanic sound systems, the major English vowel shift, treated by April McMahon, and umlaut, dealt with by Gregory Iverson and Joseph Salmons.

Among the models of language change which have of late been the object of great interest among linguists is grammaticalisation which, while reaching back to at least the beginning of the twentieth century, has been given a formal framework within which it is now interpreted. The chapter by David Lightfoot looks critically at grammaticalisation while that by Elizabeth Closs Traugott examines subjectification/intersubjectification and its role in speaker exchanges.

Two chapters in the present volume concern themselves specifically with spoken language and language change. The chapter by James Milroy sees the role of the speaker as central and Raymond Hickey examines the scenario of new dialect formation with regard to the genesis of later varieties of English outside Britain (New Zealand English).

The importance attributed to contact in studies of language change has been addressed by many scholars in recent years (see Thomason 2001), some backgrounding contact as a factor in change (Lass 1997) and others demanding an objective reassessment of language contact. The chapter by Markku Filppula returns to the contrast between internal and external factors, this time with much data from Irish English. Malcolm Ross brings his interest and knowledge in this sphere to a consideration of contact in the prehistory of Papuan languages.

Broader questions of language organisation and typology are reflected in two chapters in this book, one by Bernard Comrie on typology and reconstruction and the other on reanalysis by language learners and typological change by Raymond Hickey.

When producing a book on such a popular topic as language change, it is difficult to strike on a title which has not been used before. Furthermore, the title is naturally intended to reflect the contents of the book. The present title was chosen after much deliberation and consultation with others. The editor feels that it reflects the common strand of thought which runs through the chapters. However, there is one reservation which should be made explicit here: the word *motives* in the title implies a degree of agency which may not be quite the intention of each contributor. The use of *motives* here is intended in an inclusive sense: it covers internal and external forces in language change while also encompassing the behaviour of speakers, though usually on an unconscious level.

Among the many publications broadly located in diachronic linguistics there have been some in which an author or group of contributors have decided to stand back for a moment and take stock of what insights have been reached in the field, where disagreement exists and what questions are still in need of answering. The present volume has been conceived in this spirit and can hopefully contribute, to whatever extent, to our understanding of the subject.

REFERENCES

Campbell, Lyle. 1998. *Historical linguistics: an introduction.* Edinburgh University Press.

Croft, William. 2000. *Explaining Language change: an evolutionary approach.* London: Longman.

Durie, Mark and Malcolm Ross (eds.). 1996. *The comparative method reviewed: regularity and irregularity in language change.* Oxford University Press.

Fischer, Olga, Ans van Kemenade, Willem Koopman and Wim van der Wurff. 2000. *The syntax of early English.* Cambridge University Press.

Gerritsen, Marinel and Dieter Stein (eds.). 1992. *Internal and external factors in syntactic change.* Berlin: Mouton de Gruyter.

Greenberg, Joseph H. 1978. *Universals of human language.* 4 vols. Stanford University Press.

Hopper, Paul and Elizabeth Traugott. 1993. *Grammaticalization.* Cambridge: University Press.

Labov, William. 1981. 'Resolving the Neogrammarian controversy', *Language* 57: 267–308.

Labov, William. 1994. *Principles of linguistic change,* vol. 1: *Internal factors.* Oxford: Basil Blackwell.

Labov, William. 2001. *Principles of linguistic change,* vol. 2: *Social factors.* Oxford: Basil Blackwell.

Lass, Roger. 1980. *On explaining language change.* Cambridge University Press.

Lass, Roger. 1997. *Historical linguistics and language change.* Cambridge University Press.

Li, Charles (ed.). 1975. *Word order and word order change.* Austin, TE: University of Texas.

Li, Charles (ed.). 1977. *Mechanisms of syntactic change.* Oxford: Blackwell.

Lightfoot, David. 1979. *Principles of diachronic syntax.* Cambridge University Press.

King, Robert. 1969. *Historical linguistics and generative grammar.* Englewood Cliffs, NJ: Prentice-Hall.

Nichols, Johanna. 1992. *Language diversity through space and time.* Chicago University Press.

Pagliuca, William. 1994. *Perspectives on grammaticalization.* Amsterdam: John Benjamins.

Paul, Hermann. 1975 [1880]. *Prinzipien der Sprachgeschichte [The principles of language history].* Tübingen: Niemeyer.

Pintzuk, Susan, George Tsoulas and Anthony Warner (eds.). 2001. *Diachronic syntax: models and mechanisms.* Oxford University Press.

Romaine, Suzanne. 1982. *Socio-historical linguistics: its status and methodology.* Cambridge University Press.

Thomason, Sarah G. 2001. *Language contact: an introduction.* Edinburgh University Press.

Part I

The phenomenon of language change

1 On change in 'E-language'

Peter Matthews

In a view that is widespread among linguists, change in language is not simply change in 'speech': what is affected is 'a language', and by that is meant a system, at an underlying level, that in any community constrains the forms that speech behaviour can take. As a system changes so the speech in that community, which is partly determined by it, also changes. But a historian is not concerned directly with observed shifts in how people behave. We are seen instead as trying to explain how languages, as underlying systems, change from one state to another. We may speculate that they are subject to specific structural laws. We may posit laws of history by which changes in their structure have to follow one route rather than another. In this light, we develop theories in historical linguistics of a sophistication quite unheard of in most other fields of history.

The distinction between speech and language goes back to Saussure, and arguably beyond. In the terms, however, in which Chomsky has recast it, every individual speaker has what he calls an 'I-language', and the underlying changes are among I-languages developed by a changing population in successive periods. In any individual, the one formed in childhood will determine, in part, how that individual will speak; and that speech, in turn, will be part of the experience by which new members of the community form their own I-languages. When I-languages are different, we will expect to see shifts in the way a population speaks. In corresponding terminology, these will be shifts in an 'E-language': in a language as it is 'externalised'; but our primary concern is not, in this view, with E-language. I-languages are seen as subject to laws. In Chomsky's account, their structure is at its 'core' constrained by our genetic inheritance. For Chomsky himself, the central problem is then to explain how languages can vary. For historians who follow this lead, it is to explain how speakers in one period can develop an I-language different from the ones developed in an earlier period.

The answer must, in part, lie in the speech that they experience. Let us suppose, for example, that a word is borrowed from a neighbouring language. In Saussurean terms, this is an element in a new 'état de la langue'; in Chomsky's terms, there is at least an additional lexical entry in the minds of new speakers.

But how does it come to be there? The 'language' we are positing would not, at one stage, have included it. Therefore, to the extent that speech is determined by that system, it too would not have included it. But then, despite that, it would be borrowed by some speakers; others would follow their example; and, in time, it would become an element indistinguishable from others in the speech that children were exposed to. It would therefore become part of the 'language' as they came to know it; and this is again the system that would be reflected in their speech from then on. In such cases at least, it seems that, for the underlying system to be different, speech must change first. In Chomskyan terms, a difference in I-language would then follow from a difference in the experience on which its development is based.

A conclusion like this is again quite widely implied. But it is reasonable to ask, at that point, why a change in language has to be conceived of at two separate levels. The word, in cases like this, would be borrowed by some speakers, whose example would be followed by other speakers. These could as naturally include those of new generations. Why are changes not straightforwardly at just one level?

Let us turn for comparison to another field of social history. As speech changes so too, for example, do the things that people drink; and, once upon a time, no one in Britain drank tea. Therefore, if we must talk after the manner of linguists, we will say that the community's drinking habits were determined, in part, by an underlying system in which tea was not an element. Then some members came into contact with societies whose systems, we will say, were different, and, despite the one in which we say they were brought up, they acquired a habit of tea-drinking from them. This habit they brought home and introduced to other members of their own society. But these at first were people who, like them, would have to have been brought up to the earlier system. So, if they too started drinking tea, it would be because, despite that system, they were curious or it was recommended to them; because it was a new fashion; because they found they liked it. Such explanations bear directly on the behaviour of specific individuals, in response to that of other individuals. Then, at a later stage, some members of the community would be familiar with tea-drinking from their childhood. Therefore, if we still talk in the manner of linguists, we will say that their behaviour is constrained by a new system of drinking habits, in which tea, although in practice some might never touch it, had a place like that which it has had since. They would thus have 'internalised' a set of rules concerning times and circumstances in which it was drunk, what forms of silver or crockery were used in drinking it, and so on. But it is not at all clear why we should be obliged to talk in that way. Is it not sufficient to say simply that some people started to drink tea, at specific times or in specific circumstances, using specific kinds of vessel, and other people imitated them? This explanation is again in terms of the behaviour of individuals, in response to that of other individuals. What else is there, that we have to explain in terms of changes at an underlying level?

But when it comes to change in language, linguists do talk in just such a manner. The issue is an old one, with which Roger Lass, to whom this essay is dedicated, has long been familiar. But recent work, ostensibly at least Chomskyan, has raised it in what seems to be a new form.

Let us begin with Ian Roberts's conception of a 'step' in syntax. The context in which it was defined is that of Chomsky's theory as it developed in the 1980s, and the changes that were of special interest were those in which a parameter of 'Universal Grammar' could be seen as reset. These are, as Roberts put it, 'diachronic relations among I-languages' (1993: 159). An E-language was described, in contrast, as 'some set or corpus of sentences' (158), and another kind of relation is, accordingly, 'between the E-language of one generation... and the I-language of a subsequent generation'. A step, however, is a mere relation between E-languages. This is, as Roberts saw it, 'the traditional notion of change', and can involve 'the appearance of a new construction, or a significant change in the frequency of a construction, in a set of texts'. But when 'a language takes a new step' this does not 'necessarily imply' a change (in alternative terminology) in 'the grammar'. Changes in the 'traditional' sense are thus the nearest equivalent, in linguistics, of a change in actual habits of drinking. Their explanation must, in part at least, be independent of I-languages or 'grammars', since these may not change. But, of course, when such a step is taken, the experience of a later generation of speakers will be different. Therefore the 'grammar', as they develop it, may, in the light of their experience, be different also.

I will return to Roberts's formulation in a moment. But a theory of change in 'grammars' has also been developed, for some twenty years, by David Lightfoot. Since 1990 he too has appealed to Chomsky's theory of parameters; and, for most resettings, we must again envisage differences in the speech experienced by successive generations of children. These must be due to 'nongrammatical factors' (1999: 225). 'Some changes', more precisely, 'take place while grammars remain constant' (1991: 160), relating, as he put it, 'to the ways in which grammars are used rather than to their internal structure' (1991: 166). These might be 'explained by claims about language contact or socially defined speech fashions' (1999: 166) or, as in his first book on syntactic change, by 'foreign influence, expressivity and "after-thought"' (1979: 381). But, once they happen, changes in the speech that children hear may subsequently 'trigger' changes in the 'grammar' itself.

Two questions naturally arise. The first concerns the kinds of 'triggering' change we must allow for. In what ways, for example, can the speech of a community be influenced, independently of 'grammars' that its members are already said to have, by 'socially defined speech fashions'? What kinds of 'step', in

Roberts's definition, can be explained entirely by what Lightfoot calls a 'non-grammatical' factor?

Whatever the answer, these are changes that affect the speech of individuals, regardless of their 'grammars', in response to their perception of the speech of other individuals. It is therefore reasonable, again, to ask what other explanation is needed. What is a change in language other than, in Lightfoot's words, a change in 'socially defined speech fashions'?

The first question cries out for an answer. But, although such theories are ostensibly Chomskyan, it seems clear that the relation of E-language to I-language cannot be as Chomsky himself originally conceived it. In his account, the former was 'the object of study in most of traditional or structuralist grammar or behavioral psychology'; and, since different structuralists, for a start, did not define 'a language' in the same way, that is perhaps not wholly illuminating. But whatever the definition of E-language, it was 'now regarded as an epiphenomenon at best' (Chomsky 1986: 25). For Roberts, as we have seen, it was 'some set or corpus of sentences'; for Lightfoot, in a passage I have not yet cited, it is 'external linguistic production' (1999: 66). But it is of the essence of their theory that such external production, or the character of such sets of sentences, can change independently of 'grammar' or I-language. Therefore, if this is what Chomsky also meant by an E-language, it cannot be merely epiphenomenal.

If we grant this, we are left with a theory that in part at least is like the one developed by Eugenio Coseriu (1958) in the heyday of European structuralism. I have remarked on this parallel elsewhere (2001: 114f., 150f.), and will not labour it. But 'a language', in Coseriu's account, could be identified not only as a system, but as a system plus a set of 'norms' by which it is realised. The system of Latin included, for example, a *k* phoneme. But there were also norms by which it was realised, variably as, among other things, a front velar or a back velar. Change in 'a language' can then have its origin in individual departures from a norm. For example, a phoneme that was normally realised by a velar might sometimes have been realised, before front vowels, by an affricate. This might increasingly become a new norm; but, at that stage, such a change was still at the level of realisation only. Only later might the system itself change, as in the history of Romance, to a state in which the affricates realise a new phoneme.

In Coseriu's account the system was one of 'possibilities': it distinguished 'routes', or ways of speaking, that are 'open' to a speaker from others that implicitly are 'closed' (1962: 98). His examples were not from syntax; but the structures constituting an I-language will, in a similar sense, define a set of possible forms of sentences. Some arrangements of words, to speak in the most neutral manner, will be open and others closed, all else being equal, to the speaker whose language it is. But the frequency with which an open route is taken may then vary independently. A specific arrangement of words might come to be 'used', for example, much more rarely. This would be one kind of step in Roberts's definition: 'a significant change', in his terms, 'in the frequency of a construction'. In Coseriu's theory, it would again be a change in norms by which constructions are realised. But, like any such step, it affects the speech to which a child of a new generation is exposed. If the construction is rare they may no longer have sufficient 'evidence', from what they hear, that the possibility is open. Therefore they may take it to be closed; and, with whatever accompanying repercussions, the 'language' they develop may come to exclude it. In this way, changes in the frequency of constructions, due to no more than a shift originally in usage, may be claimed, in Lightfoot's terminology, to trigger 'catastrophic' changes at the level of the 'grammar'. As Coseriu had put it earlier, the norms that a community follows may change to the point at which a system 'overturns' (1962: 107).

To what extent, then, might E-language, as determined by I-languages and an accompanying set of 'norms', change independently of I-languages themselves? In Coseriu's account, a change in norms would be within the 'possibilities' determined by the system. Each construction would represent a 'possibility', just as, in a case he did discuss, a pattern of word formation (1962: 78–9). But the system itself did not determine the range of words formed in a certain way. It would be a matter of norms that, for example, a noun formed from *reasonable* is realised as *reasonableness* not *reasonability*. Nor might the system determine, for example, which verbs take specific patterns of complementation. That too might be a matter of norms, and that too might change independently. The system itself would then change when new 'possibilities' are added or old 'possibilities' disappear. For example, English did not at one time have a productive formation in -*ee* (*employee, trainee*, and so on); as soon as it did, the system had to be in a new state.

But is the generativist theory quite the same? A step, in Roberts's definition, can again be a change in the frequency of a construction. But it can also be the 'appearance' of a new one. Is this also a step that does not 'necessarily imply' a change in the 'grammar'? Roberts did not confirm at this point that it was. But, if it could be, it would be a change in norms that would itself change what was 'possible' for a speaker. Only in the next stage, when it would have affected the experience of new members of the community, might the 'grammar' come to allow it.

How then do these theories account for new constructions? One answer is that they might arise directly through a process of reanalysis. A new generation of speakers would accordingly be said to have developed a 'grammar' based on reinterpretation of the speech heard from their elders. They could also be said to follow indirectly, when a parameter is reset for other reasons. In Lightfoot's account, parameters are set in accordance with specific 'cues' in speech that children experience. If a cue becomes, for example, rarer they will be set differently by a new generation. This would then have repercussions; and the appearance of a new construction could in principle be one of them. But are these the only mechanisms that we must envisage? One 'nongrammatical factor', as we have seen, is 'language contact', and it is well known that, when languages are in contact, they may converge. There is no other way to explain a 'linguistic area' or *Sprachbund*. But what exactly is the process of convergence? Speakers said to have a 'grammar' of language A will be forced to communicate with ones who speak language B. To do so they may have, in the ordinary sense, to learn B. They may, in consequence, use words from B when they are speaking A: the nature of that mechanism is not in dispute. For convergence to be possible, it seems that they must also borrow new constructions from B. That would seem to involve a step in their E-language, independent of the 'grammar' of A that they will originally have developed.

Lightfoot has as yet said very little about how 'nongrammatical factors' operate. They are simply there because, for 'grammars' to change, the speech that children hear must, at least in many cases, change first. But, if we are on the right track, an E-language would be still less of an epiphenomenon. Frequencies can change independently, as we have seen, of I-languages. This could logically include the case in which a construction disappears: its frequency, that is, will be reduced to zero. If new constructions can enter speech directly so too could, for example, an extension in the range of words with which an existing construction is used. Why, then, is the 'traditional notion' of change, as Roberts described it in the passage with which we began, not in itself sufficient?

A follower of Chomsky might reply in two ways. The most likely answer is that I-languages instantiate, in part, a Universal Grammar. We know that this exists; therefore we know that I-languages exist, in abstraction from E-languages, in every speaker; therefore we need, in addition, a theory of change in I-languages. Some changes are, moreover, inexplicable unless this theory of a Universal Grammar is assumed.

I will return to this claim in the last part of this essay. But another reply is simply to insist on the distinction between 'languages' and 'speech'. If someone, for example, drinks tea they can literally be seen to do so; and, when others imitate them, their behaviour can be seen to be similar. The abstraction implied is minimal. But when different speakers use the same construction, what they say may literally be very different. We are therefore forced to talk of abstract structures that they have in common. In Chomskyan terms, they 'know' the language that they have acquired as children, and this 'knowledge', or I-language, must in principle be different from 'performance', or observed behaviour in 'using' it.

This form of answer can again be traced at least to Saussure. But how exactly would a new syntactic construction or new pattern of word order spread through a community? Some speakers, let us say, would 'have' the pattern. That means that it would be within the constraints of the 'grammar' as they knew it. Others would not 'have' it, and, as it spreads, their number would of course diminish. But who exactly would be 'using' it? Are they only those who would be strictly said to 'have' it? Its spread, in that case, would be limited to changes in the frequency with which they 'used' it, and the 'grammars' of a newer generation who would hear them. Or could it also be acquired, directly from their speech, by others who did not 'have' it? Such speakers would thus have knowledge that they had acquired in childhood of what forms of speech are possible and not possible – but then, in later life, would pick up further forms of speech that would extend it.

If so, we must ask how they are able to do so. A pattern or construction is an abstraction and, by the argument with which we started, it cannot be 'picked up' in the same way as, we said, behaviour like tea-drinking. It would seem then that a speaker could acquire a second form of abstract 'knowledge', additional to the 'knowledge' that is originally claimed to constitute a 'grammar'. The 'external production' of language, as E-language was defined by Lightfoot, would then reflect both.

It would be easy to find ways in which these different forms of 'knowledge' might be labelled. One way is to distinguish a speaker's 'active' competence in a language, as acquired in childhood, from an initially 'passive' knowledge of the speech of people who are encountered later. But this second form of knowledge would itself then come to exercise an 'active' influence on their own speech. I explored devices like this more than twenty years ago (1979: 51–66), as one hypothesis of 'idiolectal multilingualism'. Another way is to distinguish a 'core' knowledge, much as Chomsky distinguished it in the 1980s, from a 'periphery'. The former would again be fixed in childhood; but the periphery might in principle be open, therefore new things could be added to it later in a speaker's life. This would in essence be a variant of an idea that was fashionable, thirty years ago, in generative phonology. New rules or patterns could again be tacked on without change to mental structures that a speaker has already developed. They too would therefore be reflected in speech, and this, again, would be the speech heard by the children of a following generation.

Our question, however, was why 'knowing a language' should be seen as anything other than the state of having 'picked up' certain forms of speech. Why, again, do we not talk simply of one level of 'knowledge', both developing and expanding in the same way? A community's mastery of its forms of speech would then be attested equally by both the continuities and the changes in 'E-language'.

That is, I take it, Roberts's 'traditional notion' of change – that developed by Paul (1880) in particular. But the most likely riposte would again rest on the concept of a Universal Grammar. Although Chomsky's theory is not itself concerned with change in language, it has nevertheless to be admitted that, for anyone who accepts it, much of what I have said so far is likely to seem neither here nor there. I must therefore refer to another recent essay (1998) for a fresh rehearsal of the reasons why I cannot myself take it for granted. It might be claimed, however, that the arguments for it are not only those that Chomsky himself originally proposed. Thus, in the account as popularised in Lightfoot's latest book, a 'grammar' will again develop in response to a specific set of cues that children can identify in the speech to which they are exposed. But a single cue does not determine just one aspect of a 'grammar'. Instead it will determine a whole range of them; so, if the experience of one generation of children differs crucially in one respect from that of earlier generations, the 'grammar' they develop may change drastically. This change in the 'grammar' will be reflected in E-language as observed from then on, which will in turn change in what would otherwise be unexpected ways. We can explain them only if we posit that the relation between cues and 'grammars' is as Universal Grammar determines.

Lightfoot's examples are from the history of English, a field I know at best at third hand. I will therefore restrict myself to asking how far such an explanation could in principle be convincing.

Let us first assume, for the sake of argument, that Chomsky is right. According to the theory that he elaborated in the 1980s, the properties that distinguish languages are then reduced, as far as possible, to different settings of genetically inherited parameters. But single parameters would not determine single properties. In setting, for example, the 'null subject' parameter children did not merely develop a language with or without null subjects. The relation would instead be one of what biologists call 'pleiotropy', in which a setting might be expressed by several characters that, at first sight, seem quite unconnected. By a 'character' we mean, for example, a construction or some individual pattern of word order. It therefore seems that Lightfoot too has got to be right. A cue will 'trigger' the setting of a parameter; and, when its setting changes, this will affect, potentially at least, all characters by which it may be expressed. The appearance of new characters might then be no more than a repercussion, as I put it earlier, of a change whose causes, in the 'triggering' experiences of children, are quite different.

This is indeed a very powerful theory. But it is not clear that it is necessarily what Chomsky's theory leads us to expect. Nor is it clear how Lightfoot's theory would be other than invulnerable.

The first doubt is suggested directly by my allusion to pleiotropy. For it does seem likely that the relation between languages and Universal Grammar would be very complex. Certain languages might be identified as having, for example, characters *a, b* and *c*. We might therefore conjecture, still in terms of Chomsky's theory as it was in the 1980s, that this reflects, in part, a setting of a parameter P. But we might not then be worried by the discovery of other languages that have *a* and *b* but not *c*, or *b* but not *a* or *c*, and so on. We would simply conjecture that these differences reflect the setting of other parameters. The character identified as *a* might thus reflect a setting not of P alone, but of P and at least one other. The settings that are responsible for *b* and *c* would both be partly different. In this way we could account successfully for all the fine diversity of structures that is actually found. But it is less clear why historians should expect such structures to change suddenly and drastically. Could a single change in speech provoke a simultaneous change in many different parameters? If not, we might expect the changes we observe to be more gradual, as the expression of any that are reset is inhibited, at any stage, by that of others that have not been.

This is a question only; but it seems one that is at least worth raising. For if change were gradual, this would at best be a competing theory of what Winfred Lehmann, or Sapir before him, called 'drift'. One crucial change, relating to what Lightfoot calls a 'cue', would take place at the level of E-language. We would then expect that other changes of specific kinds should follow. But, of course, it would be easy to find explanations if they did not. Thus, in particular, some further 'nongrammatical factor', triggering change of a quite different kind, might be found to intervene.

But let us assume, in fairness, that the effect is instant. We would thus envisage crucial changes in cues; and, precisely because the expression of parameters is as complex as we have supposed, such a change, initially at the level of E-language, would then trigger changes, at the level of the underlying 'grammar', that cannot be other than pervasive. These will ensue directly in the 'grammars' of new members of the speech community. We should therefore expect their speech to differ strikingly from that of older members. We might also predict the same effects, in any other language, if the same cue were affected in the same way.

The problems then lie in the other factors that in principle could intervene. Let us suppose, for example, that a pattern *c* has formerly been common. That is in part because, we say, the older speakers have a 'grammar' that allows it. Then, for some extraneous reason, a new set of speakers form a 'grammar' whose parameters exclude it. Would we expect, in that case, not to find *c* in their speech? One possibility is that, in addition to a 'grammar' which excludes *c*, they might also be said to have one that allows it. This is again a hypothesis of 'idiolectal multilingualism', and, in a sophisticated version, we might again distinguish 'grammars' that develop in childhood, when an individual is in contact with a limited set of speakers, from subsidiary 'grammars' that develop in the course of wider contacts later. It might therefore be that younger speakers merely 'use' *c* less than older speakers, that they 'use' it most in 'accommodation' to older speakers, and so on. All the familiar effects of variation might thus be explained. But still, according to our hypothesis, there is a 'grammar' whose parameters have been reset; and, as more and more speakers have it, *c* will be doomed.

Such forms of explanation are explored by Lightfoot himself (1999: 92ff.). But another factor might again be the 'periphery'. In Chomsky's account, a part of each I-language follows from the setting of parameters: this was the 'core' as he defined it in the 1980s (1986: 147). Let us suppose, then, that our younger speakers have a 'grammar' whose core will exclude *c*. But the core of a 'grammar' is not claimed to be the whole of it: it is for that reason in particular that I have continued to put Lightfoot's term in inverted commas. Could it be claimed then that the periphery of their I-language nevertheless allows *c*?

It is hard to know the answer, since the scope of a 'periphery' has not been explicitly constrained. We were told originally that it covers 'exceptions', such as irregular morphology or idioms. For Chomsky's purposes, there was indeed no motive to say more. But constructions can also be exceptional. In English there are, for example, scattered patterns of inversion: after *neither* or *nor* (*Nor was I*), sporadically after *then* (*Then came the floods*), and so on. How exactly, then, would we describe their history? The pattern of *Then came the floods* was normal in the days of a 'verb-second' order; so the parameters would be said to have been set accordingly. Then their setting would have to change; this might be explained, in the terms that Lightfoot suggests, by changes in E-language such that some cue was no longer instanced with sufficient 'robustness'. But would this pattern thereby vanish from I-languages affected? Let us claim, instead, that it was relegated to a periphery. It would then be exceptional, and we would expect it to be restricted lexically and, in time, to become rare. But no group of speakers would at once stop 'using' it.

By invoking either of these factors, or both, we could easily explain why sudden and pervasive changes in a 'grammar' might not, in reality, lead to either sudden or pervasive changes in speech. But there are two obvious comments. Firstly, it is only if the effects were sudden that the predictions of our theory might be confirmed. If they are gradual then, at any stage in any language, other changes, which would arise perhaps from new 'speech fashions' or from other 'nongrammatical factors', could again be claimed to intervene. What changes in speech could not then, in principle, be attested?

The second comment is that gradual shifts in speech are just what we expect if change is at a level of 'E-language' only. If Chomsky's theory of I-language is right, we are again obliged to posit consequential changes at an underlying level. That is granted, and we would then have to consider whether they were likely to be local or pervasive. But do we again have any other motive, as historians, for positing an underlying 'language' of that kind?

It is appropriate to end with questions, since the theory that has provoked this essay may be further clarified or updated. But, in Chomsky's later accounts, the core of an I-language may directly 'instantiate' a Universal Grammar (1995). The more, of course, this 'core' is simply invariant, the less historians of language will be concerned with it. Where languages vary systematically it is said, conjecturally, to be a function of potential differences in their lexicon. Beyond what would be regular, it seems that there would still be a periphery; and, independent of all levels of I-language, we must then envisage Lightfoot's 'socially defined speech fashions', something like Coseriu's norms, and so on. We have to ask if there any reasons, other than a prior belief that knowledge of 'a language' must develop in the form that Chomsky says it does, why these proliferating levels should be seen as separate.

REFERENCES

Chomsky, Noam. 1986. *Knowledge of language*. New York: Praeger.
Chomsky, Noam. 1995. *The minimalist program*. Cambridge, MA: MIT Press.
Coseriu, Eugenio. 1958. *Sincronía, diacronía e historia*. Montevideo. 2nd edition, Madrid: Gredos, 1973.
Coseriu, Eugenio. 1962. *Teoría del lenguaje y lingüística general: cinco estudios*. Madrid: Gredos.
Lightfoot, David W. 1979. *Principles of diachronic syntax*. Cambridge University Press.
Lightfoot, David W. 1991. *How to set parameters: arguments from language change*. Cambridge, MA: MIT Press.
Lightfoot, David W. 1999. *The development of language*. Oxford: Blackwell.
Matthews, Peter H. 1979. *Generative grammar and linguistic competence*. London: Allen and Unwin.
Matthews, Peter H. 1998. 'Should we believe in UG?', in M. Janse (ed.), *Productivity and creativity: studies in general and descriptive linguistics in honor of E. M. Uhlenbeck*. Berlin: Mouton de Gruyter, 103–13.
Matthews, Peter H. 2001. *A short history of structural linguistics*. Cambridge University Press.
Paul, Hermann. 1880. *Prinzipien der Sprachgeschichte*. Halle: Niemeyer.
Roberts, Ian G. 1993. *Verbs and diachronic syntax*. Dordrecht: Kluwer.

2 Formal and functional motivation for language change

Frederick J. Newmeyer

1 Introduction

The goal of this chapter is to sort out the roles that 'formal' and 'functional' factors have been said to play in language change. An immediate challenge is to provide these two terms with enough content so that there is no uncertainty about what specifically is at stake in any explanation of a change that incorporates one of these two terms. It is not uncommon, for example, to encounter statements in the literature such as: 'Formal pressure was responsible for the loss of instrumental case in English' or 'Grammatical oppositions with a low degree of functionality are more likely to be lost than those with a high degree.' Unfortunately, such claims are often not accompanied by a sufficiently precise characterization of the notions 'formal pressure' or 'degree of functionality' to allow them to be adequately evaluated. Our first task, therefore, is to specify as precisely as possible what a 'formal explanation' and a 'functional explanation' might consist of.

Throughout this chapter a 'formal explanation' will designate one in which principles governing the organisation of *grammars* are said to play a central role. A 'functional explanation', on the other hand, refers crucially to properties of language *users*, in particular to their interest in producing and comprehending language rapidly, to their states of consciousness, or to aspects of their behaviour. It is important to stress that these definitions leave open the possibility that any particular language change, from its inception to its full realisation, can have both a formal and a functional dimension. Indeed, I believe that a bidimensional view has long been the mainstream way of looking at things. For example, over a century ago the Polish linguists Jan Baudouin de Courtenay and Nikolaj Kruszewski posited that sound change originates in the (user-based) exigencies of articulation and acoustics, but ultimately grammar-internal systematic pressure lead the results of these changes to be phonologised (for discussion, see Anderson 1985: ch. 3). More recently, Paul Kiparsky has

---

* I would like to thank Charles Barrack for his helpful comments on an earlier version of this paper.

provided a picture of sound change in which formal and functional factors are inseparably intertwined:[1]

> [N]atural phonological processes, originating in production, perception, and acquisition, result in inherent, functionally controlled variability of speech. 'Sound change' takes place when the results of these processes are internalized by language learners as part of their grammatical competence. Internalization as lexical representations or lexical rules is subject to structure-preservation and other relevant constraints on the lexical component, and may involve selective grammaticalisation and lexicalization of variants preferred at the optional stage. In consequence, conditions on sound change reflect functional factors.   (Kiparsky 1988: 389)

The problem of teasing out the relative weight of formal and functional factors in language change is complicated enormously by the fact that some linguists view the organisation and structure of grammar as itself a reflection of external functional pressure. This is particularly true for linguists of the Prague School and those on whom they have had the greatest influence. Indeed, members of this school have tended to refer to themselves as both 'structuralists' and 'functionalists'. André Martinet, a Prague School disciple, provided formal explanations, in that he saw language change in terms of changes in grammars and provided constraints on how and why a grammar might change. But at the same time, most of those constraints were functionally based. For example, he believed that phonological systems tended toward formal symmetry. However, he provided a functional explanation for why that appeared to be true. In his view, the function of language is communication and maximal differentiation among grammatical elements (i.e. maximal symmetry) aids the communicative process (see Martinet 1952; 1955).

While most linguists see a role for both formal and functional factors in language change, there tends to be an asymmetry between formalists and functionalists in terms of the weight each attributes to the factors characteristic of the other. Wholly reductionist views are far more typical of the latter than of the former. The functionalist Simon Dik can write that 'Saying that a certain feature of linguistic design or change cannot be functionally explained is tantamount to saying that we have not yet been able to find a functional explanation for that feature' (Dik 1986: 22).[2] I have yet to find a correspondingly 'imperialistic' statement from a formal linguist about language change. Even David Lightfoot, for example, a formalist par excellence, acknowledges that stylistic and sociopolitical factors can play an important role in change (Lightfoot 1988: 319).

---

[1] For another, rather different, example of how formal and functional factors might be said to interact in language change, see the optimality-theoretic account presented in Haspelmath (1999b).

[2] For similar remarks, see Jakobson (1928/1971: 1) and almost anything written by Michael Shapiro (see especially Shapiro 1985; 1991).

In general, formal phonologists have been more welcoming of the idea of functional factors playing a central role in language change than have formal syntacticians. Such is undoubtedly a consequence of the fact that phonologists are far more likely than syntacticians to see their object of inquiry as having properties that more or less directly reflect functional factors. For example, Michael Kenstowicz's introductory text *Phonology in generative grammar* has a chapter entitled 'The phonetic foundations of phonology', where it is remarked that 'phonological distinctions and categorizations display gaps that appear arbitrary from a purely abstract, classificatory point of view, but seem to reflect contingencies of the articulatory and acoustic systems that realize language in speech' (Kenstowicz 1994: 136). A more recent introduction observes that 'an understanding of phonological theory is impossible without at least some knowledge of the way speech is produced' (Gussenhoven and Jacobs 1998: ix). The book makes good on this observation by devoting the first chapter to speech production. One searches in vain for a formal syntax text that emphasises the degree to which syntactic systems reflect the exigencies of processing or the utility of maintaining an iconic relationship between form and meaning. The absence of such texts is a consequence of the fact that only a small minority of syntacticians explore the functional shaping of formal systems (but see Hawkins 1994 and Newmeyer 1998).

The outright rejection of the possibility of functional explanation of language change does not necessarily involve the embracing of formal explanation. Roger Lass, for example, has long militated against the possibility of *any* explanation that might be proffered for a particular change, whether formal or functional, though his guns have been trained more on the latter than the former (see Lass 1980 for an extreme statement of such a position and Lass 1997 for a more moderate one). And it should be pointed out as well that debates between formalists and functionalists regarding language change need not involve the issue of formal versus functional explanation per se. For example, the exchange between David Lightfoot and the functionalists Elizabeth Traugott and Henry Smith (Traugott and Smith 1993; Lightfoot 1995) was more over the nature of grammars than about the relative merits of functional explanations and formal ones.

Finally, it needs to be stressed that it is not necessarily the case that a language change should have either a formal or a functional explanation, or some combination of the two. Paul Postal is undoubtedly not the only linguist to believe that 'there is no more reason for languages to change than there is for automobiles to add fins one year and remove them the next, for jackets to have three buttons one year and two the next, etc.' (Postal 1968: 283). Indeed, it is now uncontroversial that social factors, such as the desire to imitate arbitrary (from a linguistic point of view) prestige forms play the dominant role in the spread of a variant through a speech community (Weinreich, Labov and Herzog 1968; Milroy 1987).[3]

This chapter is organised as follows. Sections 2 and 3 discuss the arguments for and against formal explanations of language change respectively. Sections 4 and 5 deal in like manner with functional explanations. Section 6 is a brief conclusion.

2   Formal explanations of language change

As noted above in section 1, the linguists of the Prague School (as well as other European structuralists) had a mixed formal–functional view, in which functionally motivated pressure resulted in the restructuring of formal systems. The American structuralists between the 1930s and the 1960s held a Neogrammarian view of change, but – due to the empiricist philosophy that guided them – one that was stripped of even the meagre explanatory devices to which the Neogrammarians subscribed. As a consequence, the first 'purely' formal explanations of language change arose with the advent of generative grammar in the early 1960s. The rule-centred approaches of early generative grammar were mirrored, not surprisingly, by rule-centred accounts of change. In phonology, the goal was to demonstrate that rule change led to 'simpler' grammars, though the notion of 'simplicity' was understood differently by different scholars (for characteristic work of this period, see Kiparsky 1968 and King 1969). Historical syntax consisted, more modestly, in comparing different grammars at different stages in time and, in some cases, even proposing 'diachronic grammars' linking different stages of the same language (Traugott 1969).

As formal generative theory developed in the following few decades, the subtlety and complexity of the explanatory devices increased as well. A good example of a formal explanation of language change is the account presented in Kiparsky (1995) of lexical diffusion. Specifically, he argues that lexical diffusion is the analogical generalisation of lexical phonological rules. In other words, he sees lexical diffusion as an optimisation process that eliminates idiosyncratic complexity from the system. While the full story is too complex to present here, Kiparsky's account relies crucially on such formal devices as radical underspecification, structure-building rules and rule-ordering. Kiparsky also provides a formally based account of one of the major puzzles of historical linguistics, namely how sound change could possibly be 'blind', when

---

[3] It has become the accepted view, I believe, that functional factors are crucial in the *actuation* of a linguistic change, but that linguistically arbitrary social factors explain why certain actuated changes are transmitted through the speech community, while others are not (see Croft 1995: 523; Haspelmath 1999b; Newmeyer 2001).

its results seem to respect purely structural conditions. For example, Jakobson (1929/1971) was puzzled by the fact that the same phonological changes tended to occur repeatedly in the history of the Slavic languages. His answer to this puzzle was an essentially teleological conclusion that 'elles vont selon des directions déterminées'. Kiparsky argued in reply that phonetic change is regular but the child language learner is sensitive to formal feature types already existing in the language. Hence one has the illusion of 'directed' sound change.

Any phonological change whose explanation demands a look at something 'deeper' than phonetics is ipso facto a change whose explanation requires a formal theory. Kiparsky (1995) gives the example of vowel shifts. A popular functional explanation for their occurrence is that they lead to perceptual distinctness. However, Kiparsky shows that they often have no such effect at all. In certain cases, in fact, vowel shifts simply produce 'musical chairs' effects, where the distinctness between the elements undergoing the shift is not enhanced at all. Kiparsky argues that tenseness can trigger vowel shift if it is present in the language's *phonological* representation. Vowel shifts

can thus be considered as the result of suppressing marked specifications of the relevant height features in lexical representations, resulting in the assignment of the appropriate default value of the feature in question to the vacated segment . . .

(Kiparsky 1995: 663)

Turning to syntactic change, it is axiomatic among formal syntacticians that there are no independent principles of language change. Nothing transgenerational can have a cognitive reality (on this point, see Lightfoot 1979: 151). Nevertheless, formal linguists have suggested from time to time that the child language learner is guided by strategies that, if conditions are right, will lead him or her to posit different structures from those of the adult community, thereby effecting a grammatical change. For example, Lightfoot (1979) proposed the 'Transparency Principle', which controls the distance tolerated between underlying and surface structure. If, as a result of grammatical changes over the centuries, this distance becomes too great, the resulting 'opaque' structures will be reanalysed more on the surface. Hence the categorial reanalysis in Early Modern English of modal auxiliaries, which previously had been members of the category 'Verb', into a new category 'Auxiliary'.

Transparency-motivated changes are presumed to occur when other changes in the language have rendered it impossible for the child to assign the same analysis to a sentence type that it had formerly. For example, the verb *like* originally meant 'please' in one of its uses. Sentences with *like* often occurred in the productive [object__subject] frame in Middle English. Thus we found sentences like *him liked the pears, the king liked the pears*, etc., where in both cases the initial NP was understood as object. As a result of a complex series of changes in this period of English (the loss of case endings, a change in order from SOV to SVO, and so on), the object–verb–subject analysis of the above sentences became opaque to the child language learner – there was nothing in the triggering experience to suggest such an analysis. *The king liked the pears* was therefore reanalysed as subject–verb–object, while sentences such as *him liked the pears* simply dropped out of the language.

Lightfoot abandoned the Transparency Principle in his next historically oriented book (Lightfoot 1991). Both its overly broad conceptual sweep and difficulties with its concrete empirical predictions made it too problematic. He replaced it with an idea rooted in the principles-and-parameters approach to syntax, which he had come to adopt in his formal syntactic work. The basic idea is that children, in effect, 'filter out' much of the ambient language in the process of setting the parameters that fix the essential aspects of their syntax. Specifically, the triggering experience for children's grammars is only what they observe in main clauses and the left edge of the highest subordinate clause. An ongoing change in the language that alters significantly the balance of what occurs in main and subordinate clauses can have a dramatic effect on the triggering experience and hence on the grammar that the child constructs. So, between Old English and Middle English a quantitative change in the percentage of SOV and SVO sentences heard by the child led to a qualitative change – from the former to the latter as the underlying order in the grammar.

More recently Roberts (1993) has proposed a different formal principle governing the child language learner, the Least Effort Strategy (LES) (228–9).

Least Effort Strategy:
Representations assigned to sentences of the input to acquisition should be such that they contain the set of the shortest possible chains (consistent with (a) principles of grammar, (b) other aspects of the trigger experience).

Roberts applies the LES to the explanation of certain grammaticalisation-related changes.[4] Grammaticalisation is, roughly put, the loss of grammatical independence of a grammatical structure or element. This loss of independence has lexical, semantic and phonological, consequences. Lexically, we find a 'downgrading' reanalysis from, say, full lexical category to functional category, from functional category to clitic, or from clitic to affix. Semantically, there is typically a 'bleaching' of meaning, that is a shift from the specific to the general. And phonologically, we find phonetic reduction (or 'erosion') of the element involved. The change in the English modal auxiliaries over the past thousand years illustrates all three processes. They have been reanalysed from the lexical category 'Verb' to the functional category 'Auxiliary', their meanings have become bleached (e.g. *will* originally denoted 'to desire'; *can* 'to know how'; *shall* 'to owe'; *might* 'to have power'; and so on). And they

---

[4] See also Fintel (1995) for interesting discussion of how the semantic changes observed in grammaticalisation might be handled by semantic mechanisms interfacing with formal syntax.

now occur with reduced stress and can even be cliticised to the element to their left.

Roberts starts from the observation that the two most common manifestations of grammaticalisation, the change from a full lexical item to that of an auxiliary-like item and the change from the latter to an affix, lend themselves to ready characterisation in the vocabulary of generative syntax. The former change, which can also be characterised as the change from a lexical category to a functional category, is illustrated in (1a–b) with respect to the first stages of evolution of the Romance future:

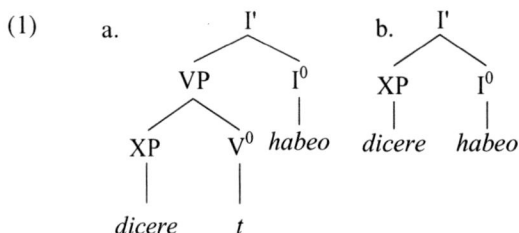

(1)   a.

I'
  VP I^0
XP V^0 *habeo*
dicere   t

b.

I'
  XP I^0
dicere   *habeo*

LES led to the elimination of the *habeo . . . t* chain and consequent reanalysis of *habeo* as an auxiliary.[5]

A current debate among formal historical linguists concerns what the child, metaphorically speaking, sees as his or her major 'task' in acquisition. The cue-based model proposed in Lightfoot (1999) is an extension of his earlier ideas discussed above, in which the child searches for specific cues in the input to act as triggers in grammar construction. An alternative view is the input-matching theory of Clark and Roberts (1993), in which children search for a grammar that generates the set of sentences that they are exposed to. The formal consequences of both approaches are discussed in Niyogi and Berwick (1995).

3   Problems with formal explanations of language change

The typical criticism of a formal explanation for language change is no different in principle than the typical criticism of formal explanations in general. The standard functionalist view is that such 'explanations' are not worthy of the word, since they do little more than reshuffle the data:

In essence, a formal model is *nothing but* a restatement of the facts at a tighter level of generalisation . . . There is one thing, however, that a formal model can never do: it cannot *explain* a single thing . . . The history of transformational-generative linguistics boils down to nothing but a blatant attempt to represent the formalism as 'theory', to

---

[5] Later in the paper (pp. 243f.) Roberts argues that the reanalysis from auxiliary to affix was also a consequence of LES.

assert that it 'predicts a range of facts', that it 'makes empirical claims', and that it somehow 'explains'...   (Givón 1979: 5–6; emphasis in original)

According to functionalists, one has not provided an explanation for any aspect of grammar until one has gone *outside* grammar – that is, to root that aspect in properties of users of grammar. Hence any account of language change that appeals crucially to grammar-internal processes would simply be excluded from the domain of explanation by most functionalists.

But not only functionalists have provided negative appraisals of formal treatments of language change. The earliest generative work, which viewed all changes as simplificatory, has been judged particularly harshly. As noted in McMahon (1994: 43), such accounts tended (ironically) to ignore the effects of changes on the entire system. McMahon points out that a change might lead to a 'simpler' grammar according to one economy measure, yet be more complex in terms of the structural interrelationship of elements in the system. Early accounts were hard pressed to deal with the latter. McMahon also provides several examples of phonological changes that could not properly be regarded as simplificatory, in any sense of the term.

The more sophisticated formal accounts of change, such as David Lightfoot has developed in the past twenty-five years, have led to more sophisticated criticism. While Lightfoot's approach relies crucially on formal principles, he does root these principles in properties of language users (in particular, language learners) – they strive to minimise opacity, they attend only to certain aspects of the input, etc. Hence his work is not subject to the charge of being merely a 'mechanical reshuffling' of the data, as was earlier work. Criticism, then, has tended to focus on the empirical predictions of his approach, in particular on whether change is as 'catastrophic' as his theory would seem to predict and on whether, as is demanded by principles-and-parameters approaches to syntax, the notion 'grammatical construction' can be dispensed with in accounts of syntactic change (for typical criticism, see Traugott and Smith 1993; Haspelmath 1999a).

Finally, Roberts's formal account of grammaticalisation has been subject to criticism. Campbell (1997: §4.2.2) suggests that LES is too restrictive to account for the bulk of reanalyses that have been implicated in grammaticalisation. In his view, few if any of the following changes are plausibly derived by simplification of the number of chain-positions in a phrase-structure tree:

(2)   a. The reanalysis of grammatical affixes as independent words.
       b. The development of definite articles from demonstrative pronouns.
       c. The development of third-person pronouns from demonstratives.
       d. The development of relative pronouns from interrogative pronouns.
       e. The development of switch-reference markers from contrastive conjunctions.

   f. The development of partitive constructions from ablative or genitive markers; the development of genitive markers from ablative or locative markers.

   g. The development of copulas from demonstratives or third-person pronouns.

   h. Shifts in irrealis forms either from or to futures, subjunctives, optatives, potential/conditionals, or imperatives.

   i. The development of existential/presentational constructions from 'have', 'give', 'be' or from locative pronouns.

   j. The development of coordinate conjunctions from 'with'.

4   Functional explanations for language change

The functional factor of longest standing that has been implicated in language change is the desire of the speaker to maximise ease of articulation.[6] For example, although many Neogrammarians tended to view sound change as an essentially random drift in phonetic space, they were aware that some changes were more likely to occur than others. Hermann Paul suggested that the more common changes tended to be 'in some respect more convenient... where greater or lesser degree of convenience is ... purely physiological' (Paul 1891: 43). Explanations of phonological change in terms of increasing ease of articulation have not diminished in popularity over the past century. For example, Lyle Campbell, in his discussion of the widespread tendency to voice stops between vowels, writes:

> This change is in some sense explained by the limitations of human muscle control, which tends to maintain the vibration of the vocal cords ... across the intervening consonant. That is, it is much easier to allow the vocal cords to continue to vibrate right through the V-stop-V sequence ... than it is to have the vocal cords vibrating for the first vowel, then to break off the vibrating for the stop, and then to start up the vibration of the vocal cords once again for the second vowel ...   (Campbell 1998: 286)

Just as assimilations of sounds are attributed to speaker ease, dissimilations have been explained in terms of benefit to the *hearer*, who prioritises maximal clarity. John Ohala in particular has stressed the listener as an agent of change (see Ohala 1974; 1981; 1987; Hombert, Ohala and Ewan 1979). In his view, listeners

---

[6] Or, more properly, 'the unproblematic functional factor'. Jacob Grimm pointed to national character as an intrinsic motivating factor in sound change: 'It may be reckoned as evidence of the superior gentleness and moderation of the Gothic, Saxon, and Scandinavian tribes that they contented themselves with the first sound shift, whilst the wilder force of the southern Germans was impelled towards the second shift' (quoted in Crowley 1994: 191). And Henry Sweet attributed the more common rounding of [a] to [o] in northern Europe than in southern to 'the result of unwillingness to open the mouth widely in the chilly and foggy air of the North' (Sweet 1900: 32).

in the process of comprehension will frequently 'undo' speaker assimilations. Occasionally they will 'over-undo', leading them to dissimilate adjacent sounds whose phonetic similarity was not rooted historically in an assimilation:

Since the listener does not have independent access to the mind of the speaker, and thus may be unable to determine what parts of the received signal were intended and what were not, he may intentionally reproduce and probably exaggerate these distortions when he repeats the same utterances.   (Hombert, Ohala and Ewan 1979: 37)

Indeed, in Ohala's view, the sounds need not necessarily even be adjacent – he argues that Grassman's Law in Sanskrit, in which the first of two (nonadjacent) aspirated sounds were de-aspirated, arose as a result of hearer overcorrection.

Processing-based arguments for change have been presented in the domain of morphosyntax as well. For example, several researchers have attempted to explain why verb-final order is more likely to give way to verb-medial order than the reverse. Vennemann (1973) points to the loss of case endings in SOV languages through phonological attrition. In such an eventuality, the shift of the verb to the middle serves to demarcate more saliently the subject from the object. A parsing-based argument for a drift to verb-mediality can be derived from the findings of Hawkins (1994). SOV languages with 'heavy' objects create considerable parsing difficulty. Processing efficiency is maximally improved by preposing the object to initial position, creating OSV order. Such a gain in efficiency is reflected cross-linguistically. As Greenberg (1963: 79) noted, 'in a substantial proportion, possibly a majority, of [SOV] languages . . . if any other basic order is allowed, it is OSV'. However, efficiency is also increased (though not as greatly) by postposing the object, creating SVO order. And as it turns out, a substantial minority of SOV languages allow SVO as an alternative order. Thus there is a ready parsing-based mechanism for 'leakage' from SOV to SVO. Now, it is *never* advantageous from the point of view of parsing for an SVO language to prepose a heavy object to a position between the subject and the verb. And hence, there is nothing based in language processing that would create 'leakage' from SVO to SOV.

More recently, Aske (1998) has put forward a rather complex information content-based argument for the seemingly greater naturalness of the move from OV to VO than from VO to OV. Very briefly, he points to discourse-based pressure for the development of a focus position after V in OV languages, leading ultimately to VO order. However, there is no corresponding mechanism for the loss of an NP after V in VO languages. Thus he posits a long-term drift to VO.

The desire of language users to establish an iconic (one-to-one) relationship between form and meaning has frequently been appealed to in explanations of language change. Indeed, such is the major explanatory device in the theory of natural morphology (Wurzel 1989; Dressler 1985). Robin Lakoff (1972) has given an iconicity-based explanation for general tendencies in the development of the Indo-European languages such as the replacement of case markers by prepositions, the development of periphrastic causatives, and the decreasing percentage of null subject languages. In her view, these are all moves toward greater semantic transparency. Along the same lines, Haspelmath (1993) gives an example of an iconicity-motivated change in the history of Latin. Citing Bybee (1985), he points to an iconicity-driven preference for derivational morphology to occur inside inflectional morphology. Old Latin developed a reinforcing particle to a suffix-inflecting demonstrative, leading to derivation occurring outside inflection. But, as Haspelmath notes, changes soon took place that resulted in the reversal of the ordering of the two types of suffix.

Croft (2000) presents a detailed picture of a set of iconicity-motivated actuations of change, which he labels 'form–function reanalysis'. A functional principle guiding speakers is to seek an isomorphic relationship between sound and meaning. Due to the complexity of the functional forces affecting grammars and their mutual interaction, in no grammars will isomorphism obtain without exception. So, one common type of innovation is for speakers to 'impose' an iconic relation where it does not exist. Croft identifies four subtypes of form–function reanalysis: hyperanalysis, hypoanalysis, metanalysis and cryptanalysis. In hyperanalysis, semantic properties of one grammatical unit are reanalysed as properties of another. An example is the loss of governed oblique case in Russian and other languages. Since in many instances the governed case is not semantically motivated synchronically, the tendency has been to reanalyse the inherent semantic value of the case as belonging solely to the verb meaning, leading ultimately to the loss of that case marker. Hypoanalysis is the reverse process of hyperanalysis. In this instance, an existing grammatical unit gains a new meaning. German umlaut, for example, was at one time purely phonologically conditioned. However, its association with pluralisation, comparativisation, etc. led it to become morphologised and identified with the semantic effects of those processes. Metanalysis is simultaneous occurrence of hyperanalysis and hypoanalysis. Here there is simultaneous exchange of the contextual and semantic values of a syntactic unit. It can be illustrated by negation in modern colloquial French. *Je dis pas* illustrates both hypoanalysis (the change in meaning of *pas* from reinforcer to negative particle) and hyperanalysis (the loss of *ne*). Finally, cryptanalysis involves the insertion of an overt marker where none is 'needed', as in pleonastic negation.

The associated changes that come under the heading of 'grammaticalisation' are more typically accorded a functional explanation than a formal one. The predominant view appears to be that semantic changes set the ball rolling and that they have a functional origin. The following characterisation is typical:

[W]e suggest that human language users have a natural propensity for making metaphorical extensions that lead to the increased use of certain items . . . Thus the paths of development leading to grammatical meaning are predictable, given certain lexical meaning as the starting point. As the meaning generalizes and the range of use widens, the frequency increases and this leads automatically to phonological reduction and perhaps fusion . . .   (Bybee and Pagliuca 1985: 76)

That is, what starts out as a cognitive property of language users (the propensity for making metaphorical extensions) is later reinforced by the 'least-effort'-based motivation of wanting to say quickly what one says often.

It is a truism to observe that if all language change were a response to functional pressure and that this pressure were uniform, then all languages would have settled on a functionally optimal state many thousands of years ago. Clearly, this has not happened. The explanation for this lack of stasis is attributed by functionalists to the existence of competing functional factors or, as they are often called, 'competing motivations'.[7] That is, some forces push language in one direction, some in another. What results is an uneasy balance, whereby languages fall into a range in which all external motivations are filled to a certain extent, but none totally. In such a situation, it is easy for one functional force to trigger a particular change at the expense of another. Hence, individual language changes are functionally motivated, even though neither individual languages nor language as a whole become more 'functional' over time. Croft provides a clear picture of how the push–pull of competing forces might affect language change:

Why does a novel variant occur . . . ? . . . The (external) functionalist model provides an answer . . . competing motivations bring about the novel variants. A grammar consists of a balance between multiple competing functional forces. . . . the system is inherently unstable. While the external motivations for stability preserve the balance most of the time, alternative resolutions of competing motivations are occasionally produced by individuals.   (Croft 1995: 524)

The idea of competing motivations goes back at least to Gabelentz (1891), who described the tension between 'striving for ease' and 'striving for clarity'. Conflicts between speaker-based motivations such as the former and hearer-based motivations such as the latter were central to Martinet's view of grammar and grammatical change. Many examples have been adduced of competing motivations in the realm of syntactic change. Haiman (1983) argues that the desire for economy (such as might result in the simplification or omission of redundant material) can come into conflict with pressure to make grammatical

---

[7] All agree that language contact is another factor preventing 'functional optimality'. For example, the current 'dysfunctional' system of English word stress is a product of the contact between Old English and Old French, each of which had fairly simple stress rules.

structures iconic. Hence languages develop deletion rules, in which understood meanings have no grammatical coding, but disallow 'unrecoverable deletions', as they constitute too grave a violation of iconicity. In the view of Dik (1989), iconicity can conflict with the prominence of participants. Thus, in indirect-object constructions, the V–DO–IDO order is an iconic one, in that it reflects the movement of the object in question from the donor to the recipient. The V–IDO–DO order, on the other hand, is also functionally motivated in that it places the more 'prominent' indirect object before the less prominent direct object. Languages resolve the conflict in different ways, some by developing only one of the two orders and some (like English) by developing both.

5   Problems with functional explanations of language change

Very few linguists would reject outright the idea that external functional pressure is a factor in language change. Yet at the same time there is a great hesitancy on the part of many linguists to make (or endorse) such statements as 'This particular language change was caused by this particular functional factor.' The reason is the existence of competing motivations, whose effect is to inject a great deal of vacuity into such statements. It will not do to claim that speaker-ease explains why one particular change occurred and hearer-ease another, unless one has a theory of form–function interactions that explain when and why the speaker 'wins' and when and why the hearer 'wins'. But no such theory exists. Likewise, to provide an explanation of why change A > B is more common than change B > A, one must do more than simply declare that the motivation for the former change is stronger than the motivation for the latter change. Rather, one is obliged to provide independent motivation to explain *why* this should be the case. Otherwise, one has accomplished nothing more than finding a different way of saying that A > B is more common than B > A.

Further undercutting any 'easy' appeal to a functional motivation for a particular change is the fact that grammars that seem to be functionally nonoptimal can persist for centuries. Perhaps the most striking example of what appears to be the retention of functionally disfavored grammars comes from the phenomenon of 'near mergers' in phonology. Halle (1962) and Chomsky and Halle (1968) noted that the theory of generative phonology allows for the possibility that two phonemes might merge at one point in history and then reappear at a later point, where the re-emerging phonemes 'remembered' what their historical antecedents had been before they coalesced. This could happen if their underlying representations were kept distinct in the intervening period. And they suggested this actually happened in the historical development of English. Three English word classes, represented by the words *meet, meat* and *mate*, were uncontroversially pronounced with different vowels in Middle English. Chomsky and Halle argued that the *meat* and the *mate* class fell together in the

Table 2.1. *The changing vowels of the* meet, meat *and* mate *class*

Type	ME class	ME value	16th century	17th century
meet	ē	[eː]	[eː]	[iː]
meat	ēā	[æː, ɛː]	[ɛː]	[iː]
mate	ā	[aː]	[ɛː]	[eː]

sixteenth century, only to separate a century later, at which point the *meet* class and the *meat* class had merged. Their scenario is illustrated in table 2.1 (I have availed myself of the presentation of the data in Labov 1994: 296). Chomsky and Halle were much ridiculed for this hypothesis on functionalist grounds: how and why would a language keep a distinction alive that played no functional role in phonemic, and hence semantic, contrast? Weinreich, Labov and Herzog (1968) and others argued that the sixteenth- and seventeenth-century systems coexisted in the speech of Londoners for a considerable period, and hence one would not have to resort to assuming that nonaudible distinctions could be kept alive underlyingly.

But Labov (1974; 1987; 1994) subsequently re-evaluated the relevant facts and came to the conclusion that they were essentially as Chomsky and Halle described them. The *meat* class and the *mate* class did, in a sense, merge and then split. Labov posited that a subliminal phonemic distinction was maintained between the members of each class. Even though speakers could not tell that the pronunciations differed, the difference was real and maintained for over a century. In other words, a 'near-merger' took place. And indeed, it would appear that among older speakers in Belfast today these vowels still stand in the relation of near-merger (Milroy and Harris 1980).

Near mergers have been identified elsewhere. For example, in Philadelphia English, [e] has been centralized to [ə] before [r], so *merry* and *Murray* are both pronounced *almost* [məriy]; *ferry* and *furry* are both pronounced *almost* [fəriy]; and so on (Labov 1994: 397f.). The pronunciations sound the same, even to trained linguists. Certainly Philadelphians deny that they are pronounced differently. But they *are* pronounced differently. Sensitive instruments can record the difference. Just as in Early Modern English, a phonemic difference is kept alive that has no functional value.

After a long discussion of near-mergers, Labov (1987: 319) concludes that they have:

important consequences for functional explanation. It appears that the communicative role of phonemic contrasts can be suspended for a considerable period of time without disrupting the integrity of the word classes and the system they participate in. There is no doubt that phonemes do function to distinguish words. But the historical development of the system of phonemes is not narrowly controlled by that communicative function. In this respect, the anti-functional position taken by Chomsky and Halle (1968) in defending flip-flip rules seems fully justified, even if that is not the actual mechanism of vowel shifting.

An extremely controversial class of functional explanations for language change involves attributing to the language user the ability to either forestall a dysfunctional change or, if the change is complete, to 'repair' its effects.[8] An example of the former was provided in Campbell (1975), who argued that Early Greek speakers blocked the deletion of intervocalic /s/, an otherwise regular sound change, when it would lead to the merger of present and future forms. The latter is illustrated by the restoration in some English dialects of second-person plural pronominal forms (*youse, y'all,* etc.). Lass (1997: 355–61) questions whether the motivations for these changes can in any sense be called 'functional'. After all, many languages do very well without overtly marked present-future or second-person singular–plural distinctions and, in the latter case, many centuries elapsed between the loss of the distinction and its reappearance in certain dialects. As William Croft observes, there exist a relatively high number of pronoun systems in the world with gaps, indicating that they are not all that unstable and, on the other hand, 'there are cases where new plural forms arose where old ones existed, and the new plural morphemes are even added onto the old plural forms (as has happened in many Turkic languages for the first and second person pronouns...)' (Croft 2000: 70).

  In summary, functional explanation is typically criticised on grounds that, more often than not, the link between the explananda and the proffered explanans is too tenuous to be convincing.

6   Conclusion

Formal explanations are those which appeal to mentally represented formal grammars and constraints on those grammars; functional explanations are those that appeal to properties of language users. Many, if not most, accounts of language change appeal to both types of explanation. The principal objection to formal explanation is to claim that it does little more than rearrange the data in more compact form – such criticism embodies the idea that in order to explain the properties of some system, it is necessary to go outside of that system. The principal criticism of functional explanation is to claim that it is vacuous. Since for any functional factor there exists another factor whose operation would lead

---

[8] Many linguists accept the possibility of therapeutic change, while rejecting 'prophylactic' change (see, for example, Lightfoot 1979; Kiparsky 1982; Labov 1994). Harris and Campbell (1995: ch. 11), on the other hand, present a lengthy defence of prophylactic change.

to the opposite consequence, the claim that some particular functional factor 'explains' some particular instance of language change has the danger of being empty.

REFERENCES

Anderson, Stephen R. 1985. *Phonology in the twentieth century*. University of Chicago Press.

Aske, Jon. 1998. *Basque word order and disorder: principles, variation, and prospects.* Amsterdam: John Benjamins.

Bybee, Joan L. 1985. *Morphology: a study of the relation between meaning and form.* Typological Studies in Language 9. Amsterdam: John Benjamins.

Bybee, Joan L. and William Pagliuca. 1985. 'Cross-linguistic comparison and the development of grammatical meaning', in Jacek Fisiak (ed.), *Historical Semantics and Historical Word Formation*. Berlin: de Gruyter, 59–83.

Campbell, Lyle. 1975. 'Constraints on sound change', in K.-H. Dahlstedt (ed.), *The Nordic Languages and Modern Linguistics*, vol. 2. Stockholm: Almqvist and Wiksell, 388–406.

Campbell, Lyle. 1997. 'Approaches to reanalysis and its role in the explanation of syntactic change', in Linda van Bergen and Richard M. Hogg (eds.), *Papers from the 12th International Conference on Historical Linguistics*. Amsterdam: John Benjamins, 57–8.

Campbell, Lyle. 1998. *Historical linguistics: an introduction*. Cambridge, MA: MIT Press.

Chomsky, Noam and Morris Halle. 1968. *Sound pattern of English*. New York: Harper and Row.

Clark, Robin and Ian Roberts. 1993. 'A computational theory of language learnability and language change', *Linguistic Inquiry* 24: 299–345.

Croft, William. 1995. 'Autonomy and functionalist linguistics', *Language* 71: 490–532.

Croft, William. 2000. *Explaining language change: an evolutionary approach*. London: Longman.

Crowley, Terry. 1994. *An introduction to historical linguistics*, 2nd edition. Cambridge University Press.

Dik, Simon C. 1986. 'On the notion "functional explanation"', *Belgian Journal of Linguistics* 1: 11–52.

Dik, Simon C. 1989. *The theory of functional grammar*, part 1: *The structure of the clause*. Functional Grammar Series 9. Dordrecht: Foris.

Dressler, Wolfgang U. 1985. 'On the predictiveness of Natural Morphology', *Journal of Linguistics* 21: 321–37.

Fintel, Kai von. 1995. 'The formal semantics of grammaticalization', *North Eastern Linguistic Society* 25 (part 2): 175–90.

Gabelentz, Georg von der. 1891. *Die Sprachwissenschaft: ihre Aufgaben, Methoden und bisherigen Ergebnisse*, Leipzig: Weigel.

Givón, Talmy. 1979. *On understanding grammar*. New York: Academic Press.

Greenberg, Joseph H. 1963. 'Some universals of language with special reference to the order of meaningful elements', in Joseph H. Greenberg (ed.), *Universals of language*. Cambridge, MA: MIT Press, 73–113.

Gussenhoven, Carlos and Haike Jacobs. 1998. *Understanding phonology*. London: Arnold.

Haiman, John. 1983. 'Iconic and economic motivation', *Language* 59: 781–819.

Halle, Morris. 1962. 'Phonology in generative grammar', *Word* 18: 54–72. Reprinted in J. A. Fodor and J. Katz (eds.), *The structure of language: readings in the philosophy of language*, 1964, Englewood-Cliffs, NJ: Prentice-Hall, 344–52.

Harris, Alice C. and Lyle Campbell. 1995. *Historical Syntax in Cross-Linguistic Perspective*. Cambridge Studies in Linguistics 74. Cambridge University Press.

Haspelmath, Martin. 1993. 'The diachronic externalization of inflection', *Linguistics* 31: 279–309.

Haspelmath, Martin. 1999a. 'Are there principles of grammatical change?' (Review article of *The development of language* by David Lightfoot), *Journal of Linguistics* 35: 579–95.

Haspelmath, Martin. 1999b. 'Optimality and diachronic adaptation', *Zeitschrift für Sprachwissenschaft* 18: 180–205.

Hawkins, John A. 1994. *A performance theory of order and constituency*. Cambridge Studies in Linguistics 73. Cambridge University Press.

Hombert, Jean-Marie, John J. Ohala and William G. Ewan. 1979. 'Phonetic explanations for the development of tone', *Language* 55: 37–58.

Jakobson, Roman 1971 [1928]. 'The concept of the sound law and the teleological criterion', in R. Jakobson (ed.), *Selected writings*, vol. 1: *Phonological studies*. The Hague: Mouton, 1–2.

Jakobson, Roman 1971 [1929]. 'Remarques sur l'évolution phonologique du russe comparée à celle des autres langues slaves', in R. Jakobson (ed.), *Selected writings*, vol. 1: *Phonological studies*. The Hague: Mouton, 6–116.

Kenstowicz, Michael. 1994. *Phonology in generative grammar*. Oxford: Blackwell.

King, Robert D. 1969. *Historical linguistics and generative grammar*. Englewood Cliffs, NJ: Prentice-Hall.

Kiparsky, Paul. 1968. 'Linguistic universals and linguistic change', in Emmon Bach and Robert Harms (eds.), *Universals in linguistic theory*. New York: Holt, Rinehart and Winston, 170–202.

Kiparsky, Paul. 1982. *Explanation in phonology*, Dordrecht: Foris.

Kiparsky, Paul. 1988. 'Phonological change', in Frederick J. Newmeyer (ed.), *Linguistics: the Cambridge survey*, vol. 1: *Linguistic theory: foundations*. Cambridge University Press, 363–415.

Kiparsky, Paul. 1995. 'The phonological basis of sound change', in John A. Goldsmith (ed.), *The handbook of phonological theory*. Oxford: Blackwell, 640–70.

Labov, William. 1974. 'On the use of the present to explain the past', in Luigi Heilmann (ed.), *Proceedings of the Eleventh International Congress of Linguists*, vol. 2. Bologna: Società Editrice il Mulino, 825–52.

Labov, William. 1987. 'The overestimation of functionalism', in René Dirven and Vilém Fried (eds.), *Functionalism in linguistics*. Amsterdam: John Benjamins, 311–32.

Labov, William. 1994. *Principles of linguistic change*, vol. 1: *Internal factors*. Language in Society 20. Oxford: Blackwell.

Lakoff, Robin T. 1972. 'Another look at drift', in Robert P. Stockwell and R. K. S. Macaulay (eds.), *Linguistic change and generative theory*. Bloomington, IN: Indiana University Press, 172–98.

Lass, Roger. 1980. *On explaining language change*. Cambridge University Press.

Lass, Roger. 1997. *Historical linguistics and language change*. Cambridge Studies in Linguistics 81. Cambridge University Press.

Lightfoot, David W. 1979. *Principles of diachronic syntax*. Cambridge Studies in Linguistics 23. Cambridge University Press.

Lightfoot, David W. 1988. 'Syntactic change', in Frederick J. Newmeyer (ed.), *Linguistics: the Cambridge survey*, vol. 1: *Linguistic theory: foundations*. Cambridge University Press, 303–23.

Lightfoot, David W. 1991. *How to set parameters: arguments from language change*. Cambridge, MA: MIT Press.

Lightfoot, David W. 1995. 'Grammars for people', *Journal of Linguistics* 31: 393–9.

Lightfoot, David W. 1999. *The development of language: acquisition, change, and evolution*. Blackwell/Maryland Lectures in Language and Cognition 1. Oxford: Blackwell.

Martinet, André. 1952. 'Function, structure, and sound change', *Word* 8: 1–32.

Martinet, André. 1955. *Economie des changements phonétiques*. Bern: A. Francke.

McMahon, April M. S. 1994. *Understanding language change*. Cambridge University Press.

Milroy, James and John Harris. 1980. 'When is a merger not a merger? The MEAT/MATE problem in a present-day English vernacular', *English World-Wide* 1: 199–210.

Milroy, Lesley. 1987. *Language and social networks*, 2nd edition. Oxford: Basil Blackwell.

Newmeyer, Frederick J. 1998. *Language form and language function*. Cambridge, MA: MIT Press.

Newmeyer, Frederick J. 2001. 'Where is functional explanation?' *Chicago Linguistic Society* 37: 146–59.

Niyogi, Partha and Robert C. Berwick. 1995. *The Logical Problem of Language Change*, A. I. Memo 1516. Cambridge, MA: MIT Artificial Intelligence Laboratory.

Ohala, John J. 1974. 'Phonetic explanation in phonology', in Anthony Bruck, Robert A. Fox and Michael W. La Galy (eds.), *Papers from the Parasession on Natural Phonology*. Chicago: Chicago Linguistic Society, 251–74.

Ohala, John J. 1981. 'The listener as a source of sound change', in Carrie S. Masek, Roberta A. Hendrick and Mary Frances Miller (eds.), *Papers from the Parasession on Language and Behavior*. Chicago: Chicago Linguistic Society, 178–203.

Ohala, John J. 1987. 'Explanation in phonology: opinions and examples', in Wolfgang U. Dressler, Hans C. Luschützky, Oskar E. Pfeiffer and John Rennison (eds.), *Phonologica 1984*. Cambridge University Press, 215–25.

Paul, Hermann. 1891. *Principles of the history of language*, translation of 2nd edition. London: Longmans, Green and Co.

Postal, Paul M. 1968. *Aspects of phonological theory*. New York: Harper and Row.

Roberts, Ian. 1993. 'A formal account of grammaticalization in the history of Romance futures', *Folia Linguistica Historica* 13: 219–58.

Shapiro, Michael. 1985. 'Teleology, semeiosis, and linguistic change', *Diachronica* 2: 1–34.

Shapiro, Michael. 1991. *The sense of change: language as history*. Bloomington: Indiana University Press.

Sweet, Henry. 1900. *The history of language*. London: J. M. Dent and Co.

Traugott, Elizabeth C. 1969. 'Toward a theory of syntactic change', *Lingua* 23: 1–27.

Traugott, Elizabeth C. and Henry Smith. 1993. 'Arguments from language change', *Journal of Linguistics* 29: 431–7.

Vennemann, Theo. 1973. 'Explanation in syntax', in John Kimball (ed.), *Syntax and semantics*, vol. 2. New York: Seminar Press, 1–50.

Weinreich, Uriel, William Labov and Marvin I. Herzog. 1968. 'Empirical foundations for a theory of language change', in W. Lehmann and Y. Malkiel (eds.), *Directions for historical linguistics*. Austin: University of Texas Press, 95–188.

Wurzel, Wolfgang U. 1989. *Inflectional morphology and naturalness*. Kluwer: Dordrecht.

Part II

Linguistic models and language change

3   Metaphors, models and language change

Jean Aitchison

1   Introduction

'A myth in the widest sense is a story or image that structures some epistemic field . . . But the function of the myth, as a structuring device . . . is in principle independent of its truth value. Its utility derives from its perceived truth or explanatory or gap-filling efficiency' (Lass 1997: 4).

These wise words come from Roger Lass's critical survey of the practice of historical linguistics, and his discussion of standards which should be adopted in historiographical activities such as reconstructing and explaining (Lass 1997). He explores in a coherent and enlightening way, 'some of our central myths and rituals' (1997: 8), and discusses how we form our theories. The overall book is a culmination of decades of enquiry into the nature of the discipline of linguistics, and his writings en route have become essential reading for today's historical linguists (e.g. Lass 1980, 1986, 1993).

As part of his discussion, Lass explores metaphor. Metaphors, he notes, are often thought of as vague sloppy things, as compared with good theories. 'But one could argue on the contrary that theory often (maybe normally) is the formalization of metaphor' (1997: 32), he suggests. By considering the English Great Vowel Shift, he shows 'how metaphors can populate history with new objects and kinds, and provide both access to interesting new worlds, and great field-internal success' (1997: 33).

The usefulness of metaphor in theory building has of course long been recognised, in a variety of scientific fields. 'The most impressive contribution to the growth of intelligibility has been made by the application of suggestive metaphors', Jonathan Miller pointed out in a discussion of medical images (1978: 9). The heart, for example, was once thought of as a furnace: the perception of it as a pump was a major step forward (Marshall 1977). And from wax tablets onward, human memory has been described in terms of writing surfaces (Draaisma 2000).

In descriptions of language, a number of recurring metaphors are found, which have arguably influenced our view of language and language change. Some well-known metaphors are the 'family' metaphor, especially in relation to language cognates; the 'game' metaphor, which became widely known from Saussure (1916); the 'chain shift' metaphor, as a description of linked changes, usefully discussed by Lass (1997).

Such metaphors raise questions. These may seem obvious, even simple-minded, yet they are not routinely asked by linguists. First, why have the particular metaphors associated with language arisen, and what accounts for their success? Second, have our language metaphors helped or hindered our understanding of language?

In order to answer these, some preliminary issues need to be outlined, about the definition, types and sources of metaphor.

2   Definition

Metaphor, according to Aristotle, is 'the application to one thing of a name belonging to another'. This much-quoted definition is in Aristotle's treatise *De Arte Poetica* (1457b). Accordingly, metaphor is traditionally associated with poetry.

Yet Aristotle's definition has held back metaphor studies. It is defective in two ways. First, non-poetic examples abound, as is now generally recognised: 'Metaphor is pervasive in everyday life...Our ordinary conceptual system is...fundamentally metaphorical in nature', Lakoff and Johnson point out (1980: 3).

Second, Aristotle's definition is too narrow. It inspired a long-standing but in-conclusive debate as to whether metaphor topics are like or unlike their source domains. But from the mid twentieth century onward, it became clear that simple source–target comparisons break down. Instead, an interactional view-point is essential: two frames interact, rather than two words. Both target and source domains participate in the overall, intertwined picture (e.g. Black 1962, Tourangeau and Sternberg 1982). For example: 'slow asphyxiation: the life is ebbing out of local government' (*Guardian* 2/6/00). Here a whole domain, that of local government, is viewed as a patient in a terminal state, and it is hard to see which particular 'name' (in Aristotle's sense) has been misapplied.

3   Types

Metaphors have deservedly received considerable attention in recent years (e.g. Gibbs 1994; Goatly 1997; Ortony 1993; Steen 1994). They can at first sight be usefully divided into those which are intentionally open-ended and those in which alternative interpretations are closed off.

Open-ended metaphors are a 'lure' to the imagination: the reader or listener is invited to provide a number of possible layers of interpretation. These are typical of poetry. T. S. Eliot's metaphor of the Church as a hippopotamus is famous (Eliot 1920). This could be interpreted as the Church's size, its slow-movingness, its preference for avoiding conflict by sinking out of sight when challenged, and so on. The possibilities expand, the more the reader thinks about them. Such metaphors fit in with 'spreading activation' theories of comprehension, in which the mind activates multiple interpretations in ever-widening ripples (McClelland and Rumelhart 1986).

Closed-off metaphors are those whose interpretation is obvious, often because they are explicitly explained, as: 'Hollywood money isn't money. It's congealed snow, melts in your hand', as Dorothy Parker once claimed (Augarde 1991). Such metaphors are typically found in newspapers, especially in sections of the paper that journalists feel need livening up, such as finance: 'Retailers squeezed', 'share prices took a roller-coaster ride', 'Country house prices are rocketing', and so on. Scientific metaphors seem at first sight characteristically closed off, and this includes some linguistic ones: 'Now we come to the irregular verbs. A menagerie of nearly 200 words coming in many shapes and sizes' (Pinker 1999: 57).

The richness of poetic metaphors therefore apparently contrasts with the clarity of scientific ones. Yet this is an oversimplification. These types overlap, in two main ways. First, poetic metaphors may be as closed off as scientific ones, as with the recurring idea that 'life is a bubble', just as factual metaphors may be rich and multi-layered: 'Numerous modern studies ... have demonstrated that, far from being transparent, scientific language functions with the same complexity as literary discourse does' (Papin 1992: 1253).

A second way in which poetic and factual metaphors overlap is in the lack of a precise fit between source and target. Readers may be lured on to draw conclusions that are unmerited, or, alternatively, they may fail to recognise important facets of the subject under discussion because of the narrow mindset caused by powerful metaphors: 'In allowing us to focus on one aspect of a concept ..., a metaphorical concept can keep us from focusing on other aspects of the concept that are inconsistent with that metaphor' (Lakoff and Johnson 1980: 10, cf. Aitchison 1997).

4   Metaphor sources

Arguably, human language has always used metaphor. At an abstract level, image schemas are built into the human mind. Everywhere 'up' is good and 'down' is bad, as in *up-market* vs. *down-market*, *top of the heap* vs. *bottom, high* vs. *low* in relation to mood, quality, life, and so on (Johnson 1987).

At a more concrete level, the body is a universal source of metaphor presumably from the origin of language. This is possibly how words were extended to cover the world at the beginning of human speech (Aitchison 1996; Heine 1997). Word meanings move outwards from the body: *the foot of the mountain, the head of the organisation, the ribs of the ship*; they also move inwards from actions near the body: thoughts are *turned over*, ideas are *inwardly digested*, and so on. The human body was the most fruitful source of metaphor in a study which spanned three centuries (Smith et al. 1981), and is still possibly so today. For example, the economy is frequently discussed in terms of health: *funds were haemorrhaging out of the lira, dollar makes tentative recovery, the ailing tourist industry, a very sick balance-sheet* (Knowles 1996, 1999).

Other metaphorical universals have been proposed: anger everywhere is heat (Lakoff 1987), though it varies as to whether the heat is wet or dry (Aitchison 2003), life everywhere is a journey (Lakoff and Turner 1989), and so on.

At a superficial level, the concerns of particular centuries give rise to idio-syncratic metaphors. In the eighteenth century, time-pieces exerted a strong fascination: 'the human body is a watch, a large watch, constructed with such skill and ingenuity, that if the wheel which makes the seconds happens to stop, the minute wheel turns and keeps on going round...' (La Mettrie 1748, quoted in MacCormac 1985: 11). Today of course the computer image has taken over as perhaps the most widely used metaphor, with phrases such as *software, hardware, input, output, flame, spam*, and so on, which have become part of everyday speech.

However, minds can become stuck in particular grooves, based on old-fashioned, outdated ideas, as with the four humours which date from Galen in the second century AD. This idea survived and was popularised by Robert Burton in *The anatomy of melancholy* (1621). It inspired false medical ideas for centuries, and is still found today in phrases such as *black mood, sanguine temperament, phlegmatic personality*, and so on.

In language too, metaphors have a habit of hanging on, and if not outdating their usefulness, at least creating false images, as will be explained.

5   Language metaphors

A number of language metaphors have been coined, with varying degrees of success. The best known will be outlined below. Later, the reasons for their success – or lack of it – will be discussed.

5.1   Conduit

A major metaphor for language is the 'conduit' image, which dates from John Locke in the late seventeenth century, when he envisaged language as a water-pipe: 'For Language being the great Conduit, whereby Men convey their Discoveries, Reasonings and Knowledge, from one to another' (Locke 1690/ 1975: book 3, ch. 11, sect. 5). This metaphor was probably based on Locke's understandable admiration for London's recently established water supply.

'Locke's influence on eighteenth-century thought is immeasurable', it has been claimed (Harris and Taylor 1997: 137). Locke laid down the foundations for the long-standing belief that the main function of language is the transfer of thoughts and information. Communication is envisaged as an event in which a sender transmits a message through a channel to a receiver. This 'conduit' metaphor has provided a host of related communication metaphors, as Reddy (1979/1993) points out, with examples such as *Try to get your thoughts across better*, *None of Mary's feelings came through to me with any clarity*, and so on.

5.2 Tree

Another major and well-known model is that of a tree. The so-called *Stamm-baumtheorie* was popularised by August Schleicher in the mid nineteenth century, and has dominated historical linguistic thought. It represents a group of related languages as a 'family tree' with a primary ancestor 'mother' language, which then split, in a series of neat divides, into a set of offspring 'daughter languages', which in turn split into further offspring, as in a genealogical tree – though Schleicher's tree was initially represented sideways, as an extending and splitting horizontal branch (Schleicher 1861–2; Bynon 1986).

The idea of a tree also gave rise to the standard way of diagramming relations within sentences, an S-node at the top of a page splits into, say, NP and VP, which further subdivides, in a tree structure which eventually covers the page. What has changed over the years is the labels for the nodes, not the basic splitting structure.

5.3 Waves and ripples

Johannes Schmidt's *Wellentheorie* 'wave theory' envisaged language changes as spreading out, like ripples on a pond (Schmidt 1872, Bynon 1977). Saussure enthusiastically endorsed this theory: 'Un ouvrage de Johannes Schmidt... ouvrit les yeux des linguistes en inaugurant la théorie de la continuité ou des ondes (Wellentheorie).... Ainsi la théorie des ondes... nous éclaire sur les lois primordiales de tous les phénomènes de différenciation' (1968 [1916]: 287). This image has not been particularly popular until recently. Those few linguists who worked to promote it in the interim were not pre-eminent (e.g. Bailey and Shuy 1973).

5.4 Game

A widely used and celebrated language model is that of a game of chess, which originated with Ferdinand de Saussure. He used this famous image to point out some seminal linguistic ideas, above all the insight that substance must be distinguished from form, and that the internal relationship between the pieces was supremely important: 'si je remplace des pièces de bois par des pièces d'ivoire, le changement est indifférent pour le système: mais si je diminue ou augmente le nombre des pièces, ce changement-là atteint profondément la "grammaire" du jeu' (1968 [1916]: 43).

Wittgenstein (1958) carried the notion of a game further, using it in a number of ways, including the notion of a game as rule-governed:

We can also think of the whole process of using words ... as one of those games by means of which children learn their native language. I will call these games 'language-games' and will sometimes speak of a primitive language as a language-game... (1958: 1.7)

The idea of a game has also generated further metaphors, such as turn-taking in conversations being likened to a ball going to and fro: 'Conversation is like playing tennis with a ball made of Krazy Putty that keeps coming back over the net in a different shape', says Professor Maurice Zapp, in David Lodge's novel *Small World* (1984/1985:25).

5.5   Chain

The notion of a chain-shift (drag chain or push chain) was popularised by Martinet (1955), though linked changes had of course been recognised much earlier, with Grimm's Law, and the Great Vowel Shift. This (as noted above) has been well discussed by Lass (1997).

5.6   Plants

The idea that languages might be like 'organic bodies', usually plants, recurs at intervals, particularly in the nineteenth century:

Languages are to be considered organic natural bodies, which are formed according to fixed laws, develop as possessing an inner principle of life, and gradually die out because they do not understand themselves any longer, and therefore cast off or mutilate their members or forms. (Franz Bopp 1827, in Jespersen 1922: 65)

Some years later, Jakob Grimm suggested that language might be like a tree, his point being that plants require space and nourishment:

Does not language flourish in a favorable place like a tree whose way nothing blocks? ... Also does it not become underdeveloped, neglected and dying away like a plant that had to languish or dry out from lack of light or soil? (Grimm 1851)

Saussure also toyed with this plant analogy:

De même que la plante est modifiée dans son organisme interne par des facteurs étrangers: terrain, climat, etc., de même l'organisme grammatical ne dépend-il pas constamment des facteurs externes du changement linguistique?... Est-il possible de distinguer le développment naturel, organique d'un idiome, de ses formes artificielles, telles que la language littéraire, qui sont dues à des facteurs externes, par conséquent inorganiques?

(Saussure 1968 [1916]: 41–2)

Saussure additionally used a plant metaphor to distinguish between diachronic and synchronic linguistics: 'la section longitudinale nous montre les fibres elles-mêmes, et la section transversale leur groupement sur un plan particulier; mais la seconde est distincte de la première' (Saussure 1968 [1916]: 125).

The plant metaphor is rarely used seriously these days. Yet it is sufficiently well known for John Simon to argue against it in a popularising book:

Why does language keep changing? Because it is a living thing, people will tell you . . . it is a living organism that, like a live plant, sprouts new leaves and flowers . . . let us concede that language is indeed a living plant – a rhododendron, say. Well, a rhododendron can be depended upon to sprout rhododendron leaves and rhododendron flowers. At no point will it start sprouting petunia blooms or *Ficus* leaves.   (Simon 1981: 17–18)

5.7   Buildings

The metaphor of language as a city or house possibly began with Wittgenstein:

Our language can be seen as an ancient city, a maze of little streets and squares, of old and new houses, and of houses with additions from various periods; and this surrounded by a multitude of new boroughs with straight regular streets and uniform houses.

(1958: I.18)

The linguist Charles Fillmore (1979) likens language to a house:

The house of language that we live in is a large house, with many rooms. We do not know yet how many rooms we have, or exactly what kinds of furnishings we will find.

(Fillmore, personal communication)

Such metaphors are not at first sight major ones. Yet building metaphors, the 'building blocks' of language, are implicitly found in the writings of structural linguists (my boldings):

Using the phoneme and the morpheme as their **basic units**, linguists have been able to **build** a comprehensive theory of the expression side of language.   (Gleason 1961: 11)

Language . . . is a **complex of structures** of various kinds. The analysis of a language must proceed by separating out the **various parts**, but a full understanding of language cannot be gotten if they are left as detached details unrelated to one another. The various elements are of significance and interest primarily because they **fit together** into one integrated system.   (Gleason 1961: 373)

5.8   Dominator model

The terminology of linguistic theory, it has been claimed, reflects a 'dominator model' (Junker 1992). On linguistic trees, higher nodes dominate lower nodes, and the relationship of *c-command* is defined in terms of dominance, within the theory known as 'government and binding'. This is in fact an extension of the tree metaphor, already outlined.

5.9   Other metaphors

Various other metaphors are found, often fleeting ones. Wittgenstein, for example, talks about a language labyrinth: 'Language is a labyrinth of paths. You approach from *one* side and know your way about; you approach the same place from another side and no longer know your way about' (1958: I.203).

6   Success of static metaphors

The most successful of these metaphors for language have been static ones. Locke's conduit metaphor contributed strongly to the idea that language should be controlled in a watertight pipe. This and other 'still life' metaphors have been more readily adopted than the more realistic 'wave' metaphor, even though the latter was championed by Saussure.

Yet the success of static metaphors is not accidental. The conduit image would not have been influential, had it not tied in with existing viewpoints. Metaphors which thrive in a culture need to be in accord with the general *Zeitgeist*, and they have to fit with each other. In short, they have to achieve cultural resonance and avoid cognitive dissonance or 'frame conflict'.

Metaphors are not for the most part coined in isolation. In biology, Paton (1992) has argued that larger global metaphors generate their own metalanguages, which become part of a complex hierarchy of derived images, as Lass emphasises: 'The point is obvious', Lass comments. He spends time on it, he says, because 'the obvious is not always that easily seen, and as practitioners of any field we are so immersed in our own metalanguage that we may not notice (a) that much more is metaphorical than we think, and (b) how important these metaphors are as devices for framing our thinking, and how much of our theory they actually generate' (1997: 41–2).

This has been true for centuries. Locke's ideas caught on, and influenced thought primarily because they coincided with existing views: this static viewpoint has subconsciously been built into the national consciousness, and covertly maintained, even in the writings of linguists, as will be outlined below.

7   Maintenance of the static viewpoint

When Locke promoted his waterpipe metaphor, insecurity about English was at its height. The fluidity of English was contrasted with the apparent permanence of Latin, and calls were made to fix English in a similar way. As Edward Waller said (mid seventeenth century):

> Poets that lasting marble seek,
> Must carve in Latin or in Greek.
> We write in sand, our language grows,
> And like the tide, our work o'erflows.
> (Waller, 1904, in Bailey 1991: 54–5)

Particularly at the end of the seventeenth century and beginning of the eighteenth, the influential writers Daniel Defoe, Joseph Addison and Jonathan Swift all strongly urged that English should have a fixed standard. Defoe, for example, proposed that a formal body would be appointed to:

polish and refine the English tongue, and advance the much neglected Faculty of Correct Language, to establish Purity and Propriety of Stile, and to purge it from all the Irregular Additions that Ignorance and Affectation have introduc'd. (Defoe 1697)

In 1711, Joseph Addison said he had often wished that:

certain Men might be set apart as Superintendants of our Language, to hinder any Words of Foreign Coin from passing among us; and in particular to prohibit any French Phrases from becoming Current in this Kingdom. (Addison, 1711, in Bolton 1966: 102)

Best known of all the would-be purifiers is Jonathan Swift, who in 1712 wrote to the Lord Treasurer, with 'A Proposal for correcting improving and ascertaining the English tongue':

I do here...complain...that our Language is extremely imperfect, that its daily improvements are by no means in proportion to its daily Corruptions... and if it were once refined to a certain Standard, perhaps there may be ways found out to fix it for ever.
(Swift, 1712, in Bolton 1966: 107)

Swift is often praised as a high-minded individual who wished to preserve the language for the benefit of mutual understanding, yet the truth is more mundane: he wanted his own work to survive. He noted that if English could be fixed, then:

our best Writings might probably be preserved with Care, and grow into Esteem, and the Authors have a Chance for Immortality. (*Ibid.*)

In addition to concern about the survival of his own work, Swift's desire to keep the language 'pure' tied in with his idiosyncrasies: he was obsessed with personal cleanliness, something unusual in his time. As Thomas Sheridan commented, describing Swift:

He was one of the cleanliest men that ever lived. His hands were not only washed, as those of other men, with the utmost care, but his nails were constantly kept pared to the quick... As he walked much, he... cleansed his feet with the utmost exactness.
(Sheridan, in Glendenning 1998: 226)

These eighteenth-century purists were therefore picking up on current worries, and promoting them in order to further their own interests.

The nineteenth century saw further attempts to fix language, though from a somewhat different angle. Richard Chenevix Trench, an influential archbishop of Dublin, expressed his bizarre belief that the language of 'savage tribes' had slithered down from former excellence. He regarded language as a 'moral barometer', and claimed that 'with every impoverishing or debasing of personal or national life goes hand in hand a corresponding impoverishment and debasement of language'. He quoted with approval a German, F. Schlegel, who claimed:

The care of the national language I consider at all times a sacred trust and a most important privilege of the higher orders of society. Every man of education should make it the object of his unceasing concern, to preserve his language pure and entire.

(Trench 1856: 5)

His assumption apparently was that God had given language to humans perfect, and they needed to preserve it so, otherwise it would collapse.

Trench's bizarre views on language extended to meaning also: he deplored meaning change, claiming that words which altered their meaning 'bear the slime on them of the serpent's trail' (Trench 1855: 41). He worried about the effect not only on language, but also its speakers:

This tendency of words to lose the sharp, rigidly defined outline of meaning which they once possessed, to become of wide, vaguer, loose application instead of fixed, definite and precise, to mean almost anything, and so really to mean nothing, is ... one of those tendencies ... which are at work for the final ruin of a language and, I do not fear to add, for the demoralization of those that speak it.   (Trench 1856:192)

These influential views spread widely. Even in the twentieth century respectable writers on language have used labels such as 'weakening', 'bleaching', 'verbicide', 'distortion' to refer to it. 'The problem with verbicide is that words no longer die: having been drained of their vitality ... they become zombies' (Hughes 1988: 14).

Only relatively recently has this notion of 'bleaching' become outmoded and been replaced by the idea of polysemy. Typically, a word develops several layers of meaning, we now realise:

Meanings expand their range through the development of various polysemies ... these polysemies may be regarded as quite fine-grained. It is only collectively that they may seem like weakening of meaning.   (Hopper and Traugott 1993: 100)

This understanding of polysemy has come even later than the general understanding of the role of language variation in language change, which developed particularly via Labov's seminal work (Labov 1972, 1994).

7.1   Successful linguistics metaphors

Saussure's notion of language as a game, such as chess, tied in not only with the general belief that language should be controlled, but also with the prevailing notion of games as neat, tidy and rule-governed: games were organised events, as shown by Alice's complaints about the croquet game in Wonderland, where the mallets were live flamingos, and the croquet balls live hedgehogs. Just as she had got the flamingos head down, 'it was very provoking to find that the hedgehog had unrolled itself, and was in the act of crawling away':

'I don't think they play at all fairly,' Alice began, in a rather complaining tone, '... and you've no idea how confusing it is all the things being alive.'   (Carroll 1865/1988: 83)

Games, then, were rule-governed objects, and played with static implements.

Linguists did of course realise that language rules were not water-tight: 'All grammars leak', commented Edward Sapir (1921: 38). But leakiness implies a few drops squeezing out at the edges, not a need to regard language as anything other than neat and tidy overall. And the role and nature of the leakiness was not explored.

Of course, games have other properties apart from having rules. But these other properties fed into the idea of overall control. For example, games also have aims. Here, the transfer of information fitted in as a primary aim. Additionally, games need to have conventions for orderly interaction. Here again language fits in with the game idea, as people take it in turns to speak. A further property of games is that a governing body rules the rules: again, this ties in well with the notion of linguistic constraints.

All in all, the game metaphor fitted language well, it seemed, with aims, rules, conventions of interaction and constraints. But in all this, language was tidied up, and change was hard to comprehend, so much so that bizarre theories were thought up to explain language change, such as the claim by generative linguists that children, rather than adults, change the language (e.g. King 1969).

A few lone voices, such as Malinowski, Firth and Whorf, tried to counteract the neat and tidy structuralist viewpoint, but their insightful yet unsystematic attempts at 'loosening up' language were only marginally successful: 'Whorf's examples clearly demonstrate that Western languages, based on segmentation – verbs and nouns, subjects and objects – are best suited to describing systems at rest and are profoundly deficient in accounting for dissipative structures – systems in movement, in turbulence, or under stress', notes Papin (1992: 1258). The static view of language, current in general thought, was therefore adopted subconsciously by professional linguists. This damaged our view of historical linguistics for decades.

But what about the other metaphors around, such as a wave? 'If a concept is structured metaphorically, the presence of multiple conflicting metaphors is a serious problem', notes Murphy (1996: 187). But in most instances, as in language, minor metaphors are simply ignored: they may be acknowledged, but they do not disrupt the major viewpoint. The wave metaphor was for a long time marginalised, and language change was treated as if it did not truly exist.

Linguists were presumably not consciously distorting their field. They were subconsciously fitting their ideas in not only with long-held views about language, but also about the world at large: '"Nature on the rack", passively open to human investigation and detached observation, is indeed a construct deeply embedded in our thought and language systems', it has been claimed (Papin 1992: 1258), and the failure to explore certain metaphors may have slowed down the development of science (Bohm and Perat 1987). This is due to the western mind-set: 'One of the most developed skills in contemporary Western civilization is dissection: the split-up of problems into their smallest possible components. We are good at it. So good, we often forget to put the pieces back together again' (Prigogine and Stengers 1984: xi).

8   Conclusion

Linguists have largely pooh-poohed views of the general public on language, often quoting Bloomfield (1944) who condemns 'secondary responses' (utterances about language) made by self-styled yet ignorant linguistic 'experts'. Yet, as this discussion has shown, linguists themselves have been unwittingly drawn into the net created by such people, and while pouring scorn on them, have themselves fallen into the trap of assuming language is neat and tidy.

But in recent years, an increasing number of linguists, like Lass, have been exploring metalinguistics, views about language, and also the theoretical underpinnings of our subject. This paper has tried to follow in their footsteps, by showing how linguists' use of metaphor has misled them, and how in order to move forward, we need to be aware not only of the ways in which we have been misled, but also the deeper causes of these false trails.

The final message is that we must all be on our guard when faced with enticing metaphors. As Palmerston said in 1839 (quoted in Crystal 2000: 247): 'Half the wrong conclusions at which mankind arrive are reached by the abuse of metaphors, and by mistaking general resemblance of imaginary similarity for real identity.'

REFERENCES

Aitchison, Jean. 1996. *The seeds of speech: language origin and evolution*. Cambridge University Press.
Aitchison, Jean. 1997. *The language web: the power and problem of words*. Cambridge University Press.

Aitchison, Jean. 2003. *Words in the mind: an introduction to the mental lexicon*. 3rd edition. Oxford: Blackwell.

Augarde, Tony (ed.). 1991. *Oxford dictionary of modern quotations*. Oxford University Press.

Bailey, Charles-James N. 1982. 'The garden path that historical linguistics went astray on', *Language and Communication* 2: 151–60.

Bailey, Charles-James N. and Roger W. Shuy (eds.). 1973. *New ways of analysing variation in English*. Washington: Georgetown University Press.

Bailey, Richard W. 1991. *Images of English: a cultural history of the language*. Cambridge University Press.

Black, Max. 1962. 'Metaphor', in M. Black, *Models and metaphors*. Ithaca, NY: Cornell University Press, 25–47.

Bloomfield, Leonard. 1944. 'Secondary and tertiary responses to language', *Language* 20: 45–55.

Bohm, David and David Perat. 1987. *Science, order and creativity*. New York: Bantam.

Bolton, W. F. (ed.). 1966. *The English language: essays by English and American men of letters*, 1490–839. Cambridge University Press.

Bynon, Theodora. 1977. *Historical linguistics*. Cambridge University Press.

Bynon, Theodora. 1986. 'August Schleicher: Indo-Europeanist and general linguist', in Theodora Bynon and and Frank R. Palmer (eds.), *Studies in the history of western linguistics: in honour of R. H. Robins*. Cambridge University Press, 129–49.

Carroll, Lewis 1988 [1865]. *The complete works of Lewis Carroll*. London: Penguin.

Crystal, David and Hilary Crystal. 2000. *Words on words: quotations about language and languages*. London: Penguin.

Defoe, Daniel. 1697. 'Of academies', in *An Essay upon projects*, in James T. Boulton (ed.), *Selected writings of Daniel Defoe*. Cambridge University Press, 1975.

Draaisma, Douwe. 2000. *Metaphors of memory: a history of ideas about the mind*, trans. P. Vincent. Cambridge University Press.

Eliot, Thomas Stern. 1969 [1920]. 'The hippopotamus', in *The complete poems and plays of T. S. Eliot*. London: Faber and Faber.

Fillmore, Charles. 1979. Paper presented at the University of Salzburg, Summer Linguistics Institute.

Gibbs, Raymond W. 1994. *The poetics of mind: figurative thought, language and understanding*. Cambridge University Press.

Gleason, Henry A. 1961. *An introduction to descriptive linguistics*, revised edition. New York: Holt, Rinehart and Winston.

Glendenning, Victoria. 1998. *Jonathan Swift*. London: Hutchinson.

Goatly, Andrew. 1997. *The language of metaphors*. London: Routledge.

Grimm, Jakob. 1984 [1851]. *On the origin of language*, trans. R. A. Wiley, Leiden: Brill.

Harris, Roy and Taylor, Talbot J. 1997. *Landmarks in linguistic thought*, vol. 1. *The western tradition from Socrates to Saussure*, 2nd edition. London: Routledge.

Heine, Bernd. 1997. *Cognitive foundations of grammar*. Oxford University Press.

Hopper, Paul J. and Elizabeth C. Traugott. 1993. *Grammaticalization*. Cambridge University Press.

Hughes, Geoffrey. 1988. *Words in time: a social history of the English vocabulary*. Oxford: Basil Blackwell.

Jespersen, Otto. 1922. *Language, its nature, development and origin*. London: Allen and Unwin.

Johnson, Mark. 1987. *The body in the mind: the bodily basis of meaning, imagination and reason*. University of Chicago Press.

Junker, Marie-Odile. 1992. 'Metaphors we live by: the terminology of linguistic theory', *Natural Language and Linguistic Theory* 10: 141–5.

King, Robert D. 1969. *Historical linguistics and generative grammar*. Englewood Cliffs, NJ: Prentice-Hall.

Kittay, Eva F. 1987. *Metaphor: its cognitive and linguistic structure*. Oxford: Clarendon.

Knowles, Frank. 1996. 'Lexicographical aspects of health metaphors in financial text', *Proceedings of EURALEX 96*, Gothenberg University, 789–96.

Knowles, Frank. 1999. 'Lexicographical and collocational aspects of health metaphors in financial text', *Moscow University Bulletin* 3: 75–85.

Labov, William. 1972. *Sociolinguistic patterns*. Philadelphia: University of Pennsylvania Press.

Labov, William. 1994. *Principles of linguistic change,* vol. 1: *Internal factors*. Oxford: Blackwell.

Lakoff, George. 1987. *Women, fire and dangerous things*. University of Chicago Press.

Lakoff, George and Mark Johnson. 1980. *Metaphors we live by*. University of Chicago Press.

Lakoff, George and Mark Turner. 1989. *More than cool reason: a field guide to poetic metaphor*. University of Chicago Press.

Lass, Roger. 1980. *On explaining language change*. Cambridge University Press.

Lass, Roger. 1986. 'Conventionalism, invention, and "historical reality": some reflections on method', *Diachronica* 3: 15–42.

Lass, Roger. 1993. 'How real(ist) are reconstructions', in *Historical linguistics: problems and perspectives*. London: Longman, 156–89.

Lass, Roger. 1997. *Historical linguistics and language change*. Cambridge University Press.

Locke, John. 1975 [1690]. *An essay concerning human understanding*. Oxford: Clarendon Press.

Lodge, David. 1985 [1984]. *Small World*. London: Penguin.

MacCormac, Earl R. 1985. *A cognitive theory of metaphor*. Cambridge, MA: MIT Press.

Marshall, John C. 1977. 'Minds, machines and metaphors', *Social Studies of Science* 7: 475–88.

Martinet, Antoine. 1955. *Economie des changements phonétiques*. Berne: A. Francke.

McClelland, James L. and David E. Rumelhart. 1986. *Parallel distributed processing: exploration in the microstructure of cognition*, vol. 2. Cambridge, MA: MIT Press.

Miller, Jonathan. 1978. *The body in question*. New York: Random House.

Murphy, Gregory L. 1996. 'On metaphoric representation', *Cognition* 60: 173–204.

Ortony, Andrew. 1993. *Metaphor and thought*, 2nd edition. Cambridge University Press.

Papin, Liliane. 1992. 'This is not a universe: metaphor, language, and representation', *Proceedings of the Modern Languages Association* 107.5: 1253–65.

Paton, Ray C. 1992. 'Towards a metaphorical biology', *Biology and Philosophy* 7: 279–94.

Pinker, Steven. 1999. *Words and rules: the ingredients of language*. London: Weidenfeld and Nicolson.

Prigogine, Ilya and Isabelle Stengers. 1984. *Order out of chaos*. New York: Bantam.

Reddy, Michael J. 1993 [1979]. 'The conduit metaphor: a case of frame conflict in our language about language', in Ortony, 164–201.

Richards, Ivor A. 1936. *The philosophy of rhetoric*. Oxford: Oxford University Press.

Sapir, Edward. 1921. *Language*. New York: Harcourt, Brace, World.

Saussure, Ferdinand de. 1968 [1916]. *Cours de linguistique générale*. Paris: Payot.

Schleicher, August. 1861–2. *Compendium der vergleichenden Grammatik der indogermanischen Sprachen*. Weimar: Böhlau.

Schmidt, Johannes. 1872. *Die Verwandtschaftverhältnisse der indogermanischen Sprachen*. Weimar: Böhlau.

Simon, John. 1981. *Paradigms lost*. London: Chatto and Windus.

Smith, Michael K., Howard R. Pollio and M. K. Pitts. 1981. 'Metaphor as intellectual history: conceptual categories underlying figurative usage in American English from 1675–1975', *Linguistics* 19: 911–35.

Steen, Gerard. 1994. *Understanding metaphor in literature*. London. Longman.

Sweetser, Eve E. 1990. *From etymology to pragmatics: metaphorical and cultural aspects of semantic structure*. Cambridge University Press.

Tourangeau, Roger and Robert J. Sternberg 1982. 'Understanding and appreciating metaphors', *Cognition* 11: 203–44.

Trench, Richard Chenevix. 1855. *On the study of words*, 6th edition. London: J. W. Parker.

Trench, Richard Chenevix. 1856. *English past and present*, 3rd, revised edition. London: J.W. Parker.

Wittgenstein, Ludwig 1958 [1953]. *Philosophical investigations*, trans. by G. E. M. Anscombe. Oxford: Basil Blackwell.

4   Log(ist)ic and simplistic S-curves

David Denison

1   Introduction

The technical term *S-curve* goes back at least to 1839 (*OED*, as two words), and
in the context of linguistic change certainly to 1954 (Altmann et al. 1983: 105).
The importance of S-curves is now generally taken for granted in historical
linguistics.[1] Devitt, for example, asserts that '[t]he S-curve pattern of diffusion
occurred throughout [her] data' (1989: 75). Here is a more recent example
concerning early Modern English morphosyntax (Nevalainen 2000: 339):

> I need to be able to measure the degree of supralocalisation and subsequent standardisa-
> tion of a linguistic variable. The measure I shall use will be the completion of an S-curve
> by the feature in question in the data examined.

In Nevalainen's paper, many graphs need just five or six data-points to reveal
a jagged but nevertheless recognisably S-shaped form. I myself have long assumed 'that the time course of the propagation of a language change typically
follows an S-curve', as Croft expresses it (2000: 183). In this chapter I wish to
question why this might be so, what it means and why perhaps, in the end, it
is actually rather *un*expected. In touching on explanations of language change
and notably the shape that changes take, there is a risk (or one might well say,
the hope) of echoing some of Roger Lass's published work: there can be few
topics in historical linguistics that he has not profitably addressed at some time
or other.

Change tends to proceed slowly at first, then after a while it speeds up.
That seems uncontroversial enough. Linguistic change is always occasional

---

* I first started reflecting on S-curves in Denison (1999), a lecture delivered at a conference on
medieval English under the title 'Slow, slow, quick, quick, slow'. This chapter is in part a
reworking of that paper. I have developed the discussion of S-curves proper and compressed some
speculations about the overall chronological shape of change in English. I am grateful to Helena
Raumolin-Brunberg for some references and for her friendly and stimulating disagreement, to
Ted Briscoe for two preprints, to Edmund Weiner of the *OED* for looking into early uses of the
term *S-curve*, and to Malcolm Campbell for help with graphics.

[1] Helena Raumolin-Brunberg (personal communication, 19 Sept. 2000) wryly implies, however,
that relatively few S-curves of long-term historical data are actually available, apart from graphs
based on Ellegård's famous DO material (1953).

and sporadic to begin with. We might imagine plotting some imaginary change as in (1), where at first only the conservative form is found, so that the proportion of an innovatory form (as against the conservative form) is zero. After the first occurrence, the curve slowly climbs through single-figure percentages until the innovation is being used on maybe 20–25 per cent of the available occasions (20 per cent is the usual transition point chosen in such illustrations). All the time its rate of increase is increasing – the curve is getting steeper – and after a while its progress is very rapid:

(1)   The beginning of a change

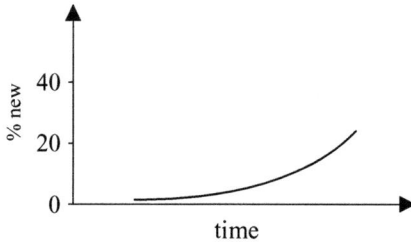

Why has the rate of change been speeding up? What happens next? A common-sense view might be that we make our linguistic choices by **analogy**, modelling our behaviour on what we hear around us. A change must start somewhere. Use with one word – for a change which can be located at word level, such as a sound change – might eventually be generalised to a second, then to a third, and so on, and as the number of relevant words showing the change and acting as models reaches a 'critical mass', it makes sense that the remainder should be drawn into the change with increasing speed. The rate goes on increasing until the remaining pool of unchanged words is altogether used up. 'Critical mass' is the imagery of nuclear fission. It suggests that linguistic change ought to go 'slow, slow, quick, quicker, bang!', something like (2):

(2)   The big bang?

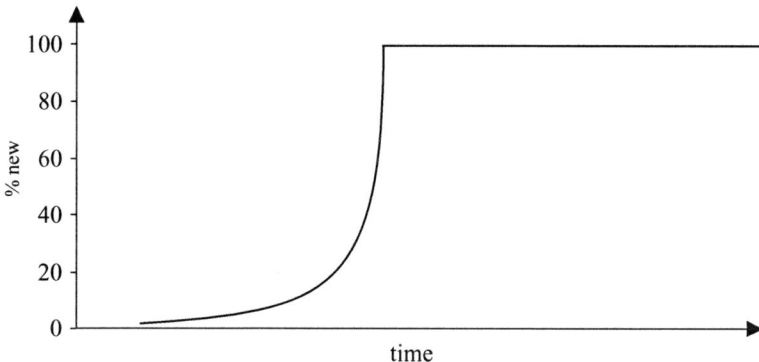

In diagram (2), the rate of change rises exponentially until the new form completely ousts the old. Of course, you can't use a form on more than 100 per cent of the available occasions, so when the proportion hits 100 per cent, the curve just becomes a horizontal line again.

Trouble is, this does not generally happen. Our common-sense thought experiment does not seem to reflect linguistic history very well at all. What actually happens much of the time is more like 'slow, slow, quick, quick, slow'. After the phase when the new form gains ascendancy rather rapidly, the process of change slows down again as the last remnants of the older state linger on. The result might look something like this:

(3)   An idealised graph of change

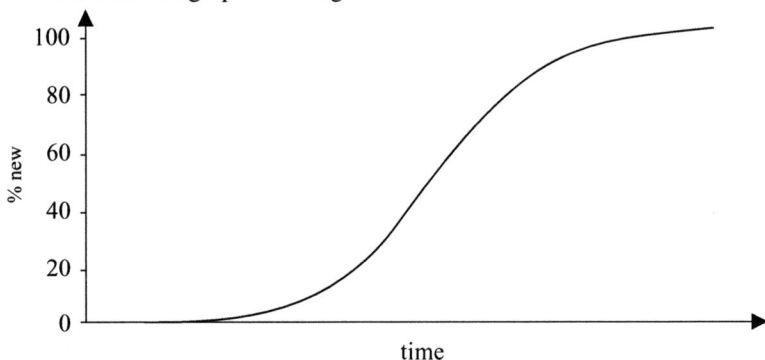

The whole thing can last hundreds of years altogether, indeed may never be wholly completed, but the bulk of the change is located within a much narrower slice of time where the slope is steeper. We need a concrete example.

The standard reference works (see Denison 1993: 428) all point to 1795 as the date of the earliest occurrence of the English progressive passive, as in the modern type:

(4)   A road *was being built.*

Then there is a rash of further occurrences in the decades immediately following. The construction seems to spring rather quickly into use, albeit at first a rather limited and socially constrained use. Earlier examples keep turning up, however:[2]

(5)   I have received the speech and address of the House of Lords; probably, that of the House of Commons *was being debated* when the post went out. (1772)

---

[2] Examples (5) and (6) are due to Roger Higgins (via Warner 1995), and (7) to Linda van Bergen (personal communication, 27 Oct. 1999).

(6)   The inhabitants of Plymouth are under arms, and everything *is being done* that can be. (1779)

(7)   and while you *are being lampoon'd* in ballads and newspapers, I mean to cut a figure in the history of England (1790)

Nakamura (1998) claimed to have a seventeenth century example, which I do not find convincing, and in Denison (1999: 54) I toyed with an apparent example from 1709 which subsequently proved to be a modern editorial creation. In a way that makes the point. What it strongly suggests is that if enough suitable texts had survived from the eighteenth and maybe also the seventeenth centuries, and if we had the resources to go through them all, we might well be able to show the characteristic early life of a linguistic innovation, with occasional, sporadic occurrences leading eventually to a more rapid take-up. Early use of the progressive passive *is* sporadic, and the very earliest one might be ca 1770, like (5), or some earlier date. It doesn't matter too much (at least for this kind of story.) But I am sure the beginning of the steeper part of the rise would be in the late 1790s and early 1800s. In Pratt and Denison (2000) we have tried to give a sociohistorical account of this period (and I have also speculated on a possible regional origin for the construction).

That is the transition from 'slow, slow' to 'quick, quick': I have chosen this example to illustrate an S-curve, because in this instance we would probably be justified in going on to complete a whole graph like that in (3), since arguably there were old and new forms in genuine competition:

(8)   A road *was building*.

(9)   (= (4)) A road *was being built*.

Unusually in syntax, these are forms which seem to be virtually synonymous. Between the late eighteenth century and the present day, type (8) has been replaced by type (9), at first occasionally, then in the mid to late nineteenth century with great rapidity. In fact Nakamura (1998) judges from his evidence of diaries and journals that the majority usage was already type (9) for people born after 1800, therefore leaving written records after the 1820s or so. However, type (8) did not die out in the nineteenth century:

(10)   A trans-provincial highway *is building* through southern British Columbia from the mountains...to Hope in the Fraser River Valley. (1916 [*OED*])

Sporadic examples continue to be found. The speed of change returns from 'quick, quick' to 'slow' again, and the (8) type, sometimes known as the **passival**, may never quite die out.

2   Why an S-shaped curve?

Why do we get S-curves rather than big bangs? The case which is usually made (see e.g. Labov 1994: 65–6, who traces it back to Bloomfield) runs roughly as follows. That rush to follow analogy is utterly misleading, since we are dealing here with gradual processes which take a long time to go through, even in the rapid phase. It's much more like evolution by natural selection, where repeated minuscule statistical preferences gradually add up over the generations to a large cumulative difference. Change requires **variation**, the existence of an alternative way of saying roughly the same thing. There would be no change at all unless there were some small advantage in the new form, whether structural or social. The net advantage of the new form must be small, as – if for no other reason – inertia and the need to communicate with older generations mean that the old form has something going for it as well. The change proper gets going – the transition from **innovation** to **propagation** – if the new form acquires a social value (Croft 2000: 185–6).

Now, speakers reproduce approximately what they hear, including variation, and even apparently including the rough proportions of variant usage they hear around them.[3] However, if there is some slight advantage in the new form over the old, the proportions may adjust slightly in favour of the new. Thus the *status quo* is not reproduced with perfect fidelity. The speaker has (unconsciously) made a slightly different choice between variants – albeit a statistical choice, reflected in frequencies of occurrence. And this effect of choice is greatest when the two variants are both there to choose from. In the very early stages of a change, so the argument runs, the new form is rare, so the pressures of choice are relatively weak and the rate of change is slow. In the late stages of a change, the *old* form is rare, so that the selective effect of having two forms to compare and choose between is again weak, and once again the rate of change is slow. Only in the middle period, when there are substantial numbers of each form in competition, does the rate of change speed up. Hence the S-curve.

What of the mathematics? Labov shows how an S-curve is produced by the cumulative frequencies of the binomial distribution (1994: 65). He mentions too that other mathematical functions have this shape, including the cumulative normal distribution and the logistic function. Altmann et al. had looked at three different functions that produced similar S-shaped curves, preferring the logistic function, in which the rate of change is proportional to the frequencies both of old forms and new (1983: 106–9) – cf. the plausibility argument above. Kroch also uses the logistic to model linguistic S-curves (1989a, b, etc.), arguing that it provides a good empirical fit, that its mathematics are simple, and that in the possibly analogous case of population biology, the logistic can actually be derived theoretically from one particular proposal for a mechanism of change.

---

[3] Labov talks of **probability matching** (1994: 580–6, also cf. 1994: 65–6, 595), an interesting concept which I cannot go into here.

Niyogi and Berwick are more cautious, or perhaps more catholic, in their choice of mathematical function (1997: 715):

> We note that...the logistic shape has sometimes been *assumed* as a starting point, see, e.g., Kroch [(1989b)]...On the contrary, we propose that language learning (or mislearning due to misconvergence) could be the engine driving language change. The nature of evolutionary behavior *need not* be logistic...Sometimes the trajectories are S-shaped (often associated with logistic growth); but sometimes not...

Briscoe (2000a) reviews some models of population, speaker–hearer interactions and language learning. The assumptions made can sometimes lead to logistic or logistic-like diffusion of an innovating grammar through a population. Note too that the term **logistic** may also be used for distributions of S-shaped appearance, without commitment to the underlying mathematics.

Of course the scenario I sketched out a little earlier is merely another thought experiment, but the suggested time course of change with its distinct phases does seem to correspond to observable facts. We know from experience that we don't suddenly wake up one morning and find that everyone is using a novel syntactic construction or pronouncing the diphthong /eɪ/ differently. Even successful innovation takes time to catch on. As for the 'quick, quick' phase of the main part of a change, there are examples where the rate of increase in frequency is sharp enough to be perceptible; I think here of the rapid growth of non-present-tense *may* in the last couple of decades, most notoriously in the form of counterfactual *may have* at the expense of traditional *might have*:

(11)   I suppose history *may have been* different had we done so, or had we entered at a different rate or discussed the rate with others when we entered (1999 Chris Patten, *The Guardian Saturday Review*, p. 9 (16 Oct.))

And we know that there are often stubborn relic forms left over 'after' language change: think of the remaining irregular plurals in Modern English (*children, feet, deer*, etc.) when nearly all other nouns have gone over to a single regular pattern, or the fossil syntax of such PPs as *the whole world over* after the general loss of post-positional prepositions.

3   The axes of the graph

However, not everything about S-curves is clear to me. I want now to turn to the vertical scale in those hypothetical graphs. What are the percentages percentages *of*? There are a number of possible answers to this question.

The percentages could be percentages of relevant linguistic contexts in some corpus (ideally in *all* speech events in the whole language during the relevant period, though of course we could never observe them). There are all sorts of different linguistic contexts we could use to subdivide this potentially huge mass of data. For example, some changes are supposed to spread by **lexical**

diffusion, that is, word by word through the relevant lexemes of the language. Labov argues that some (not all) sound changes work like that, namely those involving 'the abrupt substitution of one phoneme for another' such that the newer form 'will usually differ by several phonetic features' from the older (1994: 543), while Lass (1997: 141 n. 41) suggests that all phonological change at least starts with lexical diffusion.[4] Then we would be counting proportions of the relevant words which have succumbed to the change at a given time.

Suppose that the small impetus towards change has to do with some structural disadvantage in the old form (Labov: 'a tendency for one or the other type of form to be misunderstood more than the other', 1994: 586), then after the change had taken place in a majority of contexts, reduction in numbers of the old form would perhaps reduce the pressure for change, allowing the rate of transfer to the new form to slow down again. Or words that are particularly salient, or maybe especially frequent or infrequent, or of a particular form, might resist the change for reasons which had not applied – or at least did not apply so strongly – to those words which had succumbed early on. Even if the impetus towards change is not structural but to do with social convention (Croft: 'the desire of hearers to identify with the community to which [a speaker of particular variants] belongs', 2000: 183), then according to Labov (1994: 66) there would still be the same slow-down towards the end.

However, *lexical* diffusion is not the only kind of diffusion through linguistic space. Another example would be the spread of a syntactic change through particular construction types, though that could hardly be plotted as a percentage. Let's return to the question of the vertical axis in an S-curve of change.

Pragmatic contexts present a special case of linguistic context, slightly outside the more structured systems of phonology, lexis, syntax, etc. Percentages don't seem so appropriate here either, as it seems strange to try to enumerate the registers, but the informal principle of spread 'through the language', register by register, has some intuitive appeal. Suppose the new usage begins life as merely a private family usage, or as slang, or as a colloquialism, for instance. If it generalises beyond its original context, it might be expected to appear next in a related register, and so to spread through the language. Again, from 'slow, slow' to 'quick, quick' is easy to motivate, but back to 'slow' again needs reasoning which may be (in every sense) slightly *post hoc*, probably to do with salience: the last to go on resisting a change from above would be the least salient contexts, and in change from below, perhaps the most salient. For the concept of changes from above/below as both social and mental phenomena, see Labov (1994: 78).

---

[4] Note that Labov claims that the process of lexical diffusion – as opposed to regular sound change – 'is most characteristic of the *late* [my italics: DD] stages of an internal change . . . or of borrowings from other systems ("change from above")' (1994: 543).

Variation is very common in the speech of an individual. Some of that variation may depend on individual lexemes or on particular linguistic contexts, as already discussed. However, there is also sometimes an element of statistical variation for which no direct link can be established to any particular conditioning factor. For a given word in a given context, the speaker may use one form on X% of available occasions, and another form for the remainder – **orderly heterogeneity**. Perhaps this means that there is some subtle conditioning factor or constellation of factors which has not yet been identified by scholars, or perhaps it's an irreducibly random choice with an overall statistical pattern, like radioactive decay. This kind of variation is the staple of Labovian sociolinguistics. The question then arises, does an individual's usage change as he or she gets older, or is overall change through time in a language merely a function of changes in the population, with older speakers becoming inactive and dying, and younger speakers continually entering the community? I believe that speakers do change their usage during adult life (see now Croft 2000: 48–9, 55–9 for some discussion), so that language change has an individual as well as a social component, but I do not know whether the former typically follows an S-curve. S-curves of linguistic change would not normally be plotted through the lifetime of an individual speaker (outside language acquisition studies, anyway), as scholarly practice is to produce composites of the usage of many speakers (or writers).

Chambers thinks that one kind of change in the individual *does* involve an S-curve. He cites the phenomenon (1992: 695) in connection with his study of six Canadian youngsters acquiring Southern England English:

The typical pattern . . . is the S-curve, with phonological changes occurring slowly for the first 20% or so of possible instances and then rising rapidly to about 80% before tailing off towards categoricity. The empirical basis underlying the S-curve is the sparsity of speakers caught in the middle three fifths, 20–80%, at any given time, in contrast to the clusters of speakers found at either end. These figures are taken to signify that speakers must sporadically acquire new pronunciations for about 20% of the available instances as the basis for generalizing a rule, and that, once the process becomes rule-governed, about 80% of the instances will be affected immediately, with some portion of the remaining instances, usually the less frequent ones (Phillips 1984), resisting change and perhaps remaining as residue.

Here a synchronic (apparent time) distribution of speakers with respect to some complex rule is apparently assumed to correspond diachronically to the time course of the adoption or dropping of that rule. This, then, is a very different explanation from Labov's for the S-curve, depending as it does not on statistical competition between variants but on catastrophic (in the Thomian sense) reorganisation of a speaker's internal grammar, much more along the lines promoted by Lightfoot for syntactic change in general and – though with a much more functionalist bias – by Stein for a syntactic change dependent on phonology (1990: 218–20, 300–1). Some recent work tends to abstract away from observed usage and envisage the spread of *grammars* through a population, thus e.g. Briscoe (2000a, b). There is disagreement as to whether an individual may have access to more than one grammar at a time. For further discussion of differing interpretations of the relationship between an individual's usage and S-curves see also Croft (2000: 187–8).

If we consider communities of speakers we have some more explicit modelling of language contact between individuals, notably Lesley and James Milroy's ideas about social networks (e.g. L. Milroy 1987; J. Milroy 1993). So there can be propagation via weak ties between social networks, and inhibition of change by strong ties within a social network. We need some mechanism for tying such models of social contact into the arguments about selectional pressure. Percentages could be the proportions of speakers in the community at any time who show (at least some? majority? invariable?) usage of the new form.

What constitutes a community is an interesting question. Are we, for instance, looking at the relatively small numbers of interlocutors in a local social network, or the whole population of medieval England, grown to some 4–5 million by renaissance times, or the hundreds of millions of current speakers of English world-wide? Croft has some comments on the natures of different types of community (2000: 187). I note that Briscoe uses relatively small population sizes in his computer simulations of language change because 'networks of strong and regular linguistic interaction are probably limited to group sizes of around 100–150' (2000a: 7). Grouping historical data may reveal overall trends; equally, lumping disparate data together may conceal the true path of change. Thus, for example, Kroch and Taylor's explanation of verb-second syntax (1997) depends crucially on separate treatment of certain Middle English dialects.

For completeness I should point out that the horizontal scale is not without controversy. Does one plot the data against the time of composition (or writing), or is the relevant time the birthdate of the writer? This question is clearly connected to our previous discussion of whether language development continues during the adulthood of speakers – or rather, how significant such development is when set against the norms established in childhood and adolescence.[5]

4   Syntactic illustrations

We see, then, that there are various different senses in which a change could be said to have the shape of an S-curve. I turn now to some illustrations from the

[5] The x-axis need not even represent time at all. Devitt changes it at one point to *texts* (1989: 38–46), arranged so as to get a monotonic rise in frequencies of the innovating form. If the resulting graph is S-shaped, she claims it represents diffusion in apparent time across speakers.

history of English of certain points of view I have mentioned, mainly using the syntactic data with which I am most familiar.

Many years ago I argued that a syntactic innovation, the prepositional passive, spread by lexical diffusion. That is the very characteristic English construction seen in

(12)   Fran will be frowned at

first found in the thirteenth century. One piece of evidence for lexical diffusion concerned a particular prepositional verb, LETEN *of* 'think of, regard'. Both the verbal part and the preposition in LETEN *of* had idiosyncrasies which made that particular combination a likely point of entry for the new passive construction (see Denison 1993: 141–3), even if the very earliest attested prepositional passive happens to involve a different item. If the construction did indeed spread by lexical diffusion, an obvious route would be from LETEN *of* to the closely related prepositional verbs LETEN *by*, SETTEN *of/by*, TELLEN *of/by*, all of which mean 'regard, esteem, think of', and all of which are semantically and even phonologically similar. Sure enough, all of these combinations are prominent among the early examples:

(13)   no prophete *is* so mychel *leten of* in his owene cuntre as...(ca 1400)
         'No prophet is so well regarded in his own country as...'

Visser lists by century the prepositional verbs which permit such passives (1963–73: §§1947–57). Allowing for his errors, by 1300 there was one such verb, by 1400 another 22, by 1500 another 64, and so on. If we count by type (particular combinations), then, we get the lower half of an S-curve, and the same would be true if we counted by token (actual examples), though here we would be plotting absolute numbers rather than relative frequencies. It isn't clear what 'completion of the change' could be, however, short of every conceivable verb–preposition combination having a passive, or – better – every one with appropriate semantic roles for its nominal arguments (which in any case is not an invariant set), so I am unwilling to attempt the upper half of the S. More important, this would not be an S-curve based on proportion and therefore on the notion of competition between variants, but one based on absolute frequency; the underlying mathematics of such a graph are quite different.

Having looked at a change with perhaps only the first half of an S-curve, I can refer to the recent paper by Cynthia Allen (2000) which examined the alleged suddenness of the change in the twelfth century by which verb-final order was lost from English. The upshot of her analysis is that there is no good evidence of 'sudden death', and that gradual obsolescence was at least as plausible a scenario. This would be the second half of an S-curve, and one where competition between variants is plausible. It is probably the case that complete or near-complete S-curves are outnumbered by changes which show just part of the S-curve, whether the part-curves result from the impossibility of obtaining numerical evidence or from disruption or reversal of a change.

Another ME innovation is periphrastic DO, the use of DO as a dummy auxiliary verb with the infinitive of a lexical verb, first found (in my opinion) in the thirteenth century:

(14)   toward þe stude þat þe sonne In winter doth a-rise. (ca 1300)
         'towards the place that the sun in winter does arise'

A paper by Ogura (1993) has argued that lexical diffusion is the route for the spread of this construction through the language, whereas Kroch (1989a, b, etc.) has argued that the right way to visualise the spread of the construction is not verb by verb but syntactic context by syntactic context. I don't propose to get involved in that particular disagreement. Both are compatible with an S-curve. Kroch's approach has a number of interesting consequences for us:

- he employs a mathematical transformation of one kind of S-curve which allows one to develop a measure of rate of change and perhaps of starting-point;
- he finds that the S-curves for different syntactic contexts (e.g. interrogatives, negatives) show the same rate of change, his so-called Constant Rate Hypothesis;
- he finds that the S-curves for DO in different syntactic contexts show discontinuities in the late sixteenth century – something which for him demands an explanation in terms of syntactic restructuring at that time;
- the frequency of affirmative declaratives starts off as it should with a slow rise, but then rather than accelerating up an S-curve it dies away again until it has virtually disappeared from the language by 1800 – which shows that not all changes proceed irreversibly; presumably the steady favouring impetus had disappeared.

For diffusion through pragmatic contexts, we might consider some other scholarly writings on periphrastic DO, for example the contention that in Chaucer's English it was particularly appropriate for use with children (Tieken-Boon van Ostade 1990), which I am unconvinced about, or work by Rissanen (1991, etc.) and others on the **registers** in which the periphrasis occurs at different periods. For recent and subtle analysis of Ellegård's (1953) figures see Warner's ongoing work (2000), and for revision of the data Nurmi (2000).

Finally, back to society. Labov and his followers have given myriad examples of diffusion of linguistic change through the strata of a modern society. Various scholars from Helsinki have begun to demonstrate it from a period of around five to three centuries ago with the Corpus of Early English Correspondence project. Going back earlier still, we can mention something like the replacement of native forms like *hi, her(e)* and *hem* by the Scandinavioid personal pronouns *they, their* and *them*, a development which involves both lexical and geographical diffusion. Lexical because they typically appear in a given dialect area in the order subjective, then genitive, and last of all objective, and geographical because over time the isoglosses which divide old and new forms on the map move southwards. Geographical diffusion through the country can be seen as an example of spread through the community of speakers, though to treat the England of Middle English as a single speech community is perhaps a bit dubious.

5 Variables and variants

I do have other problems with S-curves. The original justification for them was the ecological competition between two variants competing to perform the same linguistic function. Immediately we have problems with sound changes in the vowel space, where at the phonetic level at least there is the possibility of continuous variation and hence no *two* competitors. This can perhaps be tackled at the phonological level with some kind of feature analysis which allows an abstraction away from the analogue kind of continuous change to a quantised stepping between discrete states. In Lass's discussion of the size of such quanta is the claim that 'the units of change are generally very small (though not of course infinitely so)' (1997: 222), which would militate against simple binary competition lasting over a long time period. But even with the syntactic phenomena I am more at home with, it is a rarity to find competition between one old form and a single replacing form. Let me review some of my examples in this connection.

Progressive passive. Types (8) and (9) are close to being a binary choice, but there were also other means of expression, including actives, non-progressive passives, and so on.

Counterfactual *may have*. The *may have* of (11) begins to replace *might have*, but *could have* is a third possibility in some positive contexts:

(15)   How different her own life *might have been* if she'd had a brother – a 'bro' who *may have grown up* to be bigger and stronger than Dad, who *could have put* a stop to the violence. (2000 Anna Davis, *Melting* (Sceptre), 152)

Example (15) is a convenient one to cite because it shows alternation between *might have* and *may have* in an epistemic context, but also has *could have* in a clause with a possible epistemic reading beside its deontic one. Note, however, that because of scope differences, *could have* is not an alternative to *might/may have* in negatives, so that the number of variants available depends crucially on the syntactic context.

Prepositional passive. If type (12) was an innovation, what did it replace? An active with the indefinite pronoun *man* or *me* as subject? That is indeed a close equivalent in function to a passive, but it wasn't the only one, and after the fifteenth century it was no longer in contention, yet the prepositional passive continued to spread.

Periphrastic DO. The innovation of type (14) is mainly in competition with simple tensed forms, but it only gives part of the picture of the history of the periphrasis if – as is often done – the only clauses counted are those with no auxiliary or with DO, since the other auxiliaries are changing in frequency as well. I demonstrated in Denison (1993: 467–8) that even before periphrastic DO had become common, negatives showed a statistically significant preference for the presence of an 'operator' (broadly, an auxiliary verb or main-verb BE or HAVE) over the use of a simple lexical verb alone.

Just as gravitational attraction between two bodies is easier to calculate than the so-called three-body problem, so competition between two variants is easier to model than competition among three or more. In linguistic work, at least, I am not aware of serious attempts to model competition among multiple variants. Even a work like Niyogi and Berwick (1998) which plots three-dimensional graphs of dynamical systems is doing so only as part of an attempt to model systems with two linguistic variants. Nevalainen explicitly mentions that one of her case studies of standardisation, the spread of present indicative plural *are* at the expense of the older *be*, ignores a third variant, plural *is* (2000: 342).[6]

Here is another question as yet unresolved for me, also concerned with the number of variants under consideration. Consider the advent of the form *of* used in positions where traditional grammar demands *have*. This is now increasingly common. If we plot written language, we can treat *have* and *of* as old and new variants, respectively, and very probably find the lower half of an S-curve relating their use. (I have not done this: it would demand a major corpus investigation of extremely common forms in so-far untagged material.) The earliest example I have found, (16), is a little isolated chronologically from the early cases noted in *OED* s.v. *of* joc. '(being erroneous in Received Standard) or dial. var. HAVE v.', (17)–(18) (and, why, incidentally, must all instances be 'jocular'?):

(16)   Had I known of your illness I *should not of written* in such fiery phrase in my first Letter. (1819)

(17)   Soposing seven hundred and sixty [servants] *to of advertised* and the same number *not to of advertised*. (1837 [*OED*])

(18)   I never *would of married* in the world, ef I *couldn't of got* jist exactly suited. (1844 [*OED*])

[6] Raumolin-Brunberg points out that she and Nevalainen have also sometimes created a binary opposition by plotting the innovative form against all the others (personal communication, 19 Sept. 2000).

This is the typical sporadic, slow start of an innovation, and it should be possible in principle to plot the increasing proportion of *of* in written texts. There remains the question of whether to treat contracted *'ve* as representing *have* or as a third variant. But the real problem comes if we try to plot the history of these forms in recent speech, where – I would guess – unstressed [əv] would vastly outnumber both [hæv] and [ɒv] and yet couldn't in any individual case be ascribed with confidence to either the conservative or the innovative underlying form. The existence of the unstressed [əv] form is probably crucial to the development of stressed [ɒv] in such patterns, precisely because it is equivocal, and its high frequency is part of its importance. To ignore the equivocal examples would therefore be a gross distortion of the evidence, and yet they could not be counted either as old or new.

Another problem with S-curves is that of synonymy: are we entitled to treat variants as members of a single variable, that is, as equivalent alternative expressions of 'the same thing'? Outside the realms of phonology, perhaps morphology and just possibly lexis, that is very much a moot point. To call two syntactic forms fully equivalent is to make a very bold claim indeed. The pioneering investigations of the Helsinki sociolinguists rely perhaps on selecting changes which can plausibly be reduced to competition between two variants. I wonder how often this can be done.

6   Conflation of S-curves: the shape of English

We could start to pull the camera outwards and backwards. Diffusion of a syntactic change through different words and/or contexts could be looked at from afar as the overall progress of that change in the language. (Aitchison (1991: 85–7) suggests that S-curves for a given change tend to be made up of overlapping little S-curves, each representing one linguistic environment.) It makes language change sound rather like a fractal, in that it might be self-similar at any magnification, though probably not in other aspects of the mathematical functions which can model language change. Maybe if we moved even further away, all the syntactic changes could be subsumed into one big curve, all the sound changes into one big curve, then linguistic changes of all kinds into one big change. Maybe the history of the English language is, crudely speaking, one big S-curve.

That may sound silly: no percentage scale would make any sense if you tried to conflate different changes into a single curve. What I had in mind was superposing a number of graphs to see where they bunch in historical time, rather like looking at isoglosses in the hope of spotting a significant dialect boundary. And rather than the S-curves themselves, peak values of the *rate* of change (first differential of the S-curve) would have to be plotted to see whether they tend to coincide. This whimsical idea of gathering together a lot of S-curves came about because in playing with the 'slow, slow, quick, quick, slow' catch-phrase, I realised that it is often applied implicitly to the shape of the English language as a whole, under the frequently made assumption that Old English and (late) Modern English are relatively invariant, whereas Middle (and possibly early Modern) English show rapid change of all kinds.

Does such a view stand up to examination? Immediately we run up against the problem of periodisation (Blake 1994, and see now also Lass 2001). Old English did not spring fully armed out of nowhere in about 700; it came at the end of a long period of Germanic development which can be reconstructed in many respects with great certainty. Most of the extensive surviving writings either come from the narrow early West Saxon or late West Saxon bands, or they are later copyings of earlier texts. And the transition to early Middle English is masked by a paucity of surviving texts from the crucial time. The geographical spread of the documents is also very patchy, with later documents like the essential *Second Continuation* of the *Peterborough Chronicle*, or *Ormulum*, not corresponding very well to anything much in Old English. Furthermore, we might well argue that in many respects, the later Middle English and the early Modern English periods (under their standard labels) really belong together, for example as far as phonology, morphology and even syntax are concerned. Undiluted, unmodernised Shakespeare is not an easy read for present-day schoolchildren.

Having made those obvious cautionary noises, I then tried in Denison (1999) to separate the major domains of linguistic study, and drew the conclusion that for many of them Middle English was not a specially active period of change, apart perhaps from nominal morphology and lexis. Roger Lass wrote (1997: 304) that 'Languages may vary all the time, but they change in bursts.' Although I'm happy to accept that general statement, on balance I think it's unhelpful to apply it to a whole period of English like Middle English – some 400 years – and to every domain of linguistics.

7   Concluding remark

The catch-phrase 'slow, slow, quick, quick, slow' refers, I gather, to the fox-trot. Here's what one of the *OED*'s citations has to say about that dance:

(19)   The Fox-Trot is a dance of many steps, and to the casual observer everybody seems to have different ones. (1919 [*OED*])

Much the same goes for S-curves and the scholars who draw them. The S-curve is neither as simple nor as uniform a phenomenon as is sometimes assumed. Given too the simplistic picture of variation it sometimes reflects (and requires), the S-curve should not be seized on too readily as *the* general shape of language change.

REFERENCES

Aitchison, Jean. 1991. *Language change: progress or decay?*, 2nd edition. Cambridge University Press.

Allen, Cynthia L. 2000. 'Obsolescence and sudden death in syntax: the decline of verb-final order in early Middle English', in Bermúdez-Otero et al. (eds.), 3–25.

Altmann, Gabriel, H. von Buttlar, W. Rott and U. Strauss. 1983. 'A law of change in language', in B. Brainerd (ed.), *Historical linguistics*. Quantitative Linguistics 18. Bochum: Brockmeyer, 104–15.

Bermúdez-Otero, Ricardo, David Denison, Richard M. Hogg, C. B. McCully (eds.). 2000. *Generative theory and corpus studies: a dialogue from 10 ICEHL*. Topics in English Linguistics 31. Berlin and New York: Mouton de Gruyter.

Blake, Norman F. 1994. 'Premisses and periods in a history of English', in Francisco Fernández, Miguel Fuster and Juan José Calvo (eds.), *English historical linguistics 1992: papers from the 7th International Conference on English Historical Linguistics, Valencia, 22–26 September 1992*. Current Issues in Linguistic Theory 113. Amsterdam and Philadelphia: John Benjamins, 37–46.

Briscoe, Ted. 2000a. 'An evolutionary approach to (logistic-like) language change', MS, Computer Laboratory, University of Cambridge.

Briscoe, Ted. 2000b. 'Evolutionary perspectives on diachronic syntax', in Susan Pintzuk, George Tsoulas and Anthony Warner (eds.), *Diachronic syntax: models and mechanisms*. Oxford University Press, 75–105.

Chambers, J. K. 1992. 'Dialect acquisition', *Language* 68: 673–705.

Croft, William. 2000. *Explaining language change: an evolutionary approach*. Longman Linguistics Library. London and New York: Longman.

Denison, David. 1993. *English historical syntax: verbal constructions*. Longman Linguistics Library. London and New York: Longman.

Denison, David. 1999. 'Slow, slow, quick, quick, slow: the dance of language change?', in Ana Bringas López et al. (eds.), *'Woonderous Ænglissce': SELIM Studies in Medieval English Language*. Vigo: Universidade de Vigo (Servicio de Publicacións), 51–64.

Devitt, Amy J. 1989. *Standardizing written English: diffusion in the case of Scotland, 1520–1659*. Cambridge University Press.

Ellegård, Alvar. 1953. *The auxiliary 'do': the establishment and regulation of its growth in English*. Gothenburg Studies in English 2. Stockholm: Almqvist and Wiksell.

Kroch, Anthony S. 1989a. 'Function and grammar in the history of English: periphrastic do', in Ralph Fasold and Deborah Schiffrin (eds.), *Language change and variation*. Current Issues in Linguistic Theory 52. Amsterdam and Philadelphia: John Benjamins, 132–72.

Kroch, Anthony S. 1989b. 'Reflexes of grammar in patterns of language change', *Language Variation and Change* 1: 199–244.

Kroch, Anthony and Ann Taylor. 1997. 'Verb movement in Old and Middle English: dialect variation and language contact', in Ans van Kemenade and Nigel Vincent (eds.), *Parameters of morphosyntactic change*. Cambridge University Press, 297–325.

Labov, William. 1994. *Principles of linguistic change*, vol. 1: *Internal factors*. Language in Society. Oxford and Cambridge, MA: Blackwell.

Lass, Roger. 1997. *Historical linguistics and language change*. Cambridge Studies in Linguistics 81. Cambridge University Press.

Lass, Roger. 2001. 'Language periodization and the concept "middle"', in Irma Taavitsainen, Terttu Nevalainen, Päivi Pahta and Matti Rissanen (eds.), *Placing Middle English in context*. Topics in English Linguistics 35. Berlin and New York: Mouton de Gruyter, 7–41.

Milroy, James. 1993. 'On the social origins of language change', in Charles Jones (ed.), *Historical linguistics: problems and perspectives*. London and New York: Longman, 215–36.

Milroy, Lesley. 1987. *Language and social networks*, 2nd edition. Language in Society 2. Oxford: Blackwell.

Nakamura, Fujio. 1998. 'A word on the history of the English passive progressive', paper read at the 10th International Conference on Historical Linguistics, Manchester.

Nevalainen, Terttu. 2000. 'Processes of supralocalisation and the rise of Standard English in the early Modern period', in Bermúdez-Otero et al. (eds.), 329–71.

Niyogi, Partha and Robert C. Berwick. 1997. 'A dynamical systems model of language change', *Linguistics and Philosophy* 20: 697–719.

Niyogi, Partha and Robert C. Berwick. 1998. 'The logical problem of language change: a case study of European Portuguese', *Syntax* 1: 192–205.

Nurmi, Arja. 2000. 'The rise and fall of periphrastic DO in early Modern English, or "*Howe the Scotts will declare themselv's*"', in Bermúdez-Otero et al. (eds.), 373–94.

Ogura, Mieko. 1993. 'The development of periphrastic *do* in English: a case of lexical diffusion in syntax', *Diachronica* 10: 51–85.

Phillips, Betty. 1984. 'Word frequency and the actuation of sound change', *Language* 60: 320–42.

Pratt, Lynda and David Denison. 2000. 'The language of the Southey-Coleridge circle', *Language Sciences* 22: 401–22.

Rissanen, Matti. 1991. 'Spoken language and the history of *do*-periphrasis', in Dieter Kastovsky (ed.), *Historical English syntax*. Topics in English Linguistics 2. Berlin and New York: Mouton de Gruyter, 321–42.

Simpson, John A. and Edmund S. C. Weiner. 1992. *OED = The Oxford English Dictionary: CD-ROM Version*, 2nd edition. Oxford University Press.

Stein, Dieter. 1990. *The semantics of syntactic change: aspects of the evolution of 'do' in English*. Trends in Linguistics/Studies and Monographs 47. Berlin and New York: Mouton de Gruyter.

Tieken-Boon van Ostade, Ingrid. 1990. 'The origin and development of periphrastic auxiliary *do*: a case of destigmatisation', *NOWELE* 16: 3–52 [originally published in *Dutch Working Papers in English Language and Linguistics 3*, 1988].

Visser, F. Th. 1963–73. *An historical syntax of the English language*, 4 vols. Leiden: E. J. Brill.

Warner, Anthony R. 1995. 'Predicting the progressive passive: parametric change within a lexicalist framework', *Language* 71: 533–57.

Warner, Anthony R. 2000. 'Change and rate of change in *do*', plenary lecture given at the 11th International Conference on English Historical Linguistics, Santiago.

5 Regular suppletion

Richard Hogg

1 Introduction

One of my very first linguistic delights came in a Latin class at school, when I discovered the principal parts of *ferre*. That a word could conjugate as: *fero ~ ferre ~ tuli ~ latum* was an unexpected pleasure, even when years later I found out that *tuli* and *latum* were merely forms of the same verb. I am not too sure that every linguist has that same feeling. I have been inspecting a variety of historical linguistics handbooks to see what they have to say about suppletion. Indeed, even Microsoft Word was no help, since it suggested that what I should have written was either *supple ion* or *simpleton*.

More seriously, Lehmann (1992), for example, does not even index the term. And in this he is not alone, for there are others in the same position, including Lass (1997) and Campbell (1998). And others mention the term merely in passing: thus Trask (1996) does little more than refer to the term, whilst others use the term in a context which is different from that with which I am concerned here, for example Anderson (1992). Perhaps not surprisingly, the morphologist who comes closest to today's issues is Matthews (1991: 139–40).

One question to be asked, quite obviously, is why, even amongst morphologists, the issue of suppletion has been relatively ignored. The answer to this, I believe, is two-fold. Firstly suppletion is ignored because, wherever it occurs, it is felt to be a one-off, a fun idiosyncrasy and no more. And, secondly, because suppletion is not felt to have any interesting formal properties. It is well known (or at least supposed), for example, that by definition suppletion is irregular. What I want to argue here is that this is not always true. Sometimes suppletion can be regular or, and even more interestingly, result in regularity. To support my argument, I shall look at four cases, all rather different from each other.

2 *Bad*

The belief that *worse* is the comparative suppletive form of *bad* is probably so engrained in the minds of most speakers of English that it almost requires some will-power to recall that this has not always been the case. And the fact that *bad* is first recorded at the very end of the thirteenth century would scarcely be believed if it were not for the fact that the *OED* tells us so.

The normal view is that *worse*, together with its superlative *worst*, is merely the suppletive form of *bad*. This would be consistent with the view that *bad*, like *good*, is an adjective which in Indo-European systematically forms its comparison by suppletion. But there are obvious problems with such a view. The claim that *bad* forms its comparison with *worse, worst* looks sensible only if we don't attempt to consider the history of these forms. Thus, as I mentioned earlier, *bad* is only recorded from the end of the thirteenth century. The *OED* suggests that the word is related to OE *bæddel* 'hermaphrodite, effeminate man', and adds that for reasons of taboo this is almost certainly the reason that *bad* is not recorded earlier. There is the further implication, I think, that the compared forms *bædra, bæddest* were part of the paradigm of a quite regular OE *bæd*.

On the other hand, the normal view is that in Old English *wyrsa* and *wyrsta* were the compared forms of *yfel* (= PDE *evil*). The question to be asked, therefore, seems to be: in Old English of which positive form were *wyrsa* and *wyrsta* the compared forms? Let us suppose, for example, that the positive form was *yfel*, as the handbooks and dictionaries tell us. What, then, were the compared forms of the unattested, but surely occurring *bæd*? Well, there appears to be a suitable candidate, for the *OED* states that the forms *badder* and *baddest* occurred between the fourteenth and eighteenth centuries. It is only reasonable to suppose that earlier examples of *badder, baddest* are unattested for the same taboo reasons as explained the absence of *bæd*.

Nevertheless, it might be argued, there is no real problem. But surely there is. As far as I can tell, the only compared forms of *evil* in PDE are *more, most evil*. That is to say, *worse* and *worst* are the compared forms only of *bad*. Since we have also seen good reason to suppose that at one time the compared forms of *bad* were regular, this rather implies that there was also a stage at which both *evil* and *bad* could have used *worse, worst*. We can show what most probably was the development by means of the following diagram:

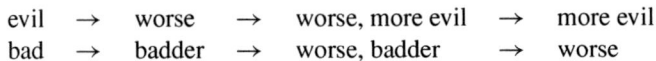

| evil | → | worse | → | worse, more evil | → | more evil |
| bad | → | badder | → | worse, badder | → | worse |

I have not attempted to put dates on these changes, since I have engaged in sufficient speculation already.

But if this diagram is in any way accurate, then further questions have to be asked. Perhaps the simplest of these is the question of why *evil* lost its suppletion. The answer is likely to be semantic. That is to say, the suppletion began to be lost as *evil* lost its primary meaning as the opposite of *good* and started to become restricted to a religious or non-secular meaning. This, of course, implies that suppletion is only found in lexical items with core meaning.

How, on the other hand, did *bad* come to adopt the suppletion? I think it is over-simple just to say that it took over the forms after the specialisation of *evil*. After all, if we consider either Dutch or German, in both of which the cognate forms lost their generalised status of being antonyms of *good*, none of the modern equivalents to *evil*, such as Dutch *slecht* or *erg* and German *böse*, have acquired the suppletion. Furthermore, it is not true that *badder* has been entirely lost from English: it is still found in children's language.

Does this mean that we must follow, for example, Szemerényi (1996: 202) who talks of 'The ever-self-renewing process of suppletivism'? Rather than simply accepting such a situation, it may be that we should search for a more principled explanation. This is not to say some suppletion is the result of 'renewal', as we shall shortly see. However, in the current case there may also be an issue of paradigm identity.

That is to say, there has to be some doubt about how close the relationship between *worse* and positive *bad* has been. The evidence from Dutch and German rather implies that *worse* could have become separated from the positive form and consequently been lost, for in both languages the compared suppletive forms have been lost. Is it not conceivable that something similar could have happened in English, given that the loss of the link between *evil* and *worse* was weakened for semantic reasons? However, the availability of *bad* was more possible because of the weakening of the taboo connotations. Of course, as in Dutch and German, it would have been equally possible to lose *worse*. But the fact that it was retained, even at the expense of *badder*, is an intriguing demonstration of linguistic fondness for irregular forms at the expense of regular ones.

3   *Went*

The loss of *ēode* and its replacement by *went* during the ME period is often noted, but it is less often discussed. Perhaps the reason for this is that the change is seen as merely the replacement of one suppletion by another. In that context, then, the only interesting feature is the creation of a new preterite for *wend*, namely *wended*. We shall see in a moment that it is of some interest that the development of *wended* appears firstly in the sixteenth century.

There are two points to consider in relation to this replacement. The first, which we can deal with quite quickly, is to note that relatively recent suppletion is not uncommon. Thus the present case can usefully be compared with Italian *vado* 'I go' ~ *andiamo* 'we go'. As Szemerényi (1996: 301–2) states, 'The opinion is often encountered that suppletivism is something primitive. This is at once contradicted by the fact there are fairly recent examples of it . . .'

However, I want to concentrate here on another aspect of the preterite of *go*. If suppletion is a highly marked process, then it would be assumed that there would be some overall tendency to avoid it wherever possible. If we look at the chronology of the loss of *ēode* and the use of *went*, then we can observe that the use of *went* and the loss of *ēode* is more or less complete by about 1500. But there is another preterite form which is relevant, namely northern, particularly Scots, *gaid, gaed*. Here is an example from the *OED*:

(1)   [He] led her with him quhair euer he gaid (Dalrymple, 1596)

My impression is that such a form persists in Scots.

Obviously, a form such as *gaed* is explicable as a new preterite formation on the basis of the present tense, and this is done by adding the regular dental suffix. The analogy is simple and *gae:gaed* now parallels, for example, *tae:taed* 'toe, toed', see OED **toe** *n*. The failure of this apparent simplification in most dialects of English, with its elimination of a suppletion, furthermore a suppletion which itself has been caused by the loss of an older suppletion, suggests that in fact suppletion is not an undesirable characteristic. Of course, a caveat has to be entered at this point. This can only be true of core, highly frequent, elements of the lexis. Yet this example demonstrates a preference for suppletion over obvious regularity.

4   *Syndon*

So far we have considered an example, in the case of *bad*, of one suppletive variation replacing another and then, in the case of *went*, a new suppletion being preferred over a regular formation. The third case is rather different again and consequently shows a different issue.

In Old English, as in other Indo-European languages, the verb *bēon* 'be' was multiply suppletive. But it is not that issue *per se* that I want to consider here. Rather, I want to explore the form of the present indicative plural, for the history of that form in Old English is particularly interesting. This part of the paradigm derives from the IE root *-*es* and its regular development therefore is to *synd* (with some irrelevant variation of the root vowel) or *synt*, where the final devoicing appear to have been frequent in unstressed positions. These two forms correlate well with the forms which appear in the other West Germanic languages.

None of the above causes any problems, since it merely shows the persistence of the inherited suppletions. However, there appears, alongside *synd/synt*, a further very common variation, namely *syndon*. As Brunner (1965: §427A1) states, this form presents the present indicative form which is found with preterite-present verbs, as, for example, in *cunnon* 'they know'. As in all the other handbooks, Brunner is content with this account, since, of course, it quite clearly demonstrates the origin of the new inflection which *syndon* has received. From a Neogrammarian perspective, which these handbooks present, this is entirely unexceptional. Yet, it has to be said that it is also unrevealing. Certainly, in Old English the class of preterite-present verbs remained a morphological category, although in some cases membership of the category was rather precarious: for example, in Northumbrian *þearf* 'need' has a plural form *ðorfeð* which is one of the forms associated with regular weak and strong verbs.

In this context, the presence of *syndon* raises a range of issues. If we assume, firstly, that a new inflection has, for some so far unexplained reason, been provided for earlier *synd*, then we have to ask whether or not the fact that the inflection is *-on* is itself of any significance. Clearly another inflection, namely *-aþ*, would have been possible. That, for example, is the shape of the example *ðorfeð* cited above (with some typical Northumbrian variation of no relevant importance). But the preference for *-on* is presumably a further sign of the viability and synchronic strength of the preterite-present morphology, see Warner (1993: 142–3). Furthermore, as both Warner and, earlier, Prokosch (1939: §65) state, the preterite-present verbs are frequently associated with stativity. This stativity is also expressed in the copulative verb, and therefore the link between preterite-presents and the copula is more transparent than a link between the copula and the essentially active 'regular' verbs could ever be. And so it turns out the choice of *-on* rather than *-aþ* is straightforward and unsurprising.

So far, therefore, there is still no problem. But that is to ignore the central issue. As I stated earlier, we have examined one case where one suppletive form is favoured over another, and one case where a new suppletion is preferred over a regular formation. The rise of *syndon* is different, because although it shows the introduction of what we can now agree is a regular formation, this is not the result of the loss of suppletion, nor does the introduction of a regular formation itself cause the loss of suppletion. Indeed, our earlier examples may help us to realise that the loss of suppletion is an unusual event. Therefore the situation here is, in that sense, normal.

Yet it is impossible to leave matters there. The usual view of suppletion, I would suggest, is that suppletive forms are unanalysable. They appear to be more or less frozen idioms, and of course that is one reason why suppletion is usually ignored. Thus, if we were to consider Old English forms such as, say, *eart* 'thou art', then there is no sense in attempting to analyse the form as bimorphemic: what could the two morphemes possibly be? Or, to take one of our previous examples, how could we find two morphemes in PDE *worse*? But if that is the case, then surely it also follows that the same will be true of *synd*. That seems reasonable enough. But does it not then follow that *syndon*, also, should be monomorphemic? Yet there is, obviously, a second morpheme there, for *-on* can be nothing else other than a second morpheme in a bimorphemic word, as it is demonstrably in any preterite-present verb, such as in the example *cunnon* which I mentioned earlier.

This, regrettably, starts off a paper chase all of its own. Alongside the *-es* root from which *synd* is ultimately derived, there was a further root available for the present tense of the copula in Old English. This, of course, was the root *bheu-*, which provides not only the infinitive form *bēon* but a complete present-tense paradigm, including, and this is the point of present interest, a plural form *bēoþ*.[1]

The question to ask at this point is whether or not this form should, like *synd*, attract the morpheme *-on*. Rather than simply going straight to the evidence and thereby providing an indisputable empirical result, it is, as will become clearer later, more helpful to firstly weigh up the theoretical consequences of whatever evidence there might be. Clearly, the simplest, least awkward situation would leave *bēoþ* unaltered. Indeed, it might be argued that this would be what we might expect. After all, the condition of suppletion, it would seem reasonable to claim, is both wholly irregular and not subject to any kind of paradigmatic pressure. At the start of this chapter, this might have been a sensible claim. But surely our discussion of *syndon* has demonstrated that even suppletive forms can be subject to external paradigmatic pressure. So this will no longer do.

Even so, the claim that *bēoþ* would remain unaltered still retains substantial force. Firstly, if we were to argue that it would attract the morpheme *-on*, that would mean that we had to allow for the existence of paradigmatic levelling from *syndon*. But this does not appear to occur anywhere else. Take, for example, the third person singular, which in the two roots occurs as *is* and *biþ*. Now in Northumbrian Old English the inflectional morpheme, historically *-að*, is frequently replaced amongst regular verbs by *-as*, hence alongside *lufað* we find *lufas* 'he loves'.[2] Should we not, therefore, find **bis* alongside *bið*, or, since the replacement in regular verbs causes complete confusion, **ið* alongside *is*? But as I have indicated, neither of these apparent possibilities ever occurs. Indeed, I would suggest that they are absolutely excluded. Yet paradigmatic pressure, apparently, would have allowed them, especially given the confusion apparent in the regular paradigms. And thus, secondly, there appears to be a principled explanation for the failure of paradigmatic pressure. Since the fundamental principle about suppletion is that the different suppletive examples are supposed to be exactly that, then there can be no method by which changes in one suppletive example could affect any other example. That is to say, there can be no paradigmatic pressure since every such paradigm is isolated from

---

[1] For discussion of some of the variety of views on the semantic distinction, if any, between the two roots, see Mitchell (1985: §§651ff.).

[2] Here, and elsewhere in the remainder of this chapter, when I shall be dealing mainly with Northumbrian forms, I shall ignore many of the specifically Northumbrian variations, although they may seem strange to readers more used to West Saxon, or even Mercian, forms. It has to be accepted that such variations are of no relevance to the issues at hand. For a clear conspectus of the variations, see Brunner (1965: §427).

every other one. Perhaps there is the suspicion in the minds of some readers that the actual empirical data are not quite as straightforward as one would expect. Why, otherwise, have I pursued this paper chase for so long? Yet I still do not want to reveal that data. I still believe that the most important task is to assess the theoretical implications. Let us, therefore, suppose that *bēoþ* does not remain unaltered. Let us suppose that a new form is provided. The first question, then, is what that form would be. Of course, one possibility would arise by the mere addition of *-on*. But before we consider the implications of that possibility, there is an alternative which we should consider.

To do this we need firstly to look at *bēoþ* in more detail. It is immediately obvious that the final consonant of the form is related to the regular inflection *-aþ* as in *rīdaþ* 'he rides'. It is perhaps even more obviously related to the inflectional form of a contracted verb such as *sēoþ* 'he sees'. The question, therefore, which must be asked is whether or not *bēoþ*, like *sēoþ*, should be analysed as bimorphemic, assuming, that is, that *sēoþ* is indeed bimorphemic. If that is so, then presumably it would be possible to substitute *-on* for *-þ*. The result of this would be *bēon*. This, of course, is identical to the present subjunctive plural. I don't want to pursue this possibility at present, for reasons which will eventually become clear. It will suffice simply to say that there is no evidence to support such an option.

Instead, let us follow the path which would lead to the addition of *-on* to *bēoþ*. We have already observed that such a shift could be explained on the basis of paradigmatic pressure, but that that would be a somewhat shaky foundation. Nevertheless, let us assume that this is what happens. It might, for a moment, be thought that such a result would merely parallel *syndon*. However, it does not seem to me that that is unequivocally true. It will be recalled that we previously discussed the issue of whether *syndon* was monomorphemic or bimorphemic. That, in fact, was what started this paper chase off.

At that earlier stage we made no attempt to reach a decision on this question of internal morphemic structure. Perhaps the reason we did not do so is now clear. For with the possibility of a parallel form *bēoþon* the difficulty is doubled. Thus if we assume a bimorphemic structure *synd+on*, then given what we have already observed about the structure of *bēoþ*, we would be compelled to suggest a trimorphemic structure *bēo+þ+on*. Even monomorphemic *syndon* would, I think, have to be paralleled by *bēo+þon*.

Perhaps the moment has now arrived when we should look at the actual data. If we simply consider the data from West Saxon, of whatever date, then the problem seems factitious, since the only form (leaving aside minor ortho-graphic variation) is *bēoþ*. That would argue in favour of the view that each suppletion is entirely autonomous, which might be held to be the standard view. Unfortunately the situation looks very different in Northumbrian and, to a lesser extent, in the North Mercian *Rushworth 1*. In Northumbrian there do exist historical forms, usually of the shape *bīað* (where the variation in stem vowel is at present unimportant).[3] But such forms are clearly less frequent than Northumbrian *biðon* (also *bioðon*).

It would divert too far from my present concerns to do more than note that the stem vowel (or diphthong) here can only be explained by assuming that in Northumbrian the vowel of the third person singular has been extended to the plural. Let us concentrate, rather, on what such data reveal for the particular variation which I have been discussing. Quite clearly, it demonstrates that it is indeed possible for paradigmatic pressure to be applied across different suppletive roots. On the other hand, if we accept that *biðon* has been formed on the parallel with *syndon*, it is really quite difficult to accept that *biðon* could have a tripartite morphemic structure. One reason for claiming this is that it would be most appropriate to assume that *syndon*, which is found in all dialects, is earlier than *biðon*, which is found only in the most northerly dialects. Now since *syndon* clearly develops by simple addition to a root, the later and dialectal parallel for *biðon* must also be an addition to a root. But if that is so, then the root form must be *bið-*, and that has to be monomorphemic.

The consequence of this, of course, is that we can no longer persist with an analysis of the present tense of *bēon* which is inflectionally identical to that of a verb such as *sēon*, since we have had to assume that a form, in West Saxon terms, such as *bēoþ* is unlike *sēoþ* 'they see' because only in the latter is there an overt synchronic inflection. As it happens, this is an excellent point at which to move on to the final example of suppletion which I want to discuss here, since that last issue will turn out to be the crucial feature of this fourth example.

5   *Be*

At the risk of repetition, let me summarise where we have got to so far. We have seen one case, *bad*, where one suppletion replaces another; one case, *went*, where suppletion is favoured over regularity, and now one case, *syndon/biðon*, where a suppletive form adopts an additional regular inflection. The final case I want to consider, namely that of Old English *bēo* 'I am', offers another, and different, variation, albeit one which is quite closely related to the first case, which we have just discussed. This case is in fact one that I have discussed previously; see Hogg (1980) for details. My excuse for returning to it now is two-fold: partly I want to flesh out the rather sparse nature of that account; more importantly I want to attempt to show how the facts which I discussed there can be included in a more systematic overview of suppletion as a whole.

We need to start this part of our discussion by examining the two suppletive forms of the first-person-singular present indicative of *bēon* as they appear in

---

[3] See again footnote 2 for such typically Northumbrian variation.

Old English. For 'I am' Anglian (i.e. Mercian and Northumbrian) has *(e)am*, which is essentially the same as West Saxon *eom*. For 'I be' West Saxon has *bēo*, which is the historically expected form. But this is not the form which appears in Anglian. Instead, we find the form *bēom*.

The question to be asked, quite obviously, is what the origin of Anglian *bēom* might be. Most handbooks are silent on the issue, one of the few to offer an explanation is Wright (1925: §548), who suggests that *bēom* is based on the parallel with *eam*, from which it receives its final consonant; see also the less helpful comments in Campbell (1959: §735a) and Brunner (1965: §374). I suppose that this is correct, but it is not without its problems. One reason for supposing that the basis of the argument is correct is that in most other West Germanic languages – which have the oddity of combining the two suppletive structures, so that we find, in Modern German, a single paradigm which contrasts *ich bin* and *du bist* with *er ist* – it is noteworthy that the first-person form has final *-n*, deriving from earlier *-m*.

Yet, we need to be aware of the problems. It is, of course, true that what we are observing is at first sight merely parallel with the third case we considered above. But it is worth looking in more detail at the paradigm which results. It is as follows:

(2)   1sg   *bīom*
       2sg   *bist*
       3sg   *bið*
       pl   *biðon/bioðon*

The real question to ask here is what the status of the final *-m* might be. Is it an inflection? Or is *bīom* an unanalysable single morpheme? When we were considering the case of *biðon* above, we took the view that *-ð-* was the final element of the root morpheme. It would seem strange to do anything else here.

Unfortunately that will not do, and the reason for that I first outlined in Hogg (1980), although I hope that the remarks which follow below present a more sophisticated view. However, the basic problem remains. This is that the presence of final *-m* does not, in Anglian, remain restricted to the two copular verbs. Rather, what we find is that there is a further class of verbs which sometimes – not, it has to be said, frequently, but sufficiently often to be significant – show the same presence of final *-m*. These are the so-called contracted verbs. Thus we have forms such as *flēom* 'I flee', *sēom* 'I see'.

The first important point to make here is that there is absolutely no possible source for the final *-m* of these contracted verbs other than the final *-m* of the two copular verbs: there is no other verb class, or even single verb, which has such a characteristic, nor could it reasonably be supposed to have developed historically, for presumably the only possible source would be the subjunctive, and that is implausible for too many reasons that do not need discussion here.

The second point which has to be made is rather different, and gets close to the heart of the problem. Once a form such as *sēom* has emerged, we have to ask what its internal morphological structure might be. As I argued in that earlier paper, we are actually obliged to assume that *-m* is a new inflectional suffix. That, of course, is of some interest in itself, but it is not the most relevant feature for our present concerns. Rather, the implication of the fact that the type *sēom* must be bimorphemic is that the source from which it emerges must also be capable of internal segmentation. But that source can only be *bēom*. But in section 3 above I conclude that *bēom* had to be monomorphemic. This now looks less plausible. But it leaves us in a difficulty. For if *bēom* is monomorphemic, then by definition the final *-m* must simply be an unanalysable part of the stem. And if that is so, then there is no ready explanation of how that final *-m* could be transferred to a form such as *sēom* and transmogrify into an inflectional suffix.

The problem can be summarised as follows. The form *syndon* must be the result of the addition of the morpheme *-on* to an unanalysable root *synd*. Therefore, when the same addition creates the new form *biðon* from *bið*, this can only occur if *bið*, equally, is an unanalysable root. But when *-m* is added to *bēo* to give *bēom*, this final *-m* cannot but be an inflectional suffix, because it is transferrable to contracted verbs such as *sēo* to produce *sēom*, etc. If we compare the resultant paradigm of *sēon*:

(3)   1sg   *sīom*
        2sg   *sīst*
        3sg   *sīð*
        pl   *sēað*

with the paradigm of *bēon* presented above, then the inflectional status of *-m* becomes quite clear. Furthermore, it is important to note the contrast between *biðon* and *sēað*. The absence of a form such as **sēaðon* to parallel *biðon* is absolute.

6   Conclusion

In this chapter I have discussed four types of suppletive variation: (1) the replacement of one suppletion by another, the case of *bad*; (2) the preference for suppletion over regularity, the case of *went*; (3) the addition of regularity without disturbance of the suppletion, the case of *syndon*; (4) the creation of a new regular inflection on the basis of suppletion, the case of *be*.

In attempting to discuss these cases, my principal aim has always been to demonstrate that suppletion is not merely a linguistic freak which does no more than give a small amount of pleasure to a rather giggling schoolboy. There are, I believe, serious issues here, which we should not ignore. Firstly, of course, the evidence that we have considered shows that suppletive forms are not mere fossils. Rather, we must accept as true the comments by Szemerényi (1996), quoted earlier, that suppletion is a dynamic process. Secondly, we must acknowledge that new suppletions can arise in preference to regularisation. Thirdly, and particularly interesting from a synchronic point of view, it is possible for suppletive forms to acquire so-called regular formations without at the same time losing any of their suppletive character. And fourthly, suppletive forms can influence the structure of those regular forms without damaging the viability of their own character.

This collection of issues raises further questions and problems. In particular, we have been able to observe that the interaction of suppletive morphology with regular morphology is not only not clear-cut, it can also lead to contradictory analyses which all need to be accepted. This must lead us, at the least, to reflect more deeply on the organisation of the morphological system. In other words, the regular structure of the irregular process is one which has to be confronted, perhaps most of all because the suppletive process is one which emerges only in the most basic elements of the language.

REFERENCES

Anderson, Stephen R. 1992. *A-morphous morphology*. Cambridge Studies in Linguistics 62. Cambridge University Press.
Brunner, Karl. 1965. *Altenglische Grammatik*, 3rd edition. Tübingen: Max Niemeyer.
Campbell, Alistair. 1959. *Old English grammar*. Oxford: Clarendon Press.
Campbell, Lyle. 1998. *Historical linguistics: an introduction*. Edinburgh University Press.
Hogg, Richard M. 1980. 'Analogy as a source of morphological complexity', *Folia Linguistica Historica* 1: 277–84.
Lass, Roger. 1997. *Historical linguistics and language change*. Cambridge University Press.
Lehmann, Winfred P. 1992. *Historical linguistics*, 3rd edition. London: Routledge.
Matthews, Peter H. 1991. *Morphology*, 2nd edition. Cambridge University Press.
Mitchell, Bruce. 1985. *Old English syntax*. Oxford: Clarendon Press.
Prokosch, Eduard. 1939. *A comparative Germanic grammar*. Baltimore, MD: Linguistic Society of America.
Szemerényi, Oswald J. L. 1996. *Introduction to Indo-European linguistics*. Oxford: Clarendon Press.
Trask, R. Larry. 1996. *Historical linguistics*. London: Arnold.
Warner, Anthony R. 1993. *English auxiliaries: structure and history*. Cambridge University Press.
Wright, Joseph and Elizabeth Mary Wright. 1925. *Old English grammar*, 3rd edition. London: Oxford University Press.

6 On not explaining language change: Optimality Theory and the Great Vowel Shift

April McMahon

1 Explanation and motivation

Motive seems to play an essential role in the explanation of any event. It is not enough for us to know that something happened, and where, and who or what the participants were: this Cluedo model is intrinsically unsatisfactory. That is to say, it is all very well to know that Miss Murgatroyd dunnit, in the conservatory with the pinking shears, but we have a further need to know why. Police investigations, to secure a conviction, require a suspect (without a decent alibi); the opportunity to commit the crime; and a plausible motive. We are also rather particular about what counts as a motive, and therefore as an explanation. We prefer not to invoke very general factors whose relevance to the matter at hand is difficult to establish (she murdered him because mankind is sinful); and equally, we see extremely particularistic accounts as leaving something to be desired (she saw the pinking shears there and it just sort of happened). Ideally, we are searching for a middle way, where we can understand immediate actions as the result of general, but variable and nonabsolute trends. Stereotypically, looking for some cause in terms of sex or money might fit the bill. However, we have to be careful that our attempts at explanation do not become circular, so that we simply resort to relabelling: saying someone committed murder because they are the murdering type, and claiming this as a generalisation which provides us with a motive, is not likely to be hailed as an outstanding success.

Linguists work in a rather similar way when it comes to explaining sound change. Very broad, general principles (of the 'ease of articulation' variety, for instance) are insufficient since they do not always provoke immediate remedial action. On the other hand, setting out the specific circumstances which led to a specific result is likely to be seen as descriptive rather than explanatory. Again, we are in search of something in between: motives which generalise over sets of cases, but which allow exceptions.

This could be a made-to-measure description of the main apparatus of Optimality Theory. Whereas earlier generative phonologies involved both language-specific rules and universal constraints on rule applications, OT subsumes both in the set of constraints. Constraints are universal, and innate: but they are not absolute. Instead, compromise is factored into the model, since a higher-ranking constraint may necessitate the violation of a lower-ranking one: hence, the learner's task in language acquisition is no longer to construct rules on the basis of output data, but to assess the ranking of this set of constraints which will produce the appropriate surface forms. Learners must also, of course, acquire a lexicon of input forms. Rather than passing through a serial derivation, these are submitted to a function Gen, for 'Generator', which computes all possible permutations of each input: these candidate parses are then evaluated, in parallel, by the ranked set of constraints. Typological variation therefore results from the differential ranking of constraints in different languages.

The question is how these universal but violable constraints are involved in motivating sound change; and the sole relevant mechanism is constraint reranking. Archangeli (1997: 31) makes this point quite unambiguously: 'Under OT, the formal characterization of language change through time is that constraints are reranked.' Of course, it makes supremely good sense for OT to model change in terms of constraint reranking, for two reasons. First, cross-linguistic variation is captured in terms of different rank orders, and there seems no good reason why this should not hold diachronically as well as diatopically. Second, if we follow the standard OT assumption that constraints 'are not arbitrary stipulations plucked from the air to produce the correct results; every constraint should articulate a universal linguistic tendency' (Sherrard 1997: 45), then we are not at liberty to propose the addition, deletion or modification of constraints. If constraints are the only formal object of phonological analysis within OT, then this leaves reordering as the only possible mechanism.

The problem is, to anticipate the results of the next section, that although constraint reranking turns out to be a reasonable descriptive mechanism, it is hard to see it as explanatory: ascribing loss of a consonant to a constraint banning that consonant is in danger of falling into the same category as explaining a murder on the grounds that the perpetrator's murderous nature suddenly asserted itself (but why then?). We can write neat descriptions of successive grammars using Optimality Theory, but it encounters significant difficulties when faced with the transitions between them; that is, with change itself. This is precisely what we might expect from a formal model of this sort, given Lass's (1980: 119) observation that 'while synchronic states are (within limits) "lawful", history is by and large contingent'. And contingency is the enemy of universalism.

2   Constraint reranking and the explanation of change

2.1   Aims and claims

There is no question that universal constraints and constraint ranking can often describe what happens in sound change. It is equally true that this is all phonological rules can typically do, but the difference is that rules are not presented, or intended as directly explanatory: they have a language- and indeed dialect-specific role in describing processes, which require explanation externally, perhaps in terms of history, phonetics, memory or acquisition. On the other hand, the Optimality Theoretic account of sound change is not generally presented as a descriptive system: it seems categorically intended as an explanatory one. For instance, the abstract to Miglio (1998) tells us that 'This paper presents a model of the Great Vowel Shift... and offers an explanation of how it may have been triggered... The model shows how Optimality Theory... can be... an important means to explain language change... The novelty of the paper consists in explaining what may have set [the change] off... This is a natural explanation...' Sherrard (1997: 82) supports this impression with his assertion that, while rule-based phonology 'typically tells us *what* happens in a language', OT 'arguably places greater emphasis on *why what happens happens* by supplying priorities and objectives for the grammar'. An obvious difficulty arises if these claims for the explanatory nature of OT turn out not to be fulfilled. One particularly clear case involves Miglio's (1998) treatment of the Great Vowel Shift.

2.2   *The Great Vowel Shift: Miglio (1998)*

Circular chain shifts like the Great Vowel Shift present an immediate difficulty for any theory cast in terms of markedness, as OT is, since they are unconditioned, and furthermore involve swopping of feature values in the same environment, so that considerations of articulatory or perceptual preference are difficult to invoke. What sort of constraint or constraints would make the occurrence of long vowels A to Z in lexical classes A to Z maximally harmonic at time t1, but a different distribution of long vowels A to Z in lexical classes B to A at time t2, with the system of vowels remaining very substantially unchanged?

Miglio's (1998) answer is that weak points in a system, defined in terms of markedness and ultimately perceptually, can be identified as probable causes of change. Miglio argues that /ɛː ɔː/ constituted the weak spots in this case: mid long lax vowels of this type are considered by Maddieson (1984) as rare, and therefore highly marked. She proposes that, although these vowels had been part of the English vowel inventory for a long period, 'the shift and instability of these lax long vowels was perhaps primarily caused by the coming into the inventory of a bulk of lexemes with these vowels caused by the Middle English Open Syllable Lengthening [MEOSL]'; if children are sensitive to major changes in the functional load of segments, then 'these words with newly lengthened vowels may have caused the demotion of a faithfulness constraint or promotion of a markedness constraint against mid long lax vowels' (1998: 3).

Miglio (1998) requires various Faithfulness constraints like IDENT[hi], which requires input and output segments to match in their values for height, plus well-formedness constraints like *MID [-ATR], which disfavours mid lax vowels, and crucially, a cooccurrence constraint *[-ATR]mm, which expresses the markedness of long lax vowels. Although Miglio's account does not make this explicit, it would appear that the influx of words with /ɛ: ɔ:/ after MEOSL must have caused the reranking of *[-ATR]mm, which had earlier ranked too low to provoke any reaction to the marginal presence of these vowels in the system. The consequent raising of /ɛ: ɔ:/, however, only starts a chain shift because of a further constraint, Distance, which is itself composed of two constraint families, Maintain Contrast and Mindist, the latter 'requiring a minimal auditory distance between contrasting forms' (Miglio 1998: 9). This constraint, which favours the avoidance of mergers, must be ranked fairly high in Middle English to encourage the continuation of the Great Vowel Shift; where it is ranked low, vowel mergers would be predicted instead.

However, this combination of constraints still does not allow Miglio to model part of the Vowel Shift, namely the raising of /a:/ to /ɛ:/. To account for this, Miglio has to assume that the top part of the Great Vowel Shift took place, then a change in the grammar caused the demotion of *[-ATR]mm, along with the promotion or introduction of a local conjunction of faithfulness constraints referring to height and [ATR]: this 'allows /a:/ to raise, but not as far as [e:]' (1998: 11). Since precisely such a raising to [e:] does happen subsequently during the Vowel Shift, there must presumably be yet a further, later reranking, reactivating the dispreference for /ɛ:/ which, in Miglio's view, motivated the initial shift in the first place.

There are various purely historical difficulties with Miglio's account. First, MEOSL does indeed represent a source of additional vocabulary with /ɛ:/ and /ɔ:/; but MEOSL is generally accepted as preceding the Great Vowel Shift by around 300 years, or several generations of speakers, during which time /ɛ: ɔ:/ were stable members of the system. Why should such a period elapse before the onset of raising? Secondly, Miglio treats /ɛ:/ and /ɔ:/ together in her discussion of the initial raising which begins the Vowel Shift, and the various constraint rerankings she posits necessarily affect them both. However, at the end of the Great Vowel Shift, although /ɛ:/ had been removed from the system, /ɔ:/ remained. Presumably yet another reranking would have to be posited, demoting the constraint disfavouring long lax vowels after /ɛ:/ had raised but before /ɔ:/ had; or some differentiation between back and front vowels would need to be built in, resulting in more, or more complex, constraints.

With this in mind, it is important to ask what the motivation is for the particular constraints Miglio selects in her analysis of the Great Vowel Shift. In Miglio's defence, her constraints are clearly intended to be motivated, either functionally and phonetically, as in the case of Distance and its subparts, Maintain Contrast and Mindist, or typologically, as with *[-ATR]mm and *MID[-ATR], which she explicitly grounds on frequency counts from Maddieson (1984). However, one might equally analyse the Great Vowel Shift in terms of other constraints with the same type of motivation, such as those in (1).

(1)   a. V [+ high]: vowels are high
      b. NO-MERGER: keep contrastive vowels maximally distinct.

(1a) would account for a drive towards vowel raising, which might be tempered by (1b), preventing a wholesale collapse. The Great Vowel Shift could then be attributed to a reranking of V [+ high] relative to the earlier dominant NO-MERGER, which had previously kept each vowel in its place. NO-MERGER, like Miglio's Distance, is functionally and systemically motivated; V [+ high], on the other hand, like Miglio's *[-ATR]mm, is typologically based, and reflects the common emphasis in the OT literature on cross-linguistic attestation of phonological phenomena which can be attributed to a particular constraint. In this case, precisely constraint (1a) is proposed for Yokuts by Archangeli and Suzuki (1997: 200).

Since both Miglio's analysis and the rather schematic, OT painting-by-numbers one sketched above involve similarly motivated constraints, and both, in standard OT fashion, require reranking, we must confront the question of what sort of pathway an argument would take for assessing the superiority of one over the other. In rule-based phonology, an account will be judged on whether the rules proposed do or do not capture the facts of the language, with explanations coming necessarily from beyond those rules. In OT, the idea of deriving both description and explanation from the innate constraints is attractive; but there are currently so many candidate constraints which could be used and combined in so many different ways, that it is hard to see how we are to tell when we have found the right analysis. Many analyses therefore reduce to exercises in constraint invention, in the absence of any sensible limit on the form and number of constraints to be proposed.

In addition, explanation for the sound change(s) still appears to be theory-external in many cases; but the more closely phonetic factors, for instance, are incorporated into OT, the more other aspects of the theory are challenged. For instance, both Hayes (1996) and Haspelmath (1999) see many constraints as necessarily grounded phonetically. Hayes (1996: 4) proposes a model of 'Phonetically-Driven Optimality-theoretic Phonology' which differs from the standard version of OT in Prince and Smolensky (1993) in that constraints are not inherited, but invented during language acquisition. By a process of inductive grounding, a large number of constraints are hypothesised by the language learner, on the basis of 'a phonetic map of the space of articulatory difficulty' (Hayes 1996: 12). Assuming that 'the goal of a constraint is to exclude hard things and include easy things' (1996: 13), the hypothesised constraints can then be assessed for their degree of grounding, and ranked. Since Hayes's constraints are not innate, they will be language-specific, albeit limited by knowledge of universal articulatory markedness. However, inductive grounding emerges as a lengthy and complex procedure, which will be unable to deal with ungrounded constraints (and, of special relevance here, aspects of the language which were once grounded, but are no longer clearly so for reasons of diachronic development).

While Hayes (1996) sees diachronic developments and their residues as a source of exceptionality for inductive grounding, Haspelmath (1999) considers these issues as central to the formulation and motivation of constraints. Essentially, Haspelmath argues that grammatical optimality must be supplemented by user optimality in order for us to understand why we find NOCODA and ONSET very frequently in the literature, for instance, but not CODA and NOONSET. Haspelmath (1999: 5) argues that 'the best option among a range of alternatives is the one which promises the highest net benefit to speaker and hearer', and assumes that variants arising in historical change are subject to functional selection, with speakers and hearers able to judge which form suits them best, and that form ultimately coming to dominate as the new standard variant. OT constraints used to describe that resultant synchronic situation therefore have the shape they do as a result of what Haspelmath calls 'diachronic adaptation'. To take one example, NO VOICE CODA, which in a standard OT definition, would state 'Voiced coda obstruents are forbidden', is related to 'User-optimal NO VOICE CODA: Coda obstruents should be pronounced voiceless in order to avoid articulatory difficulties' (Haspelmath 1999: 13). Hence, the synchronic constraints relevant to a particular system will depend on the interaction of the history of that system with the language user's knowledge of what is 'better' or 'worse' for speakers and hearers; and Haspelmath therefore also argues that constraints are not innate. However, the notion of motivation here is verging on the teleological.

It seems, then, that we can include functional and phonetic motivation directly in (at least some) OT constraints, but must then weaken or reject claims for innateness, as Hayes (1996) and Haspelmath (1999) do, meaning that typological data is no longer so directly relevant in constraint formulation. This also weakens the common argument for OT analyses on the grounds of greater economy or parsimony: this might follow if rules plus constraints were replaced by universal constraints alone, but is significantly harder to assess if we allow any departure from this position of Prince and Smolensky (1993). If constraints are language-specific and learned, they bear much more affinity to rules; and, indeed, some OT work includes rules as well as constraints (see Blevins 1997; McCarthy 1993).

Reranking itself, however, is the main difficulty with Miglio's (1998) analysis, and with similar treatments of sound change within OT. The essential difficulty here is whether the change motivates the constraint reranking, or whether the reranking motivates the change. We might say that a constraint with visible effects in the phonology is necessarily ranked high: so the fact that vowels raise in the Great Vowel Shift is evidence for the relatively high ranking of my constraint (1a), or Miglio's *[-ATR]mm, and the fact that vowels did not raise earlier shows they were then ranked low. If the two constraints in (1) reversed their ranking first, then the Great Vowel Shift could be a response to the newly active status of 'vowels are high': but this does not explain the reranking; it presupposes it. On the other hand, if the Great Vowel Shift started for other reasons, and children learning the language ascribed the change in progress on the phonetic ground to the previously dormant 'vowels are high' constraint, then the reranking is explained, but not the change. Problems of this kind are familiar from rule-based work, where general, universal tendencies have sometimes unsuccessfully been invoked to account for sound, or indeed syntactic change: this is true, for instance, of the attribution of shifts from OV to VO, as between OE and ModE, to a principle like 'natural serialisation' in 1970s discussions of syntactic change (see Lehmann 1973; Vennemann 1974). In short, it is impossible to sensibly determine why this principle comes into play precisely when it does, and not otherwise, unless external evidence from parsing, memory limitations and so on is included. If we need reference to nonphonological factors for sound change too, whether those are phonetic or sociolinguistic, then we can still by all means say the result is a reranking of constraints, but calling the reranking explanatory is very problematic.

We might seek refuge from the complexities of this case in the intrinsic oddness of chain shifts. However, these are not particularly rare either synchronically or diachronically, and moreover initially seem promising candidates for a constraint-based analysis. Labov, surely the authority on such shifts in progress, holds that 'When a number of English dialects are charted, and when these results are compared with the array of chain shifts reported in the historical record, constraints emerge with a compelling, exceptionless character that would satisfy the most stringent demands of a universalist approach' (1994: 115–16). Some of the principles Labov formulates on the basis of both historical and ongoing chain shifts are given in (2).

(2)   In chain shifts, peripheral vowels become more open and nonperipheral
       vowels become less open.
       In chain shifts, low nonperipheral vowels become peripheral. (Labov
       1994: 601–2)

The principles are not illustrated only with English data: for instance, Labov shows that symmetrical raising and diphthongisation, though perhaps best known in the context of the Great Vowel Shift, is also manifested in Czech,

Old Prussian and Middle High German, while raising plus fronting is found in chain shifts in Germanic, Albanian, Lithuanian, and the Lolo-Burmese language Akha.

Nonetheless, Labov does provide extensive illustration and justification of the principles in the context of the ongoing Northern Cities Shift in US English. This process, which, as its name suggests, is furthest advanced in big cities like Buffalo, Cleveland and Chicago, is of particular interest because, as he states:

> It is the most complex chain shift yet recorded within one subsystem, involving six members of the English vowel system in one continuous and connected pattern. It is also a remarkable new development in English phonology: over the past millennium, most of the rotations have affected the long vowels; the short vowels have remained relatively stable. (Labov 1994: 178)

The whole pattern of the Northern Cities Shift, in its most complete form, is given in (3), with some examples of its effects. However, although this series of steps shows the consequence of the completed shift for the system, it does not reflect the order in which the steps took place: Labov (1994: 195) argues that raising and fronting of /ɑ/ appears to have been the first step, followed by subshifts of /o/, /oh/, /e/, /i/ and finally /ɑ̃/, this last stage being apparent first in recordings from the late 1970s and early 1980s. He analyses all these subshifts as involving fronting of tense vowels along peripheral paths, and backing of lax vowels along nonperipheral paths, a view which, incidentally, allows resolution of certain failures of vowels to merge when this might have appeared inevitable from ongoing changes, since a vowel on a peripheral track may pass another shifting on a nonperipheral track without colliding.

(3)   The Northern Cities Shift: i → e → ʌ → oh → o → æh → iy
        Debbie, steady = [dʌbi], [stʌdi] got = [gæht]
        massive drop = [mɛsɪv drap]

Initially, Labov's observations on chain shifts appear to fit well into an OT approach, an impression strengthened by his contention that none of these principles is exceptionless: processes exhibiting just such general but violable trends might seem naturally characterisable by OT constraints. However, there are various difficulties which make the match between chain shifts and OT less close. First, Labov (1994: 140) argues that social factors very largely determine when the principles of chain shifting are adhered to: OT constraints respond to innate, phonological universals rather than contingent social pressure. Second, chain shifts are also powerfully conditioned both systemically and phonetically: for instance, issues of avoidance of merger and preservation of distinctions are involved, while discrepancies between front and back vowel shifts may arise from the greater available articulatory space for front vowels, meaning that four degrees of height, for instance, are more readily sustainable at front than at back position. These functional and phonetic issues, as we have seen, paradoxically pose a challenge to constraint innateness.

Finally, 'synchronic chain shifts, whereby certain sounds are promoted (or demoted) stepwise along some phonetic scale in some context, are one of the classic cases of opaque rule interactions' (Kirchner 1996: 341). Although diachronic chain shifts (and chain shifts in progress, like the Northern Cities Shift) can be dealt with by assuming that the various stages are historically sequential and nonoverlapping, cases where synchronic alternations seem describable in terms of chain shifts are much more problematic for OT for reasons of apparent ordering and reciprocity. That is, a chain shift with /a/ [e] and /e/ [i] can be handled by sequential rule ordering with /e/ [i] first, to avoid the otherwise predicted merger; but in a strictly parallel instantiation of OT, this ordering cannot be modelled. Furthermore, if we dealt with /a/ [e] in a standard OT manner, by invoking constraints favouring [e] rather than [a], it is inexplicable why [e] should then simultaneously be disfavoured in the same context, being replaced by [i].

Various methods of dealing with chain shifts in OT terms have been proposed: Kirchner notes, for instance, that McCarthy analyses the Bedouin Hijazi Arabic shift illustrated in (4) as reflecting a constraint NO-V-PLACE, which prohibits place-feature specifications for short vowels in open syllables, thus producing vowel reduction, in association with various PARSE constraints and an assumption that stray elements are automatically deleted postphonologically.

(4)   Bedouin Hijazi Arabic: /a/ [i], /i/ Ø in open nonfinal syllables
       /kitil/ = [ktil] 'he was killed'
       /katab/ = [kitab] 'he wrote'

However, Kirchner argues that this approach cannot be extended to chain shifts with more than two steps, or cases where there is no deletion, as is the case in the Bantu language Nzebi, where /a/ → [ɛ], /ɛ/ → [e], and /e/ → [i]. In this case, Kirchner initially suggests the morphologically conditioned constraint 'RAISING: Maximize vowel height (in verbs when occurring with certain tense and aspect affixes)' (1996: 344), another language-specifically customised constraint of the type frequently associated with opaque alternations and historical changes. This, however, turns out to be unsatisfactory, since 'there appears to be no way to rank RAISING relative to the $PARSE_F$ constraints to permit raising of the nonhigh vowels without raising /a/ all the way to [i]' (Kirchner 1996: 345). Kirchner therefore proposes a new strategy allowing local conjunction of constraints, which is also used by Miglio in her (1998) analysis of the Great Vowel Shift: this allows multiple violations of a single constraint or related ones to be assessed, since a derived constraint will be violated only if all its component, conjoined constraints are violated. Hence, $PARSE_{low}$ and

PARSE$_{ATR}$, and PARSE$_{high}$ and PARSE$_{ATR}$ could be locally conjoined, allowing the Nzebi chain shift to be modelled.

Here, we face a proliferation of analytical techniques and of constraints within OT. Local conjunction must be added to the various novel subtypes of Correspondence and to Sympathy Theory to deal with opacity, and there seems no principled way of deciding which should be applied in particular cases beyond trial and error (see McMahon 2000 for more detailed discussion of this and other issues raised in this chapter). It is not even possible to argue that local conjunction can deal in a unified way with the entire class of chain shifts, since Kirchner (1996: 348, fn.8) himself observes that circular chain shifts do not lend themselves to analysis in this way: this would include the Northern Cities Shift, for instance, and Xiamen tone sandhi (Chen 1987), where contour tones shift in the sequence 53 → 44, 44 → 22, 22 → 21, 21 → 53. Kirchner (1996: 348) accepts that 'Unrestricted local conjunction would appear to result in excessive descriptive power'; it is also certain to increase the number of constraints, since if a violation of a conjoined constraint is more serious than violation of its components, this implies both that the conjoined constraint and the components are individually present in the hierarchy, and that the conjoined constraint outranks the component constraints. If conjoined constraints are innate, the number of constraints which require ranking will therefore rise considerably, since presumably all possible local conjunctions must be innately available unless some principled division can be drawn between those constraints which are conjoinable and those which are not. On the other hand, if children learning a language decide to conjoin innate constraints as a response to particular input data, then we must again confront the question of how innate and hypothesised constraints interact, and can be ranked into a single hierarchy.

2.3   Historical segment loss

The difficulties identified in Miglio (1998) are by no means unique to that analysis or to the OT treatment of chain shifts: many recur in constraint-based approaches to other sound changes, including segment loss. For example, Cho (1995) allows for the replacement of earlier Korean *nip* 'leaf', which was current until the eighteenth century, by the novel form *ip*, by invoking reranking of the constraint *[ni with Faithfulness. Whereas Faithfulness constraints ideally impose identity between input and output representations, *[ni prohibits the [ni] sequence at the beginning of a prosodic word. When the *[ni constraint, which presumably was earlier too low ranked to have any discernible effect, came to outrank Faithfulness, the best parse of /nip/ became [ip].

Cho's analysis again raises the question of universality. The *[ni constraint looks suspiciously language-specific; and yet, given the assumptions of the theory, it has to be seen as innate, partly because it is based on negative evidence and is therefore unlearnable as it stands, and partly because it must be available for reranking, as a parallel change could take place in another language. Even if we include only those banning constraints actually attested by their presumed effects in particular languages, rather than listing all possible segments and sequences, this will still increase the constraint inventory very significantly in more strongly innatist versions of OT. In addition, if we are to take cross-linguistic evidence seriously in formulating constraints, we can never be sure, since our descriptions of many languages are incomplete, that there is not another language in which Constraint X is 'in evidence': that is, propose a constraint for Korean today, and someone may ascribe effects in Gaelic to it tomorrow. On that basis, my analysis of the Great Vowel Shift has just validated Archangeli and Suzuki's 'vowels are high' constraint for Yokuts.

Here again, we also face the problem of why the reranking happens. If the reranked constraint causes the *ni-* sequence to simplify, why did that constraint come to rank high enough in the eighteenth century to have that effect, when it did not in the seventeenth century? Archangeli (1997: 31) tells us that:

Under OT, the formal characterization of language change through time is that constraints are reranked. A prevalent view of diachronic language change is that change occurs when there is imperfect transmission from one generation to the next. Combining these two claims implies that constraints can only be reranked when the evidence for a particular ranking is not very robust.

If this means *ni-* was already on the way out, the reranking is purely a descriptive technique for telling us things were different at two stages of Korean; and any explanation will have to come from outside the theory, in phonetics or acquisition, for instance. The constraints themselves cannot directly explain the change if their order at the time of that change does not predict the output we find, unless we are willing to countenance teleology. In general, OT seems to concentrate on internal explanations, with phonological behaviour constituting a response to the universal constraints. But the violability of these constraints, although beneficial in many ways, introduces tension here: if a change improves harmony, this should be calculated in terms of constraint ordering at the time the development began; but the constraints will subsequently be reranked in response to the change. So why was the earlier form maximally harmonic then, while the new one is now? This also raises questions for the OT view of language acquisition. If children rank the innate constraints on the basis of language-specific behaviour, discovering the right order to generate the data they hear, sound change presumably will not necessitate reranking for a particular speaker once her grammar is established; instead, reranking is something only the phonologist can discern by comparing the appropriate rankings for the stages before and after the change. However, if the explanation for certain changes lies in the acquisition process, then imperfect learning will have to be a possibility in a constraint-based system. Paradoxically, Tesar and Smolensky's (1998) acquisition algorithm may be too successful here: its results are generally good, but there seems no way of building in imperfect learning, meaning that the capacity for modelling and explaining change in OT is potentially seriously limited.

Restrictions on possible rerankings should also delimit possible sound changes. Since little attention has been paid to change in OT until relatively recently (perhaps because evidence on prosodic change from earlier language stages is notoriously difficult to interpret, and the strengths of OT lie outside the segmental alternations which have been the focus of most studies of sound change), it is only possible at this stage to provide some questions which might guide further research. Since the power of OT is largely defined by the interaction of constraints, the restrictiveness of the model will depend on the provision of answers to these questions (along with other areas requiring further attention, such as the incorporation of language-specific phonological rules). For instance, is there a limit on the number of constraints which can be involved in the reranking responsible for a given change? Does reranking to a point high in the hierarchy cause more visible effects, or predictably different effects, from a change which leaves a constraint still ranked relatively low? Are there particular points in the constraint hierarchy where reranking preferentially occurs?

Precisely parallel problems arise for other analyses of segment loss, such as Green's (1998) account of the simplification of the [kn] cluster in the history of English, which equally relies on reranking. Green defends his approach, and the analysis of sound change under OT in general, by arguing that 'An OT approach to sound change predicts that the same sorts of sound changes will happen over and over again cross-linguistically, which rule-based approaches to sound change do not' (1998: 2). It would seem, however, that reranking is descriptive at best, fortuitous at worst, and post hoc either way, so long as the constraint set is in principle unrestricted, and the reranking itself depends on external factors, whether phonetic, functional, or sociolinguistic.

3   Learning the limits

The root of many of these problems may be precisely the much vaunted reduction in OT to a single formal object, in place of the older system of rules and constraints. This kind of reductionism is by no means unique to OT, or even to linguistics: evolutionary biologists have also grappled with the temptation to put all phenomena into one category. In their case, there is a tendency to see all biological phenomena as adaptive; that is, as arising from mutation, variation and natural selection. However, biologists are trying to resist that temptation.

In this connection, Sober (1990: 764) argues that ' "Why do rhinoceri have horns?" is a very different question from "Why do rhinoceri have precisely the number of horns they do?" ' Whereas horns in general are possibly adaptive in terms of self-defence, and therefore a product of natural selection, Sober holds that the number of horns in different species is the result of 'purely historical factors concerning the state of the two ancestral populations'.

What Sober recognises here is that some opaque characteristics only become transparent in historical context. Sometimes that means we just need to describe things synchronically on a species-specific basis. In phonology too, we may need language-specific rules (or, perhaps, language-specific constraints) to deal with some of the products of history, and we write those rules in a particular way, and not in one of the myriad other possible ways, because the language behaves that way, and not one of the myriad other possible ways. Things in English are the way they are because of where English has come from, and what has happened to it along the way. There have been various historical accidents. English could quite easily have ended up like German. German did, after all. The problem for biologists is that adaptive stories, albeit of different degrees of plausibility, can always be told; just as phonologists can always come up with constraints, albeit of different degrees of plausible universality. Biologists are trying to find principled distinctions between what is adaptive and what is not. They recognise that the vital step is to stop trying to cram everything into a single conceptual category, when some of the material plainly won't fit.

All this is, essentially, a corollary of studying history at all: 'the search for historical laws is...mistaken in principle. Laws apply..."other things being equal." But in history, a sequence of real, individual events, other things never are equal' (Simpson 1964: 128). Lass (1980: 138), who quotes Simpson with approval, develops the theme further, observing that 'the problem with language is not merely a matter of complex individuals (whether speakers, communities, or languages themselves...) facing simple (and known) contingencies; we really have no idea of what the contingencies are, and whether they are even implicated in language change.' Where we can identify the contingencies, as in the obvious case of language contact, we are still in no position to predict how individual language structures will be affected, or explain why languages and speakers respond to apparently similar situations in radically different ways.

This is no reason to give up on the enterprise of working historically; it is simply the case, as Lass (1980) recognised well before the advent of Optimality Theory, that we must recognise the limits on what we can do, and obey certain strictures in attempting to do it. There are two elements to this prescription. First, explanation of change, in its truest sense, may be beyond OT, and indeed any other formal linguistic theory. The cause of the model is not served if its practitioners continue, nonetheless, to claim that they are providing explanations. Lass notes that we tend to talk about 'explanations' when we mean 'models' or 'metaphors', and to claim that we have shown 'why X happened' when what we have really done is linked X up in a 'network' with Y, Z, etc., and thus created a more or less plausible and imaginatively pleasing picture of 'how (*ceteris paribus*) X could happen'. This is all really relatively harmless...; at least it is if we can bring ourselves to see clearly what we actually do, and avoid terminological subterfuge and defensive pretence. (1980: 157–8)

Even if we cannot achieve full explanations, we can, Lass argues, provide some insight into why some event took place; but when we do, we are apt to become passionately sure that the model providing the insight is right, and perhaps convince ourselves that it provides all the answers:

The critical factor is the 'Aha!' feeling that comes from the imposition of order on some domain... If an explanation, model, analogy, or whatever fails to evoke the feeling of 'illumination', then it's a failure, however rational it seems to be; and by the same token, if the feeling is evoked, we are tempted to fight like hell to hold onto the source of it. (1980: 158)

However, this degree of insight is only valuable if we can convince people working outside our particular model of its worth: 'if the community of believers want to make a case for others joining them, they should be obliged to proceed in a particular way: above all, they must break out of the protective hermetic circle defined by their particular community as an institution' (Lass 1980: 155–6).

This is all rather prescient, and leads to two conclusions particularly relevant to OT. First, its practitioners have to realise and accept that, while OT may do an extremely good job of dealing with some phonological phenomena, it is not a Theory of Everything. Some aspects of phonology, especially in the historical domain, will require system-specific tools to describe and systematise them, which is as far as we can meaningfully go (and in this context, it might be worth stressing that while description may be the poor relation, it is not the ugly sister). OT seems at present to be falling into the old Standard Generative trap of seeing description and explanation as interchangeable concepts; but overusing terms like explanation does not make it any more likely that we are actually explaining anything, and might make those outside the model more reluctant to believe claims that do have more right to be taken seriously. Secondly, when alleged explanations are presented, they cannot be justified in purely theory-internal terms. Practitioners of OT often simply assume that their model is preferable to the alternatives, without defending this position: and the best defences often seem inadequate, since they are predicated on a form of the model without rules, additional types of constraint interaction, and the other formal mechanisms which are nonetheless frequently invoked in OT analyses. Paradoxically, recognising OT as a limited theory might make it a stronger one, and one which might be combined with other models and with external factors to provide fuller and more satisfactory motives for change.

REFERENCES

Archangeli, Diana. 1997. 'Optimality Theory: an introduction to linguistics in the 1990s', in Diana Archangeli and D. Terence Langendoen (eds.), *Optimality Theory: an overview*. Oxford: Blackwell, 1–32.

Archangeli, Diana and Keiichiro Suzuki. 1997. 'The Yokuts challenge', in Iggy Roca (ed.), *Derivations and constraints in phonology*. Oxford: Clarendon Press, 197–226.

Blevins, Juliette. 1997. 'Rules in Optimality Theory: two case studies', in Iggy Roca (ed.), *Derivations and constraints in phonology*. Oxford: Clarendon Press, 227–60.

Chen, M. 1987. 'The syntax of Xiamen tone sandhi', *Phonology Yearbook* 4: 109–49.

Cho, Young-mee Yu. 1995. 'Language change as reranking of constraints', paper presented at the 12th International Conference on Historical Linguistics, University of Manchester.

Green, Antony Dubach. 1998. 'The promotion of the unmarked: representing sound change in Optimality Theory', paper presented at the 10th International Conference on English Historical Linguistics, University of Manchester.

Haspelmath, Martin. 1999. 'Optimality and diachronic adaptation', *Zeitschrift für Sprachwissenschaft* 18: 180–205.

Hayes, Bruce P. 1996. 'Phonetically-driven phonology: the role of Optimality Theory and inductive grounding', MS, Rutgers Optimality Archive.

Kirchner, Robert. 1996. 'Synchronic chain shifts in Optimality Theory', *Linguistic Inquiry* 27: 341–50.

Labov, William. 1994. *Principles of linguistic change*, vol. 1: *Internal Factors*. Oxford: Blackwell.

Lass, Roger. 1980. *On explaining language change*. Cambridge University Press.

Lehmann, Winfred P. 1973. 'A structural principle of language and its implications', *Language* 49: 47–66.

Maddieson, Ian. 1984. *Patterns of sounds*. Cambridge University Press.

McCarthy, John. 1993. 'A case of surface constraint violation', *Canadian Journal of Linguistics* 38: 169–95.

McMahon, April. 2000. *Change, chance, and optimality*. Oxford University Press.

Miglio, Viola. 1998. 'The Great Vowel Shift: an OT model for unconditioned language change', paper presented at the 10th International Conference on English Historical Linguistics, University of Manchester.

Prince, Alan and Paul Smolensky 1993. 'Optimality Theory: constraint interaction in generative grammar', MS, Rutgers University/University of Colorado at Boulder.

Sherrard, Nicholas. 1997. 'Questions of priorities: an introductory overview of Optimality Theory in phonology', in Iggy Roca (ed.), *Derivations and constraints in phonology*. Oxford: Clarendon Press, 43–89.

Simpson, G. G. 1964. *This view of life: the world of an evolutionist*. New York: Harcourt, Brace and World.

Sober, Elliott. 1990. 'Comment on Pinker and Bloom', *Behavioral and Brain Sciences* 13: 764.

Tesar, Bruce and Paul Smolensky. 1998. 'Learnability in Optimality Theory', *Linguistic Inquiry* 29: 229–68.

Vennemann, Theo. 1974. 'Topics, subjects and word order: from SXV to SVX via TVX', in John M. Anderson and Charles Jones (eds.), *Historical linguistics*, vol. 1, Amsterdam: North Holland, 339–76.

Part III

Grammaticalisation

7   Grammaticalisation: cause or effect?

David Lightfoot

1   A nineteenth-century legacy

The central research question for nineteenth-century linguists was: how did a language get to be the way it is? Historical linguistics was the only kind of linguistics of the time. Towards the end of the century, Hermann Paul (1880: 20) was able to pontificate that 'Es ist eingewendet, dass es noch eine andere wissenschaftliche Betrachtung der Sprache gäbe, als die geschichtliche. Ich muss das in Abrede stellen' (It has been objected that there is another scientific view of language possible besides the historical. I must contradict this). What changed for the nineteenth-century linguists was a language and a language essentially was an inventory of words. There was more to it than that, of course, but everything else was attributable to either a universal 'logic' or individually variable 'habits', and this didn't interest contemporary linguists much. So there wasn't anything to have a history of except words, their pronunciations and their meanings.

Words are transmitted from one generation to the next and they may change their form in that transmission. Latin *pater* 'father' became *padre, père, patre, pai*, etc. in the modern Romance languages. One could characterise such changes by writing sound 'laws', for example, that a dental stop is voiced in some phonetic environment, between a vowel and a vocalic *r* in Italian and Spanish, C –> +vd / V_ṛ.

In this view, languages are the basic objects of reality, entities 'out there', existing in their own right, waiting to be acquired by speakers, essentially inventories of words. Linguists sought to quantify the degree of historical relatedness among sets of languages and historical relatedness was expressed through tree diagrams or cladograms, introduced by August Schleicher (1861). As often pointed out, the Schleicher-style cladograms, familiar from all textbooks on historical linguistics, capture only what biologists call homologies, similarities which arise through historical commonalities, and not analogies, similarities which arise from common developments. This was recognised very early and nineteenth-century linguists supplemented cladograms with 'wave' models, which represented common innovations shared by geographically contiguous languages.

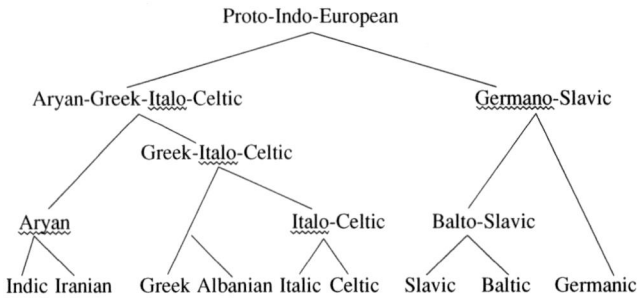

These cladograms assume that languages are like species, as articulated by Schleicher (1863), and that they derive from one another in some coherent historical or evolutionary development. But languages are not like species and we should recognise some of the idealisations involved. Trees of this kind idealise away from the fact that languages do not split sharply at some specific point and suddenly emerge in their full individuality. The splitting process is more gradual and is initiated by minor divergences. We might say that the first change which affected, say, Latin and not any of the other languages is the bifurcation point, the point at which Latin suddenly splits away. But that is not enough. Saying that French and Italian are descended from Latin glosses over the fact that they descended from different forms of Latin, and that 'Latin' is a cover term for many different forms of speech. As a result, the conventional tree models of historical linguists would require vast elaboration to be equivalent to modern, biological cladograms, which are based strictly on the molecular structure of organisms.

There is no precisely definable notion of a language, such that one can show in some non-circular way that a certain sentence is 'a sentence of English' (see Chomsky 1986; Lightfoot 1999 and others). A given sentence might be used by speakers in Texas but not by speakers in Yorkshire. Does that make it a sentence of English? Well, yes for speakers in Houston but not for speakers in Leeds. There is no general algorithm which characterises the sentences of English and there is no reason to expect to find one. Languages, rather, are conglomerations of the output of various grammars, all represented in the mind / brain of individual speakers. They are not coherent entities themselves and, in that case, there is no reason to believe that languages are entities which 'descend' from one another.

Schleicher-style cladograms also do not provide a particularly insightful way of talking about relatedness, since they deal only in terms of historical similarities. The models were developed to capture relatedness among lexicons, which were taken to be pretty much unstructured inventories of words. However, if one thinks beyond the lexicon and if one thinks of relatedness more broadly, not just in terms of similarities resulting from a common history, one would arrive at very different relations. For example, if one thinks of grammars, acquired on exposure to some relevant linguistic experience, and emerging according to the prescriptions of the linguistic genotype, 'Universal Grammar' (UG), as children set thirty or forty predefined parameters, one could compare the grammars of German speakers with those of English speakers and ask whether those grammars are more or less similar to each other than to the grammars of Italian speakers. German grammars are quite different from English grammars: they are object–verb, verb-second, and have very different scrambling properties inside VP. In fact, it is quite possible, even likely that English grammars might be more similar to grammars with which there is less historical connection. From this perspective, and looking at the parameters in the current linguistic literature, English grammars may be more similar to Italian than to German, and French grammars may be more similar to German than to Spanish.[1] There is no reason to believe that structural similarity should be even an approximate function of historical relatedness, ... assuming that there is a coherent, non-circular notion of historical relatedness to be discovered.

Nonetheless, nineteenth-century linguists focused on languages, seen often as inventories of words, which could change over time; languages, so conceived, could change in systematic ways. By the end of the nineteenth century, linguists knew that there were regularities of language change which could not be stated in purely phonetic terms, which suggested that it wasn't the language or the sounds which were changing, but rather some kind of abstract system. This matter was dealt with in a terminological move: there were regularities of 'sound change', but there could be other kinds of change which worked differently: namely, what were called 'analogical changes', which were not law-governed in the same way. Analogy was a different, more mysterious kind of regularity.

Nineteenth-century linguists focused on the products of human behaviour, rather than on the internal processes that underlie the behaviour, dealing with E-language rather than I-language in the terminology of Chomsky (1986). Not all aspects of language can be treated productively in this way, and sometimes one has to deal with the underlying processes and abstract systems. This is true for Grimm's Law, for example, which affected many consonants in a kind of *Kreislauf* or 'cycle'; it is also true of more complex changes, such as

---

[1] Linguists idealise and speak of French grammars, but a French grammar is of the same status as a French liver, as I have noted elsewhere, a convenient fiction. Individuals have livers and individuals have grammars. Grammars may be similar to each other and we may seek similarities among grammars of 'English speakers', whoever they may be exactly. In doing so, we must be ready to expect to find differences between the grammars of a man in Houston and a woman in Leeds.

the Great Vowel Shift, which changed all the long vowels of Middle English in another kind of cycle, raising all vowels by one step and making diphthongs of the highest vowels: so /swe:t/ 'sweet' became /swi:t/, /ti:m/ 'time' became /taim/ and /hu:s/ 'house' became /haus/. Grimm's Law and the Great Vowel Shift affect many sounds and represent changes in systems.

(1)   a.

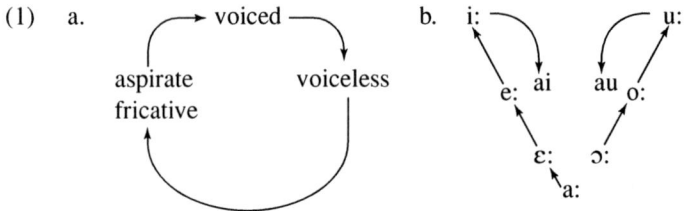

Because the Neogrammarians were working with the products of language, rather than with the internal, underlying processes and abstract systems, there were principled reasons why they worked where they did and paid little attention to change in syntactic systems. It makes no sense to think of (sets of) sentences, products of behaviour, being transmitted from one generation to another, because language acquisition is clearly not just a matter of acquiring sets of sentences. None of this bothered nineteenth-century linguists, who worked where they worked. By contrast, there was much debate about the causes of sound change.

Grimm's, Grassmann's and Verner's Laws were not general laws like Boyle's Law; therefore they required a deeper explanation. Changes were taken to be *directional*, as in biology. Rask (1818) held that languages become simpler. Schleicher (1848) identified a progression from isolating to agglutinating to inflectional types, although this was said to hold for preliterate societies, whereas Rask's drive to simplicity was relevant for literate societies. Darwin (1874: 88–92) thought that languages changed in the direction of having shorter, 'easier' forms. There was widespread agreement that language change followed fixed developmental laws and that there was a direction to change, but there was active disagreement about what the direction was. By the end of the nineteenth century there was an enormous body of work on sound correspondences between historically related languages and vast compendia of changes which had taken place in many Indo-European languages. However, there were few ideas on why those changes had happened.

The notion that languages became simpler / more natural / easier to pronounce was, first, circular. 'Simpler', etc. was what languages change to, and there was no independent definition in a framework dealing entirely with historical change. Second, the idea that languages change toward greater simplicity (or whatever) gives no account for why a given change takes place when it does – unlike the laws of gravity, etc. which apply to all objects at all times. To that extent, invoking notions of directionality was no more law-like than the laws of Grimm, Grassmann and Verner, which directionality was intended to explain.[2]

By the early twentieth century the data of linguistics consisted of an inventory of sound changes occurring for no good reason and tending in no particular direction. The historical approach had not brought a scientific, Newtonian-style analysis of language, of the kind that had been hoped for, and there was no predictability to the changes. The historicist paradigm, discussed most thoroughly in recent times by Lass (1980) – the notion that there are principles of history to be discovered, which would account for a language's development – was largely abandoned in the 1920s. Indeed, there was a virulent anti-historicism in the writing of structuralists Franz Boas, Leonard Bloomfield and Edward Sapir. They worked on language change but they abandoned *historicism*, and with it the earlier programme of seeking to explain how it was that languages became the way they are. The perceived problems related to the circularity of invoking historical principles and to the psychological claims (see note 2). Sapir (1929) wrote that the psychological interpretation of language change was 'desirable and even necessary', but that the existing psychological explanations were unhelpful and 'do not immediately tie up with what we actually know about the historical behavior of language'. Bloomfield (1933: 17) complained about the circularity of Paul's psychologising, saying that there was no independent evidence for the mental processes other than the linguistic processes they were supposed to explain. The historicist paradigm was not really refuted or shown to be wrong; rather, it was abandoned as yielding diminishing returns. Work on language change continued to flourish, but structuralists, by and large, did not appeal to historicist explanations.

In section 4 I shall ask what kinds of accounts of language history we can give if we take a more contingent approach. We shall shift away from a study of the products of behaviour toward a study of the states and properties of the mind/brain that give rise to those products. But first let us consider more recent work, which perpetuates aspects of nineteenth-century thinking.

2   Long-term directionality in the twentieth century

Nineteenth-century linguists viewed languages changing as objects floating smoothly through time and space, and that image continued to be adopted throughout the twentieth century. Despite the move away from historicism in the 1920s, linguists have resumed the search for historical principles. In the

---

[2] There were attempts to break out of the circularity by invoking psychology but the psychology was implausible. Grimm attributed his consonant changes to the courage and pride associated with the German race's advance over all parts of Europe. Jespersen ascribed the shift in the meaning of verbs like *like, repent*, etc. to the greater interest taken in persons than in things at one stage in the history of English. This is discussed in Lightfoot (1999: 38–9).

1970s much work recast the notion of 'drift', originally due to Sapir (1921: ch. 7). A drift for Sapir represented the unconscious selection of those individual variations that are cumulative in some direction. So he attributed the replacement of English *whom* by *who* to three drifts: the levelling of the subject–object distinction, the tendency to fixed word order and the development of the invariant word. He was concerned that in positing a 'canalising' of such 'forces' one might be imputing a certain mystical quality to this history. Certainly the modern work invoked mysticism. Robin Lakoff (1972), for example, examined changes in various Indo-European languages which yield a more 'analytic' surface syntax, and she sought to combine Sapir's three drifts into one. The phenomenon cannot be described, she pointed out, by talking about individual changes in transformational rules or whatnot:

> Rather, it must be described as a metacondition on the way the grammar of a language as a whole will change ... Speaking metaphorically, it instructs the language to segmentalize where possible ... It is not at all clear where this metacondition exists: neither as part of a grammar nor as a universal condition on the form of grammars. It is not clear how a constraint on change within one language family, a constraint which is not absolute but which is nevertheless influential, is to be thought of. But there is no other way to think of these things: either there is such a metacondition, whatever it is, or all the Indo-European languages have been subject to an overwhelming series of coincidences.   (1972: 192)

If the explanation is admittedly incoherent, then maybe the fallacy is in requiring a principled explanation for such a large-scale change taking place over such a long period. What's wrong with a series of coincidences or a series of independent events? Why should we believe that this is the only way that history could have progressed?

Only slightly less mystical is the approach to drifts based on Greenberg's word-order typologies. This distinguishes transitional and pure language types which are defined universally in terms of hierarchically ranked word-order phenomena. Languages change from one pure type to another by losing/ acquiring the relevant orders in the sequence specified by the hierarchies. A pure subject–verb–object language, for example, has verb–object order, auxiliary–verb, noun–adjective and preposition–NP/DP, and these orders are ranked in some hierarchy. A subject–object–verb language is essentially the mirror image and has the opposite orders: object–verb, verb–auxiliary, adjective– noun, and NP/DP–preposition, etc. If a language changes from the object–verb type to the verb–object type, it acquires all of the new orders in the sequence prescribed by the hierarchy: first verb–object, then auxiliary–verb, and so on.

This raises the question of how a child attains a language which is exactly half-way between the subject–verb–object and subject–object–verb types; how does she know whether this is a subject–verb–object language changing to subject–object–verb or vice versa? How does she know that her generation must push the language a little towards, say, a subject–verb–object type? It seems that the only conceivable answer is to postulate a racial memory of some kind, such that the child knows that this is a subject–verb–object language changing towards subject–object–verb. This is presumably what Robin Lakoff had in mind in postulating a 'metacondition on the way the grammar of a language as a whole will change'.

Whether or not an individual change is part of a larger drift, its cause must be found locally. Sapir stressed this and avoided the mystical quality that he warned against. The replacement of *whom* by *who* is part of the general drift towards invariable words and the loss of the case system, but Sapir nonetheless isolated four reasons for this particular change: first *whom* was felt not to belong to the set of personal pronouns, which have distinct subject/object forms, but to a set of interrogative and relative pronouns, which show no such distinction; second, the emphatic nature of interrogative pronouns militates in favour of their invariableness; third, an objective form rarely occurs in initial position; and fourth, [hu:m] was alleged to be phonetically clumsy before the alveolar stops of *do* and *did*. I am not interested here in the validity of this account but in the form that Sapir felt an explanation should take: there were local reasons for the change. This is very different from the ideas of the 1970s typologists, who argued that notions like the subject–object–verb-to-subject–verb–object continua constituted diachronic explanations (Vennemann 1975); for them, the drift was the explanatory force, rather than being something which required explanation, and no local causes were needed.

The typologists remained faithful to the methods of the nineteenth century. They retained the same kind of historical determinism and they dealt with the products of the language capacity rather than with the capacity itself, like their nineteenth-century predecessors. The goal remained one of finding what Lass (1980) called 'straightline explanations for language change', generalisations which would hold of history. And they were not successful.

A recent variant on this approach offers historicist accounts in a biological guise. Bauer (1995) argued that Latin was a thoroughgoing left-branching language, which changed into a thoroughgoing right-branching system in French. Where Latin has a head to the right of its complement (*exercitum duxit, deorum munus*, etc.), French has its head to the left (*il conduisit l'armée, le présent des dieux*). She explains the change through 'an evolutionary concept of language change': 'languages evolve in the direction of features that are acquired early' (1995: 170). She says that 'Latin must have been a difficult language to master, and one understands why this type of language represents a temporary stage in linguistic development' (1995: 188), but she gives no reasons to believe this and she gives no reason why early languages should have exhibited structures which are hard to acquire.

The same logic, another throw-back to nineteenth-century thinking, shows up in the evolutionary explanations of Haspelmath (1999b); see the commentary on this paper by Dresher and Idsardi (1999). If a diachronic change is 'adaptive', one needs to show how the environment has changed such that the new phenomenon is adaptive in a way that it wasn't before. However, proponents of this kind of evolutionary explanation do not do this; instead, they set up universal 'tendencies' by which any change is 'adaptive'.

Another line of work has emphasised the alleged unidirectionality of change. Grammaticalisation, a notion first introduced by Meillet, is taken to be a semantic tendency for an item with a full lexical meaning to be bleached over time and to come to be used as a grammatical function. Such changes are said to be quite general and unidirectional; one does not find changes proceeding in the reverse direction, so it is said. Grammaticalisation of this type does undoubtedly occur and there are many examples (Hopper and Traugott 1993). Grammaticalisation is a real phenomenon but it is quite a different matter to claim that it is general, unidirectional or an explanatory force. If there were a universal tendency to grammaticalise, there would be no counterdevelopments, when bound forms become independent lexical items. When grammaticalisation takes place, it is explained when one points to local factors which promoted the new grammar, new triggering experiences, changes in cues, or what Kiparsky (1996) calls the 'enabling causes'.

This is the stance taken by Olga Fischer (1997) in her reanalysis of grammaticalisation approaches to the development of *have to* in English. She reports work by Adrienne Bruyn (1995), who has shown that

> the grammaticalisation processes which are said to be so typical for pidgins developing into creoles are not at all so straightforward in Sranan, when looked at in more detail. It could be the case, as Bruyn shows painstakingly, that a particular process was aborted before it was completed . . . or that it was heavily supported or even instigated by substratum features . . . or that it does not develop in the way it is expected to, or that the development is much more abrupt than is usual in grammaticalisation cases. Her investigation shows that it is important at each stage to take into account the synchronic circumstances, which will ultimately decide what will happen. In other words, there may not be such a thing as an *in*dependent process of grammaticalisation.
>
> (Fischer 1997: 180)

Grammaticalisation, challenging as a *phenomenon*, is not an explanatory force. We have no well-founded basis for claiming that languages or grammars change in one direction but not in another, no basis for postulating algorithms mapping one kind of grammar into another kind ($G_x \rightarrow G_y$). The fact that we observe locative case endings coming to be used with partitive force in some language does not mean that it cannot be otherwise. Van Gelderen (1997), Janda (2001), Joseph (2001), Newmeyer (1998: ch. 5) and others offer careful studies showing changes which run counter to grammaticalisation, 'de-grammaticalisation', where affixes or minor categories become full lexical items.[3] Imperious blanket

---

[3] Janda (2001) offers many references. He also has good critical discussion of how fundamental the issue of unidirectionality is for grammaticalisationists and how cavalier some of them have been in dismissing changes which appear to run counter to their predispositions. Newmeyer (1998: ch. 5) examines studies which use reconstructions as *evidence* for 'grammaticalisation theory', despite the fact it was *assumed* in the very reconstruction.

denials that such changes occur, as in the writings of Haspelmath (1999a, c, etc.), do not remove them from history.

If we observe a lexical verb being reanalysed as a functional category in one language, one needs a local cause. One cannot invoke principles of history as explanatory forces nor is it appropriate to explain the change by invoking some principle of UG which favours the new grammar (*pace* Roberts 1993; see Lightfoot 1999: section 8.3 for discussion). The search for principles which require that a particular type of grammar change historically into another type has led nowhere, not surprisingly.

3 Grammars and time

If we switch our perspective from language change to grammar change, from E-language to I-language, from the products of the language system to the system itself, we explain grammatical change through the nature of the acquisition process. A grammar grows in a child from some initial state (UG), when she is exposed to primary linguistic data (PLD) (2). So the only way a different grammar may grow in a different child is when that child is exposed to significantly different primary data.

(2)   PLD (UG —> grammar)

The explanatory model is essentially synchronic and there will be a local cause for the emergence of any new grammar, namely a different set of primary linguistic data. Time plays no role. St Augustine held that time comes from the future, which doesn't exist; the present has no duration and moves on to the past, which no longer exists. Therefore there is no time, only eternity. Physicists take time to be 'quantum foam' and the orderly flow of events may really be as illusory as the flickering frames of a movie. Julian Barbour (2000) has argued that even the apparent sequence of the flickers is an illusion and that time is nothing more than a sort of cosmic parlor trick. So perhaps linguists are better off without time.

Let us consider the kinds of explanations that are available, and then ask whether we can or should be more ambitious. In the next section I will consider an instance of grammaticalisation, changes affecting modal auxiliary verbs in English, offering local causes for the various changes and not invoking any general tendency to grammaticalise as an explanatory force.

4 English auxiliary verbs

One view of English modal auxiliary verbs like *can, could, may, might, will, would, shall, should* and *must* is that they are ordinary verbs at a deep level of analysis. Well, not really just ordinary verbs, but verbs with various exceptional features to account for the way in which they behaved differently from real verbs like *grab* and *understand* (Ross 1969). So a modal auxiliary may be fronted in a question, but a verb like *understand* may not (3); a modal may occur to the left of a negative particle, unlike a verb (4); a modal may not occur with a perfective (5) or progressive (6) marker, unlike a verb; a modal may not occur in the infinitival complement to another verb (7), nor as the complement of another modal (8), unlike a verb like *try*; and no modal may occur with a direct object, whereas some verbs may (9).

(3) a. Can he understand chapter 4?
     b. *Understands he chapter 4?
(4) a. He cannot understand chapter 4.
     b. *He understands not chapter 4.
(5) a. *He has could understand chapter 4.
     b. He has understood chapter 4.
(6) a. *Canning understand chapter 4, ...
     b. Understanding chapter 4, ...
(7) a. He wanted to try to understand.
     b. *He wanted to can understand.
(8) a. He will try to understand.
     b. *He will can understand.
(9) a. *He can music.
     b. He understands music.

The different behaviour, in this view, was allegedly due to features attached to lexical items: one feature specified that some verbs (the modals) could move around a subject NP / DP in an interrogative; others specified that modals had no perfective or progressive forms, and so on.

The distribution of these modal auxiliaries is peculiar to modern English. For example, the French verb *pouvoir* 'can' behaves the same way as a regular verb like *comprendre* 'understand' with respect to movement in a question (10) and negation (11). Unlike *can, pouvoir* may occur as a complement to another verb (12), even to another modal verb (13), and may take a clitic direct object (14), and to that extent it behaves like ordinary, common-or-garden verbs in French. In French grammars, the words which translate the English modals, *pouvoir, devoir*, etc., walk like verbs, talk like verbs and are verbs, just like *comprendre*.

(10) a. Peut-il comprendre le chapitre?
         'Can he understand the chapter?'
      b. Comprend-il le chapitre?
         'Does he understand the chapter?'
(11) a. Il ne peut pas comprendre le chapitre.
         'He cannot understand the chapter.'
      b. Il ne comprend pas le chapitre.
         'He doesn't understand the chapter.'

(12)   Il a voulu pouvoir comprendre le chapitre.
         'He wanted to be able to understand the chapter.'
(13)   Il doit pouvoir comprendre le chapitre.
         'He must be able to understand the chapter.'
(14)   Il le peut.
         'He can it', i.e. understand the chapter.

Furthermore, not only may languages differ in this regard, but also different stages of one language. Sentences along the lines of the ungrammatical utterances of (3–9) were well-formed in earlier English. In that case, if the differences between Old and Modern English were a function of several exception features with no unifying factor, we would expect that these features came into the language at different times and in different ways. On the other hand, if the difference between modern and Old English reflected a single property, a categorical distinction, then we would expect the trajectory of the change to be very different. If the differences between *can* and *understand* in (3–9) were a function of the single fact that *understand* is a verb while *can* is a member of a different category, Inflection (I), then we would expect (3b), (4b), (5a), (6a), (7b), (8b) and (9a) to have dropped out of people's language in parallel, at roughly the same time.

If we attend just to changing phenomena, the change consists in the *loss* of various forms, not in the development of new forms; people ceased to say some things which had been said in earlier times. Before the change, all of the utterances in (3–9) might have occurred in a person's speech, but later only those forms not marked with an asterisk. That fact alone suggests that there was a change in some abstract system. People might start to use some new expression because of the social demands of fashion or because of the influence of speakers from a different community, but it would be quite a stretch to claim that people ceased to say certain things for that sort of reason. There might be an indirect relationship, of course: people might introduce new expressions into their speech for external, social reasons, and those new expressions (e.g. analogues to (3b) and (4b) with the periphrastic *do*) might entail the loss of old forms. However, when we find changes involving no new expressions, only the loss and obsolescence of some forms, then that needs to be explained as a consequence of some change in an abstract system. This methodological point is fundamental.

If one focuses on the final disappearance of the relevant forms, one sees that the various forms were lost at the same time. The most conservative writer in this regard seems to have been Sir Thomas More, writing in the early sixteenth century. He used many of the starred forms in (3–9) and had the last attested uses of several constructions. This means that his grammar treated *can*, etc. as verbs in the old fashion (15), and the fact that he was using *all* the relevant forms and his heirs did not, suggests that his grammar differed from theirs in one way and not that the new grammars accumulated various unrelated features. The uniformity of the change suggests uniformity in the analysis. There was a single change, a change in category membership: *can*, etc., formerly verbs which moved to I in the course of a derivation, came to be analysed as I elements (16). The fact that there was a single change in grammars accounts for the bumpiness: several phenomena changed simultaneously.

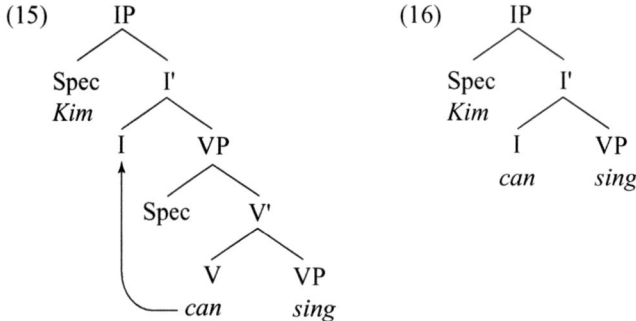

(15)

```
            IP
          /    \
      Spec      I'
      Kim      /  \
             I      VP
                   /  \
               Spec    V'
                      /  \
                    V      VP
                  — can    sing
```

(16)

```
            IP
          /    \
      Spec      I'
      Kim      /  \
             I      VP
            can    sing
```

The change in category membership of the English modals indicated the catastrophic nature of change, not in the sense that the change spread through the population rapidly (as many changes do), but that phenomena might change together in a way which required explanation. The notion of re-analysis of an abstract grammar and, later, of resetting grammatical parameters was a way of unifying disparate phenomena, taking them to be various surface manifestations of a single change at the abstract level.

The cause of the change in grammars is other changes which preceded the change in category membership, notably the fact that the modal auxiliaries became distinct morphologically, the sole surviving members of the preterite-present class of verbs. There were many verb classes in early English and the antecedents of the modern modals were preterite-presents. What was distinctive about the preterite-presents (so-called because their present-tense forms had past-tense or 'preterite' morphology) was that they never had any inflection for the third person singular, although they were inflected elsewhere: *þu cannst, we cunnan, we cuðon*. Nonetheless, they were just another class of verbs and the forms that were to become modal auxiliaries belonged to this class, along with a number of other verbs which either dropped out of the language altogether or were assimilated to another more regular class of verbs. For example, *unnan* 'grant' was lost from the language and *witan* 'know' simply dropped out of the preterite-present class, coming to be treated like nonpreterite-presents. After the simplification of verb morphology, verb classes collapsed and the only inflectional property of present-tense verbs eventually came to be the -*s* ending for the third person singular, and the preterite-present verbs had always lacked that property. The preterite-presents did not change in this regard, but a great mass of inflectional distinctions had disappeared and now the preterite-presents were isolated; they looked different from other verbs in lacking their one morphological feature, that -*s* ending.

The morphological distinctiveness of the surviving preterite-presents, the new modals, was increased by the general loss of a separate subjunctive mood. The past-tense forms of the preterite-present verbs were identical in many instances to the subjunctive forms and, as a result, some old past tense forms like *could, should* and *might* survived with subjunctive-type meanings rather than indicating tense. While *loved* is related to *love* pretty much exclusively in terms of tense in present-day English, the relationship between *can* and *could* is sometimes one of tense (17a) and sometimes has nothing to do with tense (17b). And *might* is never related to *may* in terms of tense in present-day English (18a, b); in earlier times, however, *might* did serve as a past tense – the thought of (18c) would need to be expressed as *might not have intended* in present-day English. So *might, could, should*, etc. came to take on new meanings which had nothing to do with past time, residues of the old subjunctive uses.

(17) a. Kim could understand the book, until she reached page 56.
      b. Kim could be here tomorrow.
(18) a. *Kim might read the book yesterday.
      b. Kim may / might read the book tomorrow.
      c. These two respectable writers might not intend the mischief they were doing. (1762 Bp Richard Hurd, *Letters on Chivalry and Romance* 85)

As a result of these changes, the preterite-present verbs came to look different from all other verbs in the language. If UG provides a small inventory of grammatical categories, then elements are assigned to a category on the basis of their morphological and distributional properties. Morphological changes entail new primary linguistic data which may trigger new category distinctions. In this case, we know that, following the morphological changes, the surviving verbs of the preterite-present class were assigned to a new grammatical category, and that change was complete by the early sixteenth century.

There were two stages to the history of English modal auxiliaries (Lightfoot 1999: ch. 6). First, a change in category membership, whereby *can*, etc. ceased to be treated as verbs and came to be taken as manifestations of the Inflection category; this change affected some verbs before others, but it was complete by the sixteenth century. Consequently, for a sentence like *Kim can sing*, early grammars had structures like (15), where *can* is an ordinary verb, but later grammars had structures like (16), where *can* is a modal, generated as an instance of I. Second, English lost the operation moving verbs to a higher Inflection position (e.g. in 15). This change was completed only in the eighteenth century, later than is generally supposed (Warner 1997). At this point, sentences with a finite verb moved to some initial position (3b) or to the left of a negative (4b), became obsolete and were replaced by equivalent forms with the periphrastic *do*: *Does Kim understand this chapter? Kim does not understand this chapter*, etc. Also sentences with an adverb between the finite verb and its complement became obsolete: *Kim reads always the newspapers*.

The two changes are, presumably, related in ways that we do not entirely understand: first, the Inflection position was appropriated by a subclass of verbs, the modal auxiliaries and *do*, and the V-to-I operation no longer applied generally to all tensed clauses. Somewhat later, the V-to-I movement operation was lost for all verbs other than the exceptional *be* and *have* and I was no longer a position to which verbs might move.

An intriguing paper by Anthony Warner (1995) shows that there is a further stage to the history of English auxiliaries, involving changes taking place quite recently, and this turns out to be of theoretical interest. It has often been observed that VP ellipsis is generally insensitive to morphology. So one finds ellipses where the understood form of the missing verb differs from the form of the antecedent (19).

(19) a. Kim slept well, and Jim will [sc. sleep well] too.
      b. Kim seems well behaved today, and she often has [sc. seemed well behaved] in the past, too.
      c. Although Kim went to the store, Jim didn't [sc. go to the store].

There is a kind of sloppy identity at work here. One way of thinking of this is that in (19a) *slept* is analysed as [*past+*$_V$*sleep*] and the understood verb of the second conjunct accesses the verb *sleep*, ignoring the tense element. However, Warner noticed that *be* works differently. *Be* may occur in elliptical constructions, but only under conditions of strict identity with the antecedent form (20). In (20a, b) the understood form is identical to the antecedent, but not in the non-occurring (20c, d, e).

(20) a. Kim will be here, and Jim will [sc. be here] too.
      b. Kim has been here, and Jim has [sc. been here] too.
      c. *Kim was here, and Jim will [sc. be here] too.
      d. *If Kim is well behaved today, then Jim probably will [sc. be well behaved] too.
      e. *Kim was here yesterday, and Jim has [sc. been here] today.

This suggests that *was* is not analysed as [*past+*$_V$*be*], analogously to *slept*, and *be* may be used as an understood form only where there is precisely a *be* available as an antecedent; not *was* or *is*, but just *be*, as in (20a). Similarly for *been*; compare (20b) and (20e). And similarly for *am, is, are, was, were*.

Words are stored differently in the mental lexicon. Irregular words are stored individually but words formed by a regular, productive process are not. In forming compounds, one accesses lexical entries. So, for example, one may access irregular plurals (*mice eater, men hater*) but not regular plurals (**rats eater,* *boys hater); instead, one has *rat eater* and *boy hater*. The idea here is that the various forms of *be* are listed individually in the lexicon, like *mice* and *men*, and they are not composed by productive lexical processes. Our tentative conclusion, then, is that *was, been*, etc. have no internal structure and occur in the lexicon as unanalysed primitives.

Warner goes on to note that the ellipsis facts of modern English were not always so and one finds forms like (20c, d, e) in earlier times. Jane Austen was one of the last writers to use such forms and she used them in her letters and in speech in her novels, but she did not use them in narrative prose (21a, b.). These forms also occur in the work of eighteenth-century writers (21c), and earlier, when verbs still moved to I (21d).

(21) a. I wish our opinions were the same. But in time they will [sc. be the same]. (1816 Jane Austen, *Emma*, ed. by R. W. Chapman, London: OUP, 1933: 471)
      b. And Lady Middleton, is she angry? I cannot suppose it possible that she should [sc. be angry]. (1811 Jane Austen, *Sense and Sensibility*, ed. C. Lamont, London: Oxford University Press, 1970: 237)
      c. I think, added he, all the Charges attending it, and the Trouble you had, were defray'd by my Attorney: I ordered that they should [sc. be defrayed]. (1740–1 Samuel Richardson, *Pamela*, London: 3rd edition 1741, vol. 2: 129.)
      d. That bettre loved is noon, ne never schal. (c1370 Chaucer, *A Complaint to his Lady*, 80.)
         'so that no one is better loved, or ever shall [sc. be].'

These forms may be understood if *were* in (21a) was analysed as *subjunctive+be* and the *be* was accessed by the understood *be*. In other words, up until the early nineteenth century, the finite forms of *be* were decomposable, just like ordinary verbs in present-day English. So the ellipsis facts suggest.

Warner then points to other differences between present-day English and the English of the early nineteenth century. Present-day English shows quite idiosyncratic restrictions on particular forms of the verb *be*, which did not exist before the late eighteenth or early nineteenth century. For example, only the finite forms of *be* may be followed by *to*+infinitive (22); only *been* may occur with a directional preposition phrase (23); and *being* is subcategorised as not permitting an *-ing* complement (24).

(22) a. Kim was to go to Paris.
      b. *Kim will be to go to Paris.
(23) a. Kim has been to Paris.
      b. *Kim was to Paris.

(24) a. I regretted Kim reading that chapter.
      b. I regretted that Kim was reading that chapter.
      c. *I regretted Kim being reading that chapter.

Restrictions of this type are stated in the lexicon and these idiosyncrasies show clearly that *been, being*, etc. must be listed as individual lexical entries. However, these restrictions are fairly new in the language and we find forms corresponding to the non-occurring sentences of (22–24) up until the early nineteenth century:

(25) a. You will be to visit me in prison with a basket of provisions;...(1814 Jane Austen, *Mansfield Park*, ed. J. Lucas, Oxford University Press, 1970: 122.)
      b. I was this morning to buy silk. (1762 Oliver Goldsmith, *Cit W*: 158.) (meaning 'I went to...', not 'I had to...')
      c. Two large wax candles were also set on another table, the ladies being going to cards. (1726 Daniel Defoe, *The Political History of the Devil*, Talboys, Oxford: 1840: 336.)
      d. ...he being now going to end all with the Queene...(1661 Samuel Pepys, *Diary* II 129.1 (30 June).)
      e. One day being discoursing with her upon the extremities they suffered ...(1791 Daniel Defoe, *Robinson Crusoe*, vol.2: 218.)
      f. ...and exclaimed quite as much as was necessary, (or, being acting a part, perhaps rather more,) at the conduct of the Churchills, in keeping him away. (1816 Jane Austen, *Emma*: 145.)
      g. Their being going to be married. (1811 Jane Austen, *Sense and Sensibility*, ed. R. W. Chapman, Oxford University Press, 1923: 182.)
      h. The younger Miss Thorpes being also dancing, Catherine was left to the mercy of Mrs Thorpe. (1818 Jane Austen, *Northanger Abbey*, ed. R. W. Chapman, Oxford University Press, 1923: 52.)

Warner concludes that after the change

was continues to carry the information that it is third singular past finite indicative. The point is that it does not do so as a consequence of inflection or inflectional relationships, but is essentially monomorphemic. The relationship *was: be* becomes fundamentally different not only from regular verbs *loved: love*, etc. but also from that of irregular or suppletive verbs (*slew: slay, went: go*), which are in some sense essentially compositional, as the contrast of behaviour in ellipsis shows.   (Warner 1995: 538)

Whether the change affects *be* alone or also *have*, it is clearly restricted to a very narrow class of lexical items. The analysis, however, reflects quite general properties and the change relates to the matter of category membership. Forms of *be* cease to be analysed as a verb with the usual morphological structure.

Grammars have quite small sets of categories and individual lexical items are assigned to one or other of these categories. Evidence suggests that items are assigned to grammatical categories on the basis of their morphological properties. If a given item becomes morphologically distinct from other items in its category, then it is liable to be assigned to a new category. This is what was involved in the earlier changes involving the modal auxiliaries, formerly preterite-present verbs. As a result of changes affecting the preterite-present class of verbs and the subjunctive mood, these items became morphologically distinct from other verbs and were assigned to a new category, Inflection; similarly with the changes affecting *be* in the eighteenth century.

If we ask why the change took place, we get some insight into the grammatical property involved. The change in the internal structure of *be* forms was preceded by two other changes.

First, the operation moving verbs to an Inflection position, V-to-I, was finally lost in the eighteenth century, as manifested by the obsolescence of sentences like (3b) and (4b). The loss of V-to-I movement further distinguished the modal auxiliaries from main verbs, with the modals continuing to occur in the old positions, initially and to the left of a negative; *be* patterns with the modals in this regard: *Is she happy?* and *She is not happy.*

Second, Warner shows that the pronoun *thou* and the accompanying inflectional forms in -*(e)st* were lost from informal spoken English in the eighteenth century. *Thou* had the use of French *tu*, directed to children, intimates and inferiors. It was lost for social reasons, as speakers abandoned a linguistic manifestation of these social distinctions. The obsolescence of *Thou shalt, Thou shouldest*, etc. removed the last inflectional property of modal verbs which was shared with ordinary verbs.

Modals had become very different from verbs in the course of changes that we have linked to their change in category, completed by the sixteenth century. They ceased to have nonfinite forms, ceased to have mood and tense forms, ceased to have complements, etc.; that showed that they were recategorised as Inflection elements. The loss of the second-person-singular forms constituted a further step: the last remaining inflectional commonality shared by modals and ordinary verbs was lost. This last change also affected the verb *be*, which had shown no symptoms of the category change affecting the modals: *be* did not lose its nonfinite forms in the way that *can* did, nor did it lose its mood and tense forms, nor its ability to be followed by a complement. Now, however, *be* became distinct from ordinary verbs in that it continued to move to I and on to C, while main verbs lost this ability, and it did not look like a verb any more in terms of its finite inflectional properties.

The first of these changes affected all verbs – they ceased to move to I overtly – and the second change affected all verbs and (modal) elements generated in the Inflection position. Neither change affected *be* in particular, but their effect was to single out *be* and make it less like a verb. As a result of these changes, *be* differed from verbs in that it could occur in high functional positions like I and C, and it lacked the only morphological properties characteristic of verbs, the universal third-person-singular marker in *-s* and the usual past-tense *-ed* marker.

It is plausible that these were the changes which led children to treat *be* differently. Now it ceased to look like a verb and ceased to have the internal structure of a verb. *Be* did not undergo the category change that the modals underwent by the sixteenth century: *be* was never associated intrinsically with the (finite) Inflection position in the way that modals are, and *be* continues to occur in nonfinite contexts (*I want to be happy, Being happy is a good thing, Be happy*, etc). This shows that the finite forms of *be* move to I and are not base-generated there like the modals. In the eighteenth century main verbs ceased to move to I but the finite forms of *be* continued to do so. As a result, *be* no longer walks like a verb and no longer talks like a verb. The evidence suggests that, in addition, in the nineteenth century *be* ceased to show the paradigmatic properties of verbs. *Be* was no longer categorised as a verb; instead, its inflectional paradigm was individually specified as a series of lexical items, stored individually in the mental lexicon. This was the grammatical change.

One can think of this in terms of ideas of the Minimalist Program. Chomsky (1995) adopts a strict lexicalist view: not only does derivational morphology (*destruction*) result from lexical operations, but so also does inflectional morphology (*destroyed*). Verbs, all verbs, are taken from the lexicon fully inflected. Inflected forms of a verb have an internal structure resulting from lexical operations; they are drawn from the lexicon and then need to be *checked* against the relevant features of abstract functional heads. For example, the form *loves* has a third-person-singular feature, which is checked in an Inflection position; so *loves* must move to the I position. For Chomsky, the checking may take place in the overt syntax (in French) or covertly at Logical Form (LF) (in English); this distinction corresponds to the idea that a V moves to I in the syntax in French, while I lowers on to V in the morphology in English.

However, there are problems with this approach. For example, it does not account for the fact that both the sentences of (26) reflect ungrammatical forms.

(26) a. *Kim not understands the chapter.
      b. *Kim understands not the chapter.

The ungrammaticality of (26a) suggests that checking may not be 'procrastinated' until LF and therefore must take place in the syntax. However, the ungrammaticality of (26b) shows that checking may not take place in the syntax in English and that the inflectional feature is not 'strong'.

Lasnik (1999: ch. 5) offers a hybrid approach: the Inflection position may contain an affix or strong features. Features must be checked in the syntax, whereas an affix must be attached to a verb at Phonetic Form (PF). Because this attachment takes place at PF, it is a phonological operation and requires adjacency: I-lowering is a morphological operation (Lightfoot 1993). Under this view, a verb with features raises overtly to an I position with features and the verb's features are thereby checked. A bare verb with no features, on the other hand, has an affix lowered on to it from an adjacent position at PF.

This entails that a finite French verb and *have* and *be* in English are pulled fully formed from the lexicon and move to an appropriate functional position in which their features may be checked. Main verbs in English, on the other hand, have no features in the lexicon and an affix lowers on to them at PF. Now the reason for the ungrammaticality of (26) is that the inflected *understands* is not in the lexicon, since main verbs in English generally are bare and acquire their inflectional properties through lowering at PF. (26b) does not occur because *understands* does not exist in the lexicon and therefore may not move in the syntax to check its features in I. Nor may an affix lower on to an uninflected *understand* to yield (26a), because of the intervening *not*. *Be* and *have*, however, move to functional positions and therefore are featural, each form fully inflected in the lexicon, like French verbs.

Now we have the distinction that we need. *Be* and *have* are fully formed in the lexicon but regular verbs in English are bare, acquiring affixes at PF. Before that lowering takes place, the abstract *sleep* of *slept* is identifiable as a distinct unit and therefore is an appropriate antecedent for ellipsis in (19a) *Kim slept well, and Jim will [sc. sleep well] too*. This reveals how elements are stored in the mental lexicon: *is* is stored in just that form while *slept* is not stored as such but is created in the course of a derivation. If all verbs were treated the same way, as in Chomsky (1995), there would be no obvious way to make the distinction between those which may be antecedents for ellipsis under conditions of sloppy identity (*sleep*, etc.) and those which may not (*is, are* and other forms of *be*).

Lasnik keyed the distinction between affixal and featural verbs to whether the verb moves, but there is more to the story than this. Modal elements are featural and are generated in I, not moving there. Finite *be*, on the other hand, clearly moves to I, because *be* may also occur in other, nonfinite positions if I is filled with a modal (27).

(27)   Kim might still be reading that chapter.

So forms of *be* (and *have*) move to I; they are and always have been featural. They have always moved to I at all stages of their history but it was only in the late eighteenth century that they came to be stored atomically and developed the odd properties discussed here. We conclude that if a verb is featural, it moves to I. However, a featural item may be base-generated in I (modern modals) and may or may not be stored atomically: *was* is not a verb and it is stored atomically in modern grammars.

What is important about this story is that, while the changes we have discussed only involve the verb *be*, they have the hallmarks of grammatical change. There are several surface changes, all involving *be*, which can be attributed to one analytical notion. The changes reflect quite general properties of the grammar, here relating to category membership. We can identify the structural property which is relevant and we can tell a plausible and rather elegant story about why and how the grammatical change might have come about. We distinguish how items are stored in the lexicon.

We see, again, that morphology has syntactic effects. It is particularly important in defining category membership; children assign items to categories on the basis of their morphology. We have explained the change by pointing to changes in the trigger experience which led to the new morphological structure of *be* forms. Those changes in the trigger are a function of prior grammatical shifts, relating to the change in category membership of the modal auxiliaries and the loss of V-to-I movement; there are links among the changes and we have another domino effect. Again we have local causes and we do not need to appeal to internal motivating factors. As Warner notes, 'the shift in the primary linguistic data caused by the decline of *thou* seems substantial enough for there to be no reason to suppose that internal strategies should be assigned a major determining role' (1995: 543).

While morphology clearly influences category membership, one finds a stronger claim in the literature. It is sometimes argued that richly inflected languages differ in a fundamental way from poorly inflected languages like English and Chinese. In this context, it might be argued that grammars with rich inflectional systems, like those of French speakers, list forms individually in the lexicon and do not form them by general operations. On the analysis offered here, this would entail that there would be no bare forms available to syntactic operations and one would find various lexical restrictions on particular forms, as we saw for *be* in present-day English in (22–24) above. In grammars like those of present-day English speakers, on the other hand, there are fewer individual listings. Plural nouns in *-s* and third-person-singular forms of verbs in *-s* are composed derivationally through phonological lowering, and they are not listed in the lexicon fully formed. As a result, the bare form of the noun and of the verb, shorn of its affixal ending, is available to various grammatical operations and it is not possible to state lexical restrictions on particular third-person-singular forms.

However, the material of this section shows that this is not correct and it suggests that how items are stored in the lexicon is neither a function of movement nor a simple function of morphological richness. Main verbs and *be* could occur in ellipses without strict identity with their antecedent up until the nineteenth century. This suggests strongly that their forms were not stored atomically, even though they were richly inflected in the early stages of the language; instead, they were formed by operations applying internal to the lexicon. Consequently, we conclude that the way elements are stored in the lexicon has many syntactic consequences, but that distinction represents variation which is independent of whether an item moves to an Inflection position and independent of whether an item is richly inflected.

In affecting a narrow class of words, the change described here is small scale. It can be understood in terms of prior changes, including the highly contingent loss of *thou* forms, and it reflects ways in which items may be stored in the mental lexicon. It is a function of earlier changes. In this section I have tracked some changes affecting the English modal auxiliaries, changes which might be labelled 'grammaticalisation'. I have shown local causes for each of the changes in grammars, taking grammars to be individual, internal systems existing in individual brains. There was nothing inevitable about these changes: the equivalent words in French and Swedish did not undergo parallel changes, because there were no parallel local causes. Grammaticalisation theory has nothing to say about small-scale changes like these. The problem with postulating general historical tendencies is that they are too 'Cyclopean' (to adopt a useful term from Watkins's 1976 critique of typological analyses) and too gross to be enlightening, and they predict that languages should undergo parallel historical changes.

If changes in category membership are relatively common (whatever that means), they still need local causes. Identifying local causes enables us to understand the details of the change, as we have illustrated here. This case study suggests that category changes may result from morphological changes. Not many of the world's languages have a richly recorded history, but many that do have undergone morphological simplification, sometimes with category changes. If our historical records included languages with increasing morphological complexity, we would be in a stronger position to relate morphological and categorial changes. However, given the records that we have, we can see the precariousness of seeking to explain categorial changes by general historical tendencies.

5   Chaos

From the Greeks to Newton, people have believed in a predictable universe. Where unpredictable behaviour was observed, for example in weather, the unpredictability was attributed to lack of knowledge: if we just knew more, we would have better weather forecasts. Recently, however, scientists in various fields have found that many systems are unpredictable but they do follow courses prescribed by deterministic principles. The key to understanding how systems may be determinate and unpredictable – an oxymoron from the point of view of classical science – lies in the notion of sensitive dependence on initial conditions.

Predicting final outcomes – or indeed anything beyond the very short-term – becomes impossible. Chaos incorporates elements of chance, but it is not random disorder. Rather, chaos theory tries to understand the behaviour of systems that do not unfold over time in a linearly predictable manner. When viewed as a whole, these systems manifest definite patterns and structures. However, because the evolution of a chaotic system is so hugely complex and so prone to perturbation by contingent factors, it is impossible to discern its underlying pattern – its attractor – by looking at a single small event at a single point in time. At no single point can future directions be predicted from past history.

So it is with the emergence of a new species in evolutionary change, with changes in the political and social domain, and in grammar change. Change is not random, but we are dealing with contingent systems and we offer retrospective explanations, not predictions. Grammatical change is highly contingent, sensitive to initial conditions, chaotic in a technical sense. Linguists can offer satisfying explanations of change in some instances, but there is no reason to expect to find a predictive theory of change, offering long-term, linear predictions.

The emergence of a grammar in a child is sensitive to the initial conditions of the primary linguistic data. If those data shift a little, changing the distribution of the cues, there may be significant consequences for the abstract system. A new system may be triggered, which generates a very different set of sentences and structures. There is nothing principled to be said about why the cues should shift a little; those shifts often represent chance, contingent factors. Contingent changes in the distribution of those cues may trigger a grammar which generates significantly different sentences and structures, and that may have some domino effects, as we have seen.

Changes in languages often take place in clusters: apparently unrelated superficial changes may occur simultaneously or in rapid sequence. Such clusters manifest a single theoretical choice which has been taken differently. If so, the singularity of the change can be explained by the appropriately defined theoretical choice. So the principles of UG and the definition of the cues constitute the laws which guide change in grammars, defining the available terrain.

Any given phenomenal change is explained if we show, first, that the linguistic environment has changed in such a way that some theoretical choice has been taken differently (say, a change in the way that a case is realised), and, second, that the new phenomenon (perhaps a split genitive form) must be the way that it is because of some principle of the theory and the new case system.

Sometimes we can explain domino effects of this type. Linguists have argued that a changing stress pattern may leave word-final case markings vulnerable to neutralisation and loss. If morphological case marking motivates movement, for example movement of an underlying postverbal DP to a preverbal position (yielding object–verb order), then loss of the morphological marking may entail loss of object–verb word order. In that event, one establishes a link between a change in stress patterns and loss of object–verb word order. However, to say that there may be domino effects is not to say that there is a general directionality of the kind sought by nineteenth-century linguists and by modern typologists and grammaticalisationists.

What we cannot explain, in general, is why the linguistic environment should have changed in the first place (as emphasised by Lass (1997) and others). Environmental changes are often due to what I have called chance factors, effects of borrowing, changes in the frequency of forms, stylistic innovations, which spread through a community and, where we are lucky, are documented by variation studies. Changes of this type need not reflect changes in grammars. But with a theory of language acquisition which defines the range of theoretical choices available to the child and specifies how the child may take those choices, one can predict that a child will converge on a certain grammar when exposed to certain environmental elements. This is where prediction is possible, in principle.

We have an interplay of chance and necessity, and appropriately so; changes are due to chance in the sense that contingent factors influence a child's PLD and make the triggering experience somewhat different from what the child's parent was exposed to. Necessity factors, the principles of UG and the cues, define the range of available options for the new grammar. So we take a synchronic approach to history. Historical change is a kind of finite-state Markov process: changes have only local causes and, if there is no local cause, there is no change, regardless of the state of the grammar or the language some time previously. In that way, the emergence of a grammar in an individual child is highly sensitive to the initial conditions, to the details of the child's experience. So language change is chaotic, in a technical sense, in the same way that weather patterns are chaotic. The historian's explanations are based on available acquisition theories, and in some cases our explanations are quite tight and satisfying. Structural changes are interesting precisely because they have local causes. Identifying structural changes and the conditions under which they took place informs us about the conditions of language acquisition; we have indeed learned things about properties of UG and about the nature of acquisition by the careful examination of diachronic changes. Under this synchronic approach to change, there are no principles of history; history is an epiphenomenon and time is immaterial.

REFERENCES

Barbour, Julian. 2000. *The end of time*. Oxford University Press.
Bauer, Brigitte. 1995. *The emergence and development of SVO patterning in Latin and French*. Oxford University Press.
Bloomfield, Leonard. 1933. *Language*. New York: Holt.
Bruyn, Adrienne. 1995. *Grammaticalization in creoles: the development of determiners and relative clauses in Sranan*. Studies in Language and Language Use 21. Dordrecht: ICG Printing.

Chomsky, Noam. 1986. *Knowledge of language: its nature, origin and use.* New York: Praeger.

Chomsky, Noam. 1995. *The minimalist program.* Cambridge, MA: MIT Press.

Darwin, Charles. 1874. *The descent of man.* [2nd edn, 1889] New York: D. Appleton.

Dresher, Elan and William Idsardi. 1999. 'Prerequisites for a theory of diachronic adaptation', *Zeitschrift für Sprachwissenschaft* 18.1: 212–5.

Fischer, Olga C. M. 1997. 'On the status of grammaticalization and the diachronic dimension in explanation', *Transactions of the Philological Society* 95.2: 149–87.

van Gelderen, Elly. 1997. *Verbal agreement and the grammar behind its 'breakdown': minimalist feature checking.* Tübingen: Max Niemeyer.

Haspelmath, Martin. 1999a. 'Are there principles of grammatical change?' *Journal of Linguistics* 35.3: 579–96.

Haspelmath, Martin. 1999b. 'Optimality and diachronic adaptation', *Zeitschrift für Sprachwissenschaft* 18: 180–205.

Haspelmath, Martin. 1999c. Why is grammaticalization irreversible? *Linguistics* 37.6: 1043–68.

Hopper, Paul and Elizabeth Traugott. 1993. *Grammaticalization.* Cambridge University Press.

Janda, Richard D. 2001. 'Beyond "pathways" and "unidirectionality": on the discontinuity of language transmission and the counterability of grammaticalization.' *Language Sciences* 23. 2-3: 265–340.

Joseph, Brian. 2001. 'Is there such a thing as grammaticalization?', *Language Sciences* 23. 2-3: 163–86.

Kiparsky, Paul. 1996. 'The shift to head-initial VP in Germanic', in H. Thrainsson, S. Epstein and S. Peters (eds.), *Studies in comparative Germanic syntax,* vol. 2. Dordrecht: Kluwer, 140–79.

Lakoff, Robin T. 1972. 'Another look at drift', in Robert P. Stockwell and Ron Macauley (eds.), *Linguistic change and generative theory.* Bloomington: Indiana University Press, 172–98.

Lasnik, Howard. 1999. *Minimalist analysis.* Oxford: Blackwell.

Lass, Roger. 1980. *On explaining linguistic change.* Cambridge University Press.

Lass, Roger. 1997. *Historical linguistics and language change.* Cambridge University Press.

Lightfoot, David W. 1991. *How to set parameters: arguments from language change.* Cambridge, MA: MIT Press.

Lightfoot, David W. 1993. 'Why UG needs a learning theory: triggering verb movement', in Charles Jones (ed.), *Historical linguistics: problems and perspectives.* London: Longman [reprinted in Battye and Roberts (eds.), 1995 *Clause structure and language change.* Oxford University Press].

Lightfoot, David W. 1999. *The development of language: acquisition, change and evolution.* Oxford: Blackwell.

Newmeyer, Frederick J. 1998. *Language form and language function.* Cambridge, MA: MIT Press.

Paul, Hermann. 1880. *Prinzipien der Sprachgeschichte.* [1970] Niemeyer: Tübingen.

Rask, Rasmus. 1818. *Undersøgelse om det gamle Nordiske eller Islandske Sprogs Oprindelse.* Copenhagen: Gyldendalske Boghandlings Forlag.

Roberts, Ian G. 1993. 'A formal account of grammaticalization in the history of Romance futures', *Folia Linguistica Historica* 13: 219–58.

Ross, John R. 1969. 'Auxiliaries as main verbs', in W. Todd (ed.), *Studies in philosophical linguistics*, series I. Evanston: Great Expectations.

Sapir, Edward. 1921. *Language*. New York: Harcourt.

Sapir, Edward. 1929. 'The status of linguistics as a science', *Language* 5: 207–14.

Schleicher, August. 1848 *Über die Bedeutung der Sprache für die Naturgeschichte des Menschen*. Weimar: Hermann Böhlau.

Schleicher, August. 1861–2. *Compendium der vergleichenden Grammatik der indogermanischen Sprachen*. Weimar: Hermann Böhlau.

Schleicher, August. 1863. *Die darwinische Theorie und die Spachwissenschaft*. Weimar: Hermann Böhlau.

Vennemann, Theo. 1975. 'An explanation of drift', in C. N. Li (ed.), *Word order and word order change*. Austin: University of Texas Press, 269–305.

Warner, Anthony R. 1995. 'Predicting the progressive passive: parametric change within a lexicalist framework', *Language* 71.3: 533–57.

Warner, Anthony R. 1997. 'The structure of parametric change, and V movement in the history of English', in Ans van Kemenade and Nigel Vincent (eds.), *Parameters of morphosyntactic change*. Cambridge University Press, 380–93.

Watkins, Calvert. 1976. 'Toward Proto-Indo-European syntax: problems and pseudo-problems', in S. Steever, C. Walker and S. Mufwene (eds.), *Diachronic syntax*. Chicago Linguistic Society, 305–26.

8   From subjectification to intersubjectification

Elizabeth Closs Traugott

1   Introduction[1]

When the history of historical linguistics in the twentieth century is written, one recurrent theme will surely be the hypothesis that certain types of change are unidirectional. This hypothesis takes many forms, but is probably most widely associated with historical cross-linguistic, typological work, much of it devoted to the correlations among changes in meaning and morphosyntax known as grammaticalisation (see e.g. Greenberg 1978; Lehmann 1995 [1982]; Hopper and Traugott 1993; Bybee, Perkins and Pagliuca 1994). Critics of the hypothesis have pointed out that unidirectionality is not exceptionless and can be reversed (Joseph and Janda 1988; Newmeyer 1998; Lass 2000, among others). Being social as well as cognitive, and subject to contingencies such as production, perception, transmission and social evaluation, no change is likely to be exceptionless. Unidirectionality is a strong tendency manifested by particular sets of changes. The present study is a further contribution to the debate on unidirectionality, with focus on evidence for it in semantic change. The hypothesis is that intersubjectification, in the sense of the development of meanings that encode speaker/writers' attention to the cognitive stances and social identities of addressees, arises out of and depends crucially on subjectification. Schematically, subjectification > intersubjectification, not intersubjectification > subjectification. This is a semasiological hypothesis about constraints on the kind of changes that individual lexemes may undergo. It also has implications for onomasiological constraints on shifts of meaning from one conceptual domain to another, e.g. from the domain of spatial position to politeness marker in Japanese, but not vice versa.

[1] An earlier version of this chapter was presented as a paper at the Workshop on Historical Pragmatics, 14th International Conference on Historical Linguistics, Vancouver, August 1999. For a fuller study of the phenomena under discussion, see Traugott and Dasher (2002). Many thanks to Raymond Hickey for comments on an earlier draft of this chapter, and above all to Richard Dasher for discussion of subjectification and intersubjectification, and most especially for the data on Japanese cited here.

2   Subjectivity and subjectification

Subjectivity as a synchronic (and partially diachronic) phenomenon plays a role in Bréal's work (1964 [1900]: ch. 25) and was later elaborated on in Bühler (1990 [1934]) and Jakobson (1957), and with Kuroda's (1973) seminal work on Japanese expressions of physical sensation. However, it is perhaps most frequently associated with Benveniste who distinguished 'sujet d'énoncé' (syntactic subject) and 'sujet d'énonciation' (speaking subject). Crucially, he raised the question whether 'language could be called language' unless it was deeply 'marked... by the expression of subjectivity' (1971 [1958]: 225). Subsequent work by Lyons (1982, 1994) and Langacker (1985, 1995) established subjectivity as a major topic of synchronic study (see several papers in Stein and Wright 1995, and, on Japanese, Iwasaki 1993, Maynard 1993, among many others). As Lyons put it: 'the term subjectivity refers to the way in which natural languages, in their structure and their normal manner of operation, provide for the locutionary agent's *expression of himself and his own attitudes and beliefs*' (Lyons 1982: 102, italics added). This 'expression of self' may be instantiated lexically or grammatically. Most obviously space and time deictics are subjective when grounded in the speaker/writer (SP/W),[2] as are performative uses of speech-act verbs.[3] But many other aspects of language are subjective as well, such as the use of aspect – aspectual phases are not inherent in the event structure, but represent the SP/W's perception of the described event, for example, whether it is perfective or imperfective. Likewise 'adversative' adverbs like *however*, 'stance' adverbs like *frankly* (speaking) or *obviously* express the SP/W's attitude toward the content of the proposition, and discourse markers like *in fact* or *well* express the SP/W's perception of the connectivity between propositions. Scalar adverbs like *even, merely* reflect the SP/W's relative ranking of alternatives within a set.

In historical linguistics much attention has recently been paid to changes resulting from what is called 'subjectification'. One line of research on subjectification is associated with Langacker and has focused on perspectival shifts from a 'syntactic subject' to a 'speaking subject', as evidenced by the development of raising constructions from control verbs such as *promise, be going to do X* (directional movement for a purpose) (e.g. Langacker 1990, 1995, 1999). Another is associated with myself and has focused on how meanings tend to become increasingly based in the SP/W's subjective belief state or attitude toward what is being said and how it is being said (Traugott 1989, 1995, 1997, 1999a), as for example in the development of (D)iscourse (M)arker uses of adverbs

---

[2] As noted by Fillmore (1997[1971]) and frequently since, deictic properties can, however, be projected onto objects like cars and desks, based on speakers' normative uses of those objects.
[3] This definition excludes primarily institutional speech acts, such as Supreme Court findings, royal decrees, etc.

such as *after all*, and performative uses of locutionary verbs such as *promise, recognise*. According to this view, subjectification is the mechanism whereby meanings come over time to encode or externalise the SP/W's perspectives and attitudes as constrained by the communicative world of the speech event, rather than by the so-called 'real-world' characteristics of the event or situation referred to. It is one of the effects of the mechanism of 'invited inferencing' (Traugott 1999b) – the process by which conversational implicatures are semanticised over time – in this case, of implicatures regarding SP/W's attitudes to the ongoing discourse and its purposes that arise out of the strategic stances SP/Ws adopt in the speech event.

Although a particular historical record may not provide evidence due to lack of sufficient time depth, in principle, any semantically subjective lexeme or grammatical morpheme can be hypothesised to have originated semasiologically in a form with nonsubjective meaning.[4] Certainly, where the historical record gives evidence of earlier meanings, the direction of semantic change is from nonsubjective > subjective meaning. Examples include the development of perfect aspect in English (Carey 1995), the rise of performative uses of nonperformative verbs such as *promise* (Traugott 1997), and such changes as *even* 'smoothly, uniformly' to scalar particle (König 1991). A particularly rich area is the development of epistemic meanings of modals (e.g. epistemic *must* from deontic *must*, see Traugott 1989 on modal verbs, Hanson 1987, Swan 1988, Powell 1992 on modal adverbials). Another area is developments in the domain of adversatives such as *but* < OE *butan* 'outside' (Nevalainen 1991), or adverbials such as *anyway, besides*. Among many recent historical studies of Japanese, three may be mentioned here as paying special attention to subjectification: Akatsuka (1997) on the development of *-tewa*, a marker of negative conditionality expressing SP/W's assessment of the undesirability of the event described in the apodosis; Onodera (2000) on the development of *demo* as a sentence-initial adversative DM; and Suzuki (1998) on the recent development of the noun *wake* 'reason' into a particle expressing 'the speaker's ("explanatory") attitude toward the utterance' (1998: 69).

Subjectification is a matter of degree at least pragmatically, as can be seen not only from increases in subjectivity over time of both deontic and epistemic modality (Nordlinger and Traugott 1997), and of *in fact*, the history of which can be summarised as: manner adverb > adversative adverb (expressing contrast to someone else's or to the locutor's own prior proposition) > elaborating DM which signals that what follows is a stronger argument than what precedes, with respect to SP/W's rhetorical purpose at that point in the discourse (Schwenter and Traugott 2000: 12).

---

[4] This, like all generalisations about 'natural' change, excludes deliberate coinages.

A particularly interesting example of increased subjectification is provided by Brinton in a study of the development of *only*. Building on Nevalainen (1991),[5] Brinton (1998: 26) summarises the early development of *only* as in (1):

(1)   numeral ONE > polysemous adj./adv. ONLY > exclusive focusing ONLY

The development of *an-lice* (< *an* 'one' + *-lic* 'in-form/appearance' + *-e* 'adverbial marker') 'unique(ly), splendid(ly)' to an exclusive focus marker is a case of subjectification in the sense that preempting a lexeme to the class of scalar focus particles involves using that lexeme to express the SP/W's relative ranking of alternatives within a set. In this case, 'exclusiveness [with its] implicature of the meaning of "oneness"' (Brinton 1998: 27) is semanticised to express the SP/W's exclusion of other possibilities from a set. A Middle English example is:

(2)   I n'am but a lewd compilator of the labour of olde astrologiens, and have it translatid in myn Englissh *oonly* for thy doctrine.
        'I am but an unsophisticated compiler of the work of old astrologers, and have translated it into English only for your enlightenment'.
                                        (Chaucer, Astrolabe p. 662, line 61)

In her article Brinton focuses on the further development of *only* into a DM (she calls it a 'conjunction/pragmatic marker') with an adversative meaning akin to 'however'; of this DM use she says: '[i]n its conjunctive sense, *only* likewise rejects a presupposition, but in this case not the presupposition set of the focus item, but the presupposition of the entire preceding clause' (Brinton 1998: 28). A seventeenth-century example is:

(3)   I do fully see the evidence of all that which you have said, and therefore I must needs be perswaded of it. I do heartily thanke God for it, and will endevor myselfe to put it in practise continually. *Only* here is the difficulty, how a Schoolemaster may do this, to teach his Scholler so to proceede with understanding, and how to give a reason of every matter which they learne, to make use of all their learning.
                                (Brinsley, Ludus Literarius 44 (Brinton 1998: 24))

Here Brinsley uses *only* to defease any conversational implicature from his hearty thanks that his endeavour will be easy. Like other DMs *only* signals the SP/W's attitude to the connectivity between what precedes and what follows. As Brinton mentions, many of the unambiguous early examples of this

---

[5] This in turn builds on Rissanen (1967).

new meaning of *only* appear in the context of metalinguistic comment on the 'communicative situation, most often the progress of the argument' (1998: 28).[6]

In sum, a strong empirically testable hypothesis about semantic unidirectionality is:

(4)   nonsubjective > subjective

3   Intersubjectivity

In both lines of research on subjectification, little attention has been paid to the second of Benveniste's dimensions: intersubjectivity. Benveniste saw not just the speaker but the speaker–addressee dyad as the fundamental condition for linguistic communication, and characterised this relationship as one of 'intersubjectivity' – in communication each participant is a speaking subject who is aware of the other participant as speaking subject: 'discourse . . . is language in so far as it is taken over by the man who is speaking and within the condition of intersubjectivity, which alone makes linguistic communication possible' (Benveniste (1971 [1958]: 230). Speakers constitute themselves as 'subject' in saying 'I' and in contrasting themselves with 'you'.

More recent uses of the term 'intersubjective' assume audience interpretation and understanding. For example, Schiffrin argues that subjectivity and intersubjectivity 'emerge from an interaction between what an actor does – including actions intended to be perceived and designed as such and actions not so intended – and an audience's interpretation of all available information' (Schiffrin 1990: 142). And Nuyts (1998) uses 'inter-subjectivity' in referring to evidence known to or accessible to a larger group of people who share the same conclusion as the SP/W.

Another way to construe intersubjectivity is in parallel with subjectivity, an approach that appears to be more consistent with Benveniste's original concept. From this perspective, intersubjectivity is the explicit expression of the SP/W's attention to the 'self' of addressee/reader in both an epistemic sense (paying attention to their presumed attitudes to the content of what is said), and in a more social sense (paying attention to their 'face' or 'image needs' associated with social stance and identity).

This view of intersubjectivity depends crucially on a distinction between the roles of SP/W and addressee/reader (AD/R) in the world of the speech event from possible roles that the same individuals may, and often do, play as referents in the described situation (the conceptualised world that is talked about). Intersubjectivity involves SP/W's attention to AD/R as a participant in the speech event, not in the described situation. Consequently, at least in

---

[6] In other words, this change involves not only subjectification but also the development of discourse-related meanings (what Sweetser 1990 calls 'speech act meanings').

English, intersubjectivity is not necessarily a characteristic of all expressions that make reference to the second person, even though first and second person are deictics. For example:

(5)   I will drive you to the dentist

verbalises little if any attention on the part of SP/W toward the image or other needs of AD/R in that person's role as an interlocutor in the speech event. However, in the expression:

(6)   *Actually*, I will drive you to the dentist

the word *actually* indexes SP/W's attitude toward AD/R and the content of the proposition *I will drive you to the dentist*; for example, it addresses or anticipates AD/R's sense that being driven to the dentist is not necessary, or AD/R's expectation that someone else will drive them – in other words, it implicates potential or actual disagreement and signals the speaker's attempt to mitigate it.[7]

Polite behaviour involves 'continual sounding out of reciprocal image needs of *ego* and *alter*' (Held 1999: 22). As is well known, in languages with contrasting formal and intimate second-person pronouns (T-V languages), AD/R's image needs must be explicitly addressed; therefore explicit attention must constantly be paid to intersubjectivity. In languages with honorific systems like Japanese, SP/W selects appropriate honorific forms both on the basis of SP/W's social standing relative to the referents of an expression ('referent honorifics'), and on the basis of the SP/W–AD/R relationship independent of the referents ('addressee honorifics') (Brown and Levinson 1987 [1978]; Dasher 1995). In either case the choice of expression is both subjective (dependent on the point of view of SP/W) and at the same time intersubjective (dependent on SP/W's conceptualisation of his or her relationship to AD/R and AD/R's image needs at the time of the speech event).

4   Intersubjectification

From a historical perspective, in so far as subjectification involves recruitment of meanings not only to encode but also to regulate attitudes and beliefs, it inevitably involves intersubjectivity to some degree. But while subjectification is a mechanism whereby meanings become more deeply centred on the SP/W, intersubjectification is a mechanism whereby meanings become more centred on the addressee. On this view intersubjectification is the semasiological

---

[7] Aijmer (1986: 128) suggests that in spoken language *actually* can 'create contact with the listener' or 'rapport', e.g. 'I am telling you this in confidence', clearly an intersubjective reading (but not characterized in terms of adversativity).

process whereby meanings come over time to encode or externalise implicatures regarding SP/W's attention to the 'self' of AD/R in both an epistemic and a social sense. The hypothesis is that, for any lexeme L, intersubjectification is historically later than and arises out of subjectification.

Note that this view of intersubjectification depends crucially on my definition of subjectification in section 2. There is of course some overlap with Langacker's approach. However, since he is primarily concerned with perspectivisation of the grammatical subject, intersubjectification as a regular process will not grow directly out of subjectification as he construes it. In this and other respects our views of subjectification have different consequences for semantic change despite Langacker's (1999: 150) claim that the approaches are essentially the same.

The development of *let's* is a case in point. Its history is *let us* 'allow us (imp.)' > *let's* > 'I propose (hortative)' > 'mitigator/marker of "care-giver register"' (Traugott 1995), in other words a shift along the lines of *Let us go, will you,* > *Let's go, shall we,* > *Let's take our pills now, Roger.* In the first phase of the development of *let's go* the action is preempted to the SP/W, shifting the subject of *let* from *you* to *we/I*. In both Langacker's and my view this change would be a case of subjectification. In Langacker's view *Let's take our pills now* would be further subjectification because the speaker comes to be conceptually off stage, since she is not a participant in the pill-taking (note, however, that the second person singular is shifted for social deictic purposes to first person plural). On my analysis, the last stage is a case of intersubjectification because, having preempted the subject, SP in the newer use positions him- or herself as empathetic to AD's possible objection to the projected activity (in this case, pill-taking) in the here and now of the ongoing discourse.

Evidence both for the unidirectionality of the development from subjectification to intersubjectification, and for the addressee-orientation involved in the later stage, comes from the history of several DMs in English that serve the function of hedges, for example *actually* 'effectively' > 'adversative' > 'reinforcer of prior utterance' > 'hedge', and of more explicit politeness markers such as *pray* in *Pray, give me leave* from *I pray (you)* (here intersubjectivity is encoded into *pray*, with the loss of the personal pronouns).

What is perhaps the most prototypical of all hedges in English, *well*, has been shown by Jucker (1997) to have a history in keeping with the hypothesis put forward here. Jucker finds the origins of *well* in Old English in an epistemic adverbial 'certainly, definitely':

(7) Cwæð he: *Wel* þæt swa mæȝ, forþon hi englice ansyne habbað.
     Said he: Well that so   may, because they angelic faces   have
     'He said: "Well may that be so, since they have the faces of angels"'
                              (Bede's Eccl. Hist. ii.i. (Schipper) 110 [Jucker 1997: 100])

This epistemic meaning of *well* can be regarded as a subjectification of the manner adverb, a change that appears to have occurred before the period of the historical Old English record.

In Middle English as evidenced by the Helsinki Corpus and the works of Chaucer, Jucker finds that *well* begins to appear in a DM function and can be understood as 'if this is so, OK then'. Even though the first examples are represented within narratives, it is clear that they are intersubjective in their represented function, typically reflecting awareness of AD/R in a face-threatening, adversative situation. Jucker points out that in the early examples of the DM meaning in his data, *well* is always followed directly by identification of the speaker and the speech act, i.e. an 'inquit' (contrast (7) which follows the inquit), and treats the DM primarily as a 'frame marker and text-sequencing device' (Jucker 1997: 99), while recognising that it may also convey some interpersonal meanings; but as the following example shows, it is clearly interpersonal (intersubjective) in intent:[8]

(8)   '...Trusteth me,
        Ye shul nat plesen hire fully yeres thre...
        I prey yow that ye be nat yvele apayd'
        '*Wel*', quod this Januarie, 'and hastow ysayd?
        Straw for thy Senek, and for thy proverbes'
        ' "...Trust me, you will not please her for even three years...I pray you
        not to be displeased". "Well", said January, "have you said enough? I
        don't give a straw for your Seneca and your proverbs" '
                (Chaucer, Canterbury Tales, Merchant 1561–67 [Jucker 1997: 99])

This DM that at first occurs only in represented discourse is generalised to nonrepresented discourse by the sixteenth century, according to Jucker.

Similar kinds of intersubjectification have been noted in the domain of DMs in Japanese. Onodera (2000) notes an onomasiological meaning shift from interjections such as *na* expressing speaker 'exclamation' ('speaker's basic emotion in his/her inner world', 2000: 41) to addressee-oriented 'summons'. Another example of the progressive development of subjectification and intersubjectification is provided by Japanese *sate* (Traugott and Dasher 2002: ch. 4). In Modern Japanese its function is similar to some of the functions of English *so*. In formal letters it signals the shift from the formulaic initial greeting to the topic of the letter. In colloquial speech, it may carry expressive value as a mild hedge, and is translatable as *well*.

---

[8] Jucker makes an interesting very fine-grained analysis that highlights a shift from represented speech to unmediated speech. To what extent this is a happenstance of the corpus and the particular types of texts represented in it deserves further study.

Like *so* (< Old English *swa* 'thus'), *sate* originated in Old Japanese[9] as an anaphoric deictic adverb of manner that links a described event in q to a characteristic of a previously described event in p:[10]

(9) Yuki sabu-mi/   saki-ni   Fa[11] saka-nu/
     snow cold-REASON /   bloom-COP   TOP   bloom-NEG /
     ume-no   Fana /   yosi   kono-koro   Fa /
     plum-ASSOC flower / as: is (ADV) for-a-while   TOP /
     sate mo   aru-ga-ne /
     thus INCL-FOC   be-CAUSE /
     'O plum flower that does not bloom because of the coldness of the
     snow, for a while it is all right (= as is) that you may be thus.'
     (Man'yoosyuu X: 2329 [Takagi et al. 1957–60, vol. 3: 147])

By Late Old Japanese *sate* begins to be used clause-initially. Here it signals that the whole proposition p, not just a constituent of it, is to be taken as a condition or reason for further argument:

(10) Kono koyasu-gahi   ha   asi-ku
      this   safe-birth-shell (amulet) TOP   bad/poor-ADV
      tabakari-te   tor-ase-tamahu-nari.
      fashion (devise)-GER   take-CAUSE-RESP-COP
      Sate   ha   e-tor-ase-tamaha-zi.
      For-that-reason TOP   POTEN-take-CAUS-RESP-NEG
      'It is that [you] have had [the men] use clumsy methods to make this
      amulet. For that reason/so [you] are unable to have [them] get it'
      (Taketori Monogatari [Matsuo 1961: 146.1])

At first *sate* in this new discourse-connective meaning functions primarily at a local discourse level, i.e. connecting narrative events within a larger episode. Later, it appears frequently at the beginning of narrative sections serving a 'global' discourse function.[12] In other words, it comes to mark an episode boundary not unlike OE *gelamp* 'it came to pass' (Brinton 1996) or English *so* in some of its uses. By Middle Japanese, *sate* also comes to be used to express

---

[9] Approximate dates for periods of Japanese are: Old Japanese: 710–1100, Middle Japanese: 1100–1610, Early Modern Japanese: 1610–1870; Modern Japanese: 1870–present.

[10] In the following examples, F stands for a bilabial fricative (that in preliterary times was most likely a stop). The following abbreviations are used: ADV = adverbial, ASSOC = associative case, COP = copula, GER = gerund, INCL-FOC = inclusive (focus particle), NEG = negative, PERF = perfective, PROB = probability marker, Q = interrogative particle, RESP = respectful form, TOP = topic. / indicates a verse line break (each verse line is made up of five syllables).

[11] The particle *Fa* developed into the MdJ topic particle *wa*.

[12] For the distinction between local and global discourse functions, see Schiffrin (1987). Interestingly, she does not record global functions for *so* in her data.

SP/W's special emotional involvement in regard to q (further subjectification) or (as a hedge) toward AD/R (intersubjectification):

(11)   Ge-ni   omosiro-ku   mo   nobe-rare-tari,
        Truly   enjoyable-ADV   INCL:FOC   tell-RESP-PERF
        satesate nani-no   yoo   yaran
        (and)so   what-ASSOC   matter   PROB-Q
        'Truly you have told it well; *so* what is your business here?'
                                    (Shizen koji, Noh play by Kannami
                                    [Yokomichi and Omote 1960:100.11])

In (11) there is no deictic reference back to a p, and *sate* may additionally function as a mild hedge – SP seeks to preserve AD's image needs as he begins to pose a direct question. Nowadays *sate* has become one of the standard formulaic expressions used to mark the beginning of the body of a letter immediately after a sentence of formal greetings. In addition to a subjective function (marking discourse management, specifically topic-shift) it also has an intersubjective function since, by using it, the writer is following communicative norms of the genre that affect the reader's image needs.

Japanese culture has for centuries been known as one that is highly conscious of the addressee and of addressee status. It may therefore come as a surprise that subjectification is here considered a prerequisite to intersubjectification. There is, however, extensive evidence of the robustness of the directionality of this requirement from the history of honorifics (Dasher 1995: ch. 2; Traugott and Dasher 2002: ch. 6). It has long been pointed out that in Japanese addressee honorifics derive from referent honorifics (Tsujimura 1968; Lewin 1969). Referent honorifics are respectful or humiliative markers pointing to the social positions or relationships, as conceptualised by SP/W, of the referent of the subject and sometimes other participants in the described event. In so far as they arise out of verbs of receiving, eating or drinking, lifting up, and so forth, referent honorifics clearly involve subjectification as they index SP/W's strategic choice in assigning respect to the referents of the subject and other arguments in the clause, e.g. Old Japanese *itadaku* 'elevate' (< *ita* 'summit' + *daku* 'embrace') > Late Middle Japanese '[humiliative subject] receives/eats/drink'; Old Japanese *kudasu* 'send down' + *-raru* 'passive, potential' > Early Middle Japanese 'command' > Late Middle Japanese '[respectful subject] gives'. In the history of *kudasaru*, we find not only a shift from a non-subjective verb ('send down') to one which indexes the SP/W's conception of the donor's relation to him- or herself, but in later Japanese, the donee comes to be restricted to either the SP/W or a member of the SP/W's group. While there is necessarily some intersubjectification that accompanies the development of referent honorifics, especially when the addressee is conceptualised as a participant in the described event, the development of addressee honorifics involves a far greater degree of intersubjectification. Addressee honorifics do not index the social status of a participant in the described event; rather, they index SP/W's conceptualisation of AD/R's social standing relative to SP/W through, for example, polite or elevated speech styles. What was typically a referent honorific indexing a humiliative subject comes to be used as a politeness marker indexing respect for AD/R, for example, Early Middle Japanese *mairasu* '[humiliative subject] give' > Late Middle Japanese 'give [polite]'.[13]

In sum, the hypothesis in (4) needs to be extended as follows:

(12)   nonsubjective > subjective > intersubjective

(12) is to be understood not as a necessary path of development, but as a possible one. It is a unidirectional tendency, and therefore the reverse: intersubjective > subjective > nonsubjective is not expected. Furthermore, although it may in some instances be difficult to determine whether a new meaning is strictly subjective before it becomes intersubjective, nevertheless, nonsubjective > intersubjective > subjective is hypothesised not to be likely, on the grounds that it is SP/W who preempts meanings for strategic purposes (note that when innovations spread to AD/Rs, evidence for the acquisition of the new meaning derives from them in their roles as SP/Ws).

As in the case of most 'paths', written as they are in linear form, it is to be expected that the older meanings survive alongside the newer ones as polysemies (Hopper 1991 has referred to this kind of phenomenon that arises at the morphosyntactic level as a result of grammaticalisation as 'layering'). Likewise, as in the case of most 'paths', intersubjectivity is not the only possible path for subjectivised items to take. It appears that the more contentful subjectivised meanings are, the more available they are for generalisation, especially in idioms. For example *come* has been generalised in a wide number of constructions which still, however, retain some of the original deictic semantics, e.g. *come to one's senses, go out of one's mind*, and they may never be intersubjectified.

5   Concluding comments

Intersubjectification results in the development of meanings that explicitly reveal recipient design: the designing of utterances for an intended audience (see Clark and Carlson 1982) at the discourse level. There cannot be intersubjectification without some degree of subjectification because it is SP/W who designs the utterance and who recruits the meaning for social deictic purposes. Like subjectification, it is part of a mechanism of recruiting meanings to express and regulate beliefs, attitudes, etc. Therefore intersubjectification can be considered to be an extension of subjectification rather than as a separate mechanism.

---

[13] From the end of the Late Middle Japanese period the form was -*masu*.

A unidirectional tendency such as subjective > intersubjective can be, and indeed in this chapter has been, referred to metaphorically as a 'path' or 'trajectory' of change. Like many other conduit metaphors (see Reddy 1993 [1979]) for aspects of language, this metaphor has sometimes been construed as a literal conduit (e.g. a neurological path) in the mind or even in the grammar (see discussion of this point in Lass 2000). However, 'path' and 'trajectory' are not to be taken literally, and most specifically not as a claim about processes in the linguistic system; they name the typical structural or functional outcomes of the mechanisms that language users employ in the negotiation of discourse. The selection of these terms in the metalinguistics of historical linguistics is just another example of speakers' tendency to recruit terms that initially refer to some relatively objective element in the physical world to language itself (but in this case, SP/W is a linguist developing a metalanguage for specific discourse purposes rather than the typical language user who uses language relatively unconsciously!).

As a semasiological change, the unidirectionality of intersubjectification is independent of the frequency with which encoding either ego- or alter-orientation is favoured within a particular culture, group, or text type in any particular language or at any particular time. Norms for using encoded inter-subjectivity will differ according to social and political ideology. Japanese and other languages with addressee-honorific systems will inevitably evidence more overt intersubjectification than languages that do not have such a system. By hypothesis, however, we can expect that universally, given the right semantics, any lexical item may be recruited for increasingly subjective and ultimately increasingly intersubjective meanings. These meanings are usually correlated with procedurals[14] that do the work of verbalising SP/W's rhetorical strategy and attitude to it and the participants in the communicative event.

Since the hypothesis is that in the semasiological history of a lexeme subjec-tive and intersubjective meanings develop relatively late, or in any event later than non(inter)subjective meanings, the question can naturally arise whether a stage of the language must be reconstructed in which there is no linguis-tically encoded subjectivity or intersubjectivity. Lass (2000) has argued with respect to the unidirectionality posited in the study of grammaticalisation that if grammatical forms were to be shown always to derive from lexical ones, then uniformitarianism would be violated because there is no 'lexical-only' lan-guage. Setting aside the observation that grammaticalisation starts not in lexical items as independent entities, but in constructions, this form of argument does not hold. All known languages exhibit coded subjectivity and intersubjectivity

---

[14] The term 'procedural' is borrowed from Relevance Theory (see Blakemore 1987) to refer to lexemes that are primarily pragmatic rather than contentful in function and that serve to specify the relation of what is said to the context, linguistic and nonlinguistic.

(some more than others, but nevertheless all). It is possible that in its earliest evolutionary stages language did not do so, but the uniformitarian principle is not understood to cover this period. Because encoded (inter)subjective meaning is relatively late for a particular lexeme it does not follow that it is logically necessary to posit a stage A of some specific language where all of the lexemes are at the same pre-intersubjective (or pre-subjective) developmental stage.[15] No language is at some stage A the repository of all the lexical items at stage B. Different lexemes develop at different times. On the assumption that no language appeared as a full-fledged system, all that is required by the hypothesis of semantic unidirectionality is that the earlier and later meanings of a lexeme conform to the pattern hypothesised; that is, that the mechanisms, motivations and constraints on change have been the same over the millennia that human beings have used language.[16]

Whether the hypothesis of semantic unidirectionality from subjectification to intersubjectification posited here is correct is an empirical question about forces that lead to language change and should be tested against as diverse a set of languages as possible, given the limitations on access to historical data.

A topic for future inquiry is what happens to subjectivised and intersubjectivised terms. My hypothesis is that the more procedural, i.e. pragmatic, they are the more likely they are to be replaced. This seems to be especially true of DMs, and primarily those markers that are intersubjective. For example, many of the pragmatic markers discussed in Brinton (1996), e.g. Old English *hwæt*, have simply disappeared, as have addressee honorifics in Japanese like *haberi* 'be [polite]'. That intersubjective markers tend to be replaced, does not mean that they are necessarily short-lived – as we have seen, *well* appears to have had a robust life of about four hundred years alongside its manner-adverb form, and does not show any sign of disappearing. What it does mean is that, by hypothesis, intersubjectification is a semasiological end-point for a particular form–meaning pair; onomasiologically, however, an intersubjective category will over time come to have more or fewer members, depending on cultural preference, register, etc.

REFERENCES

Aijmer, Karin. 1986. 'Why is *actually* so popular in spoken English?', in Gunnel Tottie and Ingegard Bäcklund (eds.), *English in speech and writing: a symposium*. Uppsala: Almqvist and Wiksell, 119–29.

---

[15] Thanks to Paul Kiparsky for drawing my attention to this point.

[16] Deutscher (1999) has pointed out that there are two potentially conflicting views of uniformitarianism, one diachronic, according to which the 'forces of language change' have remained constant, the other synchronic, according to which languages in the past were the 'same in principle' as languages in the present. Given these two interpretations of the term, Lass's concern about uniformitarianism appears to be synchronic; what I am proposing here is that what we need is uniformitarianism in the diachronic interpretation.

Akatsuka, Noriko. 1997. 'Negative conditionality, subjectification, and conditional reasoning', in Angeliki Athenasiadou and René Dirven (eds.), *On conditionals again.* Amsterdam: Benjamins, 323–54.

Benveniste, Emile. 1971 [1958]. 'Subjectivity in language', in *Problems in general linguistics*, trans. Mary Elizabeth Meek. Coral Gables: FL: University of Miami Press, 223–30 (originally published as 'De la subjectivité dans le langage', in *Problèmes de linguistique générale*, Paris: Gallimard, 1958, 258–66).

Blakemore, Diane. 1987. *Semantic constraints on relevance.* Oxford: Blackwell.

Blank, Andreas and Peter Koch (eds.). 1999. *Historical semantics and cognition.* Berlin: Mouton de Gruyter.

Bréal, Michel. 1964 [1900]. *Semantics: studies in the science of meaning*, trans. Mrs Henry Cust. New York: Dover.

Brinton, Laurel J. 1996. *Pragmatic markers in English: grammaticalization and discourse function.* Berlin: Mouton de Gruyter.

Brinton, Laurel J. 1998. ''The flowers are lovely; only, they have no scent': the evolution of a pragmatic marker', in Raimund Borgmeier, Herbert Grabes and Andreas H. Jucker (eds.), *Historical pragmatics: Anglistentag 1997 Gießen Proceedings.* Gießen: WVT Wissenschaftlicher Verlag, 9–33.

Brown, Penelope and Stephen C. Levinson. 1987 [1978]. *Politeness: some universals in language usage.* Cambridge University Press.

Bühler, Karl. 1990 [1934]. *Theory of language: the representational function of language*, trans. Donald Fraser Goodwin. Amsterdam: Benjamins (originally published as *Sprachtheorie*, 1934, Jena: Fischer).

Bybee, Joan, Revere Perkins and William Pagliuca. 1994. *The evolution of grammar: tense, aspect, and modality in the languages of the world.* University of Chicago Press.

Carey, Kathleen. 1995. 'Subjectification and the English perfect', in Stein and Wright (eds.), 83–102.

Clark, Herbert H. and Thomas B. Carlson. 1982. 'Hearers and speech acts', *Language* 58: 332–73.

Dasher, Richard. 1995. 'Grammaticalization in the System of Japanese Predicate Honorifics', PhD Dissertation, Stanford University.

Deutscher, Guy. 1999. 'The different faces of uniformitarianism', paper given at the 14th International Conference on Historical Linguistics, Vancouver.

Fillmore, Charles J. 1997 [1971]. *Lectures on deixis.* Stanford University: CSLI Publications.

Greenberg, Joseph H. 1978. 'How does a language acquire gender markers?', in Joseph H. Greenberg, Charles A. Ferguson and Edith Moravcsik (eds.), *Universals of human language*, vol. 3. Stanford: Stanford University Press, 249–95.

Hanson, Kristin. 1987. 'On subjectivity and the history of epistemic expressions in English', in Barbara Need, Eric Schiller and Anna Bosch (eds.), *Papers from the 23rd Regional Meeting of the Chicago Linguistic Society.* Chicago Linguistic Society, 133–47.

Held, Gudrun. 1999. 'Submission strategies as an expression of the ideology of politeness: reflections on the verbalisation of social power relations', *Pragmatics* 9: 21–36.

Hopper, Paul J. 1991. 'On some principles of grammaticization', in Elizabeth Closs Traugott and Bernd Heine (eds.), *Approaches to grammaticalization*, vol. 1: 37–80. Amsterdam: Benjamins.

Hopper, Paul J. and Elizabeth Closs Traugott. 1993. *Grammaticalization.* Cambridge University Press.

Iwasaki, Shoichi. 1993. *Subjectivity in grammar and discourse: theoretical considerations and a case study of Japanese spoken discourse.* Amsterdam: Benjamins.

Jakobson, Roman. 1957. *Shifters, verbal categories, and the Russian verb.* Cambridge, MA: Harvard University Russian Language Project.

Joseph, Brian D. and Richard D. Janda. 1988. 'The how and why of diachronic morphologization and demorphologization', in M. Hammond and M. Noonan (eds.), *Theoretical morphology: approaches in modern linguistics.* San Diego: Academic Press, 193–210.

Jucker, Andreas H. 1997. 'The discourse marker *well* in the history of English', *English Language and Linguistics* 1: 91–110.

König, Ekkehard. 1991. *The meaning of focus particles: a comparative perspective.* London: Routledge.

Kuroda, S.-Y. 1973. 'Where epistemology, style, and grammar meet: a case study from Japanese', in Stephen R. Anderson and Paul Kiparsky (eds.), *A Festschrift for Morris Halle.* New York: Holt, Rinehart and Winston, 377–91.

Langacker, Ronald W. 1985. 'Observations and speculations on subjectivity', in John Haiman (ed.), *Iconicity in syntax.* Amsterdam: Benjamins, 109–50.

Langacker, Ronald W. 1990. 'Subjectification', *Cognitive Linguistics* 1: 5–38.

Langacker, Ronald W. 1995. 'Raising and transparency', *Language* 71: 1–62.

Langacker, Ronald W. 1999. 'Losing control: grammaticalization, subjectification, and transparency', in Blank and Koch (eds.), 147–75.

Lass, Roger. 2000. 'Remarks on (uni)directionality', in Olga Fischer, Anette Rosenbach and Dieter Stein (eds.), *Pathways of change: grammaticalization in English.* Amsterdam: Benjamins, 207–27.

Lehmann, Christian. 1995 [1982]. *Thoughts on grammaticalization,* Munich: Lincom Europa (originally published as *Thoughts on grammaticalization, a programmatic sketch,* vol. 1. Arbeiten des Kölner Universalien-Projekts 48. Cologne: University of Cologne, Institut für Sprachwissenschaft, 1982).

Lewin, Bruno (ed.). 1969. *Beiträge zum interpersonalen Bezug im Japanischen.* Wiesbaden: Otto Harrassowitz.

Lyons, John. 1982. 'Deixis and subjectivity: *Loquor, ergo sum?*', in Robert J. Jarvella and Wolfgang Klein (eds.), *Speech, place, and action: studies in deixis and related topics.* New York: Wiley, 101–24.

Lyons, John. 1994. 'Subjecthood and subjectivity', in Marina Yaguello (ed.), *Subjecthood and subjectivity: the status of the subject in linguistic theory.* Paris: Ophrys, 9–17.

Matsuo, Hajime. 1961. *Taketori monogatari zensyaku [Completely annotated edition of the Taketori Monogatari (mid Tenth Century)].* Tokyo: Musashino Shoin.

Maynard, Senko K. 1993. *Discourse modality: subjectivity, emotion, and voice in the Japanese language.* Amsterdam: Benjamins.

Nevalainen, Terttu. 1991. *BUT, ONLY, JUST: Focusing adverbial change in Modern English 1500–1900.* Helsinki: Société Néophilologique.

Newmeyer, Frederick J. 1998. *Language form and language function.* Cambridge, MA: MIT Press, Bradford Books.

Nordlinger, Rachel and Elizabeth Closs Traugott. 1997. 'Scope and the development of epistemic modality: evidence from *ought to*', *English Language and Linguistics* 1: 295–317.

Nuyts, Jan. 1998. 'Subjectivity as an evidential dimension in epistemic modal expressions', paper presented at the 6th International Conference on Pragmatics, Reims.

Onodera, Noriko O. 2000. 'Development of *demo* type connectives and *na* elements: two extremes of Japanese discourse markers', *Journal of Historical Pragmatics* 1: 27–55.

Powell, Mava Jo. 1992. 'The systematic development of correlated interpersonal and metalinguistic uses in stance adverbs', *Cognitive Linguistics* 3: 75–110.

Reddy, Michael J. 1993 [1979]. 'The conduit metaphor – a case of frame conflict in our language about language', in Andrew Ortony (ed.), *Metaphor and thought*, 2nd edition. Cambridge University Press, 164–201.

Rissanen, Matti. 1967. *The uses of* one *in Old and Early Middle English*. Helsinki: Société Néophilologique.

Schiffrin, Deborah. 1987. *Discourse markers*. Cambridge University Press.

Schiffrin, Deborah. 1990. 'The principle of intersubjectivity in communication and conversation', *Semiotica* 80: 121–51.

Schwenter, Scott and Elizabeth Closs Traugott. 2000. 'Invoking scalarity: the development of *in fact*', *Journal of Historical Pragmatics* 1: 7–25.

Stein, Dieter and Susan Wright (eds.). 1995. *Subjectivity and subjectivisation in language*. Cambridge University Press.

Suzuki, Ryoko. 1998. 'From a lexical noun to an utterance-final pragmatic particle: *wake*,' in Toshio Ohori (ed.), *Studies in Japanese grammaticalization*. Tokyo: Kurosio Publishers, 67–92.

Swan, Toril. 1988. *Sentence adverbials in English: a synchronic and diachronic investigation*. Oslo: Novus.

Sweetser, Eve V. 1990. *From etymology to pragmatics: metaphorical and cultural aspects of semantic structure*. Cambridge University Press.

Tagaki, Ichinosuke, Tomohide Gomi and Susumu Ohno (eds. and annot.). 1957–60. *Man'yoosyuu [Man'yoshu, The Ten-Thousand Leaves (before 760 AC)]*, 4 vols. Tokyo: Iwanami Shoten.

Traugott, Elizabeth Closs. 1989. 'On the rise of epistemic meanings in English: an example of subjectification in semantic change', *Language* 57: 33–65.

Traugott, Elizabeth Closs. 1995. 'Subjectification in grammaticalization', in Stein and Wright (eds.), 31–54.

Traugott, Elizabeth Closs. 1997. 'Subjectification and the development of epistemic meaning: the case of *promise* and *threaten*', in Toril Swan and Olaf Jansen Westvik (eds.), *Modality in Germanic languages*. Berlin: Mouton de Gruyter, 185–210.

Traugott, Elizabeth Closs. 1999a. 'The rhetoric of counter-expectation in semantic change: a study in subjectification', in Blank and Koch (eds.), 177–96.

Traugott, Elizabeth Closs. 1999b. 'The role of pragmatics in semantic change', in Jef Verschueren (ed.), *Pragmatics in 1998: Selected Papers from the 6th International Pragmatics Conference* 2. Antwerp: International Pragmatics Association, 93–102.

Traugott, Elizabeth Closs. and Richard Dasher. 2002. *Regularity in Semantic Change*. Cambridge University Press.

Tsujimura, Toshiki. 1968. *Keigo no Si-teki Kenkyuu [Historical Studies of Japanese Honorifics]*. Tokyo: Tokyodo.

Yokomichi, Mario and Akira Omote (eds. and annot.). 1960. *Yookyoku-syuu [Selected Noh Plays]*. Nihon Koten Bungaku Taikei, series, vol. 40. Tokyo: Iwanami Shoten.

Part IV

The social context for language change

9   On the role of the speaker in language change

James Milroy

1   Introduction: internal and external factors in change

It is true, I think, that in what might be called the dominant tradition in historical linguistics, it has been assumed that languages change within themselves as part of their nature as languages. The 'external' agency of speaker/listeners and the influence of 'society' in language change have tended to be seen as secondary and, sometimes, as not relevant at all. Roger Lass has been a prominent, but balanced, defender of the traditional view. He has correctly pointed out (1980: 120) that in the tradition, it has been assumed that it is languages that change and not (necessarily) speakers who change languages. More recently (1990: 370), he has commented that language change is not something that speakers 'do' to their language, and that 'endogenous change is part of the nature of the beast' (1997: 208). He has also (largely correctly) suggested in various publications that speaker-based explanations have been unsatisfactory because of the attribution to speakers of qualities that they may not actually have. In some such accounts the speakers appealed to are disembodied abstractions who can be made to 'do' almost anything the researcher wants them to. Much more generally, however, the idea of endogenous or internally triggered change is so deeply embedded in our subject that it feeds into what can be called the *discourse* of historical linguistics. In this discourse, individual languages are typically presented as changing within themselves rather than being changed through the agency of speaker/ listeners. The language user is not incorporated into the discourse. I will refer again to this discourse later in this chapter.

Since all languages change, it has been natural to assume that endogenous change is in the nature of the beast and to seek explanations preferentially from within the properties of language and languages. The priority of endogenous explanation was greatly encouraged by the rise of comparative linguistics in the nineteenth century, as this provided a model of languages changing within themselves and either *becoming* other languages in the course of time, or *giving birth to* other languages in and of their own nature, with no central role for other factors, such as language contact. For clarity we can break up this assumption of endogenous change into four related parts:

1. change originates within 'language' as a phenomenon;
2. change takes place within single languages unaffected by other languages;
3. change is more satisfactorily explained internally than externally;
4. change is not necessarily triggered by speakers or through language contact.

What we need to notice here is that these views do not depend on observed fact, because no one can directly observe the diachronic process of linguistic change. Rather, they depend on a *hypothesis* that lies behind much of the reasoning of historical linguistics – the hypothesis that language is the kind of abstract object that can change within itself or perhaps *bring about* change within itself. This is a general nineteenth-century view. Although it is true that the Neogrammarians paid lip-service to the importance of speakers (see Awedyk 1997), they are chiefly remembered for the idea of exceptionless sound laws and the claim that sound change is phonetically gradual. Both of these positions are expressed as language-internal: in the discourse, the abstraction 'language' is subject to laws (*Gesetze*), and it is languages that change phonetically gradually – not speakers who change languages phonetically gradually.

The assumption of endogeny, being generally the preferred hypothesis, functions in practice as the *default* hypothesis. Thus, if some particular change in history cannot be shown to have been initiated through language or dialect contact involving speakers, then it has been traditionally presented as endogenous. Usually, we do not know all the relevant facts, and this default position is partly the consequence of having insufficient data from the past to determine whether the change concerned was endogenous or externally induced or both: endogeny is the *lectio facilior* requiring less argumentation, and what Lass has called the more *parsimonious* solution to the problem.

It is also the most accessible solution because linguistic 'facts' from the past may be accessible or reconstructable when social 'facts' are not. We cannot, for example, say much about the social embedding of the First Germanic Consonant Shift. Yet, the simpler and most accessible solution may not always be the right solution, and it does not follow from these points that in general we do not need social and/or cognitive insights for the best explanations possible. The prioritising of endogeny has led to extremely important insights into language change: it may be thought to have stood the test of time and allowed historical linguistics to claim the status of a science. But we need also to notice that in the twentieth century this point of view has been sanctified by the Saussurean internal/external dichotomy and the exclusion of external descriptions from linguistics (Saussure 1983 [1916]: 20). This distinction amounts to an axiomatic one, and I will return to it below.

As historical databases are relatively impoverished, we might expect the newer discipline of quantitative sociolinguistics to cast some light on the matter. After all, it has access to rich and plentiful data. If it is possible (as claimed) to detect linguistic changes in progress, it should therefore be possible to examine them in great detail. But again, it seems that the hypothesis of endogenous change cannot be verified or falsified by these methods either. An important stumbling block is the fact that when language in use is observed by empirical methods, social factors are also observed at the same time, and language use is intricately – perhaps inextricably – bound up with these social factors. The hypothesis cannot be directly tested by laboratory methods either (although some have tried this) because language change is not synchronic and does not take place in laboratories. Neither can it be tested by studies in speech communities, because the linguistically homogeneous and unvarying speech community in which it could be convincingly tested does not exist in the real world and, further, no language, or variety of language, ever exists in a vacuum in which speakers of other languages, or of other varieties, have had absolutely no contact with the variety concerned. Languages in use do not get sealed up in airtight containers. Similarly, there is no known society that has no social and linguistic differentiation within it, and in which language variation is *never* indexical of social differences. To test the hypothesis wholly empirically, we would have to devise an experiment in which a community with no social differences and homogeneous speech is totally isolated from other communities for perhaps a century, and then examine it for changes. Yet, even if this were possible, we still might not be able to verify the reality of endogenous change. Therefore, in view of all these things, I think we may reasonably say that *it is in the nature of the beast to resist satisfactory explanations of how it can change within itself*.

The idea that language changes independently of speakers and society is, it seems, an inference based on comparison of data – not on direct observation or identification of change. It also happens, however, that this view is much encouraged by certain axiomatic positions, including the genetic metaphor of language descent and the Saussurean doctrine mentioned above – the methodological separation of internal from external explanations and the exclusion of the latter from language theorising. These are not trivial matters, and they have had the effect of privileging the doctrine of independent, endogenous, internally triggered linguistic change within individual languages, which are reified as internally coherent structures independent of other languages.

It is important to notice in all this that the doctrine of endogenous change cannot be logically falsified either. I want therefore to emphasise that it is not my purpose to demonstrate that there is no such thing as endogenous influence on change or that all aspects of change are external (I have been accused of saying that language change is entirely social, so I want to put that right). I have been talking here about *empirical* demonstrations, and there are limits to the use of empiricism. As Wang (1969) so memorably put it, we can't prove that a platypus does not lay eggs by showing a photograph of a platypus not laying eggs. So we can't prove that language change is not endogenous by showing examples of language change not being endogenous. If we define carefully what we mean by 'internal', we may still argue powerfully that some changes originate language-internally, and it is clear that all changes must at least *involve* language-internal factors. All that I am saying here is that purely endogenous change cannot be empirically demonstrated to take place. I will go on to suggest that speaker/ listeners play a vital role in language change, and that language changes in response to changes in external conditions. But no sociolinguist, as far as I know, has ever suggested that we can ignore internal linguistic constraints in the study of language change or that language change is merely speaker change.

2   Actuation

Ultimately we are concerned with solving the *actuation problem* or at least making progress in understanding it, and there is a serious empirical difficulty with this also. We cannot observe an innovation – more correctly, we cannot differentiate an observed innovation that will ultimately lead to a linguistic change from innovations that don't lead to linguistic changes – but we have a great deal of evidence that suggests that some types of change are more likely and more frequent than others. One type of frequent change arises from *assimilation to place of articulation*: for example, velar consonants are frequently fronted in the environment of front vowels. The question of causation naturally arises here. The change seems to be 'natural' and frequently attested, and many linguists seem to be quite happy to say that palatalisation of velars before front vowels in some dialect took place *because* the front position of the following vowel influenced the velar (back) consonant and moved it forward. It is true that this is not enough as an internally based explanation because it does not explain why *the front vowel did not back to the position of the preceding velar*, but sidestepping this for the moment, we also have to notice a difficulty arising from the standard account of the *actuation problem*. This is that completed linguistic changes arising from palatalisation have taken place at particular times, and not at other times at billions of moments throughout history when they could just as readily have taken place for exactly the same articulatory reason. Similarly, nasalisation of vowels before nasal consonants, or any one of a host of other common types of synchronic variation can be present in uses of language at virtually any time. Language is inherently variable. Why, then, does this variation lead to change in some cases, but not in others? That seems to me to be the key question, and it implies that many linguists who have pronounced on language change have not actually been talking about change. They have often satisfactorily shown how an innovation can come about, but they have not explained how it can become embedded in language as a change at some times and places, but remain only a synchronic variant at others.

As an example, let us consider nasalisation of vowels. We can easily notice that this is quite common in English, and is audible in most varieties in the environment of a following nasal consonant and also in some varieties elsewhere. Sometimes, in casual styles in certain environments, the vowel is nasalised, and *the nasal consonant is also deleted*. In expressions like 'I *don't* remember', 'I *can't* remember', the negative auxiliaries are frequently reduced to stop consonant + nasalised vowel + glottal stop: there is no [n] and no [t]. To notice that this quite regularly happens might be considered illuminating in explaining the widespread nasalisation in other languages such as French, in which the vowel was historically nasalised and the nasal consonant (with, possibly, a following consonant) deleted, exactly as it variably is in English *can't* and *don't*. What we have not explained, however, is why this nasalisation represents a set of completed linguistic changes in French, but remains only a variant in English. I doubt if we will ever be able to explain this difference purely language-internally, however many language-internal arguments we may produce, and – if my doubt is well-founded – it seems to me that we also require language-external information to explain why the French changes took place at the times and places that they did, and not at other times and places. As this lies so deep in history, however, we may never collect sufficient information to explain exactly how a synchronic variant became a diachronic change.

In practice, linguists who have worked language-internally have had to make reference to external matters, but often without sufficient attention to the analysis of these external matters – matters that ultimately depend on a distinction being drawn between the *speaker* and the *system* (Milroy and Milroy 1985; J. Milroy 1992), and which involve social matters, among others. Consider how Bloomfield's (1933: 390) explanation of the abruptness of the change from alveolar to uvular [r] in north-west Europe falls down in this way. 'Aside from its spread by borrowing', he says, '[this] could only have originated as a sudden replacement of one trill by another.' The 'sudden replacement' is of course a synchronic innovation, not (yet) a change, and the exclusion of 'change by borrowing' does not make sense in the context, because each (speaker-)act of 'borrowing' must have involved the same 'sudden replacement' as the putative original one did. Borrowing must be speaker-based (or user-based), and the 'change' itself must have involved what Bloomfield calls 'borrowing'. The axioms of the subject, however, and hence its discourse, required Bloomfield to separate sound change from borrowing: at that time they were by definition distinct phenomena that could not be associated.

The distinction between *innovation* and *change* seems to help in clarifying this variant of the actuation problem. In this account, speaker innovations involving, for example, vowel nasalisation by speakers or the perception of nasalised vowels by listeners (see Ohala 1993) would take place repeatedly in speaker usage at any time largely below the level of conscious speaker awareness, but the innovation would feed into a language change only at a particular time. This would be a linguistic change in the sense that future generations would use a nasalised vowel where there had formerly been a vowel + nasal consonant, and would not insert the nasal consonant in the relevant environments. Here, linguistic change (change in the system) is defined as a separate issue from speaker-based innovation, and the problem becomes one of explaining how innovations that are constantly taking place feed into the system only at particular times and places.

The actuation problem is the ultimate *because* problem, from which all 'because' statements ultimately derive. When linguists make statements about velars being fronted in front environments and describe the change as 'conditioned', they are making 'because' statements, even when they claim that they are not interested in the actuation problem. Within traditional historical linguistics, the conditioning environment – which is a language-internal environment and not a situational social environment – is the 'cause' of the sound change: it has 'actuated' the change. Thus, Verner's Law voicing in Germanic is explained by Germanic accent shift: if accent shift had not happened, VL voicing would not have happened; therefore there is some form of causal relationship between accent shift and VL voicing, even if there were other factors involved that are now irrecoverable. Thus, *endogenous explanations are in themselves proposed solutions to the actuation problem.* The position we are arguing here is that they may not be sufficient. Linguistic change is multi-causal and the etiology of a change may include social, communicative and cognitive, as well as linguistic, factors. Thus – seemingly paradoxically – it happens that, in order to define those aspects of change that are indeed endogenous, we need to specify much more clearly than we have to date what precisely are the exogenous factors from which they are separated, and these include the role of the speaker/ listener in innovation and diffusion of innovations. It seems that we need to clarify what has counted as 'internal' or 'external' more carefully and consistently than we have up to now, and to subject the internal/external dichotomy to more critical scrutiny.

3   The discourse of endogeny

Lass (1997: 377n.) proposes a variant of the Saussurean doctrine mentioned above, suggesting that there are 'two complementary kinds of historical linguistics: "structural" and "psychosocial" ', the first kind being 'privileged'. It is true that the basis of the subject is structural – it aims to explain how language structures and systems change, and not exclusively how cognitive and social factors (relating to speakers) change them. It is perhaps relevant, though, that Lass here names the subject as 'historical linguistics' and not 'the study of linguistic change': seen as 'subjects' these two could be somewhat different, and this may make a difference to the kind of questions we ask about them. The methodology of traditional historical linguistics did not primarily address a theory of language change, and, at the risk of some over-simplification, we may say that it asked the question: 'How do we compare states of language in the past with a view to reconstructing even more ancient states?' It was at first about discovery, not 'theory', and was explicitly devoted to comparative reconstruction of past structural states of language. Sociolinguistic methodology remains comparative, in that the language of different social groups is compared, and 'real-time' data may be used comparatively to help to determine what changes are in progress, but the *immediate* focus is exclusively on how and why particular linguistic changes take place and not on how languages have changed through history (relevant as this sometimes becomes). That is to say that the focus is on a dynamic *process* rather than on the products of change in the past and the reconstruction of such products. We may rephrase the overriding aim as: 'How do we describe the process of linguistic change?' But notice that we cannot actually observe this process: we cannot 'observe' language change in progress (even though it is sometimes claimed that we can). This is because we cannot observe dynamic processes directly in abstract objects: we can observe the products of change, as historical linguists always have. The claim can therefore be rephrased as a claim that we can *detect* change in progress in synchronic states by comparing outputs or products of variation in present-day states of language. Here the nonrandom nature of variation is crucial: this was the key insight of Weinreich, Labov and Herzog (1968).

It should also be noticed that quantitative sociolinguistics remains, for the most part, structuralist. Perhaps it should not be, but it is. The methodology is in many ways an outgrowth of mid-twentieth-century structuralism and is focused on phenomena usually seen as internal to languages – phonological mergers, splits and chainshifts. It is specially devoted to gaining access to *variation* in language by studying the speech of real speakers, and it is claimed that much of this variation is in some way structured and regular within language systems – that some form of organisation lies behind the superficially unpredictable patterns of variation. The graphs and diagrams that are used display distributions of variants within language systems: in this speakers are the access points to the systems and not in themselves the main object of inquiry. Thus, the aims of quantitative sociolinguistics are just as intralinguistic as any other approach. They do, however, contemplate social input to change, and this has been explicit from the days of Martha's Vineyard onward: according to Labov (1972), a change arising from social factors will feed into the system with internal structural repercussions, e.g. the implementation of a chainshift.

The movement of the [socially triggered: JM] linguistic variable within the linguistic system always led to readjustments of other elements within phonological space.

(Labov 1972: 179)

This is language-internal structuralism (and I don't know where we are to draw the line here between socially triggered changes and internal structural ones). But, before the 1960s, there was little or no systematic study of the possible roles of speakers in social interaction as initiators or carriers of change, and it is reasonable to hope that sociolinguistic studies may help us to understand how language systems move from one state to another. Change in language is change in linguistic systems, not change in speakers. But it is possible that processes of systemic change may be detectable by comparative methods in communities of speakers through study of innovation and diffusion of changes in speaker/ listener interaction, and to that extent, it can be described as social. One thing that has been demonstrated is that linguistic change is *socially gradual* (insightful scholars such as Whitney knew this over a century ago, but could not demonstrate it as clearly as we can now), and the Neogrammarian axiom that sound change is *phonetically* gradual may be reinterpreted or modified in these terms.

As we have noticed, historical linguistics over the last two centuries has developed a discourse by means of which its findings and theories are communicated. This discourse is based on assumptions about monolinear development in single languages, the capability of a particular language to become another language, and quasi-genetic relationships to 'sister languages'. Social and cognitive factors are largely excluded from the discourse, and the sparseness of the historical data-base further encourages this. It may be that sociolinguistic and speaker-based approaches, being based on synchronic data-bases, need to be expressed in a subtly different kind of discourse derived from a partly different set of underlying axioms.

One characteristic of a discourse is that certain underlying assumptions are shared by the participants and not questioned: they are not immediately available for critical scrutiny and may not always make sense to outsiders. The discourse of historical linguistics is still very much set in a traditional mould, in which languages bring about changes within themselves, without the immediate agency of language users. Examples are easy to find. I used a part of the accepted discourse above when I said that velars front to palatals. Actually, velars can't do anything except be themselves as products of the organs of speech. It is not literally true that they can 'front' or do anything else – it is speakers who can move their tongues from one position to another – but such an expression is accepted as part of the discourse. A nonlinguist who happens to know that the velum is a place of articulation might wonder what on earth I'm talking about: once a velar, always a velar: how can it *become* anything else? Similarly, how can Old English [a:] *become* Early Modern English [o:]? How can one sound *become* a different sound? Sound changes are not literally changes of sound: they are structural correspondences between one sound and another sound that appears in its place at a later date.

The discourse of endogeny can lead us into great difficulties when we smuggle in speaker-based assumptions without acknowledging them. As an example, consider these comments by Gasperini (1999: 37) on the collapsing of three original cases into the Latin ablative:

> In fact, the concentration of the functional load of three original cases into one ending resulted in semantic ambiguity ... to which Latin has responded by enlarging and regulating the usage of prepositions.

I am not picking out this author for criticism: I'm merely using a recent example of the discourse – one in which I am also quite capable of participating. In this quotation, the image suggested is one of an overarching authority (the language) that oversees and regulates changes in order to make itself less liable to ambiguity: 'Good heavens!', says the language, 'I'm becoming ambiguous. I'd better use my prepositions to make myself clearer!' What is important is that the agency in this discourse is the language, and not the speakers of the language. It is the language, not the speaker, that carries out the 'repair' or the 'therapy', putting right some putative damage that has come about through language change, and the appeal here to functional load is again characteristic – as it also is in arguments about the avoidance of phonological merger. It seems to me illogical to argue about function in this way in a discourse that elevates the language and not the speaker to prominence, because ambiguities that are dysfunctional must surely arise in *speaker* usage (pragmatic ambiguity is a speaker/listener phenomenon) and can only be found to be dysfunctional when speakers misunderstand them. But it is the language-based mode of the discourse here that interests me. I have often thought that when linguists make statements like this, they must really have in mind the speakers of the language, but choose to put it in terms of the language – as a kind of shorthand that stands for 'speakers of the language'. That's why I call it a discourse: perhaps we are intended to assume that it was really the speakers who wanted, for example, to resolve an ambiguity, but I do not seem to have been right. Some historical linguists do appear to mean that it was indeed the language that carried out the repairs and modifications.

If it is difficult to imagine the abstract object 'language' attempting to repair a malfunction in itself (or allowing the malfunction to come about in the first place), it is also very difficult to see how speakers can be adduced in certain kinds of functional argument. Perhaps the speakers, and not the language, carried out the repair of ambiguities arising from the merger of three cases. Plausible – but not as straightforward as it appears, because an appeal to speakers in cases of what are described as functional changes can stir up a hornet's nest of difficulty. There is no reliable evidence that speakers are much bothered by structural or lexical ambiguities, as the situational context of conversation virtually always resolves any theoretical ambiguity that may be present. When it doesn't, strategies of conversational repair are always available: thus, we might speculate that the speakers of Latin supplied prepositions in acts of conversational repair – *not* language repair – in everyday discourse. When Hockett (1958: 152) mentioned that ambiguity is 'not common', this looked wrong in the light of later arguments by Chomsky, but he was right in the assumption that what are technically structural ambiguities are usually immediately and unconsciously disambiguated by conversationalists, and so they do not matter very much. In the practical conduct of conversations in monolingual situations, structural ambiguity may be common, but pragmatic ambiguity is rare. Speakers do not normally have problems with *my aunt's murder* and *flying planes can be dangerous* because these structurally ambiguous sequences virtually always occur in contexts that disambiguate them. Nor – for the same reason – do speakers commonly have problems with wholesale mergers of vowels that were at one time distinct.

Conversation analysts are constantly demonstrating how conversationalists use strategies for repairing miscomprehensions when they do occur. In the light of what we now know about speakers' ability to manage conversations, arguments, for example, about whether *languages* practise therapy or prophylaxis (Lightfoot 1979) seem to me to become meaningless, and this is because of the presuppositions of the discourse within which these arguments are carried out. Why should there ever be a time in which, as a result of merger, rule loss, etc., the language functions so inadequately that it must somehow be repaired? Can we confidently specify such a time in the history of English, for example? If so, when exactly was this time? Certain sociopolitical events that lead to massive language contact and code-mixing may indeed cause difficulties for speakers in making themselves understood in day-to-day matters and may lead to substantial linguistic changes (*despite* speakers but also *because of* them), but such matters are airily ignored by certain theorists: for them language change is monolingual and unidirectional, and, except for the occasional re-setting of a parameter, continuous. Language contact is excluded, and endogenous explanations are preferred. Whatever the imperfections of a language may be at any or all times, why – in a discourse that assumes unidirectional and continuous descent of languages – can it not be assumed that language users make sure that language resources always remain adequate (if never ideal) for the purposes of carrying out conversations? Where are these dysfunctional monolingual states that we hear so much about?

Of course, it is not true that all language situations are monolingual or that language descent is always unidirectional or continuous. There are population movements, and there is language and dialect contact, which is contact between *speakers* or users of different languages and dialects. People have to make adjustments in such situations, and important language changes seem to have been triggered because of this necessity. But speakers are not interested in bringing about language change for its own sake, and nothing I have said is intended to imply this. They are more interested in resisting changes. As for the argument in which languages bring about changes within themselves, it is difficult to demonstrate that speakers 'look after' the language that they use. However, it is more plausible to assume that they do something like this than to assume that languages allow themselves to degenerate and then carry out acts of self-medication. However speculative it may seem, it is more plausible to assume, in the Latin example discussed above, that it was the speakers (and perhaps writers), rather than the language, who extended the use of prepositions.

4   Socially triggered change: an example

Now I would like to refer to some recent research in which references to speakers and their social settings appear to be necessary in any attempted explanation of the variation and change encountered by the analyst. I know of numerous relevant cases, but I have space here for only one. This is research on African American Vernacular English (AAVE) in Detroit, carried out by Bridget Anderson and Lesley Milroy (Anderson and Milroy 1999). It is important to remember here that even within sociolinguistics it has been repeatedly claimed that AAVE is invariant throughout three million square miles of territory. These results show that there is variation in AAVE. Underlying the interpretation of these results is the view that we have been expressing since 1980 or before, which is that to understand how linguistic changes are implemented we need to take full account of the forces in society which encourage language maintenance or resistance to change. The traditional discourse has been entirely about change and not about maintenance; matters such as language focusing, dialect levelling and language standardisation are not part of the central discourse of historical linguistics (in that discourse, changes take place over time in single continuous strands of development). Associated with the social side of the question are the identity functions of language and the indexical meaning of variants within social groups. To the extent that social functions remain the same – to the extent that there is little or no identity change – the variants will retain their functions as markers of the group, and change from outside the group will be resisted. This study concerns the monophthongisation of the diphthong in, e.g., *right, wide* in AAVE in inner-city Detroit.

Monophthongisation of /ai/ is a well-known and well-researched characteristic of Southern American English speech – both black and white. It is a very salient geographical marker, and its history suggests that for at least a century /ai/ has been monophthongized *in following voiced contexts* in both white and black speech. Monophthongisation before voiceless obstruents as in *right, life*, however, is more recent and is not generally found among southern black speakers (Wolfram and Schilling-Estes 1998). For white speakers, however, the internal linguistic diffusion of the vowel change has worked through the voiced environments and has finally encompassed the voiceless ones, much in the manner of C.-J. Bailey's 'Wave Model' (1973). The result is that any threatened split in the system that might have taken place has been cancelled, and the prior phonemic structure is maintained, with monophthongal rather than diphthongal pronunciation throughout. Retrospectively, it appears as an unconditional change: in reality it was always subject to conditions.

Therefore, changes in history that appear retrospectively to have been unconditional may in fact have been subject to internal conditioning during the process of change, and also to social conditioning. This relative resistance of voiceless obstruent environments to change is attested elsewhere in English: it is a prominent feature of Belfast English, where phonemic splits in /a/ and /e/ in the past have actually resulted from resistance to change in the voiceless stop environment (J. Milroy 1981). Failure of monophthongisation of /ai/ in (especially) voiceless stop environments is also attested in the north of England, where monophthongisation is otherwise widely attested (see, for example, Bailey 1973: 88). What is important here, however, is that AAVE speakers in the south have not shared in the change before voiceless obstruents. Southern AAVE is reported to retain the diphthong in items of the type *right, life*, and in this respect it is differentiated from southern white English.

A purely linguistic description of the change toward monophthongisation would state that the change has been spreading through voiced environments and is now reaching the voiceless ones, and general tendencies of 'drift' or 'waves' of change or 'natural' change might be argued for as endogenous phenomena. But this would not take all our knowledge into account in this case. We can hardly ignore the fact that the pattern is sharply socially differentiated. In a social interpretation that recognises that small linguistic differences can be seized on by social groups as indexical and emblematic, the retention of the diphthong is indicative of belonging to a group and differentiation of southern AAVE speakers from southern white speakers. This is a case of language maintenance of exactly the same *socially* functional kind that we studied in Belfast (see L. Milroy 1987).

In the current study, however, there is clear evidence that inner-city Detroit AAVE speakers, in contrast to southern AAVE speakers, are adopting the monophthong that they have hitherto resisted in voiceless obstruent environments. Table 9.1 shows the generational progression of the change.

The cells are uneven in numbers (there are 14 speakers in one of them), but the trend is clear. There is a reversal of preference for the monophthong between the older and younger age groups. There is also evidence that Detroit AAVE speakers are adopting other features of southern white English that they seem to have resisted in the south (for example, fronting of /u:/ in, e.g., *boot*). Thus, these *southern* changes are happening in the *north*. But what is interesting here is that

Table 9.1. Detroit AAVE /ai/
monophthongisation before voiceless
obstruent by age group (M: male;
F: female)

	aː	ai	% monophthong
1 M (age 79)	0	14	0
2 F (60–80)	6	38	14
2 M (25–45)	67	8	89
14 F (20–40)	202	65	76
4 M (14–17)	39	13	75
4 F (14–17)	27	4	87

there is a population of southern white speakers in Detroit also, and they are monophthongising throughout /ai/, as expected. So the AAVE speakers, who are also monophthongising, are not maintaining the symbolic differences that were socially functional in the south in differentiation from white southerners. Their social and geographical situation has changed, and the indexical functions of language differentiation have also changed. What is important now is no longer differentiation from southern white groups, but differentiation from northern speakers. Ultimately, the reasons for these particular changes are ideological. There is *no* language-internal reason for this particular configuration of change.

Diphthongal /ai/ is rather interesting in this respect, as Michigan speakers share to a great extent in the phenomenon known as Canadian Raising, and the centralised nucleus in voiceless obstruent environments is extremely salient. The vowel is most definitely a diphthong, and the differentiation from the low vowel monophthong could hardly be more clear. The indexical situation has changed. It is no longer important that AAVE speakers should differentiate themselves from southern white speakers. The important outgroup now is the northern majority, and participation in this last stage of the southern shift – hitherto resisted – is now allowed, assuming the function of an identity marker in terms of the ethnic and social make-up of a northern city. In endogenous terms, all that we could say is that the long-term change toward monophthongisation is going to completion. But the social information here enables us to say much more.

Of course it might not have happened in that way. The change toward monoph-thongisation might never have happened at all, but – more relevant here – it might have failed to spread to the voiceless obstruent environment, and a phone-mic split would have ensued. For this to happen, however, the argument here is that there would have had to be a configuration of socially based identity factors that favoured that particular outcome. The history of the English vowel system is full of splits, mergers and changes that have halted at some point, and residues that are not easy to explain in purely linguistic terms. The most famous of these are the words *great, break* and *steak* in mainstream British and American English, which have been stabilised in the /e:/ class rather than the /i:/ class, but there are many other intransigent cases. Although the social conditions of these changes are not directly recoverable or recoverable only in very general terms, it seems likely that changes in social conditions led to the circumstances in which these configurations of variants were stabilised in particular phoneme classes. Thus, it may have been social, rather than internal linguistic, factors that resulted in phonologically unpredictable residues of the kind mentioned.

5   Concluding remarks

Well – is it in the nature of the beast to change independently of speakers in social situations? Have I demonstrated that it is not? No – I am sure that I have not. There may be no empirical way of showing that language changes independently of social factors, but it has not primarily been my intention to demonstrate that endogenous change does not take place. The one example that I have discussed has shown that there are some situations in which it is necessary to adduce social explanations, and this may apply very much more widely. I happen to think that social matters are always involved, and that language-internal concepts like 'drift' or 'phonological symmetry' are not explanatory, but I have no space to discuss these things here.

There is, however, still some difficulty in specifying what is internal and what is external, and I have not dealt with this question either. References to the organs of speech and phonetic processes, for example, may be ambiguously language-based and speaker-based. Speakers, after all, have organs of speech. Mental and cognitive arguments about language change can also be ambiguous in so far as language is a mental phenomenon, and it is speakers who have minds. But I have been most concerned here with social aspects of language, and these concerns in particular make it desirable to reconsider, and examine very closely, the axiomatic status of the Saussurean internal/external dichotomy. This seems to me to be much more difficult to maintain than it has been in the past. It is time, I feel, to release historical linguistics – at least partly – from its iron grip.

REFERENCES

Anderson, Bridget and Lesley Milroy. 1999. 'Southern sound changes and the Detroit AAVE vowel system', paper delivered at NWAVE XXVIII: Toronto, October 1999.
Awedyk, Wieslaw. 1997. 'Traditional historical linguistics and historical sociolinguistics', in Jahr (ed.), 37–44.

Bailey, Charles-James N. 1973. *Variation and linguistic theory*. Arlington VA: Center for Applied Linguistics.

Bloomfield, Leonard. 1933. *Language*. New York: Henry Holt.

Gasperini, Lucia. 1999. 'Diachrony and synchrony of the Latin ablative', *Diachronica* 16.1: 37–66.

Hockett, Charles F. 1958. *A course in modern linguistics*. New York: Macmillan.

Jahr, Ernst Håkon (ed.). 1997. *Language change: advances in historical sociolinguistics*. Berlin: Mouton de Gruyter.

Jones, Charles (ed.). 1993. *Historical linguistics: problems and perspectives*. London: Longman.

Labov, William. 1972. *Sociolinguistic patterns*. Philadelphia: University of Pennsylvania Press.

Lass, Roger. 1980. *On explaining language change*. Cambridge University Press.

Lass, Roger. 1990. 'Exaptation in language evolution', *Journal of Linguistics* 26: 79–102.

Lass, Roger. 1997. *Historical linguistics and language change*. Cambridge University Press.

Lehmann, Winfred P. and Y. Malkiel (eds.). 1968. *Directions for historical linguistics*. Austin: University of Texas Press.

Lightfoot, David. 1979. *Principles of diachronic syntax*. Cambridge University Press.

Milroy, James. 1981. *Regional accents of English: Belfast*. Belfast: Blackstaff.

Milroy, James. 1992. *Linguistic variation and change*. Oxford: Blackwell.

Milroy, James and Lesley Milroy. 1985. 'Linguistic change, social network and speaker innovation', *Journal of Linguistics* 21: 339–84.

Milroy, Lesley. 1987. *Language and social networks*, 2nd edition. Oxford: Blackwell.

Ohala, John J. 1993. 'The phonetics of sound change', in Jones (ed.), 237–78.

Saussure, Ferdinand de. 1983 [1916]. *Course in general linguistics*, trans. R. Harris. London: Duckworth.

Wang, William. 1969. 'Competing changes as a cause of residue', *Language* 45: 9–25.

Weinreich, Uriel, William Labov and M. Herzog. 1968. 'Empirical foundations for a theory of language change', in Lehmann and Malkiel (eds.), 95–195.

Wolfram, Walt and Natalie Schilling-Estes. 1998. *American English: dialects and variation*. Oxford: Blackwell.

Part V

Contact-based explanations

10   The quest for the most 'parsimonious' explanations: endogeny vs. contact revisited

Markku Filppula

1   Introduction

In his book *Historical linguistics and language change* (see Lass 1997) and in a number of influential papers (see, e.g., Lass and Wright 1986; Lass 1990a, b), Roger Lass has put forward the argument that, whenever there is a possibility of dual or multiple origin for a given feature, endogeny is always to be preferred to language contact because it provides the most 'parsimonious' explanations for linguistic innovations. According to Lass, this methodological principle can also be applied to the various 'Extraterritorial Englishes' (ETEs) such as American English, South African English, or Hiberno-English: most of their distinctive characteristics are best explained as perfectly normal internal developments rather than as results of influence from languages other than English.

In this chapter I will discuss some lexical and structural evidence from some varieties of English spoken in, or near, the (formerly) Celtic-speaking areas of the British Isles which shows that, although Lass's methodological principle is a useful tool, it does not suffice to account for some of the problematic linguistic phenomena found in these varieties. More specifically, I will argue that the case for contact influence remains strong even with respect to some features which have formal parallels both in earlier English and in the various Celtic 'substratum' languages. I will begin by trying to explicate what is meant by the 'Principle of Parsimony', as I have chosen to call Lass's position here (I prefer 'principle of parsimony' to 'law of parsimony', which, though perhaps better established, sounds antiquated at least for linguistic purposes). This preamble will be followed by a discussion of some problematic cases which can be explained either in terms of endogenous growth or contact influence.

2   The principle of parsimony

One of the most explicit formulations of the Principle of Parsimony (PP) is to be found in Lass (1997). Writing on Afrikaans word order in certain types of subordinate contexts, Lass first notes that Afrikaans normally follows the verb-final pattern familiar from German and some other West Germanic languages. Consider (1) from Lass (1997: 198):

(1)   ek   het   gesê,   dat   ek   siek   *was*
        I   have   PP-say   that   I   sick   was
        'I said that I was sick'

However, in some contexts the conjunction can be left out and the verb moved into V2 position, as in (2) (quoted from Lass 1997: 198):

(2)   hy het gesê, hy *was* siek

This feature of Afrikaans has, as Lass points out, often been attributed to English influence. Among the factors which support interference from English, he mentions long-standing contacts between Afrikaans and English in South Africa, extensive bilingualism and mutual borrowing, the existence of a parallel feature in American Flemish, and finally, the fact that speakers of Afrikaans themselves typically consider this feature to be a stigmatised 'anglicismus' (Lass 1997: 199). Lass's own conclusion, however, is altogether different: for him, endogenous development is in this case a more likely source than contact because similar word order variation is found in German and Frisian. This is shown by the examples in (3) and (4), respectively (both quoted from Lass 1997: 199). Neither of these languages have had such close contacts with English as Afrikaans has in the South African setting.

(3)   *German*
        a. ich sagte, daß ich krank *war*
        b. ich sagte, ich *war* krank
(4)   *Frisian*
        a. hy   sei,   det   er   it   net   verdwaen   *scoe*
           he   says   COMP   he   it   NEG   do-again   *shall*
           'he says that he won't do it again'
        b. hy sei, hy *scoe* it net verdwaen

In situations like this, when a given feature is shared by a language (or variety) and (at least some of) its genetically closely related varieties, endogeny – or, to be more precise, common inheritance in this case – provides a more parsimonious account of the facts and is therefore to be preferred to language contact. Lass formulates this in terms of a general methodological principle as follows:

Therefore, in the absence of evidence [for either endogeny or contact – MF], an endogenous change *must* occur in any case, whereas borrowing is never necessary. If the (informal) probability weightings of both source-types converge for a given character, then the choice goes to endogeny.   (Lass 1997: 209)

Lass's principle can be said to be directed against scholars whom he describes as 'contact romantics', who, as Lass puts it, seek to derive 'the maximal number of characters in a given language from contact sources' (Lass 1997: 201). The PP could in fact be considered a variant of the well-known Occam's Razor, which precludes one from postulating more entities than is necessary (for discussion of the use of Occam's Razor in historical linguistics, see Hock 1991: 538–40). In cases where endogeny and foreign influence provide equally plausible explanations for a given feature, contact influence constitutes the 'unnecessary' entity and must therefore give way to endogeny.

For a historical linguist, the situation described above is not at all uncommon, and some methodological guidelines such as the PP are needed in order to distinguish between rival sources. What is important, though, is that prior to evoking this or any other principle all the necessary homework has been done to sort out the possible sources of a given feature. This is something that Lass himself emphasises when he writes:

I am not trying in any way to rule out syntactic borrowing; but merely suggesting how any suspect case ought to be investigated. Above all, one should never take apparent similarity, even in cases of known contact with evidence for other borrowing, as probative until the comparative work (if it's possible) has been done. The conclusion might be that anything can be borrowed, and often is; but in a given case it's always both simpler and safer to assume that it isn't, unless the evidence is clear and overwhelming.

(Lass 1997: 201)

In the following, I will discuss a couple of lexical and syntactic examples which are meant to test the validity of the PP and also to illustrate some of the complications which may arise when one tries to find a unitary source for a given feature. My examples are drawn from the context of contacts between English and one or another of the Celtic languages spoken in the British Isles. I will start off with a brief description of the main features of the Celtic–English contacts and of some of the methodological problems involved.

3   The general nature of the Celtic–English contacts

Linguistic contacts between the Celtic languages and English span a very long period, starting from the first encounters between the British Celts and the invading Germanic tribes in the latter half of the fifth century. The traditional wisdom is that, because of the political and social hegemony of the Anglo-Saxons, the linguistic influences went rather one-sidedly from English to Celtic, and whatever impact the Celts had on the English language was restricted to a handful of loanwords and a number of place-names and names of rivers. Along with the later differentiation of the Insular Celtic languages, linguistic contacts between English and Celtic have come to embrace several Celtic languages, each with its many regional and social varieties. And of course, English itself has similarly branched out into numerous subvarieties, which adds to the extreme complexity of the contact setting(s), with the dating and precise nature of contacts varying greatly from one region to another. A further influential factor is the large-scale language shift from Celtic languages to English which has taken place in most of the formerly Celtic-speaking areas in Scotland, Wales, Cornwall and Ireland over the last few centuries. What also complicates the picture is the nature of the transmission and acquisition of English, which has ranged from 'naturalistic' acquisition, as in Ireland and Wales at certain periods, to formal instruction in schools, as in some parts of Scotland, for example. This is then reflected in the linguistic outcome in varying degrees of influences from the substratum languages.

Besides the chequered nature and history of the Celtic–English interface, our historical linguist is faced with scant documentation of the earliest periods of contacts and their linguistic outcomes. A telling example of the difficulties encountered by scholars is Caroline Macafee's observation that, in Scottish dictionaries, there are many words which have been ascribed to Scots origin in dictionaries of Gaelic, while the same words have been labelled as being of Gaelic origin in dictionaries of Scots (Macafee 1996: xxxiv; see also Macafee forthcoming). Establishing the chronological priority in each disputable case would, as Macafee points out, help to settle the direction of borrowing but can be difficult to document in the Scottish contact setting because of the lack of early records. It is true that more evidence is available from the early modern period onwards both from the Celtic languages and from the dialects of English which emerged in the formerly Celtic-speaking areas as a result of language shift and large-scale settlements of English speakers coming from various parts of the British Isles. The varieties of English spoken in Scotland, Wales and Ireland are known to exhibit many lexical, grammatical and other features which have close parallels in the corresponding Celtic languages. This in itself does not, of course, suffice to confirm that substratum transfer has taken place, which also becomes evident from Lass's cautionary note in the quotation above.

4   Problems with lexical parallels

Macafee (forthcoming; see also Macafee 1996) provides an insightful discussion of the kinds of problems associated with lexical parallels. These had arisen during the process of the compilation of the *Concise Ulster Dictionary* (*CUD*), which sets out to record words typical of the English and Scots dialects spoken in Ulster and their etymologies. Macafee notes, first, that parallels can be of common Indo-European ancestry, and hence no borrowing in one direction or the other need be assumed. As an example, she mentions the word *cat*, which is identical in English (including Ulster dialects) and Irish. Secondly, parallels may represent mutual borrowing from a third language; such is the case with English *couple* and its Irish counterpart *cúpla* 'a pair of roof beams', which both derive from Old French. Thirdly, parallels may arise as a result of sheer coincidence. As a possible example of this category, Macafee mentions one of the dialectal Scots/English pronunciations of *balk*, which coincides with Irish *bac* 'a hob' (referring to the angular space formed by rafters). These kinds of consideration led Macafee to adopt a rather strict editorial policy with regard to putative Irish borrowings in the *CUD*. In her editor's introduction to the *CUD*, she writes:

Because the dialects we are dealing with in this dictionary are essentially English or Scots, we make the presumption that if a word, form, sense, compound, or phrase has a prior history in English or Scots then that is the source of the Ulster item.

(Macafee 1996: xxxiii)

She adds, however, that

[t]here may nevertheless be support or reinforcement from Irish, which shares a large vocabulary with English/Scots both through their common membership of the Indo-European language family, and through borrowing in both directions.

(Macafee 1996: xxxiii)

Macafee's editorial solution in cases in which the precedence has not been, or cannot be, solved was to mark a word as being found 'also in Irish, origin unknown' (1996: xxxiv).

While Macafee's stand can be seen as a carefully thought-out and justified application of the PP, this is not always so with the approach adopted in some other etymological dictionaries, including even the *OED*. Through meticulous research, Andrew Breeze has been able to show that perfectly plausible Celtic sources exist for a fair number of words labelled as being of 'obscure' or 'unknown origin' in the *OED*. Breeze's examples include Old English *deor* 'brave', for which he suggests Welsh origin (Breeze 1997); Old English *gop* 'servant', which is most likely a borrowing from Old Irish *gop* 'snout' (Breeze 1995); Middle English *brag* 'boast', which Breeze derives from Welsh *brag* 'malt' (Breeze 1994); and numerous other Old and Middle English words for which plausible Celtic sources exist. Breeze's findings can be said to cast serious doubt on the standard 'textbook' view on the tiny amounts of Celtic loanwords in English. Without going into any further detail here, it seems clear that the editors of the *OED* have been too cautious about the possibility of foreign, and especially Celtic, influence. Indeed, in many cases their judgement appears to have been based on some preconceived notion about the *im*possibility of such borrowing, instead of being based on comparative and historical research.

It is a general observation that lexicon and grammar respond differently to contact influences, and that this largely depends on the nature of the contact situation (see, e.g., Thomason and Kaufman 1988). Lexical borrowing is common enough in language maintenance situations, whereas structural borrowing typically occurs in conditions of language shift. Since the latter type of situation obtains in most parts of the Celtic areas, it is useful to examine next some of the methodological problems associated with possible structural borrowings between the Celtic languages and English.

5   Grammatical borrowing between English and the Celtic languages

It is commonly held that, at the grammatical level, English owes very little, if anything at all, to the Celtic languages. Some scholars have, however, suggested that a fair number of even the 'core' grammatical constructions of English are best explained as borrowings from Celtic. These include the 'expanded' or *-ing* form of verbs (see, e.g., Keller 1925; Dal 1952; Braaten 1967), the cleft construction (see, e.g., Visser 1955; Preusler 1956), and the so-called *do-*periphrasis (see, e.g., Preusler 1956; Poussa 1990). These suggestions have not been generally accepted for various reasons: in some cases, there is a lack of data from the relevant periods, or the timing is claimed to be wrong from the point of view of contact influences; in yet others, it seems very hard to distinguish between influences deriving from Celtic and Latin or Greek (see, e.g., Dal 1952 and Mossé 1938 on the origins of the *-ing* form). Rather than go into these vexed questions in this connection, I will here focus on the later periods of contact and use as my examples two features which have been found to be salient in the present-day dialects of English spoken in, or close to, the formerly Celtic-speaking areas.

I will begin with an example which illustrates particularly well the value of the PP as a criterion for choosing between endogeny vs. contact. This is the so-called *be* perfect in Hiberno-English (HE), which has been shown to make more extensive use of this type of perfect than most other varieties of English (see, e.g., Kallen 1989; Filppula 1999). Examples from present-day spoken HE are given in (5)-(6), both recorded from speakers who come from the counties of Kerry and Clare in the (south)west of Ireland (for further details of the HE database, see Filppula 1999):

(5)   I know they*'re gone* mad here in motorcars. (Kerry: M.C.; cited in Filppula 1999: 116)

(6)   There was a lot about fairies long ago – whether they were right or wrong – but I'm thinkin' that most of 'em *are vanished*. (Clare: M.R.; cited in Filppula 1999: 117)

Now, a perfect parallel for the HE *be* perfect can be found in Irish, which has no equivalent of the English *have* and always uses the verb 'be' (*tá*) to form a periphrastic perfect, as in (7) cited by Ó Sé (1992: 46):

(7)   Tá sé imithe.
        'Is he/it gone.'

On the other hand, the *be* perfect is also part of the grammar of English, and especially of its earlier stages. Consider, for example, the following instances found in the last subsection of the Early Modern part of the Helsinki Corpus, which covers the period 1640–1710 (for the reference codes after each example, see Kytö 1991):

(8)   This day letters *are come* that my sister is very ill. (E3 NN DIARY PEPYS VIII, 314)

(9)   [...] and that it was scarce possible to know certainly whether our Hearts *are changed*, unless it appeared in our lives; [...] (E3 NN BIO BURNETROC 147)

One could build a case for contact influence if the HE *be* perfect could be shown to exhibit some qualitative features which are not found in other dialects of English or in their earlier stages. So far at least, no conclusive evidence of that kind is available; this construction appears to be more frequent in HE than in other varieties but follows lexical and other constraints which are shared by especially the earlier English parallels. What is also important is the fact that the rivalry between *be* vs. *have* in earlier English was not settled in favour of the latter until relatively late, namely the early part of the nineteenth century (see, e.g., Rydén 1991). This, in turn, means that the superstratal model for the HE *be* perfect must have been available to the large numbers of Irish speakers acquiring English in that period. Therefore, endogenous origin is more likely than contact in explaining the presence of this feature in HE – which does not, of course, exclude 'reinforcing' influence from Irish. The latter is supported by Filppula's (1999: 119–20) observation according to which the *be* perfect is particularly common and still fairly productive in those dialects of HE which are, or have been until very recently, in close contact with Irish.

Despite the strength of evidence pointing to endogenous origin, there is a possible complication even here: the *be* perfect of English and its Irish counterpart can be considered to belong to the set of typological features shared by many West European languages, including German and French. Seen from this perspective, the English *be* perfect and its counterparts in other West European languages constitute a case of converging development, in spite of the fact that present-day Standard English has almost completely lost this feature. To turn back to HE, the areal and typological perspective does not necessarily change the story about the 'immediate' source of the HE *be* perfect but perhaps makes its occurrence in this variety more predictable. Methodologically, then, the application of the PP yields the right result in this case as far as the primary source of the feature is concerned, but if the research stops there, we miss an important aspect of the phenomenon, and our explanation, if not untrue as such, remains incomplete (cf. Thomason and Kaufman 1988: 58 on the need for 'complete' explanations).

Let us next consider another, slightly more complicated, case. Hiberno-English and some varieties of Scottish English (including Scots) are known to make extensive use of a syntactic feature which could be termed the 'absolute' use of reflexive pronouns. This involves the use of reflexives without an antecedent noun or pronoun, as in the following examples from HE and Scots:

(10)   And by God, he said, [...] he'd be the devil, if *himself* wouldn' make him laugh. (Kerry: M.C.; cited in Filppula 1999: 78)

(11)   [W]hen Cromwell came over here [...] he was s'posed to say, he'd drive the Irish to hell or Connacht [...] The Irish used to say [...] the Irish went to Connacht and left hell *for himself*. (Dublin: W.H.; cited in Filppula 1999: 78)

(12)   Is that *yoursel'*, Mr Balfour? (*Scottish National Dictionary* s.v. *your*; quoted here from Macafee and Ó Baoill 1997: 271)

Again, close parallels (though not so complete as in the case of the *be* perfect) exist in Irish and Scottish Gaelic, but also in earlier English. Though rather rare, instances like (13) and (14) can be found in the EModE part of the Helsinki Corpus.

(13)   ...in conclusion when $y = t = $ no colour could fasten vpon these matters, then he layd heinously to her charge, $y = e = $ thing $y = t = her$ *self* could not deny, that al $y = e = $ world wist was true, [...] (E1 NN HIST MORERIC 54: Heading)

(14)   Whence (ˆEdanˆ) King of those (ˆScotsˆ) that dwelt in (ˆBritainˆ), jealous of his successes, came against him with a mighty Army, to a place call'd (ˆDegsastanˆ); but in the fight loosing most of his men, *himself* with a few escap'd: [...] (E3 NN HIST MILTON X, 146: Heading)

Given the existence of earlier English parallels, the PP invites us to conclude that this feature must be of endogenous origin. Yet, it is interesting to note that Macafee and Ó Baoill (1997) ascribe it to Gaelic influence in Scots, although, generally speaking, they consider the grammatical input of Gaelic to Scots to be very limited for the reasons usually cited in this context: Gaelic was in a socially inferior position to Scots, which meant that Scots speakers had no real need for linguistic borrowing from Gaelic. In this case, however, the chronological priority of the Gaelic usage favours substratal origin: emphasising forms with *féin* 'self', parallel to the Scots usage, have been documented in Gaelic since the eighth century (Macafee and Ó Baoill 1997: 271).

Besides HE and Scots, absolute reflexives are a feature of the dialects of English spoken in the Western Isles of Scotland, usually collectively termed Hebridean English (HebE). This variety forms a suitable point of comparison with HE, as it has also emerged as a result of language shift from a Celtic language, which happens to be almost identical to Irish (being an early offshoot of Irish). An important difference between HE and HebE is that the latter is of more recent vintage than HE and hence not so likely to have preserved features from earlier and especially southern English. Nonetheless, HebE displays exactly the same usage with reflexives as HE, as can be seen from the following examples drawn from Sabban's (1982) study of HebE and from my own HebE database collected from the tape and transcript archives of the School of Scottish Studies at Edinburgh University (for further details, see Filppula 1999):

(15)   *Yourself and Annie* could come and see me. (P&P, Skye; cited in Sabban 1982: 367)

(16)   And he wouldn't let anybody very young, boy or girl, if they were taking dinner, if they were around, they had to sit beside *himself* on the bench. (SA 1970/103/A/Tiree: H.K.; cited in Filppula 1999: 85)

(17)   [...] I used to say to him, 'You be careful about that money you've got, I'm sure it's *myself* that will get it after you.' (SA 1970/94/A/Tiree: D.S.; cited in Filppula 1999: 85)

Sabban's (1982) conclusion is that the most likely source of the HebE absolute reflexives is the corresponding Gaelic usage rather than that of earlier English. In a similar vein, Odlin (1997) argues for contact influence at least with respect to some aspects of the use of HebE and also of HE absolute reflexives. As one of the factors which support Celtic influence he mentions the preferred pattern of ordering in conjoined subjects involving an absolute reflexive: both HebE and HE prefer reflexive-first order, which is illustrated by Sabban's example in (15) above. Both Irish and Gaelic share this tendency; an example from Irish is given in (18) from Ó Siadhail (1980: 41):

(18) | Tá | mé | féin | agus | Ruairí | sásta. |
        |----|----|------|------|--------|--------|
        | Is | me | self | and | Ruairí | content |
        'Ruairí and I are content.'

Another distinctive feature shared by HE, HebE, and the two Celtic substratum languages is the possibility of placing the reflexive in the focus position of a cleft construction, as in (19) cited by Odlin (1997) from HebE (see also (17) above). Its Gaelic counterpart is illustrated in (20), which has been recorded from the same bilingual speaker.

(19)   And it's *himself* that told me that up in a pub. (SA 1970/105B/Tiree: H.K.; cited in Odlin 1997: 39)

(20) | agus | 's | e | fhéin | a | bh' | ann. |
        |------|-----|-----|-------|------|------|------|
        | and | is | him | self | that | was | in-it |
        'It was himself that was there.'
        (SA 1970/109/A/Tiree: H.K.; cited in Odlin 1997: 39)

The qualitative features of HE and HebE absolute reflexives, coupled with the fact that they occur in varieties whose speakers have had the corresponding Celtic patterns readily available at least until recently, compel us to conclude that at least some aspects of the uses of absolute reflexives in these varieties (including, most probably, Scots) are the result of direct contact influence. This does not exclude the possibility of conservatism with regard to those patterns which are attested in earlier English. Multiple causation, or 'fusion of endogeny and exogeny', as Lass and Wright (1986: 217) put it, is indeed a possibility which has always to be taken into account. Neither should we forget the possibility of adstratal influences between earlier English, Scots and the Celtic languages, despite the general lack of enthusiasm among historical linguists for this type of explanation (see, e.g., Thomason and Kaufman 1988: 95). As Macafee (1996: xxxiii) notes in the quotation above, 'borrowing in both directions' must have occurred in the Ulster situation, and there is no reason to assume that it has not taken place in other similar contact situations in the British Isles. The methodological lesson here is that, as in the case of the *be* perfect, we must here too examine all possible aspects of the use of the construction at issue and look hard for sociohistorical and other 'extra-linguistic' evidence before settling for explanations based on the PP or on contact-induced change, for that matter.

6   Conclusion

The discussion above has shown that, while a useful methodological starting point, the PP cannot provide the sole basis for deciding between endogeny vs. contact. Looking for the most parsimonious explanation in a given case may well be a virtue in itself, or produce the most satisfying solutions from an aesthetic perspective, but in my view it does not change the fact that the quest must always be for the *best* explanations whether more or less parsimonious. Hock's (1991) discussion of the applicability of Occam's Razor to the reconstruction of the inflectional paradigms of Old Latin offers a good point of reference here. What according to him provides the most economical explanation may not necessarily be the best:

> Given two alternative analyses, we will prefer the one which provides *greater explanation or motivation* for the postulated changes, as well as for the attested synchronic facts. Such explanations often refer to issues of over-all linguistic structure.
>
> (Hock 1991: 536; my emphasis – MF)

In a similar vein, Thomason and Kaufman (1988: 58) emphasise the importance of 'complete' explanations. They also caution against rejecting a contact-based explanation simply because a similar change has been observed to have taken place in some other setting (Thomason and Kaufman 1988: 59):

The flaw in this type of argument is its assumption that a given change that arises through internal motivation in one language can and should automatically be ascribed to the same sort of cause when it occurs in another language. Since even the most natural changes often fail to occur, it is always appropriate to ask why a particular change happened when it did.

Both Hock's and Thomason and Kaufman's remarks are relevant to the cases discussed above. Indeed, one could argue that even Lass's Afrikaans example discussed in section 2 could be explained in terms of contact influence rather than as endogenous growth. Despite the parallels in its European sister languages, Afrikaans may well have developed the optional V2 order in subordinate clauses mainly through the influence from English, which has long had a strong presence on the local scene. Be that as it may, the Afrikaans case also illustrates the methodological difficulty of choice between endogeny and contact.

Disagreements as to what weight each of the proposed methodological principles should be assigned in a given case are bound to remain part of the scholarly discourse, but certain things seem to me uncontroversial. First, as Lass (1997: 200–1) argues, apparent similarity, i.e. a mere formal parallel, cannot serve as proof of contact influence – neither can it prove something to be of endogenous origin, I would like to add on the basis of the examples discussed above. Before jumping to conclusions it is always necessary to examine the earlier history and the full syntactic, semantic and functional range of the features at issue, and also search for every possible kind of extra-linguistic evidence such as the extent of bilingualism in the speech communities involved, the chronological priority of rival sources, the geographical or areal distribution of the feature(s) at issue, demographic phenomena, etc. Secondly – again in line with Lass's thinking (see, e.g., Lass 1997: 208) – it is true to say that, from the point of view of the actual research, there is always a greater amount of homework in store for those who want to find conclusive evidence for contact influence than for those arguing for endogeny. On the other hand, even if endogeny is hard to rule out, as was shown by the examples discussed above, it does not follow that there would be no room for contact-based explanations or for those based on an interaction of factors. The linguistic history of the Celtic–English interface provides, as we have seen, good examples of all types of explanation.

REFERENCES

Braaten, B. 1967. 'Notes on continuous tenses in English', *Norsk tidskrift for sprogvidenskap* 21: 167–80.
Breeze, Andrew. 1994. 'Celtic etymologies for Middle English *brag* "boast", *gird* "strike", and *lethe* "soften"', *Journal of Celtic Linguistics* 3: 135–48.
Breeze, Andrew. 1995. 'Old English *gop* "servant" in Riddle 49: Old Irish *gop* "snout"', *Neophilologus* 79: 671–3.

Breeze, Andrew. 1997. 'A Celtic etymology for Old English *deor* "brave" ', in J. Roberts and J. L. Nelson with M. Godden (eds.), *Alfred the wise: studies in honour of Janet Bately on the occasion of her sixty-fifth birthday.* Cambridge: D.S. Brewer, 1–4.

Dal, Ingerid. 1952. 'Zur Entstellung des Englischen Participium Praesentis auf -ing', *Norsk tidskrift for sprogvidenskap* 16: 5–116.

Filppula, Markku. 1999. *The grammar of Irish English: language in Hibernian style.* Routledge Studies in Germanic Linguistics 5. London and New York: Routledge.

Hock, Hans Henrich. 1991. *Principles of historical linguistics*, 2nd edition. Berlin and New York: Mouton de Gruyter.

Kallen, Jeffrey L. 1989. 'Tense and aspect categories in Irish English', *English World-Wide* 10: 1–39.

Keller, Wolfgang. 1925. 'Keltisches im englischen Verbum', *Anglica: Untersuchungen zur englischen Philologie (Alois Brandl zum siebzigsten Geburtstage überreicht)*, 55–66.

Kytö, Merja. 1991. *Manual to the diachronic part of the Helsinki Corpus of English Texts.* Helsinki: Department of English, University of Helsinki.

Lass, Roger. 1990a. 'Where do Extraterritorial Englishes come from?', in Sylvia Adamson et al. (eds.), *Papers from the 5th International Conference of English Historical Linguistics, Cambridge, 6–9 April 1987.* Amsterdam and Philadelphia: Benjamins, 245–80.

Lass, Roger. 1990b. 'Early mainland residues in Southern Hiberno-English', *Irish University Review* 20: 137–48.

Lass, Roger. 1997. *Historical linguistics and language change.* Cambridge University Press.

Lass, Roger and Susan Wright. 1986. 'Endogeny vs. contact: "Afrikaans influence" on South African English', *English World-Wide* 7: 201–23.

Macafee, Caroline. 1996. 'Editor's introduction', in Caroline Macafee (ed.), *A concise Ulster dictionary.* Oxford University Press, xvi–xxxvii.

Macafee, Caroline. Forthcoming. 'The under-representation of Celtic etymologies in English dictionaries', *Folia Linguistica Anglica.*

Macafee, Caroline and Colm Ó Baoill. 1997. 'Why Scots is not a Celtic English', in Hildegard L. C. Tristram (ed.), *The Celtic Englishes.* Heidelberg: Universitätsverlag C. Winter, 245–86.

Mossé, Fernand. 1938. *Histoire de la forme périphrastique ETRE + participe présent en germanique. Deuxième partie: moyen-anglais et anglais moderne.* Paris: Librairie C. Klincksieck.

Odlin, Terence. 1997. 'Bilingualism and substrate influence: a look at clefts and reflexives', in Jeffrey L. Kallen (ed.), *Focus on Ireland.* Amsterdam: John Benjamins, 35–50.

Ó Sé, Diarmuid. 1992. 'The perfect in Modern English', *Ériu* 43: 39–67.

Ó Siadhail, Mícheál. 1980. *Learning Irish: an introductory self-tutor.* Dublin: Dublin Institute for Advanced Studies.

Poussa, Patricia. 1990. 'A contact-universals origin for periphrastic *do*, with special consideration of OE-Celtic contact', in Sylvia Adamson et al. (eds.), *Papers from the 5th International Conference of English Historical Linguistics, Cambridge, 6–9 April 1987.* Amsterdam: John Benjamins, 407–33.

Preusler, Wolfgang. 1956. 'Keltischer Einfluss im Englischen', *Revue des langues vivantes* 22: 322–50.

Rydén, Mats. 1991. 'The *be/have* variation with intransitives in its crucial phases', in Dieter Kastovsky (ed.), *Historical English syntax*. Berlin: Mouton de Gruyter, 343–54.

Sabban, Annette. 1982. *Gälisch-Englischer Sprachkontakt*. Heidelberg: Julius Groos.

Thomason, Sarah G. and Terence Kaufman. 1988. *Language contact, creolization, and genetic linguistics*. Berkeley, CA: University of California Press.

Visser, Gerrard J. 1955. 'Celtic influence in English', *Neophilologus* 39: 276–93.

11   Diagnosing prehistoric language contact

Malcolm Ross

1   Introduction

The goal of this chapter is to look at the possibility of using various patterns in comparative data to reconstruct different kinds of language contact. I ask the reader to forgive a somewhat autobiographical introduction, but this is the most direct way I know of explaining why this goal is worthy of pursuit.

I spent much of the 1980s on an analysis of genetic relationships among the two hundred or so Oceanic Austronesian languages of northwest Melanesia (Papua New Guinea and the western Solomon Islands), using the classical comparative method of historical linguistics (Ross 1988). One of the things I noticed again and again was the quantity of data which was left unaccounted for. In the case of lexical items this was either because there was nothing in other languages to compare them with (that is, there were no cognate forms) or because they did not show regular sound correspondences with apparent cognates in other languages. More significantly, there were other patterns in the data which I could not account for because the comparative method does not have much to say about them. They consisted, for example, of:

  – an apparent sudden increase in phonological and morphological com-
    plexity in a single language compared with its neighbours;
  – radical differences in syntax between languages which seemed other-
    wise quite closely related;
  – similarities in semantic organisation, sometimes accompanied by syn-
    tactic similarity, which were expressed by quite different forms in the
    relevant languages.

I became aware of cases where Austronesian and Papuan languages (which were definitely not related to each other) displayed both very similar concep-tualisations of the world and very similar syntactic patterns. These phenomena will be illustrated below.

Another thing that intrigued me was that the quantity of unaccounted-for material varied enormously from language to language. Some languages were 'well behaved', in the sense that they neatly reflected the reconstructed lexicon and morphosyntax of Proto-Oceanic, whereas some others appeared remarkably ill behaved. That is, they contained much less material that I could use in comparisons and, conversely of course, much more material that I could not account for. Now, if we assume that *all* of a language reflects its history in one way or another, then it follows for these languages that I was accounting for much less of their history than in the case of a well-behaved language.

I was reasonably certain that the causes of the problem lay in contact between speakers of different languages, and I was not the first person to think this about languages in northwest Melanesia. Ill-behaved Oceanic languages have been explained as the outcomes of pidginisations involving various now defunct substrata (Capell 1943), or as the progeny of language mixing (Ross 1996).[1] I was also well enough aware of Trubetzkoy's (1930) concept of the *Sprachbund* or 'language alliance',[2] which he applied particularly in the context of the Balkans, where a number of languages share similar semantic and syntactic patterns as a result of centuries of contact. But I was frustrated with these explanations. There were several reasons for this. One was that it was not clear what terms like 'pidginisation' or 'language mixing' were intended to mean in this context. Another was that the internal workings of these alleged contact processes were opaque. Indeed, it was not even clear how many different processes I was actually confronted with, let alone how one might distinguish between them.[3]

Linguists have been talking about contact phenomena for as long as they have talked about family trees, but it was Weinreich's 1953 *Languages in contact* that started to draw them back towards the centre of historical linguistics. However, it was not until the publication of Thomason and Kaufman's (1988) book *Language contact, creolization and genetic linguistics* that a change in the linguistic climate became obvious with regard to contact-induced change. The climate change since 1988 is indicated by the growing number of publications that have been appearing on language contact. What was a trickle (e.g. Gumperz and Wilson 1971; Heath 1978; Sasse 1985; Van Coetsem 1988) has become a flood (e.g. Aikhenvald 1996; Bakker 1994; Bakker and Mous 1994; Bechert and Wildgen 1991; Dutton and Tryon 1994; Grace 1996; Haase 1992, 1993; Nau 1995; Nicolaï 1990; Prince 1998; Ross 1996; Soper 1996; Thurgood 1996, 1999).[4]

---

[1] The language mixing hypotheses about Papua New Guinea languages go back at least to 1911, and have tended to centre on Maisin, a language spoken in several scattered enclaves on the north coast of southeast Papua (the literature on Maisin is summarised in Ross 1996e).

[2] In recent literature the term 'linguistic area' is often used for a *Sprachbund*, but this is too vague and is capable of other uses. The term 'convergence area' is more specific, but entails a presupposition about process that *Sprachbund* does not.

[3] On a more theoretical level, I found it unsatisfactory that the comparative method has almost nothing to say about contact phenomena, which seemed to be the step-children of comparative linguistics.

[4] Ironically, the best-documented modern study of contact-induced change that I know from before 1988 does not appear in Thomason and Kaufman's bibliography. This is Sasse's (1985) paper on the Albanian varieties spoken in Greece.

Thomason and Kaufman (1988: 50) distinguish two main contexts of contact-induced change:
a. language shift (that is, what occurs when a group of people cease to speak one language and speak another instead);
b. bilingualism, where the speakers' second language brings about change in their first.

Both contexts entail the behaviours of speech communities, and they argue strongly that 'it is the sociolinguistic history of the speakers, and not the structure of their language, that is the primary determinant of the linguistic outcome of language contact' (Thomason and Kaufman 1988: 35). If they are correct – and I believe they are – then it follows that when we use patterns in linguistic data to diagnose prehistoric language contact, what we are diagnosing are circumstances in the history of a speech community.

Thomason and Kaufman collected together a large number of cases of contact-induced change and classified them according to their contexts, thereby laying some of the groundwork for a theory of contact-induced change. However, although they provide a classification of types of contact-induced change, they do not really provide us with a paradigm of patterns in the data which we can use to reconstruct different types of change. In other words, they do not provide a means of *diagnosing* contact. This chapter is an attempt to take a preliminary step in this direction by providing a basic paradigm of the circumstances which give rise to contact-induced change and of some of the patterns in the data that may allow us to diagnose them. How accurate such diagnosis can be will be known only after a good deal of future research.

2   Speech communities and social networks

I referred above to 'speech communities'. The concept of the 'speech community' is often used by linguists but seldom defined. The standard definition seems to be that a speech community is a community of people speaking the same language, but Grace (1996) points out that this will not work, since it is a normal human state for people to speak more than one language.[5] Instead he suggests a definition which avoids the word 'language' altogether:

A speech community consists of those people who communicate with one another or are connected to one another by chains of speakers who communicate with one another.
(Grace 1996: 172)

That is, a speech community is simply a network of relationships among speakers, in the sense in which the term 'social network' has been given currency among linguists in the work of Lesley and James Milroy (Lesley Milroy

---

[5] There are certainly more subtle definitions of speech communities, but they are fundamentally flawed: on this subject see Romaine (1982) and Dorian (1982).

1980/1987; James Milroy 1992, 1993).[6] Since 'chains of speakers' can be potentially of any length, speech community and social network are both a matter of degree. A speaker in a traditional Papua New Guinean community lives in a hamlet, which belongs to a village, which belongs to a group of villages recognised as speaking the same dialect, which belongs to a larger collection of villages speaking dialects recognised as being of the same language, and so on, up the scale. These are all speech communities.

Lesley Milroy (1980: 20, 49–52, 139–44) describes the structures of social networks using various measures of the social links between speakers, but these measures are of less importance to us here than the way relationships are clustered. Thus if a Papua New Guinean language is spoken in, say, four villages, there will be relationship links among speakers within a village, and also relationship links between speakers from the four villages. But the links within each village will be stronger and will cluster more densely than the links between villages. There are also likely to be links (through marriage and trade) with villages speaking other languages, and it is of course here that bilingualism comes into play.

It is a linguistic truism that there is no sharp boundary between the concepts of 'a language' and 'a dialect', and one can dodge the terminological problem by referring to both simply as 'lects' and to speakers who speak two or more lects as 'polylectal'. There is, of course, a sense in which even monolingual English speakers are polylectal, in that they vary their speech according to interlocutor and speech situation, but these speakers know that they only speak English. The term 'polylectal' is reserved here for speakers who are aware that the linguistic repertoire they carry in their heads consists of two or more separate lects for which in many cases they will have separate names.

The determinants of contact-induced change can largely be defined in terms of events and circumstances which affect the structure of social networks. The first question that needs to be asked is: was contact-induced change the result of the abrupt creation or re-creation of a social network? If the answer is 'yes', then the change was 'catastrophic'. If it is 'no', it was 'noncatastrophic'. The cases referred to below belong mostly to the noncatastrophic category, but a brief exemplification of the catastrophic category is in order before we move on to them.

3   Catastrophic change

Catastrophic change occurs when a new community is suddenly created out of speakers from communities with different lects or when the internal structure of

---

[6] It is implicit in the Milroys' models that any language change begins in the speech of one or more speakers who adopt an innovation. If that innovation is copied by other speakers, thereby diffusing through the network of the community, it may become what the linguist observes as a language change (Milroy and Milroy 1985).

a larger community is suddenly rearranged. For example, European colonisation in the Pacific sometimes resulted in the reorganisation of communities, either deliberately for administrative reasons or accidentally through disease. Speakers of related lects were abruptly combined into a reorganised community. This seems to have happened on two islands in southern Vanuatu, Aneityum and Erromango, where on each island several languages were apparently reduced to one (Lynch and Tepahae 1997, Taki and Tryon 1997). Each modern language contains elements that can only be attributed to more than one forebear. For example in Aneityumese there are two reflexes of the Proto-Oceanic common article *na*:

(1)   Proto-Oceanic   Aneityumese
        bakiwa   *ne-pcev*   'shark'
        topu   *ne-to*   'sugarcane'
        kutu   *ne-cet*   'louse'
        mata-   *ne-mta-*   'eye'
        pudi   *no-hos*   'banana'
        baga   *in-pak*   'banyan'
        tapuRi   *in-tohou*   'Triton shell'
        kusupeq   *in-cedo*   'rat'
        manuk   *in-man*   'bird'
        patu   *in-hat*   'stone'

Lynch and Tepahae point out that there is no conditioning of the *nV-* and *in-* variants, and suggest that they are derived from two different languages. The fact that the variants were not levelled suggests that the two languages were fused together by a rapid and violent process of social reorganisation, rather than by a slower process of koineisation.

A more extreme kind of catastrophic change in the Pacific took place in the plantation communities which were suddenly created in Queensland and elsewhere by labour recruitment. Bringing together men from different parts of Melanesia with no common language resulted in the English-based Pacific Pidgin ancestral to the present-day lingua francas of Melanesia. In other parts of the world the creation of slave communities from different African groups without a common language resulted in what Thomason and Kaufman (1988: 147–66) call 'abrupt creolisation' – shift to an imperfectly learned target language (see, for example, Ferraz 1983 on the creoles of the Gulf of Guinea). Bakker and Mous's (1994) collection entitled *Mixed languages* draws attention to other kinds of catastrophic change. One is what Peter Bakker calls 'language intertwining', which apparently occurs when a group of men with one lect marry a group of women with another lect, with a result that is a fairly consistent mixture of the two lects. For example, Michif (Bakker 1994) mixes French and Cree: most nouns are French, verbs are almost all Cree, possessive pronouns are French, and so on. Copper Island Aleut intertwines Aleut and Russian (Golovko and Vakhtin 1990; Golovko 1994). Similar to intertwining is relexification, where the morphosyntax of one language is used with the lexicon of another. This seems to occur when a polylectal group sets out to create either its own emblematic lect (like Javindo, once spoken by people of mixed ancestry in Java with Javanese morphosyntax and Dutch lexicon; Gruiter 1994)[7] or a secret or in-group language (like Anglo-Romani with English morphosyntax and Romani lexicon; Boretzky and Igla 1994).

It is obvious that our understanding of the range and types of catastrophic change is rather limited. But our ignorance is excusable, in that catastrophic contact-induced change is much rarer than noncatastrophic. In fact, one could argue that the term 'catastrophic change' is a misnomer, since in most cases the result is better characterised as language birth rather than language change.[8]

4 Noncatastrophic change and the structures of speech communities

We turn now to a more extended discussion of noncatastrophic contact-induced change. Andersen (1988: 70–4) proposes two other determinants of contact-induced change which are reflected in social network structure. He makes distinctions between 'open' and 'closed' communities and between 'tightknit' and 'looseknit' communities. (Andersen uses the terms 'endocentric' and 'exocentric', but 'tightknit' and 'looseknit' are easier to process mentally.) Essentially, an open community is one with plentiful relationship links to speakers in other communities or in a larger community, and a closed community is one where such links are few. In other words, the open/closed distinction describes a community's *external* relationships. The tightknit/looseknit distinction, on the other hand, deals with a community's *internal* relationships. A tightknit community is, for Andersen, one where speakers are bound together by tight bonds of linguistic solidarity.

Andersen sees his tightknit/looseknit distinction as having to do with speakers' attitudes rather than network structure. It seems to me, however, that each of the two parameters can be expressed in terms of both network structure and speaker attitude. If a community is 'closed' – that is, it has few external links – then this fact correlates with the attitudes of its speakers, who are likely to feel in some way separate from speakers in other communities. And if a community is tightknit – that is, drawn together by bonds of linguistic

---

[7] Another is Media Lengua in Ecuador, Quechua morphosyntax with Spanish lexicon, spoken by the descendants of Quechua speakers who are culturally alienated from both rural Quechua and urban Spanish-speaking cultures (Muysken 1994).

[8] The distinction between catastrophic and noncatastrophic change is important, because their outcomes are different. Unfortunately, Thomason and Kaufman refer rather frequently to Ma'a, a celebrated case of language contact in Tanzania (Goodman 1971; Tucker and Bryan 1974; Thomason 1983), and use it as evidence for various statements about contact-induced change. However, if Mous's (1994) fieldwork-based findings are correct, Ma'a is a case of catastrophic change – relexification to create an in-group lect – and this means that any inferences drawn from it about noncatastrophic contact-induced change are shaky.

solidarity – then this will be reflected by the strength and clustering of the relationship links among its speakers.

Although Andersen does not say so, there is an implicational relationship between the two features: a community which is closed must also be tightknit (at least, it is hard to imagine how a closed community could not have strong internal relationships). An open community, on the other hand, may be tightknit or looseknit. In other words, the two feature pairs give us three possible types of speech community structure:

a. closed and tightknit
b. open...
    i. and tightknit
    ii. and looseknit

It should be obvious that these structural characteristics are in fact not binary distinctions but gradient parameters. That is, we can speak of degrees of 'closedness' and degrees of 'tightknitness' (and probably of degrees of catastrophe as well).[9] It follows from this that our three types are simply ideal types which many communities will approximate to.

4.1   Closed communities

A substantial part of Andersen (1988) is devoted to illustrating the kinds of sound change that typically occur in the speech of closed communities. His major example is the development of 'parasitic' consonants out of the offglide occlusion of long high vowels. For example, in the early twentieth-century German dialect of Waldeck in Hesse, we find the forms listed in (2):

(2)   Waldeck dialect earlier form standard German

Waldeck dialect	earlier form	standard German	
iks	**i:s*	*Eis*	'ice'
driksiç	**dri:siç*	*dreißig*	'thirty'
biksen	**bi:sen*	*beißen*	'bite'
pikfe	**pi:fe*	*Pfeife*	'(smoking) pipe'
likp	**li:p*	*Leib*	'body'
niŋne	**ni:ne*	*neun*	'nine'
fukst	**fu:st*	*Faust*	'fist'
uks	**u:s*	*aus*	'out (of)'
rukpe	**ru:pe*	*Raupe*	'caterpillar'
ruŋmen	**ru:men*	*räumen*	'clear away'

---

[9] Although the distinction between catastrophic and noncatastrophic change is a convenient one, it probably cannot be maintained as a binary distinction. We could, for example, label the transportation of north Indian labourers to Fiji as 'catastrophic', but the koineisation which has resulted in Fiji Hindi seems to have proceeded in a more leisurely manner.

The process which Andersen infers is something like this. At an earlier stage in the development of the Waldeck lect there was phonetic variation in the degree of occlusion in the offglide of long high vowels, ranging from [i:] to [ik]. At first, the occluded form [ik] was rare, but over time variation tipped in its favour for an increasing number of speakers, until it became the norm. Now, there is variation in speakers' pronunciations in any speech community, and there is a tendency for shifts in phonetic variation to occur, resulting in sound changes which have no other particular cause. We can call this 'background change'. But the development of parasitic consonants is a change of a special kind: it results in changes in the phonological forms of the words it affects because they gain a phoneme that was not there before. In more open communities, where there is greater variability in pronunciation across the community, it is much less likely that a sound change which changes the phonological shapes of words will become the norm. In a relatively small, closed community, there is nothing to stop this.

The idea that this kind of sound change occurs in closed communities is strikingly supported by the fact that Andersen finds parasitic consonants in various geographically separated dialects of German, Dutch, Rhaeto-Romance, Provençal, Danish and Latvian. Andersen is at pains to show that these similarities can hardly be attributed to a shared substratum, and the clincher in this respect is the fact that he also finds parasitic consonants in Maru, closely related to Burmese. What all these speech communities have in common is that they were or are closed, as a result of either geographical or sociopolitical isolation.

William Thurston (1987, 1989, 1994), independently of Andersen, it seems, has also reported on similar processes characteristic of closed communities in Oceanic Austronesian lects on the island of New Britain (Papua New Guinea). However, Thurston adds another sociolinguistic dimension by suggesting that, although these processes may *arise* as background change, speakers in a closed community may, so to speak, grab hold of them as emblems of their community and of its perceived separateness from other communities speaking related lects. In this way their lect becomes an 'in-group' code from which outsiders are consciously excluded. In the lect of a small closed community, norm enforcement will be strong, and innovations that lead to increased complexity and to differences from neighbouring lects will be favoured. The lexicon is elaborated with near synonyms, often by borrowing (Thurston 1989: 556), whilst elision and assimilation result in phonological compactness, in allophony and in allomorphy, so that irregularities are accumulated and the lect becomes increasingly difficult for one's neighbours to understand or learn (Thurston 1987: 55–60; 1989: 556). All these features are illustrated in the paradigms of the inalienable noun 'father' (i.e. 'my father', 'your father', etc.) in Aria, Tourai, Lamogai and Mouk in (3) (the Takia forms are discussed below). These are Oceanic languages of the Bibling (or Lamogai) family. Reconstructed

Proto-Western Oceanic (PWOc)[10] forms are given on the left. None of the Mouk forms reflects the PWOc. Instead, they are all derived from a sequence of three morphemes: the disposable possession classifier (reflecting PWOc *le-*), a possessor pronominal suffix (reflecting the suffixes of the PWOc forms) and the noun *au* 'father', copied from the Papuan language Anêm (Thurston 1996). The origin of the first-person-singular forms in Aria, Tourai and Lamogai is unknown, but they were probably vocatives. All other forms in (3) are derived from the PWOc forms by quite complex sets of changes:

(3)	PWOc	Aria	Tourai	Lamogai	Mouk	Takia
1S	*tama-gu*	*libou*	*abo*	*ibo*	*ligau*	*tama-g*
2S	*tama-mu*	*tmem*	*pmem*	*tumom*	*lemau*	*tama*
3S	*tama-ña*	*timla*	*timla*	*tumla*	*ilau*	*taman-n*
1IP	*tama-da*	*tmada*	*pmada*	*pmarte*	*udou*	*tama-d*
1EP	*tama-mami*	*tmemi*	*pmemi*	*pmimi*	*limau*	*tama-ma(ma)*
2P	*tama-miu*	*tmomu*	*pmomu*	*pmumu*	*lumau*	*tama-m(i)*
3P	*tama-dri*	*tmarak*	*pmarak*	*pmarsek*	*uxokau*	*tama-d(i)*

In a sense, these processes, which Thurston labels 'esoterogeny', are hardly a form of contact-induced change, but rather its converse, a reaction *against* other lects. However, as they are conceived by Thurston their prerequisite is at least minimal contact with another community speaking a related lect from which speakers of the esoteric lect are seeking to distance themselves. Thurston's conception raises an interesting question: if a community is small, and closed simply because it is totally isolated from other communities, will its lect accumulate complexities anyway, or is the accumulation of complexity really spurred on by the presence of another community to react against? I am not sure of the answer to this question.

4.2   Open and tightknit communities

It is reasonably obvious that speakers in a closed community will usually be monolectal. Speakers in an open community, especially a small one, are likely to be polylectal, and we can recognise among their lects a *primary* lect and one or more *secondary* lects. The primary lect is emblematic of its speakers' identity, but it is not necessarily the lect which is spoken most often. Secondary lects are used for external communication, and in some communities many

---

[10] PWOc is the ancestor of all the Oceanic languages of Santa Isabel, the New Georgia group and Choiseul in the Solomon Islands and of Papua New Guinea except for the St Matthias group and the Admiralties. On PWOc, see Ross (1988: ch. 10). PWOc was almost certainly a dialect chain rather than a discrete language, so the reconstruction of PWOc forms here is a liberty taken for presentational purposes, but it is a small liberty only, and one that makes no difference to the argument presented here.

speakers will speak a secondary lect more often than their emblematic primary lect.

For example, in modern Papua New Guinea, the general pattern is that a village has its own emblematic vernacular as its primary lect, and a lingua franca, most often Tok Pisin, as the secondary lect of most or all of its speakers. In premodern times, the secondary lect would normally not have been a pidgin, but the lect of a neighbouring village or a lect used as a regional trade language. Often there would have been more than one secondary lect spoken in the village. This pattern has no doubt been repeated thousands of times in premodern agricultural communities, and also survives, for example, in many parts of Europe where the primary lect is a so-called 'local dialect' and the secondary lect the 'standard language'.

Such communities are both *open* and *tightknit*. A tightknit community has a strong social network and values its primary lect highly for its emblematic significance. An open community uses one or more secondary lects for external communication. It is obvious that if this polylectalism continues over a long period of time, then contact-induced change is liable to occur. What is less obvious, perhaps, is that this change will normally be quite different from the kind that occurs in closed communities, and also rather different from the changes that result from language shift.

I have coined the word 'metatypy' (Ross 1996) for the kind of change that occurs in open but tightknit polylectal communities. Metatypy is the change in morphosyntactic type which a primary lect undergoes as a result of its speakers' bilingualism in a secondary lect.[11] Metatypy is what gives rise to a *Sprachbund* or language alliance, where two or more languages are in contact over a lengthy period and become structurally more and more similar, as has happened with diverse Indo-European languages in the Balkans (Joseph 1983) and with Indo-Aryan and Dravidian languages in India (Emeneau 1980). But what happens to languages during this growth in similarity and how this process occurs are less well known. It is often assumed that languages simply grow more similar to each other, converging on some kind of mean. However, almost all case studies show a one-sided process: one language (the primary lect) adapts morphosyntactically to the constructions of another (the secondary lect), with no change occurring in the latter.

The case of metatypy that I know best is Takia, an Oceanic Austronesian language spoken on Karkar Island, about fifty kilometres NNE of Madang town, on the north coast of Papua New Guinea. Takia speakers share their island with an almost equal number of speakers of Waskia, a Papuan language of the

---

[11] Metatypy is labelled 'grammatical interference' by Weinreich (1963 [1953]) and is subsumed under 'borrowing' by Thomason and Kaufman (1988). Neither of these terms seems to capture the thoroughgoing typological change which contact can bring about: hence the term 'metatypy'.

Trans New Guinea phylum. The Takia occupy the southern half of the island, the Waskia the northern half. Takia is unambiguously Oceanic in lexicon and bound morphology, which show regular sound correspondences with cognates in other Oceanic languages. Indeed, as the PWOc and Takia paradigms for 'father' in (3) show, Takia is well behaved in this respect. But syntactically Takia is much closer to its Papuan neighbour Waskia and far from the norms of Oceanic languages. The examples in (4) illustrate the word-for-word correspondence between Takia and Waskia.

(4)　　a. Takia:　　*Kai*　*sa-n*　　　　　　　*ab*　　*lo*
　　　　　　Waskia:　*Kai*　*ko*　　　　　　　*kawam*　*te*
　　　　　　　　　　　Kai　CLASSIFIER-his　house　in
　　　　　　　　　　　POSTPOSITION
　　　　　'in Kai's house'

　　　b. Takia:　　*ŋai*　*tamol*　*an*　*ida*
　　　　　　Waskia:　*ane*　*kadi*　*mu*　*ili*
　　　　　　　　　　　I　　man　　DET　with.him
　　　　　'the man and I'

　　　c. Takia:　　*tamol*　*tubun*　　　　　*uraru*　*en*
　　　　　　Waskia:　*kadi*　*bi-biga*　　　　*itelala*　*pamu*
　　　　　　　　　　　man　(PLURAL-) big　two　　this
　　　　　'these two big men'

　　　d. Takia:　　*tamol*　　*an*　　*ŋai*　*i-fun-ag = da*
　　　　　　　　　　man　　DET　　me　he-hit-me = IMPFV
　　　　　　Waskia:　*kadi*　　*mu*　　*aga*　*umo-so*
　　　　　　　　　　man　　DET　　me　hit-PRESENT.he
　　　　　'The man is hitting me.'

　　　e. Takia:　　*Waskia*　*tamol*　*an*
　　　　　　Waskia:　*Waskia*　*kadi*　*mu*
　　　　　　　　　　　Waskia　man　DET
　　　　　'the Waskia man'

Takia generally follows Waskia in matters of phrasal and clausal syntax, but reflects PWOc bound morphology and word structure. In (4a-c), Takia has replaced the usual Oceanic pattern of the prepositional phrase with the Waskia postpositional phrase. But (4a) follows a typically Oceanic pattern of alienable possessive morphology in attaching a possessor suffix, here third-person-singular *-n* (reflecting Proto-Oceanic/PWOc *-ña*) agreeing in person and number with *Kai*, to *sa-*, a 'classifier', i.e. a morpheme which indicates the nature of the relationship between possessor and possessed.[12] However,

---

[12] In Takia there are two classifiers, but the semantic distinction between them is disappearing.

the order of constituents in a more conservative Oceanic language would be POSSESSED + CLASSIFIER-SUFFIX + POSSESSOR or POSSESSED + POSSESSOR + CLASSIFIER-SUFFIX (Lichtenberk 1985; Ross 1998), not the POSSESSOR + CLASSIFIER-SUFFIX + POSSESSED that we find in Takia. In this Takia follows Waskia. Note, though, that the correspondence is only word-for-word, not morpheme-for-morpheme: the Takia word *sa-n*, a CLASSIFIER-SUFFIX sequence, corresponds to Waskia *ko*, an ablative postposition.

Perhaps because of the lack of correspondence at the level of the morpheme, there is a slight tendency for bound morphemes to become fossilised. Thus in (4c), *tubun* 'big' reflects an early Western Oceanic pattern whereby an adjective was suffixed to agree in person and number with the noun it modified (Ross 1998). These suffixes were identical to those used to coreference a possessor. Thus *tubun* reflects earlier *tubu-n*, where *-n* is the third-person-singular suffix we encountered in the previous paragraph. Here, however, it is used instead of the grammatically appropriate plural morpheme *-di*, reflecting ongoing fossilisation.

In (4d), the Takia verb *ifunagda* is characteristically Oceanic in having a preposed subject coreferencing morpheme (the prefix *i-*) and a postposed object coreferencing morpheme (the suffix *-ag*), whilst the Waskia verb is typically Papuan: the suffix *-so* is a portmanteau marker of tense/aspect and subject coreference. However, the Takia clause has Waskia syntax. Conservative Oceanic languages are never verb-final (they may be SVO, VSO or VOS), but Takia is strictly so. The object is additionally expressed by the independent pronoun *ŋai* 'me', corresponding to the Waskia pattern rather than the Oceanic pattern where the verbal suffix alone would suffice to express the object. The Takia phrase *tamol an* 'the man' follows the pattern of Waskia *kadi mu*, whereas the definite determiner in conservative Oceanic languages precedes its noun.

In (4e) the noun *Waskia* is used as a prenominal modifier in both Takia and Waskia, but more conservative – indeed, most – Oceanic languages have only postnominal modifiers. The only phrase-initial item in the latter is the determiner, but, as (4e) shows, this occurs phrase-finally.

As noted above, although Takia syntax closely follows Waskia, Takia uses forms inherited from PWOc. This is strikingly obvious in the paradigm of 'father' in (5). Sometimes the papuanisation of Takia syntax seems simply to have entailed altering the sequence of elements. But more often an element that happens to appear in the 'right' position by Waskia standards has been reanalysed to perform a Waskia-like function. Takia did not arrive at the noun phrase sequence of HEAD NOUN + (... +) DETERMINER by simply reversing the sequence of PWOc *a tam^w ata* 'the man':[13] The sequence of events was

---

[13] A sketch of Proto-Oceanic grammar appears in chapter 4 of Lynch, Ross and Crowley (2002).

more roundabout. PWOc had a set of three deictic morphemes:

(5)   *$i\sim e$ 'this, near speaker'
        *a 'the; that, near hearer'
        *o 'that, near neither speaker nor hearer'

Used attributively, these morphemes adhered to the PWOc adjective pattern, taking a suffix agreeing in person and number with the head noun, so that 'that man' was expressed as in (6):

(6)   *a *tam^w ata*   *a-ña*
        DET   man   that-3sG
        'that man'

Over time, *a-ña* lost its deictic sense, the article *a was deleted, leaving *a-ña* to perform the determiner function, and fossilisation occurred, leaving *an* as the form for both singular and plural (this interpretation receives support from the fact that the expected plural form *adi* survives as a marker of plurality with human nouns). There were also a few phonological changes.

Takia has also developed a set of sentence-medial verbal enclitics out of PWOc conjunctions (Ross 1987; see also Ross 1994b) and postpositions from PWOc relational nouns (Ross 1996).

So far I have described some of the syntagmatic symptoms of Takia metatypy. However, metatypy also has a paradigmatic dimension. Takia has copied not only Waskia syntactic constructions, but also the internal organisation of Waskia's closed morpheme classes. In connection with (4a) and (b) it was noted that Takia has replaced Oceanic prepositions with Waskia-like postpositions. This copying also affects the paradigmatic dimension. Whereas Western Oceanic languages usually have only two or three prepositions (they express more complex relationships with relational nouns or serialised verbs), Takia has developed a set of postpositions that is remarkably similar paradigmatically – and therefore semantically – to the Waskia set. The Takia and Waskia sets are:

(7)   Takia   Waskia
        location   *na, te*   *se, te*
        location 'in'   *lo*   *i, nuŋi*
        location 'on'   *fo, fufo*   *kuali*
        ablative   –   *ko*
        instrument   *nam (= na-mi)* *se*
        referential   *o*   *ko*
        manner   *mi*   *wam*

We may call this paradigmatic and semantic reorganisation 'grammatical calquing', but noting that it is an integral part of the process of metatypy.

Metatypy is invariably also accompanied by lexical calquing; indeed, lexical calquing precedes metatypy chronologically. This is clear because (i) there are languages (e.g. Maltese) where the historical circumstances might lead us to expect metatypy, but only lexical calquing has occurred, and (ii) there are no known cases of metatypy without lexical calquing (Ross 1999). Together, lexical calquing and metatypy have constituted a profound restructuring of the language so that Takia speakers have increasingly construed the world around them in a way that matches Waskia.[14] Complex lexical items, whether compound words, phrases, or larger formulae, have been reformulated so that their component morphemes match their Waskia equivalents.

Waskia, like many Papuan languages, has compound pairs like those in (8), and these have been calqued in Takia.

(8)		'literal' meaning	Takia	Waskia
	'person'	'man–woman'	*tamol-pein*	*kadi-imet*
	'animal'	'pig–dog'	*bor-goun*	*buruk-kasik*
	'his parents'	'his mother–his father'	*tinan-taman*	*niam-niet*
	'(do) first'	'his eye–his eye'	*malan-malan*	*motam-motam*

This pattern is not found in conservative Oceanic languages. Some examples of calqued formulae are listed in (9):

(9)	'literal' meaning	Takia		Waskia	
'the palm of my hand'	'my hand's liver'	*bani-g* hand-1sG	*ate-n* liver-3sG	*a-gitiŋ* 1sG-hand	*gomaŋ* <3sG>liver
'I am dizzy'	'my eye goes round'	*mala-g* eye-1sG	*i-kilani* 3sG-go.round	*motam* eye	*gerago-so* go.round-3sG
'I disobey him'	'I cut his mouth'	*awa-n* mouth-3sG	*ŋu-tale* 1sG-cut	*kuriŋ* 3sG.mouth	*batugar-so* cut-1sG
'I am angry'	'my guts are bad'	*ilo-g* inside-1sG	*saen* bad	*a-gemaŋ* 1sG-liver	*memek* bad
'I am waiting'	'I am putting my eye'	*mala-g* eye-1sG	*ŋi-ga* 1sG-put	*motam* eye	*bete-so* put-1sG

In the last example Takia *-ga* and Waskia *bete-* even share the range of meaning: 'put, do, make'.

We could say that Takia and Waskia constitute a small language alliance. But this is not precise enough, because Takia and Waskia have not *converged*. Rather, Takia has undergone metatypy, apparently on the model of Waskia. I write 'apparently' because metatypy itself does not entail borrowing of forms, and so we sometimes cannot be sure what language was the metatypic model.

---

[14] In previous accounts (Ross 1996, 2001) I have written as if lexical calquing were an integral part of metatypy. This is true to the extent that metatypy never occurs without lexical calquing, but it is preferable to keep them separate terminologically, as lexical calquing sometimes occurs without metatypy.

It is possible that Takia underwent a measure of metatypy on the model of some other Papuan language before its speakers ever migrated to Karkar.

Metatypy has probably been very common in the linguistic history of the world. Accounts of contact are often insufficiently detailed (as a knowledge of at least two languages is required) to allow us to see if metatypy has occurred, but more comprehensive accounts have multiplied in the last decade or so, and it is clear that many of these reflect metatypy. Listed with their metatypic model and source, these include:

Maisin (Oceanic)	Korafe (?) (Papuan)	Ross (1996)
Anêm (Papuan)	Lusi (Oceanic)	Thurston (1987)
Cham (Austronesian)	Vietnamese (Austro-Asiatic)	Thurgood (1996, 1999)[15]
Tariana	Tucanoan languages	Aikhenvald (1996)
Ilwana (Bantu)	Orma (Cushitic)	Nurse (1994)
Northern Tajik (Iranian)	Uzbek (Turkic)	Soper (1996)
Qahqay (Turkic)	Persian	Soper (1996)
Albanian in Greece	Greek	Sasse (1985)
Asia Minor Greek	Turkish	Thomason and Kaufman (1988: 215–23)
Western Armenian	Turkish	Sasse (1992)
Macedonian Turkish	Macedonian (Slavic)	Friedman (1996)
Kosovo Turkish	Albanian	Friedman (1996)
Kormatiki Arabic	Cypriot Greek	Newton (1964)
Rhaeto-Romance	German or Italian	Haiman (1988)
Sauris German	Rhaeto-Romance, Italian	Denison (1968), (1977, 1988)
Mixe Basque	Gascon	Haase (1992)

The outworking of metatypy appears to follow a regular sequence. At one extreme we find languages like Anêm, a Papuan language of New Britain (Papua New Guinea), which has undergone a degree of metatypy on the model of the Oceanic language Lusi. Here lexical calquing has occurred, and the order of phrasal constituents in the clause is the same in both languages but the orders of words within phrases differ sharply (Thurston 1987, Ross 1996, to appear). Next, we have languages like Takia, where the order of words within the phrase also matches the order of the secondary lect. And finally we occasionally find language pairs in which the orders of morphemes within the word also match. Unfortunately, there is not much published data for the one case where this

---

[15] Thurgood argues for the sociolinguistic circumstances associated with metatypy in Cham. Cham metatypy on the Vietnamese model is clearly visible in the data in Moussay's (1971) Cham–Vietnamese–French dictionary of Phan Rang Cham.

is claimed to be so. This is the Indian village of Kupwar, on the Indo-Aryan/ Dravidian border, where varieties of Indo-Aryan Urdu and Dravidian Kannada have been remodelled, mainly on the basis of Indo-Aryan Marathi.[16] All three, like Takia, have largely retained their own forms, but text from one lect can, it seems, be translated morpheme by morpheme into either of the others (Gumperz 1969, Gumperz and Wilson 1971). A Kupwar Urdu example is reproduced in (10)

(10)

Kupwar Urdu:	o	gəe	t-a		bhæs	carn-e-ko
Kupwar Kannada:	aw	hog	id-a		yəmmi	mes-ø-k
	he	go	PAST-MASC		buffalo	graze- OBLIQUE-to
Standard Hindi-Urdu:	wo	bhæs	cərane-ke		liye	gəy-a th-a
	he	buffalo	graze-OBLIQUE	to		go-MASC PAST-MASC

'He went to graze the buffalo.' (Gumperz and Wilson 1971:165)

It is beyond the scope of this chapter to examine the process of metatypy in any detail (see Ross 1999), but it is not difficult to see that both lexical calquing amd metatypy are driven by a natural tendency to relieve the bilingual speaker's mental burden by expressing meanings in matching ways in both the primary and the secondary lect. The secondary lect wins out because it is the language of the larger community and is slower to change. Grammatical features of the primary lect are allowed to change because it is usually a lect's lexicon (and sometimes also its intonation) that is emblematic of its speakers' identity, not its syntax, so syntax may change without loss of emblematicity. Change begins at the level of the clause because the clause is, roughly, the unit which expresses the speech act, and speakers achieve their first reduction in burden by achieving speech-act equivalence between the two lects. Each set of changes at the next lower syntactic rank represents a further reduction in burden.

The picture of contact change in an open but tightknit community that I have presented here is obviously somewhat idealised. Although we can find plenty of cases of metatypy, we can also find cases of open but tightknit communities where metatypy has not gone as far as we might expect or where other phenomena are evident. The occurrence of metatypy and the degree of its

---

[16] There has also been some restructuring on the model of Kannada, the language of the dominant group in the village. Whether this has occurred simultaneously with restructuring on the model of Marathi or not is not known.

occurrence are obviously constrained by a number of factors, some of which are:

a. the degree of community tightknitness;
b. the degree of community openness;
c. whether the secondary lect is the primary lect of another community;
d. the relative sizes and statuses of communities speaking the primary and the secondary lects;
e. the frequency and extent of use of the secondary lect;
f. the internal structure of the community's social network;
g. which features of the primary lect are perceived as emblematic by their speakers;
h. similarity between the primary and secondary lects as perceived by polylectal speakers;
i. time depth of polylectalism.

Factors (a) to (f) all affect the maintenance of the norms of the primary lect, and (f) entails the question of whether anyone is in a position to enforce its norms and hinder innovation. Where the primary lect is spoken by a substantial community, as in a European city, and has high emblematic value for its speakers, then there will be countervailing pressure against change. If metatypy on the model of standard German were to occur, say, in some of the German dialects of Bavaria and Switzerland, some of the emblematic features of these dialects would disappear (factor (g)).

Factor (h) probably has a bearing on the speed and extent of metatypy. If the primary lects are dialects of the same language, then metatypy may be irrelevant or hard to detect. If the primary and secondary lects are structurally quite similar, as in the case of Albanian and Greek, then paradigms of morphemes will occupy similar syntactic slots and have similar semantic structures, and the paradigms of the primary lect can be more readily brought into line with those of the secondary. What is more, if their speakers perceive the two lects as variants of each other, then they may borrow bound morphemes from a paradigm in the secondary lect into the corresponding paradigm of the primary lect. This is what seems to have happened in the oft-mentioned case of Meglenite Rumanian (spoken to the north of the Greek city of Salonika), where Bulgarian person/number suffixes replaced their Rumanian equivalents on the Meglenite verb (Weinreich 1963 [1953]: 32, Thomason and Kaufman 1988: 98). At the opposite extreme are cases where the two lects are structurally very unlike. Maltese, for example, is an Arabic dialect which has undergone metatypy on the model of Italian. From Drewes's (1994) account it seems that Maltese semantic organisation reflects reshaping on the Italian model, but great differences in structure may have hindered syntactic restructuring.

There is a certain amount of literature on cases where the comparative method seems to fail because it is impossible to identify regular sound correspondences among cognate vocabulary (for a summary, see Ross and Durie 1996: 28–31). Grace (1996) suggests in his study of an area of New Caledonia that this is due to lexical borrowing over a long period of time between lects which are in a reciprocal primary/secondary relationship. That is, the primary lect of village A is the secondary lect of village B and vice versa. The very fact that the lects have survived as separate entities bears witness to the fact that their communities are tightknit, but the various lects, related to each other anyway, have come to be treated by their speakers as variants of each other rather than as separate languages, so that borrowing from one to another is relatively unconstrained. Clearly, it is a precondition in such a case that speakers do not perceive the lexicon in general as an emblematic feature of their primary lect. Cases of this kind – others are found in Australia and Papua New Guinea – represent a particular constellation of the factors listed above.

4.3   Open and looseknit communities

A looseknit community is one whose internal relationship links are relatively weak and are low in density, and a little thought shows that this is likely to be a terminal condition. When the strength and density of a community's internal links drop to the same level as its external links, it ceases by definition to be a recognisable community. When speakers no longer perceive themselves as a community, their primary lect loses its emblematic significance, and they are liable to abandon it and shift to the lect of the wider community, that is, to their secondary lect.

People in a polylectal community may well speak their secondary lect with the 'accent' of their primary lect. If they maintain this accent after the shift, then the result is that their new primary lect is a phonologically coloured version of the old secondary lect. A case where shift seems very likely is Madak, spoken in communities in central New Ireland (Papua New Guinea). Madak is clearly an Oceanic language, but its phonology now bears striking resemblance to that of its Papuan neighbour Kuot (Ross 1994). The most reasonable explanation for this is that speakers whose primary lect was either Kuot or something closely related to it shifted to their secondary lect, which was a phonologically coloured version of the Oceanic language spoken by their neighbours.[17] Significantly, Madak shows no signs of metatypy, but this need not surprise us, as metatypy affects a polylectal community's primary, but not its secondary, lect.

Haase (1993) shows how phonological features of Gascon, the Romance language spoken in the southwest corner of France, probably have their origin

---

[17] This explanation receives support from the fact that the people of New Ireland now speak Oceanic languages, except for a few small Kuot-speaking communities, but we know from archaeological evidence and from the survival of Kuot that New Ireland was once peopled by Papuan speakers.

in the phonology of Basque speakers who shifted to a secondary Romance lect. In the Gascon and Madak cases, we rely on comparison with Basque and Kuot respectively for phonological information. Where the old primary lect, or something closely related, does not survive, then shift is much harder to establish. It is also possible, of course, for a community to speak its secondary lect without an accent, so that no traces of shift remain.

Obviously language shift can occur only in a polylectal community. What happens if a monolectal community loses its sense of identity and becomes looseknit? On the account of Takia and Waskia above, the Waskia were apparently an open community speaking only Waskia, because the Takia spoke Waskia as their secondary lect. Now suppose for some reason that the Waskia had lost their sense of identity. What would have happened linguistically? They could not have abandoned their only language. The likely result would have been that in identifying more strongly with the Takia as members of the larger, combined community, they would have abandoned those features of Waskia that had distinguished them as its primary speakers from the Takia as its secondary speakers, and spoken it in the form used by the Takia. This is essentially the process of koineisation (Siegel 1985, 1993), a term derived from one of its best-documented cases, the rise of Koiné Greek, the language of the New Testament. Ancient, pre-Koiné, Greek had many dialects, each centred on an independent city state. One of these was Attic, the Athens dialect. With the absorption of the city states into the Macedonian Empire and the decline of their separate identities, Attic formed the basis of the imperial *lingua franca* which came into being through the elimination of emblematically Attic forms: Hock calls it 'de-atticized Attic' (1986: 485; see also Bubenik 1993). Jakobson (1962 [1929]: 82) argued that certain dialects of Ukrainian had simplified their vowel system as a result of being used as a lingua franca, and Andersen (1988: 49–51) suggests that the same is true of north Russian dialects. Another example of a koine is Dhuwaya, spoken by younger people at Yirrkala in northeast Arnhemland (Australia). Here, clan lects have been levelled as the result of gradual modernisation (Amery 1993).

4.4   Drawing threads together

My objective here has been to provide some means of diagnosing contact, and I hope that the symptoms to be diagnosed have been reasonably obvious from what I have written. Symptoms of noncatastrophic contact-induced change include the following:[18]

---

[18] The diagnostic symptoms listed here differ in certain respects from Thomason and Kaufman's (1988). Categories (a) and (d) do not figure in their paradigm. They assume that language shift (c) involves syntactic as well as phonological change, but their examples of shift (other than catastrophic shift) all entail difficulties of sociolinguistic interpretation, and I see no grounds for treating syntactic change as a symptom of shift.

a. If a community is *closed*, its members may complicate their lect, result-ing in phonological compactness, morphological opacity, and suppletion – basically, whatever makes the language harder to learn and understand.

b. If a community is *open, tightknit* and *polylectal*, lexical calquing and metatypy may occur, restructuring the primary lect's semantic organisation and at least part of its syntax (starting at the level of the clause) on the model of the secondary lect.

c. If a community is *open, looseknit* and *polylectal*, speakers may shift from the primary to the secondary lect, leaving either no trace or reshaping the phonology of the secondary lect on the model of the primary one.

d. If a community is *open, looseknit* and *monolectal*, its members may adopt the lingua-franca form of their lect, resulting in simplification and regularity.

A symptom which is missing from this listing is lexical borrowing. It seems that lexical borrowing is an intrinsic part of contact-induced change only when that change is catastrophic. Otherwise, lexical borrowing is not a necessary condition or concomitant of contact-induced change. I prefer to attribute lexical borrowing to *culture contact* rather than to language contact, since lexical borrowing does occur without bilingualism and *vice versa*. Despite the restructuring of the Takia lexicon, borrowing seems to be limited to a few semantic domains. And, on the other hand, the largely monolectal Japanese speech community has borrowed quite extensively from English.

The list above places metatypy under (b) and phonological change under (c). However, there are cases where metatypy is accompanied by phonological change, and this raises the question, is phonological change also an outworking of metatypy? The answer is 'no', since a majority of cases of metatypy are ap-parently not accompanied by phonological change. As far as one can tell, where phonological change accompanies metatypy, it is the result of some separate factor such as the frequent introduction of 'foreign' spouses into the group or significant lexical borrowing[19] (Ross 2001). Although this seems to introduce a complication into the diagnostic features listed above, it is only a minor one. Where metatypy occurs – with or without phonological adaptation – one can be confident that this is due to ongoing bilingualism; where phonological adaptation occurs *without* metatypy, this is due to language shift.

Finally, there are two things to note about the list above, one positive, the other negative. The positive is that the diagnostic symptoms of the four cate-gories are different and therefore distinguishable. The negative, of course, is that this is only an idealised outline of a theory of contact-induced change. Matters become considerably more complicated when we introduce a creoloid

---

[19] This has happened in Tagalog, where extensive lexical borrowing from Spanish resulted in changes in the vowel system, which in turn complicated the language's verbal morphology – all without a majority of Tagalog speakers being bilingual in Spanish.

like Afrikaans (Roberge 1993), and more complicated still when we recognise that a language can bear the marks of having undergone more than one of these changes. Maisin (an Oceanic language of Papua New Guinea), for example, has undergone metatypy, evidently in two chronologically distinct contact situations, *and* esoterogeny, probably in that order (Ross 1996). Other complex cases are outlined by Ross (1997). However, we will not get very far in devising a methodology for diagnosing prehistoric language contact unless we are willing to start with some bold but clear generalisations, and then to proceed by making equally clear generalisations about the exceptions. Only in this way will we be able to relate patterns in the data back to the varying circumstances of contact-induced change.

REFERENCES

Aikhenvald, Alexandra Y. 1996. 'Areal diffusion in north-west Amazonia: the case of Tariana', *Anthropological Linguistics* 38: 73–116.

Amery, Rob. 1993. 'An Australian koine: Dhuwaya, a variety of Yol9u Matha spoken at Yirrkala in North East Arnhemland', *International Journal of the Sociology of Language* 99: 45–64.

Andersen, Henning. 1988. 'Centre and periphery: adoption, diffusion and spread', in Jacek Fisiak (ed.), *Historical dialectology*. Berlin: Mouton de Gruyter, 39–85.

Bakker, Peter. 1994. 'Michif, the Cree-French mixed language of the Métis buffalo hunters in Canada', in Bakker and Mous (eds.), 13–33.

Bakker, Peter and Maarten Mous (eds.). 1994. *Mixed languages: 15 case studies in language intertwining*. Studies in Language and Language Use 13. Amsterdam: Institute for Functional Research into Language and Language Use (IFOTT).

Bechert, Johannes and Wolfgang Wildgen. 1991. *Einführung in die Sprachkontaktforschung*. Darmstadt: Wissenschaftliche Buchgesellschaft.

Boretzky, Norbert and Birgit Igla. 1994. 'Romani mixed dialects', in Bakker and Mous (eds.), 35–68.

Bubenik, Vit. 1993. 'Dialect contact and koineization: the case of Hellenistic Greek', *International Journal of the Sociology of Language* 99: 9–24.

Capell, Arthur. 1943. *The Linguistic Position of South-Eastern Papua*. Sydney: Australasian Medical Publishing Company.

Denison, Norman. 1968. 'Sauris: a trilingual community in diatypic perspective', *Man*, new series 3: 578–92.

Denison, Norman. 1977. 'Language death or language suicide?', *International Journal of the Sociology of Language* 12: 13–22.

Denison, Norman. 1988. 'Language contact and language norm', *Folia Linguistica* 22: 11–35.

Dorian, Nancy C. 1982. 'Defining the speech community to include its working margins', in Suzanne Romaine (ed.), *Sociolinguistic variation in speech communities*. London: Edward Arnold, 25–33.

Drewes, A. J. 1994. 'Borrowing in Maltese', in Bakker and Mous (eds.), 83–111.

Dutton, T. E. and D. T. Tryon (eds.) 1994. *Language contact and change in the Austronesian world*. Berlin: Mouton de Gruyter.

Emeneau, Murray B. 1980. *Language and linguistic area*, ed. Anwar S. Dil. Stanford University Press.

Ferraz, Luiz. 1983. 'The origin and development of four creoles in the Gulf of Guinea', in Ellen Woolford and William Washabaugh (eds.), *The social context of creolization*. Ann Arbor: Karoma, 120–5.

Friedman, Victor. 1996. 'West Rumelian Turkish in Macedonia and adjacent areas', paper presented to the Conference on Turkish in Contact, Netherlands Institute for Advanced Studies, Wassenaar.

Golovko, Evgenij. 1994. 'Mednyj Aleut or Cooper Island Aleut: an Aleut-Russian mixed language', in Bakker and Mous (eds.), 113–21.

Golovko, Evgenij and Nikolai B. Vakhtin. 1990. 'Aleut in contact: the CIA enigma', *Acta Linguistica Hafniensia* 22: 97–125.

Goodman, Morris. 1971. 'The strange case of Mbugu', in Dell Hymes (ed.), *Pidginization and creolization of languages*. Cambridge University Press.

Grace, George W. 1981. *An essay on language*. Columbia, SC.: Hornbeam.

Grace, George W. 1996. 'Regularity of change in what?', in Mark Durie and Malcolm D. Ross (eds.), *The comparative method reviewed: regularity and irregularity in language change*. New York: Oxford University Press, 157–79.

Gruiter, Miel de. 1994. 'Javindo, a contact language in pre-war Semarang', in Bakker and Mous (eds.), 151–9.

Gumperz, John J. 1969. 'Communication in multilingual communities', in S. Tyler (ed.), *Cognitive anthropology*, New York: Holt, Rinehart and Winston, 435–49

Gumperz, John J. and Robert Wilson. 1971. 'Convergence and creolization: a case from the Indo-Aryan/Dravidian border', in Dell Hymes (ed.), *Pidginization and creolization of languages*. Cambridge University Press, 151–68.

Haase, Martin. 1992. *Sprachkontakt und Sprachwandel im Baskenland: Einflüsse des Gaskognischen und Französischen auf das Baskische*. Hamburg: Buske.

Haase, Martin. 1993. *Le Gascon des Basques: contribution à la théorie des substrats*. Arbeiten zur Mehrsprachigkeit 50. Hamburg: Arbeitsstelle Mehrsprachigkeit, Germanisches Seminar, Universität Hamburg.

Haiman, John. 1988. 'Rhaeto-Romance', in Martin Harris and Nigel Vincent (eds.), *The Romance languages*. London: Croom Helm 351–90.

Heath, Jeffrey. 1978. *Linguistic diffusion in Arnhem Land*. Canberra: Australian Institute of Aboriginal Studies.

Hock, Hans Henrich. 1986. *Principles of historical linguistics*. Berlin: Mouton de Gruyter.

Jakobson, Roman. 1962 [1929]. 'Remarques sur l'évolution phonologique du russe comparée à celle des autres langues slaves', in Roman Jakobson (ed.), *Selected writings* 1. 's-Gravenhage: Mouton, 7–116.

Jespersen, Otto. 1947 [1922]. *Language: its nature, development and origin*. London: George Allen and Unwin.

Joseph, Brian. 1983. *The Balkan infinitive*. Cambridge University Press.

Lichtenberk, Frantisek. 1985. 'Possessive constructions in Oceanic languages and Proto-Oceanic', in Andrew K. Pawley and Lois Carrington (eds.), *Austronesian linguistics at the 15th Pacific Science Congress*. Pacific Linguistics C-88. Canberra: Australian National University, 93–140.

Lynch, John, Malcolm D. Ross and Terry Crowley. 2002. *The Oceanic languages*. Richmond: Curzon Press.

Lynch, John and Philip Tepahae. 1997. 'Digging up the linguistic past: the lost language(s) of Aneitym, Vanuatu', in Roger M. Blench and Matthew Spriggs (eds.), *Archaeology and language 3*. London: Routledge, 277–85.

McSwain, Romola. 1977. *The past and future people*. Melbourne: Oxford University Press.

Milroy, James. 1992. *Linguistic variation and change: on the historical sociolinguistics of English*. Oxford: Blackwell.

Milroy, James. 1993. 'On the social origins of language change', in Charles Jones (ed.), *Historical linguistics: problems and perspectives*. London: Longman, 215–36.

Milroy, James and Lesley Milroy. 1985. 'Linguistic change, social network and speaker innovation', *Journal of Linguistics*, 21: 339–84.

Milroy, Lesley. 1980. *Language and social networks*. Oxford: Basil Blackwell.

Milroy, Lesley. 1987. *Language and social networks*, 2nd edition. Oxford: Blackwell.

Mous, Maarten. 1994. 'Ma'a or Mbugu', in Bakker and Mous (eds.), 175–200.

Moussay, Fr. Gérard. 1971. *Dictionnaire Cam-Vietnamien-Français*. Phan Rang: Centre Culturel Cam.

Muysken, Peter. 1994. 'Media Lengua', in Bakker and Mous (eds.), 207–11.

Nau, Nicole. 1995. *Möglichkeiten und Mechanismen kontaktbewegten Sprachwandels*. Edition Linguistik 08. Munich and Newcastle: Lincom Europa.

Newton, Brian. 1964. 'An Arabic-Greek dialect', in Robert Austerlitz (ed.), *Papers in memory of George C. Papageotes* (*Word* 20, supplement). New York: Linguistic Circle of New York, 43–52.

Nicolaï, Robert. 1990. *Parentés linguistiques (à propos de songhay)*. Paris: Editions du CNRS.

Nurse, Derek. 1994. 'South meets north: Ilwana = Bantu + Cushitic on Kenya's Tana River', in Bakker and Mous (eds.), 213–22.

Prince, Ellen F. 1998. 'The borrowing of meaning as a cause of internal syntactic change', in Monika S. Schmid, Jennifer R. Austin and Dieter Stein (eds.), *Historical linguistics 1997: selected papers from the 13th International Conference on Historical Linguistics, Düsseldorf, 10–17 August 1997*. Amsterdam: John Benjamins, 339–62.

Roberge, Paul T. 1993. *The formation of Afrikaans*. Stellenbosch Papers in Linguistics 27. Stellenbosch: Department of General Linguistics, University of Stellenbosch.

Romaine, Suzanne. 1982. 'What is a speech community?', in Suzanne Romaine (ed.), *Sociolinguistic variation in speech communities*. London: Edward Arnold, 13–24.

Ross, Malcolm D. 1987. 'A contact-induced morphosyntactic change in the Bel languages of Papua New Guinea', in Donald C. Laycock and W. Winter (eds.), *A world of language: papers presented to Professor S. A. Wurm on his 65th Birthday*. Pacific Linguistics C-100. Canberra: Australian National University, 583–601.

Ross, Malcolm D. 1988. *Proto-Oceanic and the Austronesian Languages of Western Melanesia*. Pacific Linguistics C–98. Canberra: Australian National University.

Ross, Malcolm D. 1994a. 'Areal phonological features in north central New Ireland', in T. E. Dutton and D. T. Tryon (eds.), *Language contact and change in the Austronesian world*. Berlin: Mouton de Gruyter, 551–72.

Ross, Malcolm D. 1994b. 'Describing inter-clausal relations in Takia', in Ger P. Reesink (ed.), *Topics in descriptive Austronesian linguistics*. Semaian 11. Leiden: Vakgroep Talen en Culturen van Zuidoost-Azië en Oceanië, Rijksuniversiteit te Leiden, 40–85.

Ross, Malcolm D. 1996. 'Contact-induced change and the comparative method: cases from Papua New Guinea', in Mark Durie and Malcolm D. Ross (eds.), *The comparative method reviewed: regularity and irregularity in language change*. New York: Oxford University Press, 180–217.

Ross, Malcolm D. 1997. 'Social networks and kinds of speech community event', in Roger M. Blench and Matthew Spriggs (eds.), *Archaeology and language*, vol. 1: *Theoretical and methodological orientations*, London: Routledge, 209–61.

Ross, Malcolm D. 1998. 'Possessive-like attribute constructions in the Oceanic languages of northwest Melanesia', *Oceanic Linguistics* 37: 234–76.

Ross, Malcolm D. 1999. 'Exploring metatypy: how does contact-induced typological change come about?', keynote address to the meeting of the Australian Linguistic Society, Perth, October 1999.

Ross, Malcolm D. 2001. 'Contact-induced change in Oceanic languages in northwest Melanesia', in R. M. W. Dixon and Alexandra Aikhenvald (eds.), *Areal diffusion and genetic inheritance: problems in comparative linguistics*. Oxford: Oxford University Press, 134–66.

Ross, Malcolm D. and Mark Durie. 1996. 'Introduction', in Mark Durie and Malcolm D. Ross (eds.), *The comparative method reviewed: regularity and irregularity in language change*. New York: Oxford University Press, 3–38.

Sasse, Hans-Jürgen. 1985. 'Sprachkontakt und Sprachwandel: die Gräzisierung der albanischen Mundarten Griechenlands', *Papiere zur Linguistik* 32: 37–95.

Sasse, Hans-Jürgen. 1992. 'Language decay and contact-induced change: similarities and differences', in Matthias Brenzinger (ed.), *Language death: factual and theoretical explorations with special reference to East Africa*. Berlin: Mouton de Gruyter, 59–80.

Siegel, Jeff. 1985. 'Koines and koineization', *Language in Society* 14: 357–78.

Siegel, Jeff. 1993. 'Introduction: controversies in the study of koines and koineization', *International Journal of the Sociology of Language* 99: 5–8.

Soper, John. 1996. *Loan Syntax in Turkic and Iranian*, ed. Andras J.E. Bodrogligeti. Bloomington, IN: Eurolingua.

Taki, Jerry and Darrell T. Tryon. 1997. 'The lost languages of Erromango (Vanuatu)', in Roger M. Blench and Matthew Spriggs (eds.), *Archaeology and language*, vol. 1: *Theoretical and methodological orientations*. London: Routledge, 362–70.

Thomason, Sarah G. 1983. 'Genetic relationship and the case of Ma'a (Mbugu)', *Studies in African Linguistics* 14: 195–231.

Thomason, Sarah Grey and Terrence S. Kaufman. 1988. *Language contact, creolization and genetic linguistics*. Berkeley: University of California Press.

Thurgood, Graham. 1996. 'Language contact and the directionality of internal drift: the development of tones and registers in Chamic', *Language* 72: 1–31.

Thurgood, Graham. 1999. *From ancient Cham to modern Dialects: two thousand years of language contact and change*. Oceanic Linguistics Special Publication 28. Honolulu: University of Hawaii Press.

Thurston, William R. 1987. *Processes of change in the languages of north-western New Britain*. Pacific Linguistics B–99. Canberra: Australian National University.

Thurston, William R. 1989. 'How exoteric languages build a lexicon: esoterogeny in West New Britain', in Ray Harlow and Robin Hooper (eds.), *VICAL 1, Oceanic languages: papers from the Fifth International Conference on Austronesian Linguistics*. Auckland: Linguistic Society of New Zealand, 555–79.

Thurston, William R. 1994. 'Renovation and innovation in the languages of northwestern New Britain', in Tom Dutton and Darrell Tryon (eds.), *Language contact and change in the Austronesian world*. Berlin: Mouton de Gruyter, 573–609.

Thurston, William R. 1996. 'The Bibling languages of northwestern New Britain', in Malcolm D. Ross (ed.), *Studies in languages of New Britain and New Ireland*, vol. 1: *Austronesian languages of the North New Guinea cluster in northwestern New Britain*. Pacific Linguistics C–135. Canberra: Australian National University, 249–392.

Trubetzkoy, N. 1930. 'Proposition 16', in *Actes du premier Congrès international de linguistes à La Haye, du 10–15 avril 1928*, 18. Leiden: A. W. Sijthoff.

Tucker, A. N. and M. A. BrTan. 1974. 'The "Mbugu" anomaly', *Bulletin of the School of Oriental and African Studies* 37: 188–207.

Van Coetsem, Frans. 1988. *Loan phonology and the two tansfer types in language contact*. Dordrecht: Foris.

Weinreich, Uriel. 1963 [1953]. *Languages in contact*. The Hague: Mouton (originally published 1953 by the Linguistic Circle of New York).

12   The ingenerate motivation of sound change

Gregory K. Iverson and Joseph C. Salmons

1   Introduction

This chapter investigates the interplay between phonetic (coarticulatory) and phonological (structural) factors surrounding two of the best-studied and most complex changes in Germanic, umlaut and the High German Consonant Shift. These well-studied data sets form the springboard for our primary thesis that the boundary between phonetics and phonology is largely porous, in the specific sense that the phenomena of the latter find motivation in the particulars of the former. The idea that phonetics is not entirely separate from phonology stands in notable contrast to the classic view encoded in lexical phonology's principle of structure preservation (Kiparsky 1985) and to the separatist position taken in some current theorising in phonetics itself (Cohn and Tsuchida 1999). At the other extreme, our porosity thesis stands apart from the tenet of especially 'functional' optimality theory (Kirchner 1997), which holds that even gradient phonetic properties should be accessible within the realm of contrastive phonology. Rather than raise up impermeable barriers between phonetics and phonology or erase extant distinctions between the two domains, however, this chapter charts the development of two celebrated, nominally unrelated sound changes from their phonetic inception in coarticulation to their emergence as overt constructs of the phonology. This is our general interpretation of the familiar life-cycle of sound change, in fact: the forces of coarticulation work to shape structure, whereas structure eventually comes to override the inherently coarticulatory grounding, or ingeneracy, of phonetic naturalness.

Recent work indicates that, in its origins, Germanic umlaut is indeed ingenerate in this sense, emerging from the patterns of vowel-to-vowel coarticulation which are characteristic of stress-timed languages. In the various daughters, the source ingeneracy of umlaut is reflected in apparent irregularities relating to place-of-articulation structure of the consonants that intervene between umlaut trigger (usually /i, j/) and umlaut target, as there is a bias such that while coronals do not normally interrupt umlaut, labials can and velars often do. This bias matches the findings of phoneticians working in speech production (e.g. Butcher and Weiher 1976) who have shown experimentally that vowel-to-vowel coarticulation in nonce words is preferentially inhibited across velars, but takes place freely across intervening coronals (with higher, more front [a] in *ati* than in *aki*).

Phonologically, cross-linguistic patterns of consonantal place assimilation have been taken to justify a parallel scheme of abstract representation (cf. Rice 1994), according to which velars carry the greatest quantity of place structure (peripheral as well as dorsal), labials less (just peripheral) and coronals least (unmarked). As a phonological reflex of the ingenerate forces skewing the umlaut pattern, it is noteworthy that the same place-structure bias is recapitulated in the variable implementation of the Second Sound Shift (or High German Consonant Shift), a prosodically motivated change not rooted in coarticulation. In this nonassimilatory shift of voiceless stops into affricates and fricatives, coronals changed over a broad territory, labials over a smaller area, and velars only in a highly restricted region.

We will suggest that the markedness differential observed in such cases grows from the seeds of phonetic coarticulation, even when assimilation (or 'fossilized coarticulation', per Ohala 1993) plays no role. Germanic place-of-articulation markedness as revealed both in umlaut and the High German Consonant Shift thus reflects its basis in the ingenerate phonetics of coarticulation, one way or another. We see these events as complex phonological changes that begin as simple coarticulatory or prosodic processes, and these, in turn, form the building blocks of the now often referenced interface between phonetics and phonology.

2   *i*-umlaut

Old High German umlaut consists of several phonologically distinct components: the fronting and raising of short /a/ to [e], known as 'primary umlaut', as in (1a); the apparent absence of umlaut in 'blocking environments', as in (1b); and the general fronting of all back vowels before umlaut triggers extant in OHG, as in (1c). The forms in (1b) also reflect the appearance of 'secondary umlaut' in later Middle High German, namely, the fronting (without raising) of /a/ to [æ] in environments which blocked umlaut in OHG.

(1)   a. Primary umlaut, OHG

gast ~ *gesti*	'guest, guests'
lamb ~ *lembir*	'lamb, lambs'
fasto ~ *festi*	'solid/fast', adv. and adj.

   b. Blocking of primary umlaut, OHG (but with secondary umlaut, MHG)

maht ~ *mahti*	'power, powers' (see also dialectal *mehti*)
haltan ~ *haltis*	'to hold, you hold' (dialectally also *heltis*)
starch ~ *starchiro*	'strong, stronger' (also *sterchiro*)

c. General fronting of all back vowels before /i, j/
OHG   Modern German
gruoni   *grün*   'green'
skoni   *schön*   'beautiful'

In a number of recent papers, we argue that primary umlaut occurred chronologically prior to secondary umlaut, which we construe as a generalisation, or phonological extension, of the original process of primary umlaut. This interpretation calls attention both to the temporal and structural differentiation of umlaut, especially the differences between its primary and nonprimary manifestations, as listed in (2).

(2)   *Primary umlaut*   *Nonprimary umlaut*
       Specific phonetic conditioning   No clear phonetic conditioning
       Structure-preserving   Creates new segments
       Consistently carried through   Inconsistently carried through
       Orthographically marked early   Marked only much later
                                              (Iverson and Salmons 1996)

This more differentiated view of umlaut's unfolding yields numerous advantages, not least allowing the full range of attested umlaut data to be captured as regular sound change rather than listed as an unmotivated hodge-podge. Even previously troublesome modern dialect data come to show phonologically straightforward regularities under this new approach.

Thus, Upper German dialects are marked by the failure of umlaut to occur in words like those in (3). Of interest for the moment is the fact that the place of articulation of intervening obstruents plays a confounding role, especially when they are geminate: intervening geminate coronals seldom hinder umlaut, while labials often do and velars do so regularly.

(3)   a. Dialectal umlautless forms (Schirmunski 1962: 201–3)
          Dialect   Standard   Earlier form
       i. *muck*   *Mücke*   OHG *mucka*, OS *muggia*   'fly, gnat'
          sšduk   *Stück*   OHG *stucki*   'piece'
       ii. *khuxə*   *Küche*   OHG *kuchina*   'kitchen'
          lu:gə   *Lüge*   OHG *lugin*   'lie'
       b. Alemannic examples of blocking by place of intervening geminate
          (Lüssy 1974)
          -kx- *bucke* 'to bend down', *drucke, hucke* 'to duck, limp', *jucke* 'jump',
          lucke 'attract', *nucke* 'to go to sleep'
          -pf- *gupfe* 'to speed up', *hupfe* 'to hop', *lupfe* 'to lift', *mupfe* 'to give
          a push'
          -ts- *butze* 'to castrate, fix', *gutze* 'overshoot', *hutze* 'to jump up', *nutze*
          'to use', *stutze* 'to stop'

These previously recalcitrant data can now be taken to reflect umlaut's natural phonological evolution rather than any previously attributed analogical chaos. We turn now to the phonetic underpinnings of this view of umlaut, reviewing evidence that universal patterns of coarticulation are stronger in those environments where umlaut occurred more broadly across Germanic, but weaker in those where umlaut was less pervasive.

3   The phonetic basis of umlaut

A body of instrumental and experimental work on coarticulation suggests a starting point from which the assimilatory process of umlaut grew, and motivates key successive steps in the unfolding of the process. It is specifically the fact of low-level coarticulation between vowels which spawns assimilations like umlaut in the form of a phonological process, assimilations which eventually reach completion as sound changes. Farnetani (1997: 383–4) summarises the general relationship obtaining between coarticulation and assimilation as follows: coarticulation 'is a continuous motor process, increasing in magnitude in connected speech', while assimilation 'is a categorical change, a language-specific grammatical rule. Assimilation is a consequence of coarticulation, an adaptation of language to speech constraints.' We underscore here the notion that assimilation is taken to be a *consequence* of coarticulation, and we consider that umlaut qua sound change, in turn, is a consequence of assimilation.

The pioneering investigations of Öhman (1966) and a tradition of work on coarticulation through Keating (1988) down to the present unveils the ubiquity of vowel-to-vowel coarticulation across languages. It seems likely that i-umlaut sprang from such coarticulatory patterns, too, which most probably were present from very early on at a nascent level, presumably below the threshold of perception. The phonetics of vowel-to-vowel coarticulation, in short, prepared a rich seedbed for umlaut, and provided a programme for its later development across Germanic. Assimilation per se then grew from this bed, as a kind of exaggeration of the already extant coarticulatory patterns.

Those patterns of coarticulation still yield umlaut-like assimilations in modern West Germanic languages today, including the 'Canadian raising' phenomenon exemplified in (4).

(4)   Canadian raising: /aj/, /aw/ > /ʌj/, /ʌw/(especially when /a/ is phonetically short, as before voiceless consonants)

Cf. also Martha's Vineyard, Outer Banks English, 'English Fens' (Britain 1997), etc.

We would expect to see such adjustments first – as we do in early Germanic monophthongisations – when the vowel and triggering glide are phonetically adjacent. But modern West Germanic languages offer more striking parallels yet, extending to patterns with intervening obstruents. Butcher and Weiher (1976) conducted a study of vowel-to-vowel coarticulations in VCV sequences with three native speakers of German, using the vowels [i, a, u] interrupted by the medial consonants [p, t, k]. The major findings pinpoint 'A coarticulatory hierarchy among the vowels investigated such that [i] exerts the greatest coarticulatory influence and [a] the least' (1976: 59). Other studies have found similar patterns (e.g. Magen 1989).

To sum up: vowels regularly exhibit low-level pre-umlaut-like coarticulation with other vowels in modern Germanic languages, the strongest patterns of which happen to be just those which centuries earlier resulted in primary umlaut. Such instrumentally observed coarticulatory behaviour has repeatedly engendered subsequent patterns of vowel-to-vowel assimilations synchronically, which in turn sets the table for the patterns of historical change as recorded in Germanic. From this perspective, our view of umlaut builds directly on the familiar Ohala-esque position that complex sound changes originate in coarticulation and in other phonetically natural ways.

4   Blocking effects as the failure of coarticulation

As noted, primary umlaut in OHG was inhibited when certain consonantal structures intervened between trigger and target vowel, and umlaut failed to occur as well in modern Upper German dialects when velars, especially geminate velars, intervened between original trigger and target. If subphonemic coarticulation is the phonetic source of all umlaut, as we maintain that it is, then phonetically similar (or phonetically contradictory) intercessor consonants will play a confounding role as these come to be specified for the same quality as that which umlaut was spreading, namely, vocalic frontness. Accordingly, while primary umlaut took place over phonologically 'inert' consonants in the syllable rhyme, it was inhibited by coda approximants in the form of liquids that had been vocalised to glides (the glide /j/ otherwise induced umlaut), or by /h/ derived from /x/ (cross-linguistically, the glottal approximant /h/ takes on the oral qualities of a following vowel (in this case, /i/)). In fact, coarticulation generally over intervening obstruents follows the same pattern: Keating (1988) found that intervening consonants, normally transparent to vowel-to-vowel assimilation, inhibit coarticulation whenever those consonants are necessarily specified for the spreading features, just as the new theory of umlaut holds for the OHG blocking phenomenon discussed in connection with the examples in (3).

Parallel to the pattern observed in the Upper German umlautless residues, the previously mentioned study by Butcher and Weiher (1976) found that coarticulatory effects were relatively large over the coronal stop, while coarticulation over velars was least; more recent studies have come to similar conclusions (Recasens 1984). These restrictions correspond directly to the Upper German blocking of umlaut and accord well with the more differentiated picture of the historical data provided by ingenerate umlaut.[1] Thus, the unfolding of umlaut we present here shows that the often appealed to 'interface between phonetics and phonology' is a coherent – if complex – result of coarticulatory forces which rise gradually to the level of categorial salience, and only from there integrate into the system of phonemic contrasts.

5   Place geometry: peripherality

Throughout the history of umlaut, consonantal place structure plays a consistent role, from primary umlaut blocking through the umlautless residues of Upper German. The very same bias in place structure is central to the unfolding of the High German Consonant shift. These two ostensibly unrelated changes, perhaps the most defining phonological characteristics of German and Germanic, both reflect a geometric property of place features which Avery and Rice (1989) and Rice (1994, 1996) have termed 'Peripheral'.

The idea for an asymmetric geometry in place features builds on a bias first noted in the phonology of Korean by Iverson and Kim (1987), where, under conditions of regressive place assimilation, coronals assimilate to labials and velars, and labials assimilate to velars; but velars do not assimilate to labials, and neither labials nor velars assimilate to coronals, as exemplified in (5).

(5)   Place of articulation assimilation in Korean

	/pan+myən/	→	[pammyən]	'on the other hand'
				(< 'half+side')
	/sin-paL/	→	[sšimbal]	'shoes(-foot)'
	/han+kaŋ/	→	[haŋgaŋ]	'Han River'
	/pat+ko/	→	[pakk'o]	'receive-and'
	/os+pota/	→	[opp'oda]	'clothes-than'
	/əp+ko/	→	[əkk'o]	'carry-and'
	/kam+ki/	→	[kaŋgi]	'cold' (< 'feeling'+'energy')
But:	/nop+ta/	→	[nopt'a]	'high' (DECLARATIVE)
	/nok+ta/	→	[nokt'a]	'melt' (DECLARATIVE)
	/kuk+muL/	→	[kuŋmul]	'soup-broth'

This asymmetry derives conventionally from the spreading of marked into un-marked structure if, following Avery and Rice (1989) and Rice (1994), a node

---

[1] In further relevance to the reduction/vocalisation analysis of primary umlaut blocking, Bladon and Al-Bamerni (1976, discussed in Farnetani 1996: 388–9) develop a notion of 'coarticulation resistance'. Intervening clear /l/, specifically, does not impede coarticulation, while darker or more velarised allophones of /l/ do. This is similar to the dialectal pattern observed in Old High German, and fits with the phonological account of these data proposed in Iverson, Davis and Salmons (1994): where coda liquids reduce or vocalise, or even just velarise, blocking occurs.

Peripheral is posited in the feature geometry subordinate to Place; coronals are then unspecified for all Place nodes, labials are marked just for Peripheral, and velars contain Peripheral along with the subordinate articulator Dorsal, as portrayed in (6).

(6)   *Velars*   *Labials*   *Coronals*
       Place   Place   Place
       | |
       Peripheral   Peripheral
       |
       Dorsal

Thus, coronals take on the qualities of both labials and velars because coronals are less fully represented than either labials or velars. By the same consideration, labials take on the qualities of velars but not coronals, while velars resist assimilation to either of the other two place-of-articulation categories. This pattern is found not just in Korean, but also in English (*in Kingston >* i[ŋ] *Kingston, in Plymouth >* i[m] *Plymouth, from Kingston >* fro[ŋ] *Kingston,* but *from Toronto >* fro[m] *Toronto*, etc.), as Rice (1994) shows, drawing other support for Peripherality from developments in Romanian, Arapaho, Yurok and other languages.

For assimilations, then, assuming an underspecification model as in (6), the markedness of the representations alone takes care of what assimilates to what. But this says nothing about nonassimilatory changes, which the model would express through feature delinkings or simply feature additions, as in the creation of affricates from stops. We turn now to how the markedness relations deriving from this place of articulation hierarchy also bear, perhaps surprisingly, on the mere manner of articulation adjustments known as the High German Consonant Shift.

6   The High German Consonant Shift

Davis and Iverson (1995) show that the celebrated High German Consonant Shift, whose effects are exemplified in (7a), was primarily a prosodic event, beginning in medial position after short vowels driven by a preference for bimoraic stressed syllables. (Note the prosodic parallel to umlaut's often-presumed ties to initial stress accent.)

The shift was asymmetric with respect to place of articulation, however, as the dialect distributions in (7b) attest: most commonly affected were the coronal stops, less the labials, least the velars; these asymmetries are perhaps reflected in a varied chronology of the shift, too, changing first coronals, then labials, last velars (Franz 1883; Sonderegger 1974: 157–8).

(7)   a. Unshifted (Old Saxon) and shifted (Upper German) cognates

West Gmc	Unshifted Old Saxon	Shifted Upper German	Gloss
*t-	tehan	zëhan	'ten'
*-tt-	lātan	laȝȝan	'to let'
*-nt	lenten (MLG)	lenzo	'spring(time)'
*-Lt	herta	herza	'heart'
*p-	plegan	pflegan	'to care for'
*-pp-	appul	apful	'apple'
*-mp	damp (MLG)	dampf	'steam'
*-lp	helpan	helfan	'to help'
		helphan = [pf]	
*-rp	werpan	werfan	'to throw'
		werphan = [pf]	
*k-	korn	chorna	'grain'
*-kk-	ackar	acchar	'field, acre'
*-nk	thankon	danchōn	'to thank'
*-Lk	folk	folcha	'people'

b. Overview of the High German Consonant Shift

	Coronals	Labials	Velars
Old Saxon	t	p	K
Middle Franconian	z- -ȝȝ-	p- -ff-	k- -hh-
Rhenish Franconian	z- -ȝȝ-	p/pf- -ff-	k- -hh-
East Franconian	z- -ȝȝ-	pf- -ff-	k- -hh-
Upper German	z- -ȝȝ-	pf- -ff-	ch-- hh-
Old Saxon	d	b	G
Middle Franconian	d/t	b	G
Rhenish Franconian	d/t	b	G
East Franconian	t	b	G
Upper German	t	p	K

Davis, Iverson and Salmons (1999) show that this pattern of spread and change correlates directly with the hierarchised geometry of place-feature dependencies laid out by Rice (1994). In brief, the Old High German asymmetries reflect the amount of place structure present in feature-geometric representations, such that the strongest, or most place-structured, consonants are most resistant to the shift.

7   Peripherality and extension of the shift

From its inchoate instantiation after only short vowels, affecting /p t k/ equally, the shift generalised first to all intervocalic environments (pre-OHG [slāphan] > [slāffan] > OHG slāfan 'to sleep'), then to postconsonantal positions ([helphan] > helpfan (= <helphan>) 'to help', [dorph] > dorpf 'village'), and, eventually, albeit far less consistently, to the beginnings of words ([phlegan], [thiohan], [khorn] > pflegan 'to tend', ziohan 'to pull', kxorn 'grain' (= <chorn>)). These fully documented developments are summarised in the data set given in (8).

(8)   a. Distribution of shifted vs. unshifted labials (Sonderegger, 1974: 158)

	*p-	*-pp-	*-mp	*-lp	*-rp
Gmc	*plegan	*apla-	*kampa-	*gelpa-	*scarpa-
M Franc	plĕgan	appul	kamp	gelpa	Scarp
Rh-Franc	plĕgan	appul	kamp	gelpf/gelp	Scarpf/scarp
S Rh-Franc	plĕgan	apful	kampf; rare: kamp	gelpf	Scarpf
E Franc	pflĕgan	apful	kampf	gelpf	Scarpf
Bav	pflĕgan	apful	champf	gelpf	Scarpf
	pflĕkan		chamf	gelf	
Alem	(p)flĕgan	apful	champf	gelpf	scarpf
		afful	chamf	gelf	
	'to tend'	'apple'	'battle'	'high-spirited'	'sharp'

b. Distribution of tenues generally (Sonderegger, 1974: 159).

	Coronal					Labial						Velar			
Pre-OHG	t-	-tt-	C+t	-t-	-t	p-	-pp-	mp	lp	rp	-p(-)	k-	-kk-	C+k	-k(-)
OSax	t	tt	t	t	t	p	pp	mp	lp	rp	p	k	kk	k	k
MFranc	z	z	z	33	t/3	p	pp	mp	lp	rp	f(f)	k	kk	k	ch
Rh-Franc	z	z	z	33	3	p	pp	mp	lp/ lpf	rp/ rpf	f(f)	k	kk	k	ch
S Rh-Fr	z	z	z	33	3	p	pf	mpf	lpf	rpf	f(f)	k	kk	k	ch
E Franc	z	z	z	33	3	pf	pf	mpf	lpf	rpf	f(f)	k	kk	k	ch
Bav	z	z	z	33	3	pf	pf	mf	lf	rf	f(f)	kx	kx	kx	ch
Alem	z	z	z	33	3	pf/f	pf/ff	mf	lf	rf	f(f)	ch	kx	ch	ch
Langob	z	z	z	s(s)	s	p	p(p)	mpf	lpf	rpf	p/f(f)	k	kk	k/kx	ch

The High German Consonant Shift overall constitutes a nonassimilatory sound change that produces relatively marked segmental output (affricates) from unmarked input (simple stops). Yet it has long been recognised that nonassimilatory sound changes typically engender reductions in markedness, not increases (cf. Anttila 1972, Houlihan and Iverson 1979; Vennemann 1988; Forner et al. 1992, among others). For example, marked rounded front vowels ([ü, ö]) all became unrounded ([i, e]) in the history of English (my: si > *mice*), marked affricates ([ts, tsš]) all became less marked fricatives ([s, sš]) in the history of French (cf. *chief* < medieval French vs. *chef* < modern French), etc. The creation of an affricate series from plain voiceless stops in Old High German thus represents a distinct oddity among sound changes, not just by virtue of having neither precedent nor parallel elsewhere (cf. particularly Vennemann 1985), but also because, as nonassimilatory change, the output of the shift is invariably marked relative to its input.

A strictly structural motivation most likely lies behind the way in which the High German Consonant Shift extended from medial to initial position, but the skewed geographical distribution of the shift in initial position has continued to puzzle Germanic specialists. However, the varying content of feature representation by place of articulation on the geometric model of (5) accords exactly with the attested pattern of the shift's extension, such that less place-feature structure correlates positively with broader spread of the shift, while more structure inhibits spread.

The geographically more limited affrication of labials relative to coronals and the still more limited affrication of velars in the High German consonant shift therefore parallel Rice's (1994) observation that increased place-structure content correlates with resistance to assimilatory change. Under the general assumption that only marked features spread, and then only into less marked positions, the bias in assimilation derives automatically from phonologically underspecified geometric representation. But even though the High German consonant shift of stops to affricates is not an assimilation, it still exhibits the same asymmetries as found in place assimilation. Davis, Iverson and Salmons (1999) seek to bring nonassimilatory changes like the High German Consonant Shift into the same fold as place-biased assimilatory changes. Their observation relative to operations whose outputs are marked relative to inputs is the principle in (9):

(9)   Input Markedness Criterion Unmarked structures are affected preferentially in shifts to marked outputs.

The assimilatory biases noted previously conform to this criterion because a shift from coronal to peripheral (or from labial to dorsal) place of articulation constitutes an increase in the representational markedness of the segments affected by the change, hence coronals are more liable to assimilate than peripherals (and labials more than dorsals). Extension of the nonassimilatory High German shift into word-marginal positions meets this criterion in the same way, with the same kind of bias, because the shift's affricate output is marked relative to its simple stop input. Increased place-structure content thus correlates with resistance to assimilatory as well as nonassimilatory change under the terms of (9).

This principle further authenticates the fundamental role that markedness plays in sound change, for it complements Vennemann's (1988) 'Diachronic Maxim' interpreting sound change generally as causing decreases in markedness. While this 'fix-the-worst-first' principle holds for changes which happen to result in markedness reductions, many of them context-free, it misses the extensive class of context-sensitive changes which produce relatively marked outputs with a bias to affect unmarked structures preferentially over marked ones. Together, the Diachronic Maxim (governing changes resulting in less marked outputs) and the Input Markedness Criterion (governing changes resulting in more marked outputs) cover a fuller range of markedness-based sound changes and contribute to explanation of the observed asymmetries.

To recapitulate: the High German Consonant Shift found its original motivation in prosody, but unlike umlaut, this shift of stops to affricates is a distinctly nonassimilatory change. We argue that it is nonetheless responsive to the kind of geometric markedness that Rice proposes and is at least indirectly connected to the coarticulation-derived pattern found in umlaut blocking and in the umlautless residues.

8   Conclusions

This chapter has tried to trace a piece of the relationship between phonetics and phonology in sound change, particularly the role of peripherality, with exemplification via Germanic umlaut and the Second Consonant Shift. We find:

- Both umlaut and the High German Consonant Shift began as relatively simple changes, motivated by coarticulation and prosody. The emerging analyses fit closely with the familiar view that complex sound changes originate in low-level phonetic phenomena.
- Rice's hierarchical, apparently universal scheme of representational markedness for place of articulation properties leads to a particular diachronic generalisation: resistance to change correlates with the complexity of representation, such that unmarked structures are favoured in shifts to marked outputs, whereas marked structures are favoured in shifts to unmarked outputs.
- Though the role of phonetics can be well distinguished from that of phonology in the arena of sound change, phonetics also interacts indirectly with phonology, so that the later, structural unfoldings of both umlaut and the Second Consonant Shift still carry reflections of their phonetic origins.
- There is an identifiable range of fundamental, universally motivated structural connections between umlaut and the High German Consonant Shift.

We conclude with the observation that, in our view, the basis of phonological, structural peripherality in consonantal feature representation is itself ingenerate, i.e. the place markedness encoded in Rice's proposal and illustrated here with respect to the High German Consonant Shift is itself derivative of the coarticulatory forces at play in nascent umlaut. That is, the bias expressed in umlaut toward inhibition or 'blocking' of coarticulation across velars, less across labials, and least across coronals mirrors exactly the assimilatory as well as nonassimilatory resistance to historical change affecting consonants, and is, we believe, the phonetic grounding for the emergence of peripherals as marked consonant types. This is a significant finding, we believe, for it explains, or at least ties to considerations of coarticulation, the particular place markedness that others have merely identified.

REFERENCES

Anttila, Raimo. 1972. *An introduction to historical and comparative linguistics*. New York: Macmillan.
Antonsen, Elmer H. 1969. 'Zur Umlautfeindlichkeit des Oberdeutschen', *Zeitschrift für Dialektologie and Linguistik* 36: 201–7.
Avery, Peter and Keren Rice. 1989. 'Segment structure and coronal underspecification', *Phonology* 6: 179–200.
Bladon, Anthony and Ameen Al-Bamerni. 1976. 'Coarticulation resistance in English /l/', *Journal of Phonetics* 4: 137–50.
Braune, Wilhelm. 1874. 'Zur Kenntnis des Fränkischen und zur hochdeutschen Lautverschiebung', *PBB (Beiträge zur Geschichte der deutschen Sprache und Literatur)* 1: 1–56.
Braune, Wilhelm. 1987. *Althochdeutsche Grammatik*, 14th edition, ed. Hans Eggers. Tübingen: Niemeyer.
Britain, David. 1997. 'Dialect contact and phonological reallocation: "Canadian Raising" in the English Fens', *Language in Society* 26: 15–46.
Buccini, Anthony F. 1992. 'The development of umlaut and the dialectal position of Dutch in Germanic', doctoral dissertation, Cornell University.
Butcher, Andrew and Eckart Weiher. 1976. 'An electropalatographic investigation of coarticulation in VCV sequences', *Journal of Phonetics* 4: 59–74.
Cohn, Abigail and Ayako Tsuchida. 1999. 'Sonorant devoicing and the phonetic realization of [spread glottis] in English', paper presented at the Linguistic Society of America, Los Angeles.
Davis, Garry W. and Gregory K. Iverson. 1995. 'The High German Consonant Shift as feature spreading', *American Journal of Germanic Linguistics* 7: 111–27.
Davis, Garry W., Gregory K. Iverson and Joseph C. Salmons. 1999. 'Peripherality in the spread of the High German consonant shift', *PBB (Beiträge zur Geschichte der deutschen Sprache und Literatur)* 118.1: 69–86.
Farnetani, Edda. 1997. 'Coarticulation and connected speech processes', in William J. Hardcastle and John Laver (eds.), *The handbook of phonetic sciences*. Cambridge, MA: Blackwell, 371–404.

Forner, Monica, Jeanette K. Gundel, Kathleen Houlihan and Gerald Sanders. 1992. 'On the historical development of marked forms', in G. Davis and G. Iverson (eds.), *Explanation in historical linguistics*. Amsterdam: Benjamins, 77–93.

Franz, W. 1883. 'Die lateinisch-romanischen Elemente im Althochdeutschen', PhD dissertation, Straßburg.

Hasenclever, Max. 1905. *Der Dialekt der Gemeinde Wermelskirchen*. Marburg: Elwert.

Houlihan, Kathleen and Gregory K. Iverson. 1979. 'Functionally constrained phonology', in D. Dinnsen (ed.), *Current approaches to phonological theory*. Bloomington: Indiana University Press, 50–73.

Howell, Robert B. 1991. *Old English breaking and its Germanic analogues*. Tübingen: Max Niemeyer.

Howell, Robert B. and Joseph C. Salmons. 1997. 'Umlautless residues in Germanic', *American Journal of Germanic Linguistics* 9: 83–111.

Iverson, Gregory K. and Joseph C. Salmons. 1996. 'The primacy of primary umlaut', *PBB (Beiträge zur Geschichte der deutschen Sprache und Literatur)* 118: 69–86.

Iverson, Gregory K. 1999. 'Umlaut as regular sound change: the phonetic basis of "ingenerate umlaut"', in Edgar C. Polomé and Carol Justus (ed.), *Festschrift for W. P. Lehmann*. 207–24.

Iverson, Gregory K. and Kee-Ho Kim. 1987. 'Underspecification and hierarchical feature representation in Korean consonantal phonology', *Proceedings of the Chicago Linguistics Society* 23: 182–98.

Iverson, Gregory K. and Joseph C. Salmons. 2000. 'Zur historischen Phonetik und Phonologie des Umlauts im Deutschen', *Zentrum für Allgemeine Sprachforschung Papers in Linguistics* 15. Humboldt Universität, Berlin, 68–76.

Iverson, Gregory K., Garry W. Davis and Joseph C. Salmons. 1994. 'Umlaut blocking environments in Old High German', *Folia Linguistica Historica* 15: 131–48.

Keating, Patricia A. 1988. 'Underspecification in phonetics', *Phonology* 5: 275–92.

Keller, Rudi E. 1978. *The German language*. Atlantic Highlands, NJ: The Humanities Press.

Kenstowicz, Michael. 1994. *Phonology in generative grammar*. Cambridge, MA: Blackwell.

King, Robert D. 1969. *Historical linguistics and generative grammar*. Englewood Cliffs, NJ: Prentice-Hall.

Kiparsky, Paul 1971. 'Historical linguistics', in W. O. Dingwall (ed.), *A survey of linguistic science*. College Park: University of Maryland Linguistics Program, 576–649.

Kiparsky, Paul. 1985. 'Some consequences of Lexical Phonology', *Phonology Yearbook* 2: 85–138.

Kirchner, Robert. 1997. 'Contrastiveness and faithfulness', *Phonology* 14: 83–111.

Klatt, Dennis H. 1991. 'Voice onset time, frication, and aspiration in word-initial consonant clusters', R. J. Baken and R. G. Daniloff (eds.), *Readings in clinical spectrography of speech*. San Diego: Singular Publishing Group, 226–46.

Labov, William. 1972. *Sociolinguistic patterns*. Philadelphia: University of Pennsylvania Press.

Lerchner, Gotthard. 1971. *Zur II. Lautverschiebung im Rheinisch-Westmitteldeutschen*. Mitteldeutsche Studien 30. Halle: Niemeyer.

Lüssy, Heinrich. 1974. *Umlautprobleme im Schweizerdeutschen*. Beiträge zur schweizerdeutschen Mundartforschung 20. Frauenfeld: Huber and Co.

Maddieson, Ian. 1984. *Patterns of sound*. Cambridge University Press.

Magen, Harriet Sue. 1989. 'An acoustic study of vowel-to-vowel coarticulation in English', PhD dissertation: Yale University.

Ohala, John J. 1993. 'Coarticulation and phonology', *Language and Speech* 36: 155–70.

Öhman, S. 1966. 'Coarticulation in VCV utterances: spectrographic measurements', *Journal of the Acoustical Society of America* 39: 151–268.

Paul, Hermann, P. Wiehl and S. Grosse. 1989. *Mittelhochdeutsche Grammatik*, 23rd edition. Tübingen: Max Niemeyer.

Penzl, Herbert. 1949. 'Umlaut and secondary umlaut in Old High German', *Language* 25: 223–40.

Penzl, Herbert. 1994. 'Historiographie und Sprachgeschichte: zur Beschreibung des althochdeutschen i-Umlauts', *American Journal of Germanic Linguistics* 6: 51–62.

Prokosch, Eduard. 1917. 'Die deutsche Lautverschiebung und die Völkerwanderung', *Journal of English and Germanic Philology* 16: 1–26.

Prokosch, Eduard. 1938. *A comparative Germanic grammar*. Baltimore: Linguistic Society of America.

Recasens, Daniel. 1984. 'V-to-C coarticulation in Catalan VCV sequences: an articulatory and acoustical study', *Journal of the Acoustical Society of America* 91: 2911–25.

Rice, Keren. 1994. 'Peripheral in consonants', *Canadian Journal of Linguistics* 39: 191–216.

Rice, Keren. 1996. 'Default variability: the coronal–velar relationship', *Natural Language and Linguistic Theory* 14: 493–543.

Russ, Charles V. J. 1977. 'Die Entwicklung des Umlauts im Deutschen im Spiegel verschiedener linguistischer Theorien', *PBB (Beiträge zur Geschichte der deutschen Sprach und Literatur)* 99: 213–41.

Schirmunski, Viktor M. 1962. *Deutsche Mundartkunde*. Berlin: Akademie Verlag.

Sonderegger, Stefan. 1974. *Althochdeutsche Sprache und Literatur*. Berlin: de Gruyter.

Twaddell, W. Freeman. 1938. 'A note on OHG umlaut', *Monatshefte* 30: 177–81.

Vennemann, Theo. 1985. 'The bifurcation theory of the Germanic and German consonant shifts: synopsis and some further thoughts', in Jacek Fisiak (ed.), *Papers from the Sixth International Conference on Historical Linguistics*. Amsterdam: Benjamins, pp. 527–47.

Vennemann, Theo. 1988. *Preference laws for syllable structure and the explanation of sound change*. Berlin: Mouton de Gruyter.

13 How do dialects get the features they have? On the process of new dialect formation

Raymond Hickey

1 Introduction

The concern of the present chapter is to look at a particular type of situation found historically in the anglophone world outside England and to consider the forces which have been instrumental in determining what features the varieties at this location evince. The location in question is New Zealand for what can be termed a *new dialect formation* scenario (Trudgill et al. 2000a).

The present chapter is intended to make explicit the assumptions which lie behind the discussion of new dialect formation and so hopefully clarify the many issues of theoretical importance raised by the recent innovative work on this process by Elizabeth Gordon, Peter Trudgill and their associates. Before beginning, it is important to stress that the examination of this scenario rests on a significant premise, necessary for the discussion to be found below: speakers are unconsciously aware of features in their own variety and those which they are continually in contact with. If this premise is not accepted in principle then the arguments below will be vacuous. With regard to new dialect formation, I am in broad agreement with the statement by Trudgill et al. that 'we conclude that the shape of New Zealand English, a fascinating laboratory for the study of linguistic change, can be accounted for in terms of the mixing together of different dialects of English from the British Isles' (Trudgill et al. 2000a: 316). However, the deterministic view which sees the numerical superiority of variants as the main reason for the survival of some and the rejection of others would appear to be too simple and in need of further nuancing to include, at the very least, speakers' active, though unconscious, participation in the forging of a new variety and a more differentiated assessment of the status of the main ethnic groups in New Zealand society in the second half of the nineteenth century.

This chapter will first of all present a summary of the situation with new dialect formation and then consider what happened during focusing, i.e. at the

* I am grateful to various colleagues who provided useful comments on previous versions of this chapter. In particular I would like to mention Karen Corrigan, Lyle Campbell, James Milroy, Peter Trudgill and an anonymous reviewer of Cambridge University Press. All these provided valuable suggestions, from their particular specialities within linguistics, which have hopefully improved the chapter. As always, any shortcomings are the author's own.

stage when New Zealand English attained a stable and distinctive profile. New dialect formation concerns phonology almost exclusively. But it would appear that early forms of New Zealand English also showed considerable grammatical variation. However, this appears to have been levelled out with later generations of speakers (Peter Trudgill, personal communication).

Within the context of the present book this chapter would appear to be justified because it illustrates principles which seem to have been operative historically – random vs. predetermined transmission across generations, for example – and which are thus part of language change. These principles are worthy of consideration in the genesis of varieties of English which arose out of many other scenarios. Furthermore, certain aspects of this genesis differ in principle in the different scenarios and so provide illuminating contrast. For instance, peer-dialect in the critical phase of accent determination (up to one's teens) was present, for instance, in language-shift situations (in Ireland and South Africa) and absent in the earlier phases of new dialect formation in New Zealand (Gordon and Trudgill 1999, 2003).

2   New dialect formation

The term *new dialect formation* refers to a linguistic situation which arises when there is a mixture of dialects leading to a single new dialect which is different from all inputs. In the context of New Zealand, new dialect formation took place after initial immigration of speakers from different regions of the British Isles. This was a process of dialect mixture in which, over just a few generations, a clearly focused variety arose which was then fairly uniform and distinct from any other existing varieties of the language in question.

Due to the felicitous decision of the National Broadcasting Corporation of New Zealand to record the experiences of older people, mostly children of the first European settlers in New Zealand (Trudgill et al. 2000b: 113f.), there is now a body of acoustic data which documents the speech of New Zealanders reaching back into the second half of the nineteenth century. The Mobile Disc Recording Unit of the NBCNZ made the recordings between 1946 and 1948 and in 1989, under the auspices of Elizabeth Gordon, from the Department of Linguistics of the University of Canterbury, Christchurch, purchased copies of the recordings. These have been transcribed, catalogued and remastered so as to serve as a reliable body of data on early New Zealand English. The uniqueness of this corpus lies in the fact that it goes back as far as one can get to the founding generation of settlers in New Zealand; indeed it is unique in the context of overseas varieties of English, none of which has data as close as this to the first settlers of their particular location. The data in the recordings has been analysed meticulously by Peter Trudgill, Elizabeth Gordon and their associates (Gordon 1998) and the result of their work has been published in a number of articles in recent years (see the survey in Gordon, Campbell, Lewis, Maclagan and Trudgill forthcoming). These studies represent the most significant examination of new dialect formation to date and have thus been consulted in detail for the present chapter which looks at the assumptions and principles of new dialect formation with a view to reaching a better understanding of this process which is central to the dissemination of English during the past few centuries.

It is an essential assumption of Peter Trudgill, Elizabeth Gordon and their associates that the distinctiveness of the variety resulting from new dialect formation is an epiphenomenon arising from the interaction of forces which are not directly under the control of speakers. The new variety is in no way constructed by its speakers in order to have a distinctive form of a language spoken elsewhere which would then match other collective differences to be found in the new society at the overseas location. This point is one where the present author differs most from Peter Trudgill, Elizabeth Gordon and their associates. The linguistic profile of a new variety can, in the present author's opinion, indeed be seen as a product of unconscious choices made across a broad front in a new society to create a distinct linguistic identity. This motivation is not one which is to be found early on (in Trudgill's first and probably his second phase as well, see below). It probably does not apply to the process of koinéisation, the levelling out of salient regional features in the initial dialect mix (Gordon 1998; Bauer 1986, 2000), but it can be seen as an unconscious motivation determining the extent to which inherited ongoing linguistic change is favoured or not. Such change, as Elizabeth Gordon, Peter Trudgill and their associates readily concede, often involves the favouring of quantitatively minor variants. This in turn can be interpreted as motivated by speakers' gradual awareness of an embryonic new variety of the immigrants' language, something which correlates with the distinctive profile of the new society which is speaking this variety. If such a view has any validity, then this is only towards the end of the third stage of new dialect formation (see below) when focusing takes place, although the scene may be set in the second stage, for example with the favouring of somewhat raised short front vowels from the initial mixture of realisations (Trudgill, Gordon and Lewis 1998), something which provided the trajectory along which New Zealand English has moved since (Bell 1997).[1]

2.1   Three stages in new dialect formation

In the work of Peter Trudgill new dialect formation has been a theme since the mid 1980s (see Trudgill 1986) and recently he has refined his views on the stages

---

[1] Lyle Campbell points out that the raising of short front vowels which is so characteristic of modern New Zealand English was probably present embryonically with the input dialects of southern British English.

involved here. Essentially, Trudgill recognises three stages with the second and third subdivided into two further stages. As these divisions are central to any consideration of new dialect formation, it is worth recalling the description of the three stages offered in Trudgill et al. (2000a).

The first stage: rudimentary levelling

The first stage involves the initial contact between adult speakers of different regional and social varieties in the new location, with certain types of accommodation of speakers to one another in face-to-face interaction and thus, as a consequence, rudimentary dialect levelling. In the case of New Zealand, this stage would have lasted until approximately 1860.

For instance, a widespread 19th-century British feature which is absent from our recordings is the merger of /v/ and /w/ as /w/, giving *village* as *willage*, which was a feature of many south-of-England dialects at this time.   (Trudgill et al. 2000a: 303f.)[2]

Significantly, the feature with which Trudgill and his associates choose to illustrate the initial dialect levelling is one which involved not inconsiderable homophony in those varieties of southern nineteenth-century British English which showed it. This fact is relevant to the discussion below; but to continue, the other stages are described in the words of Trudgill et al. (2000a).

The second stage (a): extreme variability

The second stage of the new-dialect formation process, of which the ONZE [*Origins of New Zealand Corpus* – RH] corpus now provides direct rather than inferred evidence, and which would have lasted until approximately 1900, is characterised by considerable variability.   (Trudgill et al. 2000a: 304)[3]

The period they are interested in consists of the last four decades of the nineteenth century for which there is considerable demographic data available in census form, as will be discussed shortly. Trudgill et al. (2000a: 305) do concede that it was in the 'linguistic melting pots' that the greatest degree of variability was to be found and where new dialect formation was promoted. Such melting pots were urban centres, although not large by present-day European standards, and they mention Arrowtown specifically.

The conclusion from this is that new dialect formation is an essentially urban phenomenon, or, at the very least, one which requires a density of speakers from different backgrounds and importantly from all the backgrounds which are significant for the settlement of the country in question. In the context of late

---

[2] According to Lyle Campbell this variation was not present in the input to New Zealand English.
[3] The interpretation of variation with the speakers of the ONZE corpus depends crucially on the validity of the notion of *apparent time*, that is, the extent to which speakers retain the type of pronunciation they developed in their youth throughout the rest of their lives. If one does not accept this premise then it becomes difficult to extrapolate from these speakers back towards the earliest forms of New Zealand English. And of course in the situation of new dialect formation some adults may have accommodated towards other adults thus masking their original pronunciation of key variables.

nineteenth-century New Zealand the three principal backgrounds are England, Scotland and Ireland.

The second stage (b): further levelling

Inter-individual variability of this type, however, although striking and considerable, is perhaps somewhat reduced compared to what was present during the first stage. That is, in spite of all the variability we witness in the ONZE corpus, it is possible that some further levelling occurred. For example, there are some features which we can be fairly sure must have been brought to New Zealand by some immigrating speakers, and must therefore have survived the initial contact stage and have been present in early New Zealand English, but which are nevertheless absent, or almost so, from the ONZE recordings.[4]

One such feature is the use of the FOOT vowel in the lexical sets of both FOOT and STRUT, indicating a system of five rather than six short, checked vowels. As is well known, this feature was and still is normal in middle-class as well as working-class accents in nearly all of England north of a line from the Bristol Channel to the Wash – an area comprising approximately half the geographical surface of England and containing approximately half its population.   (Trudgill et al. 2000a: 306f.)

Trudgill et al. (2000a) explain the virtual absence of a five-term short vowel system, i.e. one without a STRUT vowel, demographically because the only northern county with this system and from which there was noticeable emigration to New Zealand was Warwickshire (though very little is known about this).

So a feature with such low statistical occurrence would not have any reasonable chance of surviving the process of new dialect formation.

Third stage focussing

It is only subsequently, then, in the third stage, that the new dialect will appear as a stable, crystallised variety. This crystallisation is the result of a *focussing* [italics mine – RH] process whose effects are very clear in modern New Zealand English, which has a remarkably small amount of regional variation. However, the big question is, as we have already noted, why the levelling that occurred took the precise form that it did.
                    (Trudgill et al. 2000a: 307)

In their elaboration of this focusing, Trudgill et al. state that the focusing takes place via (i) koinéisation which involves the loss of demographically minority variants and (ii) simplification which can lead to the survival of minority variants if these display more regularity than the majority variants. An example of the latter would be the use of schwa in unstressed syllables as is found in New Zealand English in words like *David, naked*. Trudgill et al. point out that only about 32 per cent of their informants from the ONZE archives had schwa in this position, i.e. speakers of Irish, East Anglian and West Country origin, but

---

[4] Lyle Campbell is doubtful about this given the lack of evidence and considers the input from the English regions to have been much more restricted.

because schwa is a less marked vowel than /i/ it survived the third stage of new dialect formation (Trudgill et al. 2000a: 311).

2.2   *The quantitative argument*

In their discussion of the survival of forms into the third stage, and hence into modern New Zealand English, Trudgill et al. emphasise that it is majority forms which survive. They stress that 'majority' refers to the numerical occurrence of a form across all dialect groupings of late nineteenth-century New Zealand and not just in the most numerous grouping, i.e. the immigrants from southeastern England. To illustrate this they discuss the demise of *h*-dropping in early New Zealand English (Trudgill et al. 2000a: 309, see also Bell and Holmes 1992; Maclagan 1998). This was found with the majority of southeastern English speakers but with only a minority of all dialect speakers at the critical phase. The southeastern English constituted the largest group (though they were just less than 50 per cent), however no feature of southeastern English could survive (even if it was 100 per cent present there) unless this feature was shared in part by another group in order to have an overall occurrence of over 50 per cent.

To strengthen their argument, Trudgill et al. discuss another phenomenon, this time a merger, which did not occur in New Zealand English.

Another southeast-of-England feature which did not survive into New Zealand English was the merger of /w/ and /ʍ/, as in *which, where, white*. (It is true that this merger is now appearing in modern New Zealand English, but this seems to be a recent phenomenon – see Bayard, 1987.) Here again, we can advance the same explanation. Although the Englishes of southeastern England and, probably, Australia, had merged *whales* and *Wales*, it was the Scottish, Irish and northern England (and probably North American) form which was the one to survive the levelling process for purely demographic reasons – and this in spite of mergers having an advantage over distinctions.

(Trudgill et al. 2000a: 310)

Two further aspects, over and beyond numerical considerations, should be added here. The first is that /h/-dropping, like the /v/ to /w/ shift (see above), is a feature which results in considerable homophony in English so that while the general principle that mergers are preferred over distinctions in contact situations holds,

Table 13.1. Survival of majority forms in New Zealand English

H-dropping			
	S-E English c. 50%	others	(Scottish 22%; Irish 20%, etc.)
with	70%	0%	
without	30%	100%	
overall:	only 35% have dropping		

this is not so when significant homophony arises as a result. The second point to make concerns the status of the voiceless labio-velar glide [ʍ]. There are strong phonological reasons for considering this as consisting of /h/ + /w/ although phonetically it is a single segment. This is in keeping with the view that sonority increases from the edge to the nucleus of a syllable and that glides – [j] and [w] – are voiced in English in accordance with their unmarked value (see Hickey 1984 for further cogent arguments in favour of this phonological interpretation). Thus the retention of /h/ and /hw/ [ʍ] in early New Zealand English increased the phonological symmetry of the emerging variety. The recent tendency to lose [ʍ] could, as in the case of southern British English in general, be a result of its restricted distribution in English, i.e. it only occurs in word-initial position and does not have a high functional load, despite such minimal pairs as *wet* and *whet*, *which* and *witch* (none of the elements of these pairs are from the same word class and any speech context is ample to distinguish them).

Trudgill et al. (2000a: 311) remark further that 'what was *not* present at the first stage, of course, was the *combination* of /h/-dropping with retention of /ʍ/ demonstrated by Mr Ritchie' (an informant from the ONZE archive – RH). Assuming that the recordings are distinct enough for this situation to be clearly recognised, then one can only conclude that this distribution is an idiosyncrasy of one speaker. There is no variety of English which has /h/-dropping and [ʍ], because /h/-dropping means that the cluster /hw/ has also been simplified to /w/.

2.3   The survival of minority variants

***Ambidental fricatives in* THINK *and* BREATHE[5].** In the discussion of third-stage focusing above, it was stated that in some cases minority variants can survive if they represent the unmarked option in a set of variants. The prime example offered by (Trudgill et al. 2000a) is the use of /ə/ rather than /ɪ/ in unstressed syllables in words like *trusted*. However, this does not appear to consider all factors in such instances. To illustrate that there is more involved here than appears initially, consider another case of survival and demise discussed by Peter Trudgill, Elizabeth Gordon and their associates.

Many of our speakers have the distinctively Irish feature of using dental plosives rather than the interdental fricatives /θ/ and /ð/. We must not, however, be surprised that this feature has been levelled out in modern New Zealand English because it was still a minority form amongst our informants, as it would also have been in Australia. (Trudgill et al. 2000a: 312)

---

[5] Because Wells (1982) does not have lexical sets for the ambidental fricatives of standard English, I use these two here and underline the segments being referred to.

But this argument is in contradiction to that used when explaining the survival of minority /ə/ in unstressed syllables (see above). The ambidental fricatives of English are cross-linguistically quite marked and are only to be found in English, Welsh, Spanish, some Italian dialects, Greek and Danish, in the context of European languages, for example. It is true that dental stops are less marked than dental fricatives (in the sense of cross-linguistic statistical occurrence and appearance in first-language acquisition), but in English the use of dental stops leads to a near merger with alveolar stops causing quasi-homophony (to English ears) in pairs of words like *tinker* and *thinker*. Indeed given the fact that over 45 per cent of the Irish emigrants were from Munster (McCarthy 2000: 272) a significant proportion of the Irish may have had a dental to alveolar merger anyway, i.e. complete homophony. The retention of English ambidental fricatives had the advantage of disambiguation for many words quite apart from it being in accord with the relative prestige of the English section of the early New Zealand population.

2.4   The interpretation of mergers

Short vowels before /r/. Peter Trudgill, Elizabeth Gordon and their associates in general support the dictum that mergers advance at the expense of distinctions in a dialect contact and new dialect formation scenario. As an instance of this they cite a common distinction found among speakers of Scottish origin in the ONZE archives, i.e. the use of distinctive values (up to three) for vowels before /r/ as in *fir, fur, fern*. 'Not only was this a minority form demographically in the original mixture, but simplification dictates that mergers normally survive at the expense of non-mergers in contact situations (Labov, 1994)' (Trudgill et al. 2000a: 314).

In the opinion of the present author this is too simplified a view of the matter: mergers are only preferred if the functional load of the distinction realised in the nonmerged situation is *low*. This is clearly the case with short vowels before tautosyllabic /r/. The distinction between /i/ and /u/ has a minimal pair *fir* vs. *fur* and for the mid front vowel one of the few pairs is *tern* vs. *turn*. The homophony is nothing near that resulting from /h/-dropping or the merger of /v/ with /w/.

Short versus long low vowels. English dialects are known for the fluctuation they show in the realisation of low vowels in two specific phonetic contexts. The first is before fricatives (Wells 1982) as in *laugh, path, grass*, where one finds [æ] or [ɑː], and the second is before a nasal or nasal plus obstruent (the latter applies above all to Romance loanwords) as in *sample, demand, plant, dance*, where either [æ] or [ɑː] is found. Trudgill et al. (1998) see evidence for two separate contexts, resulting from two distinct sound changes, in their ONZE recordings.

Excluding speakers, as we obviously must, who do not have a distinction between /æ/ and /ɑː/ – presumably as a result of West Country and/or Scottish input – as well as those with obvious north-of-England accents who have /æ/ in both sets, very many ONZE speakers consistently have /ɑː/ in the lexical set of *after, grass, path* but /æ/ in the set of *dance, plant, sample*. Out of 79 eligible speakers, 38 (48%) have this pattern. In the end, in modern New Zealand English, it was the pattern used by the other 52% of our informants which won out. But it must have been a close-run thing.

(Trudgill et al. 2000a: 315)

Here differences in numerical distribution of 2–3 per cent are named as the reason why a certain variant survived. It is questionable whether this 2–3 per cent in fact existed over the entire population of late nineteenth-century New Zealand. It may have been more but it could equally have been less. One could just as well postulate that the two-vowel system was abandoned in the dialect mixture situation of late nineteenth-century New Zealand English (on Australia in this respect, see Bradley 1991) as it did not lead to any noticeable homophony; there are few minimal pairs involving /æ/ and /ɑː/ in English and they tend to be peripheral anyway, such as *Pam* and *palm* or *cam* and *calm*.

This is precisely the type of merger which occurs in contact situations: phonotactic conditioning in the use of closely related vowels is present. Levelling occurs because language learners either do not grasp the conditioning or choose to ignore it. And they are not motivated to try and discern the conditioning as the functional load of the distinction is slight.

2.5   Numbers, distribution and status

Central to the arguments of Trudgill and his associates concerning the genesis of New Zealand English are the proportions of anglophone settlers in nineteenth-century New Zealand. The default case for any given feature of the later variety is that the input form favoured was the majority form across all the dialect groupings represented in the country. The proportions were determined using census figures covering the period up to 1881 (at which time the third stage had got under way). Figures are given in table 13.2 on the basis of McKinnon (1997).

The purely quantitative argument for the survival of dialect features throws up a number of problems straight away. Firstly, it presumes a nonstratified society so that the relative status of various immigrants can be eliminated as a relevant factor in the process. Secondly, it assumes that the proportions of immigrants from the main areas of Britain, distinguishing at least southern and northern England, Scotland and Ireland, were the same across the entire country, at least for those areas which are regarded as non-isolated. But it is much more likely for this not to have been the case. It is well known from immigration patterns in other parts of the anglophone world, such as the southeastern United States

Table 13.2. Proportions of anglophone settlers
in late nineteenth-century New Zealand

England	49%
Scotland	22%
Ireland	20%
Australia	7%
Wales	1%
N. America	1%

or Newfoundland, both in the eighteenth century and later in the United States in the nineteenth century, that immigrants from specific backgrounds clustered in certain areas. The most obvious reason for this is that those who went first passed the message about where they had settled back to those in the area they came from. Others then followed on, going to the same area at the overseas location (see further discussion below). If one assumes that this was the default case for New Zealand in the nineteenth century as well, then one can assume local proportions for the major regions of Britain which would have varied, depending on initial settlement patterns. An obvious case of this is the Otago and Southland regions of the South Island where many Scottish settled (Trudgill et al. 2000a: 305).

There is a further difficulty with the quantitative argument. It assumes that all speakers in non-isolated areas were exposed to the variants of the regional immigrants in the precise proportions in which they existed statistically for the entire country. That is, if one assumes 49 per cent English, 22 per cent Scottish and 20 per cent Irish immigrants more or less across the country, then with the purely numerical argument all non-isolated speakers must have had the proportions 49 : 22 : 20 in their immediate vicinity for them to end up making the choices across variants which the quantitative model claims to predict.

Of course Elizabeth Gordon, Peter Trudgill and their associates are aware of the difficulties of a purely quantitative model applied uniformly to the whole country. They speak of 'linguistic melting pots' (usually urban centres) where a great degree of variability was to be found and where new dialect formation was promoted. Conceding this offers a more realistic picture but it also brings into focus an additional problem for later New Zealand English, namely, how did the relative homogeneity of English spoken there develop? The answer in the opinion of the present author lies in the process of supraregionalisation, which is attested in other parts of the anglophone world, most noticeably in nineteenth-century Ireland. This phenomenon will be dealt with presently, but first a closer look at not just the numerical size of dialect groupings in nineteenth-century New Zealand but also an examination of their social status, inasmuch as this is discernible today, is called for.

2.5.1   Nineteenth-century emigration to New Zealand

In the second half of the nineteenth century emigration from Ireland, which far exceeded that of the Ulster Scots to the United States in the eighteenth century, set in (Bielenberg 2000). The first census figures in Ireland are those for 1851 and examining the figures up to the last census before the First World War (in 1911) one can see that it was the southwest and the northeast of the country (Duffy et al. 1997: 102f.) which suffered the greatest depletion in population due to emigration, although counties in the west such as Roscommon and Mayo suffered most during the Great Famine of the late 1840s. Put in stark terms, the reduction in population during the famine meant simply that there were fewer inhabitants left to emigrate.

In the period under consideration the major counties of Munster each lost between 300,000 and 500,000 inhabitants due to emigration. In the northeast of the country the somewhat smaller counties of Ulster also lost a similar number, relatively speaking, with Antrim leading here. Only a small percentage of those who emigrated left for the Southern Hemisphere, about 7 per cent for Australia and New Zealand, this contrasting strongly with 64 per cent to the United States and 25 per cent to Britain.

The New Zealand Company (originally the New Zealand Association) was an organisation formed in 1837 by the colonial reformer Edward Gibbon Wakefield (1796–1862). This company, along with the Plymouth Company (founding New Plymouth in Taranaki on the west coast of the North Island), was responsible for the initial British emigration to New Zealand from about 1840 to 1860 (Bauer 1994: 383; Rice 1992; Sinclair 1996; Simpson 1997). Scottish free-church emigrants settled in Otago and Southland on the South Island.

When considering Irish emigration to New Zealand one should first mention an early settlement from Australia which, especially in Auckland, led to a very high proportion of Irish there (over 30 per cent in 1851, Bauer 1994: 386). This was to drop somewhat later, but Auckland retained its high percentage of Irish. Australia as a source of British regional settlers was to become significant again in the gold rushes of the late 1850s and early 1860s to the West Coast and Otago, both on the South Island.

The Irish emigration to New Zealand was much slower to develop than that from England and peaked in the period from around 1870 to the outbreak of the First World War. With the outbreak of war transoceanic shipping was difficult and, afterwards, Irish independence was becoming a distinct possibility (realised in 1921), so emigration to such a distant location as New Zealand became less attractive to the Irish.

The late nineteenth-century emigration was not the type of immediate relief emigration which was to be found to Britain and America during the Great Famine (1845–8) and immediately afterwards. But it was linked up with rural conditions in Ireland. It is the agricultural depression of the 1870s which was probably a driving force for many younger, as yet childless couples (see statistics in section 2.5.4 below) to take on themselves the arduous voyage to the other side of the world.

The manner in which emigration was initiated varied in different parts of Ireland at different times. Essentially there were two types. First, there was official emigration where by some government agency or non-governmental organisation – such as a recruiting company – encouraged the Irish to try their luck abroad.[6] This was often done through advertising, extolling the advantages of life in terms of employment at the new location. The second type was what one could term individual emigration. In this situation individuals heard about prospects at some overseas anglophone location from other members of their families or from members of their local communities, usually through emigrant letters or directly in a seasonal migration scenario. Emigration of this type was most likely to keep intact the bonds of the social network in Ireland after emigration and was an added incentive bearing on the decision to leave the home country. It is the pattern to be found most clearly in Newfoundland where nearly all the Irish emigrants came from a clearly defined area, the city of Waterford and its immediate hinterland (Mannion 1977), and where the motivation to emigrate was twofold: abundant labour and transfer to an existing outpost of one's own community at the overseas location. In the absence of externally organised emigration, the second kind, based on community-internal networks, was virtually the only other type. An essential consequence of individual emigration is that it furthered the establishment of community clusters at the overseas location.

2.5.2   *How many Irish went to New Zealand?*

The percentage of Irish in the ethnic composition for the late nineteenth century in New Zealand is usually given at around 20 per cent. There are a number of sources for this (Akenson 1990: 60f.). Three authors who have concerned themselves with this question are quoted below.

1. Guy H. Scholefield in the New Zealand volume of *The Cambridge history of the British empire* (1933) gives the following statistics:

English	52%
Scottish	22.5%
Irish	21%
Total	95.5%

---

[6] One should mention that, apart from such obvious emigration as that unleashed by the gold rushes to the western part of the South Island in the 1860s, which brought some 25,000 Irish to New Zealand between 1858 and 1867 (Coogan 2000: 491; Davis 1974), there was also assisted emigration to New Zealand in the late nineteenth century. For this the Irish could travel to England, board English ships bound for New Zealand and receive assistance in becoming established there.

Table 13.3. Ethnic composition of non-Maori population (in percentages)

	Irish	Scottish	English + Welsh
1858	12.3	20.7	62.2
1861	13.1	22.1	56.4
1864	16.4	24.0	52.5
1867	18.3	23.4	50.6
1871	18.6	23.4	49.8
1874	18.0	22.9	50.2
1878	18.6	21.8	50.7
1881	18.9	21.7	50.7
1886	18.8	21.6	50.8
1891	18.7	21.7	51.1
1896	18.7	21.1	51.2
1901	18.7	21.5	52.1

2. The Australian social historian J. Lyng in 1939 gave the following figures for the non-Maori population:

English	47%
Scottish	24%
Irish	20%
Others	9%
Total	100.0%

3. James Oakely Wilson, chief librarian of the General Assembly Library, for the article on national groups for *An encyclopedia of New Zealand* gives these figures for the non-Maori population, broken down by periods:

	Irish	Scottish	English	Others
1858	11%	20%	60%	9%
1878	20%	22%	50%	8%
1901	19%	21%	51%	9%

Wilson's data are the most interesting in the present context as they show a steep rise in the late 1870s. This picture is confirmed by viewing the census returns from 1858 to 1901, given in table 13.3, which again show a culmination of Irish presence around 1880 (Akenson 1990: 63).

The kind of picture which emerges from these data is that of an Irish section of the late nineteenth-century New Zealand population of not more than 20 per cent

Table 13.4. Distribution of ethnic groups by region in 1871

	Auckland	Westland	Otago	Southland	Nelson	Hawke's Bay	Total
Ire	14.1	22.7	9.2	7.2	13.1	12.1	11.6
Sco	8.8	11.9	28.0	31.7	8.1	10.8	14.4
Eng	28.5	24.0	16.9	12.6	28.5	28.6	26.1
NZ	37.5	18.3	31.0	38.1	37.0	40.6	36.5

and only from the 1870s onwards.[7] Crucially for the present discussion, we can note that for the first phase of new dialect formation in New Zealand (up to 1860) there were only about 12 per cent Irish but that for the second phase (from about 1860 to 1900, Trudgill et al. 1998) there was on average 18.5 per cent, going on the census figures.

2.5.3   Where did the Irish settle?
It was mentioned above that the Irish tended to cluster at overseas locations given the type of individual emigration which was often practised. This clustering is in evidence in New Zealand just as in other Anglophone countries which experienced Irish emigration. Consider the figures given in table 13.4 for the distribution of the main ethnic groups from Britain in the third quarter of the nineteenth century (Akenson 1990: 54f.).

These data strongly suggest that in the area of Auckland, Westland, Hawke's Bay (all on the North Island) and in the west/northwest of the South Island the Irish were most prevalent. Indeed for all the regions listed above, there would seem to be an inverse proportion of Irish to Scottish settlers, a fact which may have its roots in sectarian animosities between Catholic Irish and Presbyterian Scottish.

2.5.4   What type of emigrants were the Irish?
The relevance of this question to the current discussion lies in the extent of influence of first-generation Irish immigrants on following generations. To illustrate what is involved here bear in mind that there was a practice of assisted emigration in the late nineteenth century and, as part of this, details concerning the status of emigrants were registered. As the late 1870s is the period of greatest Irish influx into New Zealand, the figures for 1876 are given for some 6,051 subjects (Akenson 1990: 44f.).

1. Unmarried adults (in all cases about half male/female and with an average age of between 22 and 25):

　　　　Ireland 60.8%　　　Scotland 33.4%　　　England 25%

---

[7] Trudgill and Gordon's figures would seem to be based on the 1881 census.

2. Male heads of household travelling with spouses:

    Ireland 8.5%   Scotland 15.1%   England 17.1%

3. Proportion of couples who migrated to New Zealand without children:

    Ireland 34.4%   Scotland 22.1%   England 28.8%

These data are particularly revealing. Formulated in words rather than figures: compared to the English, more than twice the Irish emigrants were unmarried on arrival, fewer than half were heads of households (the reverse of the same coin, so to speak). Furthermore, more Irish emigrated to New Zealand without children than did Scottish or English. Why should these facts be of relevance to the genesis of New Zealand English? If such a large proportion of the Irish had their children in New Zealand then much more of the entire Irish population was exposed to the embryonic variety of New Zealand English from their early childhood, or conversely fewer of them had established vernacular pronunciations from their country of origin. This means quite clearly that the influence of the Irish segment of the late nineteenth-century New Zealand population on the genesis of the later variety was probably less than the 18–20 per cent statistic would suggest. Furthermore, the possibility of unmarried individuals or childless couples influencing the incipient variety arising in other sections of the speech community would have been considerably less.

Against this background it is now understandable that certain prominent features of nineteenth-century Irish English apparently did not surface at all in New Zealand. Two of these suffice here for the purposes of illustration. (1) The well-known southwestern feature of Irish English, the raising of /ɛ/ to /ɪ/ in pre-nasal position, resulting in a *pen–pin* merger similar to that found in large parts of the southern United States, does not appear to be attested in New Zealand English. (2) The lowering of /e/ to /a/ before /r/ which is widely documented well into the nineteenth century in Ireland as in *sarve* for *serve, sarch* for *search*, etc. does not appear to have occurred in New Zealand either (Hickey forthcoming b). It should also be noted here that some features which are regarded as Scots, such as the lexical items investigated by Bauer (2000: 49f.), could equally have come from those Irish emigrants from the north of the country.

2.6   The quantitative argument again

When discussing several key features of present-day New Zealand English, Peter Trudgill, Elizabeth Gordon and their associates appeal to the quantitative argument, saying that an *overall* majority variant survives, even if it is not found with the majority of speakers within a section of late nineteenth-century New Zealand society. Some of the cases rest on a putative difference of little more than 5 per cent in the occurrence of the form which survives and that which does not (see the discussion of a distinction between low vowels before (i) a fricative and (ii) a cluster of nasal and obstruent in section 2.4 above). Here is another example from Trudgill et al. (2000a) where they discuss a feature which has a direct bearing on Irish input to New Zealand:

> Irish English and North American English are known to be characterised by having an unrounded vowel in the lexical set of LOT, whereas, as Wells (1982: 130) writes, 'in Britain the predominant type of vowel in LOT is back and rounded [ɒ ɔ]'. However, he goes on to add that we also find 'the recessive unrounded variant [ɑ] in parts of the south of England remote from London'. He further indicates (p. 347) that the vowel 'often appears to be unrounded in the west [of England], being qualitatively [ɑ], much as in the Irish Republic or in the United States'. And he also quotes from Trudgill (1974) to say (p. 339) that 'in Norfolk the LOT vowel has an unrounded variant'. This geographical pattern, with the southeast and southwest of England being areas with unrounded vowels which are separated from one another by an intervening area including London with rounded variants, strongly suggests that the [ɑ] area was formerly much bigger than it is now. This is confirmed by our New Zealand data. The fact is that unrounded /ɒ/ in LOT = [ɑ] is very common in the ONZE recordings. Of the 83 informants, 39 (i.e. 47%) use an unrounded vowel either consistently or variably. The fact that it has disappeared from modern New Zealand English has to be ascribed to the fact that users of the rounded variant were in a rather small majority.   (Trudgill et al. 2000a: 314)

In the opinion of the present author the quantitative argument in such cases is especially weak. *Ceteris paribus*, the quantitative argument holds, but how often can one assume it to have been the only factor in the fate of a variable? Firstly, it rests on the ONZE recordings and one cannot be sure that they are an accurate reflection of late nineteenth-century New Zealand English to within 1 per cent which is what one would need to make strong claims for a 5 per cent difference between occurrences of forms. Secondly, the data for emigration tell a story of regional clustering of emigrant groups so that any conclusions from absolute numbers of emigrants across the entire country, which the census returns represent (see table 13.3), would be unwarranted with differences in the range of 5 per cent or so, given the considerable geographical abstraction which the overall census figures represent.

Now if one considers that the Irish emigrants, who would definitely have had an unrounded vowel in the LOT lexical set, only had a concentration above 20 per cent in the rural region of Westland and an urban concentration significantly above 10 per cent in Auckland, then the possible retentive influence of Irish-based speech in New Zealand on [ɑ] would have been slight indeed. The status of the emigrants (see section 2.5.4 above) would offer further support for the view that the influence of the Irish on the forging of New Zealand English was much less than the absolute figure of 18–20 per cent for the end of the nineteenth century, taken on its own, would suggest.

Finally it should be mentioned that the apparent lack of syntactic features from Irish or Scottish English in the ONZE archives and, of course, in modern New Zealand English (Hundt 1998; Quinn 2000) would suggest that the influence of southeastern English English went beyond what the quantitative argument would predict, operating on the 48–50 per cent of the late nineteenth-century New Zealand non-Maori population.

2.7   The transmission of ongoing change

The concern of the present section is the transmission of linguistic change in a new dialect formation scenario. It can be best opened by considering the words of Trudgill et al. describing continuing trends in inherited features:

A number of changes, which have occurred in New Zealand English since anglophone settlement, represent continuations of changes already in progress in England and inherited from there. What is of interest to us is that all three major Southern Hemisphere varieties of English – Australian, New Zealand and South African – not only inherited the results of the changes that had occurred so far in England but also continued them after separation. There was a dynamism inherent in these ongoing changes which led to them continuing in parallel in the four different locations in the manner described by Sapir [under the heading *drift* – RH], although not always at the same speed, and not always coinciding in absolutely all details.   (Trudgill et al. 2000b: 117)

Just what does it mean to say that children inherit an ongoing change from their parents' generation? First of all, children perceive variation. But they can also see that certain variants are the preferred realisation by certain individuals and in certain environments. Furthermore, children can notice that variation is not static but dynamic in the previous generation, i.e. they notice that of, say, two variants X and Y (in a simple case of an ongoing change) variant Y is preferred under circumstances and by individuals who could in some way be interpreted as innovative in their society.

Now there are two basic ways in which a linguistic change takes place. The first is the simpler of the two and is evident when the new variant Y increases in occurrence, displacing the older variant X in the process. This type of change is common in syntax and lexis where the distinction between variants is binary, i.e. the variants are discrete.

The second way for a change to occur is along a scale ranging from an older variant X to a new variant Y. This is what one would have with children favouring a minority, innovative variant Y in the speech of their parents' generation. But this is not enough to account for the progress of scalar change. For young speakers to further the change they must realise that the variants X and Y are on a trajectory, a path of change along which they can themselves push the progressive variant Y to yield Y+, an augmented variant on that path of change. To illustrate how this operates one can consider the Dublin vowel shift for a moment as this shows this process quite clearly. Traditionally, Irish English (the supraregional standard, derived ultimately from middle-class Dublin speech) has an unrounded low back starting point in the diphthong of the CHOICE lexical set so that a word like *toy* sounds to British English ears much like *tie*. Now part of the current vowel shift in Dublin (for more details, consult Hickey 1999) is the raising of back vowels so that the word *toy* has been shifted from [taɪ] to [tɒɪ] to [tɔɪ]. But younger progressive speakers, actively participating in the vowel shift, have carried the vowel further so that something close to [toɪ] can be heard. Now one can assume that speakers with this realisation have been exposed to both [taɪ] and [tɔɪ] and have realised the situational frequency of both, and they have not only opted for the latter, as the more innovative of the two realisations, but decided to augment it. But how do speakers know how to do this? The answer surely is that they recognise the trajectory of this change, basically from low back to mid open back and carry this a little further along the path, which the change is already describing, to realise the onset for the CHOICE words as closed back, i.e. [o] as in the pronunciation of *toy* just quoted. The key question here is one of directionality. Speakers will always show realisations for a particular sound which cluster around certain values, but in a situation of language change these values will be skewed in a particular direction, namely that taken by innovative speakers in a speech community.

2.8   Favouring variants

Trudgill et al. accept individual differences in early New Zealand English but say that the distribution of variants for the second stage reflects the numerical distribution among the speakers of the first stage, *taken as a whole* (emphasis theirs, Trudgill et al. 2000a: 310). They readily admit that there were two riders to this thesis. The first is that certain ongoing linguistic changes were inherited from the British Isles. Here they assume that speakers would have favoured newer over older variants. This is an interesting contention which is not discussed further and it throws up the question of how speakers perceive what is a new variant and what an old one. However, if the newer variants were numerically less frequent than the still present older variants (as is so often the case during language change, cf. the current Dublin vowel shift discussed in Hickey 1999), then why, given their support for the numerical dominance view, did newer variants carry the day with second-stage speakers? The answer to this question, which receives support from present-day investigations such as that of current Dublin English, is that speakers are (1) unconsciously aware of the linguistic relationship between old and new variants, say lower and higher values on a trajectory in vowel space, and (2) that they are predisposed to selecting innovative variants because these represent the vanguard of change in a developing society.

2.9   An illumination of drift

The investigation of the ONZE recordings initially appeared to throw up a problem for the researchers: the majority of speakers had syllable-final /r/ but present-day New Zealand English is non-rhotic. Evidence from contemporary commentators like McBurney (Bauer 1994: 424) on New Zealand English in the 1860s shows that English on the South Island and on parts of the North Island was rhotic. Clearly it is difficult to appeal to the argument based on the removal of marked variants when attempting to explain this development, especially when the loss of syllable-final /r/ leads to homophony which is disorientating for rhotic speakers, cf. mergers like *caught* and *court*.[8] Instead Trudgill et al. offer the following account:

Rhoticity was lost in parallel in England and in New Zealand through processes which we can label with Sapir's term *drift* in its – according to us – first sense. Though non-prevocalic /r/ must have been very widespread in nineteenth-century England, it was also clearly involved in linguistic change in lower-middle-class speech in many areas: rhoticity was gradually disappearing. This is reflected in our Mobile Unit recordings. It is true that the majority of our speakers are, as we have said, rhotic. But actually, only a third are consistently so: most of our informants are variably rhotic and a number of them are only vestigially so ... English English and New Zealand English, having both been very rhotic in the nineteenth century, have both become very non-rhotic in the twentieth century, with the respective exceptions of the English southwest and of New Zealand Southland, as a result of parallel developments. The seeds of these parallel developments, moreover, can be seen to lie in the variability of the rhoticity shared between the two varieties of English in the nineteenth century. New Zealand English did not inherit non-rhoticity from English English but rather inherited an ongoing process involving loss of rhoticity.

Factually this account is acceptable as it clearly corresponds to the facts of both these varieties. What is necessary here is to take a closer look at statements like 'New Zealand English ... inherited an ongoing process involving loss of rhoticity' to see what it really means. In the opinion of the present author this interpretation of drift has a fatal flaw: it reifies language, it makes a language into a thing independent of its speakers and imputes a life of its own to the language. Of course it is a convenient abstraction to say, for instance, that 'the English language did X or Y'.[9] Naturally it is the speakers who did X or Y. The difficulty

---

[8] Lyle Campbell points out here that syllable-final /r/ was lost mostly because of the impact of the large immigration of non-rhotic speakers of English, which also happened to be the group favoured for prestige reasons, and points to the continuing abandonment of rhoticity by younger speakers in Southland and Otago because they wish to sound like the more prestigious supraregional variety of New Zealand English which is, of course, non-rhotic. Jim Milroy has also raised doubts about the avoidance of homophony argument when postulating resistance to the loss of rhoticity.

[9] In this context one can consider James Milroy's relevant comment (this volume) that 'sound changes are not literally changes of sound: they are structural correspondences between one sound and another sound that appears in its place at a later date'.

with drift is that its locus is seen in the language as a separate entity, whereas the language as something independent of its speakers is nonexistent but simply a convenient manner of conceptualising the common linguistic behaviour of a group of individuals. Such metaphorical terminology is very common and ultimately derives from the structure of human cognition and the manner in which humans conceptualise. The conclusion here is obviously that drift, if anywhere, is in the speech of the speakers. Now can one envisage this? I think the first thing is to assume that one has variation and a tendency for one variant to be preferred over another (in the simplest of situations). Now why should speakers prefer variant Y over variant X and do so consistently over generations (this is necessary to account for drift from the speakers' perspective)? A variety of reasons are conceivable here. Internal reasons, such as the spread of analogical regularity, may lead, for instance, to weak forms of verbs being favoured over strong ones as is the case in the Germanic languages, albeit with different rates, and some backsliding, in the individual languages. External reasons would have to do with speakers recognising what variant in a situation of choice is more innovative and what variant more conservative. Which individuals use what variants in what situations gives speakers of the young generation at any point in time the necessary information about what to favour as dynamic members of their society.

2.9.1   HAPPY-*tensing*

In their treatment of drift, Trudgill et al. (2000b: 124ff.) distinguish between ongoing changes, such as the loss of syllable-final /r/, and a *propensity* (emphasis mine) for change. One example they give, which New Zealand shares with the other major Southern Hemisphere varieties (Schreier, Sudbury and Trudgill forthcoming), South African and Australian English, is what is termed HAPPY-tensing, the use of a noncentralised, tense [iː] in final, unstressed position (Wells 1982: 257). Trudgill et al. (2000b: 125) give the following percentages for the occurrence of HAPPY-tensing by decade of birth in the ONZE corpus as follows: 1850s: 0%, 1860s: 25%, 1870–1889: 42%. They then conclude:

> This makes it less likely that HAPPY-tensing arrived in New Zealand from Britain at all, and more likely that it started life independently in New Zealand ... And it did not inherit an ongoing change which was introducing HAPPY-tensing. What it did inherit, apparently, was a propensity to replace /ɪ/ by /iː/ word-finally. Australian English and South African English also have HAPPY-tensing (Wells, 1982: 595, 616).
>
> (Trudgill et al. 2000b: 125)

If, as their data seem to imply, there was zero HAPPY-tensing among the older informants of the ONZE archive and if – not stated implicitly in their presentation – there was a generation which did not hear HAPPY-tensing *ever* from its preceding generation, then there is no question of it having been transmitted via the initial English input.

This leaves the question as to what *propensity* is taken to mean in the context of Trudgill et al. (2000b). An interpretation, which probably represents what is meant, is a structural imbalance which was later removed in all three major varieties of Southern Hemisphere English. To illustrate what is intended by structural imbalance allow me to paint the following scenario. A language, L_1, has a pair of alveolar stops /t,d/. The voiced member is lost by a lenition process which shifts it to /ð/, giving L_2. At this stage forms of the language are carried overseas to three geographically discontinuous areas where new dialect formation (NDF) occurs (V_{1-3}). Now assume that L_1, like English, has a contrast of voice in a series of phoneme pairs. The stage L_2 is then highly marked and there is a fair likelihood of this being redressed at some later stage in V_{1-3} (through some process like the fortition of /ð/ or the voicing of intervocalic /t/ or the like), though there can be no predicting this and the temporal coincidence of the reinstatement of /d/ would be remarkable.

L_1	L_2	→ (NDF) →	V_1	V_2	V_3
/t,d/ →	/t,ð/		/t,ð/ → /t,d/	/t,ð/ → /t,d/	/t,ð/ → /t,d/

In this scenario one could say that there is a propensity in the initial stages of V_{1-3} for /d/ to be reinstated although this propensity has no predictive power because languages can survive for long periods with 'holes' in their sound inventories, cf. /x/ which in standard German has no voiced equivalent /ɣ/ despite the importance of voice among consonants in German phonology.

Trudgill et al. (2000b: 125f.) hypothesise that the structural condition producing the propensity to change (towards H A P P Y -tensing) in the same direction in Southern Hemisphere English lay in the fact that the distinction between /ɪ/ and /iː/ is neutralised in unstressed word-final position, and that /ɪ/ can otherwise not occur in open syllables in English. The first statement is just that, a statement, i.e. it does not predict that, given the neutralisation in unstressed word-final position, English varieties should start shifting /ɪ/ to /iː/. The second statement is about stressed syllables. It is true that English does not show sound structures like /dɪ/, or for that matter/dɛ, dʌ, dɒ/, with a short vowel in an open stressed syllable. But in unstressed syllables, arising from a lack of lexical stress, short vowels do occur for high vowels and schwa, e.g. *the* [ˌðɪ], *to* [ˌtʊ], *a* [ˌə]. These considerations speak against maintaining that the presence of /ɪ/ in unstressed syllables of the H A P P Y type in input varieties of English to Southern Hemisphere English in any way represented such internal system pressure as to lead to the development of H A P P Y -tensing in all three major Southern Hemisphere varieties of English without any precedent at all in the input varieties.

Consider now that the tensing of the final vowel in words of the H A P P Y lexical set is not something which proceeded in discrete steps, though the end-point of the development is discretely different from the outset as it coalesced with the normal realisation of the /i:/ vowel in those varieties which show this tensing. So what is much more likely is that succeeding generations unconsciously perceived an increasing decentralisation, and most likely variably rather than categorically, of the final vowel which scholars later describe as a shift from /ɪ/ to /i:/.

What one is dealing with here – and in other cases of *drift* – is subphonemic variation which is later raised to a systemic level through being favoured by later generations of speakers. Hence there may be no difference in kind between a propensity for change and an ongoing change. It could simply be a matter of degree.[10] Two other cases of well-attested changes can be cited to support this. The first is actually Sapir's own original case of umlaut in Germanic. As is well known, all the Germanic languages bar Gothic show umlaut, typically in noun plurals, strong verb forms and adjectival comparisons. Umlaut is originally a phonetic process whereby the front articulation of /i/ or /j/ is anticipated in a syllable preceding this and can still be seen in modern German noun pairs like *Sohn : Söhne, Buch : Bücher*. With the loss of the triggering syllable, due in many instances to inflectional attrition, umlaut achieved systemic status and was lost or greatly reduced in later stages of some Germanic languages so that English *foot : feet, man : men* are now lexicalised instances of former umlauted plurals. The rather late occurrence of umlaut in all but one of the Germanic languages is accounted for by an appeal to drift. But this must be demystified by stating what exactly one understands by it. The only non-speculative explanation is that generations of speakers carried in their speech a subphonemic tendency to front vowels, at first only slightly, becoming phonemic at some later stage and of course appearing in writing some time after that.

The second case which can illustrate this process is that of initial mutation in the Celtic languages. The latter have a means of indicating key grammatical categories such as past tense or distinguishing between nominative and genitive which involves altering the nature of the first consonants of a word, say from stop to fricative. The details of initial mutation are much more intricate than this brief statement suggests (see Hickey, this volume, ch. 15) and the patterns of mutation in Irish and Welsh differ. In this case one is dealing also with a subphonemic tendency to weaken the articulation of initial segments (a sandhi phenomenon) which much later than the period of Common Celtic become systemic in the individual languages where it came to be recognised in writing.

The conclusion here is that umlaut in North and West Germanic and the initial mutations of Celtic are shared innovations among sets of languages *after*

---

[10] An alternative interpretation of propensity was offered by Lyle Campbell: a propensity to change may be seen as a pan-linguistic, pan-temporal tendency, a possible change available to any language. In this case an ongoing change is specific to a specific language at a specific time.

they had split up from an earlier common stage. The innovation in each case is the promotion of subphonemic phenomena to a systemic level after which they become visible in the historical attestations.

The parallel to HAPPY-tensing in New Zealand is clear: a subphonemic tendency to decentralise unstressed final /ɪ/ could have been present in the earliest forms of the variety which then was pushed along a trajectory from central to peripheral in high front vowel space, resulting in the HAPPY-tensing of present-day New Zealand English (and other Southern Hemisphere varieties of English). A slight tendency to decentralise unstressed final /ɪ/, present in input varieties of southern English in the early nineteenth century, is all one needs for HAPPY-tensing to appear across the entire Southern Hemisphere.[11]

2.10   Supraregionalisation

In section 2.5.3 above it was shown that there was considerable regional clustering in New Zealand in the late nineteenth century. All commentators on present-day New Zealand English agree that, with the partial exception of rural Southland, which has the vestigial Scottish feature of a syllable-final /r/ (Bauer 1994: 411f.), there is considerable uniformity in the English spoken throughout the country (Bayard 2000). Assuming that the regional clustering was correlated by a predominance of accents of the ethnic groups involved and given the fact that present-day New Zealand English shows virtually no regional variation,[12] some process must have occurred whereby distinctive dialect features, especially of the Irish and Scottish emigrants throughout the rest of the country, must have been levelled out with a phonetic pattern reminiscent of the southeast of England prevailing.

In their discussion of focusing in the third stage of new dialect formation Peter Trudgill, Elizabeth Gordon and their associates stress that this happened in the 'linguistic melting pots', the areas of high settler density. In those regions where the density and – significantly – the diversity of speakers was less, there must have been a stage at which younger speakers adopted the embryonic variety of New Zealand English as we know it today, a variety spreading from the areas of higher density and itself the result of the focusing process described by Trudgill et al.

---

[11] It should be mentioned here, without overstressing the point, that the Irish emigrants to New Zealand would have had HAPPY-tensing anyway. All speakers from the south of Ireland (the majority of the emigrants) have HAPPY-tensing and would have had it in the nineteenth century, not least because they would have been bilingual in Irish to a greater or lesser extent and in Irish final unstressed high vowels are always tense.

[12] Bauer (1994: 386) stresses this point but unfortunately does not suggest how the earlier regional nature of New Zealand settlement could have led to present-day NZE with so little geographical variation. See also Bartlett (1992) and Bauer (1996). Gordon and Deverson (1995: 126–34) deal with what variation there is from a present-day perspective.

Consider once more the remarks made when discussing the third stage of new dialect formation: 'the new dialect will appear as a stable, crystallised variety. This crystallisation is the result of a focusing process whose effects are very clear in modern New Zealand English, which has a remarkably small amount of regional variation' (Trudgill et al. 2000a: 307). What is noticeable here is that they seem to equate focusing with the lack of variation. But my argument here is that the latter is the result of a different process which is to be seen in many other anglophone countries and one, which for want of a better term, I have labelled *supraregionalisation* (Hickey forthcoming a).

This is a process where by dialect speakers progressively adopt more and more features of a non-regional variety which they are in contact with. There does not have to be direct speaker contact; indirect exposure to the non-regional variety can be sufficient. Supraregionalisation is distinct from accommodation which does require such contact and it is different from dialect levelling in which the input varieties lose salient or minority variants, resulting in a new mixture not present before. Dialect levelling can be assumed to have taken place in the areas of high density in New Zealand prior to both koinéisation and supraregionalisation.

Koinéisation is a process whereby a dominant variety comes to be used along-side vernaculars for means of general communication. It is the nearest of the traditionally recognised processes to, but not quite the same as, supraregionalisation. In the latter, speakers adopt features of an already present non-regional variety and by a process of lexical diffusion can replace vernacular pronunciations or grammatical structures more and more so that the original dialect loses its strongly local characteristics. There are many corollaries of supraregionalisation which may not have affected New Zealand English. For instance, in nineteenth-century Ireland vernacular pronunciations were replaced entirely in some cases, e.g. the lowering of /e/ to /a/ before /r/ alluded to above. But others were relegated to a local mode of speech and used for vernacularisation purposes, e.g. the use of *youse* (instead of *ye* or *you*) as a second-person-plural pronoun. Another corollary can be a lexical split arising through the maintenance of an older pronunciation alongside the newly adopted supraregional one. For instance, in Irish English there is a contrast between *bold* [baul] and *bold* [boːld] the former an adjective indicating a sneaking admiration for an individual.

Vernacularisation and lexical splitting, of the type just described, do not seem to have occurred in New Zealand English, perhaps because the supraregionalisation involved a variety from within the country, whereas in Ireland it was an extranational norm stemming from England. What would seem to have happened is the adoption of the focused variety of New Zealand English from areas of high density, varied settlement to areas of lower, less varied settlement, so that today there is no linguistic correlate of the regional clustering which occurred in the Irish settlement of nineteenth-century New Zealand.

3   Conclusion

The concern of this chapter has been to highlight the processes which take place in a society where several disparate input varieties have been moulded into a new form (*new dialect formation*). In this case the events at the stage of focusing, the stage at which the varieties stabilise with a distinctive linguistic profile, show similarities in that salient features indicative of minority, non-prestige groups are removed. This leads to a variety which is supraregional, i.e. no longer typical of a certain subgroup in the society in question, and it can help to account for the relative lack of regional variation in New Zealand English. This interpretation still leaves open the question whether the supraregional variety is just an epiphenomenon resulting from the alternate processes of selection and avoidance of features in early varieties or whether speakers unconsciously and collectively contribute in their choices to the emergence of a variety which promotes internal linguistic cohesion in the society using it.

REFERENCES

Adamson, Sylvia et al. (eds.). 1990. *Papers from the 5th International Conference on English Historical Linguistics*. Amsterdam: Benjamins.

Akenson, Donald H. 1990. *Half the world from home. Perspectives on the Irish in New Zealand, 1860–1950*. Wellington: Victoria University Press.

Bartlett, Christopher. 1992. 'Regional variation in New Zealand English: the case of Southland', *New Zealand English Newsletter* 6: 5–15.

Bauer, Laurie. 1986. 'Notes on New Zealand English phonetics and phonology', *English World-Wide* 7: 225–58.

Bauer, Laurie. 1994. 'English in New Zealand', in Burchfield (ed.), 382–429.

Bauer, Laurie. 1996. 'Attempting to trace Scottish influence on New Zealand English', in E. Schneider (ed.), *Englishes around the world 2*. Amsterdam: Benjamins, 257–72.

Bauer, Laurie. 2000. 'The dialectal origins of New Zealand English', in Bell and Kuiper (eds.), 40–52.

Bayard, Donn. 1987. 'Class and change in New Zealand English', *Te Reo* 30: 3–36.

Bayard, Donn. 2000. 'New Zealand English: origins, relationships, and prospects', *Moderna Språk* 94.1: 8–14.

Bell, Allan. 1997. 'The phonetics of fish and chips in New Zealand: marking national and ethnic identities', *English World-Wide* 18: 243–70.

Bell, Alan and Janet Holmes. 1992. '/H/-droppin': two sociolinguistic variables in New Zealand English', *Australian Journal of Linguistics* 12: 223–48.

Bell, Alan and Koenraad Kuiper (eds.). 2000. *New Zealand English*. Amsterdam: John Benjamins.

Bielenberg, Andy (ed.). 2000. *The Irish diaspora*. London: Longman.

Bradley, David. 1991. '/æ/ and /a:/ in Australian English', in Cheshire (ed.), 227–34.

Burchfield, Robert W. (ed.). 1994. *The Cambridge history of the English language*, vol. 5: *English in Britain and overseas: origins and development*. Cambridge University Press.

Cheshire, Jenny (ed.). 1991. *English around the world: sociolinguistic perspectives*. Cambridge University Press.

Coogan, Tim Pat. *Wherever green is worn: the story of the Irish diaspora.* London: Hutchinson.

Davis, Richard. 1974. *Irish issues in New Zealand politics.* Dunedin: Otago Press.

Duffy, Seán et al. (eds.). 1997. *Atlas of Irish history.* Dublin: Gill and Macmillan.

Gordon, Elizabeth. 1998. 'The origins of New Zealand speech: the limits of recovering historical information from written records', *English World-Wide* 19: 61–85.

Gordon, Elizabeth, Lyle Campbell, Gillian Lewis, Margaret Maclagan and Peter Trudgill. forthcoming. *The origins and evolution of New Zealand English.* Cambridge University Press.

Gordon, Elizabeth and Tony Deverson. 1995. *New Zealand English and English in New Zealand.* Auckland: New House Publishers.

Gordon, Elizabeth and Peter Trudgill. 1999. 'Shades of things to come: embryonic variants in New Zealand English sound changes', *English World-Wide* 20: 111–23.

Gordon, Elizabeth and Peter Trudgill. 2003. 'The English input to New Zealand', in Hickey (ed.).

Hickey, Raymond. 1984. 'Syllable onsets in Irish English', *Word* 35: 67–74.

Hickey, Raymond. 1999. 'Ireland as a linguistic area', in Mallory (ed.), 36–53.

Hickey, Raymond (ed.). 2003. *The legacy of colonial English: a study in transported dialects.* Cambridge University Press.

Hickey, Raymond. Forthcoming a. 'How and why do supraregional varieties arise?', in Charles Jones (ed.), *Proceedings from the Late Modern English Conference, Edinburgh, August 2001.* Frankfurt: Lang.

Hickey, Raymond. Forthcoming b. 'Historical input and the regional differentiation of English in the Republic of Ireland', in Katja Lenz and Ruth Möhlig (eds.), *Festschrift for Manfred Görlach on his 65th birthday.* Heidelberg: Winter.

Hundt, Marianne. 1998. *New Zealand grammar: fact or fiction?* Amsterdam: Benjamins.

Maclagan, David. 1998. '/H/-dropping in early New Zealand English', *New Zealand English Journal* 12: 34–42.

Mallory, James P. (ed.). 1999. *Language in Ulster.* Special issue of *Ulster Folklife* (45).

Mannion, John J. (ed.). 1977. *The peopling of Newfoundland: essays in historical geography.* St John's: Memorial University of Newfoundland.

McBurney, Samuel. 1887. 'Colonial pronunciation', *The Press*, Christchurch, 5 October.

McCarthy, Angela. 2000. '"The Desired Haven"? Impressions of New Zealand in letters to and from Ireland, 1840–1925', in Bielenberg (ed.), 272–84.

McKinnon, Malcolm (ed.). 1997. *New Zealand historical atlas.* Auckland: Bateman.

Quinn, Heidi. 2000. 'Variation in New Zealand English syntax and morphology', in Bell and Kuiper (eds.), 173–97.

Rice, G. W. (ed). 1992. *The Oxford history of New Zealand*, 2nd edition. Auckland: Oxford University Press.

Schreier, Daniel, Andrea Sudbury and Peter Trudgill. Forthcoming. 'The anglophone South Atlantic', in Ulrich Ammon, Norbert Dittmar, Klaus Mattheier and Peter Trudgill (eds.), *Sociolinguistics handbook*, 2nd edition. Berlin: de Gruyter.

Simpson, T. 1997. *The immigrants: the great migration from Britain to New Zealand, 1830–1890.* Auckland: Godwit.

Sinclair, K. (ed.). 1996. *The Oxford illustrated history of New Zealand*, 2nd edition. Auckland: Oxford University Press.

Trudgill, Peter. 1986. *Dialects in contact.* Oxford: Blackwell.

Trudgill, Peter. 1998. 'The chaos before the order: New Zealand English and the second stage of new-dialect formation', in Ernst Håkon Jahr (ed.), *Language change: advances in historical sociolinguistics*. Berlin: Mouton de Gruyter, 1–11.

Trudgill, Peter. 1999. 'Dialect convergence and vestigial variants', *Journal of English Linguistics* 27: 319–27.

Trudgill, Peter and J. K. Chambers (eds.). 1991. *Dialects of English: studies in grammatical variation*. London: Longman.

Trudgill, Peter, Elizabeth Gordon and Gillian Lewis. 1998. 'New-dialect formation and Southern Hemisphere English: the New Zealand short vowels', *Journal of Sociolinguistics* 2.1: 35–51.

Trudgill, Peter, Elizabeth Gordon, Gillian Lewis and Margaret Maclagan. 2000a. 'Determinism in new-dialect formation and the genesis of New Zealand English', *Journal of Linguistics* 36: 299–318.

Trudgill, Peter, Elizabeth Gordon, Gillian Lewis and Margaret Maclagan. 2000b. 'The role of drift in the formation of native-speaker Southern Hemisphere Englishes: some New Zealand evidence', *Diachronica* 17: 111–38.

Wells, John. 1982. *Accents of English*. 3 vols. Cambridge University Press.

Part VI

The typological perspective

14   Reconstruction, typology and reality

Bernard Comrie

1   Introduction

The immediate impetus for this contribution is an article published as Lass (1977), but which I had the privilege of hearing presented in 1975 at a meeting of the Philological Society – albeit as viewed from the perspective of a quarter century later. In this article, Lass takes a devastating look at the reliability of internal reconstruction as a method for seriously reconstructing the linguistic past. An added stimulus is the article Lass (1993), which applies similar argumentation to that used in the 1977 article to the comparative method. Perhaps somewhat surprisingly for a contribution that I am dedicating to Roger Lass, my own contribution will take issue with some of the conclusions that Lass draws in these articles, in particular the former. But I believe that the contribution is nonetheless appropriate; indeed I hope it may even be welcome, because I have learned much from trying to formulate more explicitly the points of agreement and disagreement and because I hope that my contributions, like Lass's, will push the debate forward. Moreover, as I will try to show both in the body of my contribution and to summarise in the conclusions, my approach stems from an acceptance of much of what Lass says in these two articles, while asking a different set of questions from those posed by Lass, and thus almost inevitably coming to somewhat different conclusions.

2   Reconstruction and reality

Perhaps the major point in Lass (1977; 1993) is that standard methods of linguistic reconstruction, whether internal reconstruction or the comparative method, are not reliable methods for reconstructing the linguistic past. There are examples where a literal application of internal reconstruction would correctly reconstruct the past, as in unravelling Germanic umlaut to reconstruct an earlier period where there was no phonemic alternation between back and front vowels but rather a phonetic condition that allophonically fronted back vowels in the relevant environment, or as in Saussure's reconstruction of the Indo-European laryngeals. But, equally, there are examples where this methodology would lead one hopelessly astray, as if one were to try to reconstruct a common etymon for the alternative plural suffixes -*s* and -*en* in English. And in the case of Germanic umlaut, there is no need to apply internal reconstruction, since the forms reachable by internal reconstruction are anyway attested in the historical record, and were known from well before the development of internal reconstruction as a method; at best, they could serve as some kind of test-case confirmation of the method, to be set against those cases where the method gives results contradictory to known history. Saussure's reconstruction of the laryngeals might seem more of a triumph for the method, since when Saussure carried out the reconstruction the direct evidence for (some) laryngeals from Hittite was not yet available. But if a method is known to fail in some cases, even cases of success must be weighed against such failures. In other words, at best one can say that the method of internal reconstruction succeeds only with a certain degree of reliability, with the unfortunate proviso that we are at present not really able to assess this degree of reliability.

Although the comparative method is generally considered more reliable than internal reconstruction, it too will fail in certain circumstances, even assuming that one has taken precautions to ensure that the data under consideration contain only items that are genuinely cognate, i.e. one has excluded loans in particular. As with internal reconstruction, one can point to cases where application of the method gives a result that is confirmed by historical attestation, as in the often cited example of the sibilants in Romany. Varieties of Romany show two sibilants, *s* and *š*, but when one establishes cognates across varieties one finds three sets of cognates, all found in the same phonetic environment, namely *s–s*, *š–š* and *s–š*. Literal application of the comparative method requires one to posit three sibilants for the common ancestor. This is 'confirmed' by examination of the related Sanskrit language, which indeed has three phonemically distinct sibilants in the relevant lexical items, although of course, as with Germanic umlaut, the Sanskrit situation was in fact well known long before the reconstruction of Proto-Romany was carried out. But just as with internal reconstruction, there are also cases where the literal application of the comparative method will lead one very much astray with respect to historical reality. For instance, if one takes the English words *roof, book* and *took* as pronounced in different parts of the English-speaking world, one will find areas where all are pronounced with a short vowel (parts of the USA), areas where *roof* has a long vowel but *book* and *took* have short vowels (including the varieties usually considered standard), varieties where *roof* and *book* have a long vowel but *took* has a short vowel (some varieties spoken in northern England), and varieties where all three words have a long vowel (other varieties spoken in northern England). Given that it is not possible to establish a principled phonetic environment distinguishing the cases, strict application of the comparative method would require one to reconstruct three distinct phonemes in the proto-language.

Indeed, the situation is even worse if one takes into account British varieties that have a long vowel in *roof*, short vowels in *book* and *took*, but vary between short and long vowel in *room*. But in fact we know that all items have reflexes of Middle English long close *o*, and that the variation is the result of subsequent diffusion of vowel shortening across the lexicon.

Does this then mean that these methods cannot be used in trying to reconstruct the linguistic past? I would like to suggest that the answer is that they can be used provided we remain aware of the limitations on the reliability of the methods, and that this is not inherently different from the application of any other method in any other discipline that is concerned with reconstructing the past. Methods for reconstructing the past are almost always subject to some limitation of reliability, and one must be aware of such limitations and try to reduce the effect of the limitations by simultaneous use of different methods wherever possible to provide a cross-check. An analogy from archaeology may serve as an illustration here. Radio-carbon dating is in principle a very reliable method, since it depends on the decay of radio-active carbon-14, and the decay of radio-active substances is one of the few processes known to have an absolutely constant rate independent of all environmental conditions. But radio-carbon dating in its original form relied on the assumption that the proportion of radio-active carbon in the atmosphere, the result of cosmic bombardment of the Earth's atmosphere, is constant. We now know that this assumption is incorrect. However, by comparing radio-carbon dating with other methods, such as dendrochronology (determining the age of a tree by counting the number of its rings, and then establishing a chronology by comparing particular tree ring patterns on trees that died progressively further back in time), it is possible to compensate for variations in the proportion of carbon-14 in the atmosphere at different historical periods. The method still has a fair range of uncertainty, but nonetheless it has set plausible limits on the dating of certain archaeological artefacts that have revolutionised our understanding of prehistory since the mid-twentieth century. (For further discussion, reasonably detailed though also accessible to the nonspecialist, see, for instance, Renfrew and Bahn (2000: 137–45).)

Thus, we probably need to accept that, except perhaps in certain trivial instances, it is never possible to reconstruct the past with absolute certainty; all that we can do is to do our best. In linguistics, we may well be in a worse situation than in many other disciplines, since our reconstructions are rarely subject to empirical verification, but at least we can construct arguments based on plausibility, especially when different methods converge on similar results. It may well be that many aspects of our reconstruction of Proto-Indo-European, for instance, will in fact be incorrect. But a completely negative view would not only reject the reconstruction of Proto-Indo-European, but even the assumption that there was such an entity: our assumption that the similarities among the known Indo-European languages reflects the fact that they derive from a common ancestor is in itself a reconstruction of the past, and unless and until Proto-Indo-European is attested, an almost inconceivable event, our positing of this entity remains an unconfirmed, perhaps even in practice unconfirmable, hypothesis. And here I return to agreement with Lass, in particular his statement that 'there are no algorithms for producing true accounts of... history' (1977: 18).

But even assuming that in some sense our reconstruction is correct, i.e. that we reconstruct linguistic forms that correspond to forms actually in use at some previous point in time, then there remains another problem eloquently expressed by Lass (1977: 13–14), namely that our account of the processes that lead from this earlier form or set of forms to the currently attested forms may be a gross oversimplification of the actual historical process. Lass cites the example of nasalisation in the history of French, whereby, on the basis of alternations as between *nom* /nõ/ 'name' and *nommer* /nɔme/ 'to name', internal reconstruction would posit earlier forms along the lines of /nɔm/, /nɔme/, and a historical process nasalising a vowel before a syllable-final nasal consonant, with subsequent loss of the syllable-final nasal consonant, but carrying out no change before or with an intervocalic nasal. In this case, we know from the historical record that the actual run of events was more complex than this, for instance, in that nasalisation did originally take place before an intervocalic nasal consonant but was subsequently lost in this environment.

Here I think the relevant question is what demands we are making of our reconstruction. If we are asking only that it provide a reliable reconstruction of the situation at some earlier period, then this it does, subject to the usual concerns surrounding the degree of this reliability. If we require that it also provide us with a detailed history of the intervening period, then we are making greater demands, and while we may sometimes be able to reconstruct some of that intervening history, in other cases we may not, and the reconstruction itself is then simply silent on this intervening history. The reconstruction tells us that at a certain period in the past we had the pronunciations /nɔm/ and /nɔme/; it leaves completely open the precise path by which these earlier pronunciations gave rise to the pronunciations that we find today. Thus, it is not so much that reconstruction here gives an incomplete result as that it gives a partial result. This partial result may well be correct but fail to provide any insight into other aspects of the historical processes involved, just as carbon-14 dating can give a good estimate of the date at which organic material died but fails to tell us about the uses to which the organic material was put after its death or when: if someone in the past used a long-felled tree to build a house, carbon-14 dating will tell us when the tree died, not when it was used to build the house.

To summarise this section, we may say that the aim of a historical reconstruction, in particular in linguistics though in principle equally in any other domain, is to provide a plausible hypothesis that will account for the observable data. In linguistics, as often as not, the data are all synchronic, so that most of the history is a reconstruction. This reconstruction, to the extent that it cannot be evaluated directly by comparison with an earlier state of affairs (something that is almost always impossible), is to be evaluated rather in terms of its plausibility relative to the observable data, in competition with alternative hypotheses relating to the same empirical domain. This leads to weaker claims than saying that we have algorithmic procedures for reconstructing the past, but nonetheless to interesting claims about the past. In particular, such claims become especially interesting when they are part of a set of interlocking claims based on different kinds of evidence and/or methodologies: the challenge is then not just to come up with an alternative account for one particular part of the proposed solution, but rather for the whole of the solution. In section 3, I will try to develop this idea further with reference to reconstructing even further back into the linguistic past.

But before proceeding to this, it is worth discussing one further aspect of reconstructions, particularly in regard to linguistic reconstructions. One of the controversies that arises periodically in historical linguistics is what ontological status is to be assigned to historical reconstructions in linguistics. As applied to the comparative method, for instance, one finds at the one extreme the view that a comparative reconstruction actually says nothing directly about history, but is rather simply a statement of the correspondences among a set of synchronic data. Given this interpretation, reconstructions of Proto-Indo-European, for instance, make no claim whatsoever about language states earlier than our attested documentation, but at best provide systematisation of the correspondences among the linguistic systems reflected in that documentation. On this interpretation, moreover, a host of questions become simply unaskable, especially any attempts to link the reconstructed proto-language with any particular archaeological culture, for instance. Indeed, as I have already suggested, on this assumption it is not even clear that the standard notion of the genetic (or, as I would now prefer to say, genealogical) relatedness of languages is meaningful, since the postulation of a common ancestor goes beyond the claim relating to synchronic relations among attested languages.

I will therefore adopt a realist approach to linguistic reconstruction. What we are trying to do, or at least what I am trying to do, in a linguistic reconstruction really is to reconstruct earlier stages of language. Of course, given the limitations on the data available to us such reconstructions will always be at best very partial, will often be beset by such problems as the relative chronologies of different parts of the reconstruction (did that vowel system really exist at the same time as that tense–aspect–mood system?), and will often simply be wrong. But they are our best attempts given the material at our disposal, and are always subject to replacement by better reconstructions. In some cases, of course, the materials at our disposal will be so meagre that we may acknowledge that it makes no sense to attempt a reconstruction. But this does not mean that across a wide range of cases it is not feasible to make such an attempt.

3   Grammaticalisation, typology and the origin of language complexity

One of the reasons why I wish to justify the use of linguistic reconstruction, in particular a variety of internal reconstruction, as a tool for reconstructing the linguistic past is that I have myself indulged in precisely this effort, in particular in Comrie (1992). It is now time to examine some of the ideas put forward there in the light of the discussion of the preceding sections.

Most currently spoken languages include in their grammars a substantial set of complexities that are not necessary for successful human communication and which might plausibly be attributed to the accreted residue of random historical processes. One example would be complex morphophonemic alternations, in particular those that are not directly phonetically conditioned, another would be complex morphology in general. The claim that such phenomena are not essential to human communication can be seen by examining languages that are successful means of human communication, acquired as first and often only languages, but which lack these complexities, such as (at least in some respects) creole languages (as argued, though by no means completely uncontroversially, by McWhorter (2001)), in the case of morphology also isolating languages. One question that then arises is how some languages come to have such complexities as complex morphologies and morphophonemics.

One possible answer is that they have always had these complexities, i.e. that some languages, from the beginnings of human language, just started out being complex. After all, if languages with complex morphologies, like, say, the Eskimo languages, can be acquired with relatively little difficulty by children, then they are clearly within whatever limits exist on the acquisition and use of language by human beings in general, and as soon as humans attained the level necessary for dealing with such complexity they would have been able to deal with such a language. But although such a scenario cannot be excluded a priori, the nagging question keeps coming back of where such complexity could have come from, almost as if it were improbable to accept the complexity as always having been there and at least more tempting to try to explain its origin.

Internal reconstruction, as traditionally applied in historical linguistics, is in fact an answer to part of this question. It observes that in some cases morphophonemic alternations arise from allophonic alternations made phonemic and morphophonemic by the loss of phonetically conditioning environments, for instance as the neutralisation of unstressed vowels led from Old High German /muːs/ 'mouse', plural /muːsi/ (phonetically [myːsi], by regular influence of the final high front vowel on the preceding vowel) to Middle High German /muːs/, plural /myːsə/ (where the front quality of the vowel in the plural is not predictable from the quality of the final vowel). It then suggests that other instances of morphophonemic alternations might be given a similar historical explanation. (In line with the discussion of section 2, I have weakened the claim from stating that this is an algorithm for reconstructing the past. Rather, it is in each case a hypothesis that needs to be compared for overall plausibility with competing hypotheses.)

As a result of the recent development of grammaticalisation as a tool in historical linguistics – see, for instance, Heine et al. (1991) – it has been possible to develop a more general variant of internal reconstruction, one that looks much less like an algorithm than does its traditional use in historical linguistics, but one that does enable us to come up with plausible hypotheses concerning earlier stages of language development. Grammaticalisation refers to the oft noted fact that there is a tendency in the attested history of languages for linguistic elements to develop from being less grammatical to being more grammatical. This can be observed both in relation to content and in relation to form. For instance, in Finnish comitativity is expressed by means of the postpositions *kanssa* or *kera*. Etymologically, the origins of these postpositions are well understood, the former deriving from a noun meaning 'group, company', the latter from a word meaning 'time'. In some other Balto-Finnic languages, such as Estonian, the postpositions have further developed to become case suffixes, in some languages even subject to vowel harmony. In terms of content, we can trace a development from independent lexical meaning to relational meaning. In terms of form, we can trace a development from content word (noun) to function word (postposition) to morphological affix (comitative suffix). In at least some cases, therefore, we can trace a path from less grammatical to more grammatical, and indeed the burgeoning literature on grammaticalisation has identified a large number of such instances, and also a number of grammaticalisation paths that are recurrent across the languages of the world, for instance, the use of body parts as one possible source of spatial adpositions and, subsequently, affixes. In this section, I will be concerned in particular with that part of grammaticalisation that deals with the development of morphology from lexical items.

Just like the original restricted concept of internal reconstruction as the historical unravelling of morphophonemic alternations, so we can take grammaticalisation and base on it a kind of generalised internal reconstruction that gives us access to hypotheses concerning earlier stages of the language in question, and by generalising our conclusions to earlier stages of language in general. If some instances of morphology can be shown to derive from juxtaposition of independent words, and especially in the absence of other plausible hypotheses concerning the origin of particular pieces of morphology, then other instances of morphology can at least plausibly be attributed to juxtaposition of independent words at an earlier stage. One of the advantages of this approach is that it enables us at least to approach the question of the possible origin of complex morphology and, by similar lines of argumentation, other aspects of complexity in language.

I will now turn directly to the question of reconstructing earlier stages of language that lack some of the complexities, indeed ideally all of the complexities, of all or most present-day languages, as part of a contribution to the general study of the origin and early development of human language. I should emphasise that my concern is with the development of the realisation of the human language potential, not with the development of that potential (for further discussion of this distinction, see Comrie 2000). There are clearly lots of potentials that human beings have had from the appearance of modern humans but which have only been realised much more recently, such as agriculture, domestication of animals, development of writing systems, and launching of rockets into outer space; in several cases, these potentials have been realised only through a series of intermediate stages, a point that may also be relevant in our consideration of language. Thus I do not exclude the possibility that modern humans from their first appearance may have had the same potential for human language as do contemporary people, indeed I am favourable to this view, which is of course in danger of being circular: creatures that did not have our potential for language might simply be defined as not being modern humans. But this still leaves open the question of how this potential came to be realised.

The basic assumption underlying the validity of this investigation is that it is highly unlikely that human language, with all the complexities found in present-day languages, could have arisen ex nihilo. The general principle is one widely assumed in other sciences, as when it is assumed in biology that life that did not arise ex nihilo, but rather as the result of the interaction of simpler chemical processes, i.e. the interaction of simple processes can give rise to complex phenomena. With respect to language, this means that it is unlikely that the first human language started off with the complexity of Insular Celtic morphophonemics or West Greenlandic morphology. Rather, such complexities arose as the result of the operation of attested processes – such as the loss of conditioning of allophonic variation to give morphophonemic alternations or the grammaticalisation of lexical items to give grammatical suffixes – upon an earlier system lacking such complexities, in which invariable words followed each other in order to build up the form corresponding to the desired semantic content, in an isolating language type lacking morphophonemic alternation.

(In passing, it should be noted that other kinds of complexities might also have been missing in this early language stage, for instance, complex phonetic segments. Thus, if it is the case the secondary articulations arise typically through the merger of segments, as palatalisation arose originally in the Slavonic languages through the merger of consonants with a following *j*, then it is possible that other phonetically complex segments, such as clicks, doubly articulated consonants, phonemically distinct nasalised vowels, etc., could have arisen in a similar way from an earlier stage where they were absent. I will not, however, explore this possibility in any more detail, in part because there are some examples where it is simply unclear to me, even on an intuitive basis, whether a particular phenomenon is to be regarded as a later complexity or not. For instance, we know that tone often arises on the basis of the loss of segmental distinctions, and there is a rich literature on such tonogenesis, but it is not clear to me that tone is, in the relevant sense, a complex phenomenon that was most probably lacking in the earliest human languages.)

The methodology consists essentially in stripping away all complexities that we know can be derived by the operation of historically attested processes. If it is the case that morphophonemic alternations can arise from the loss of phonetic conditioning of allophonic variants, then we strip away all morphophonemic alternations to arrive at an earlier stage lacking morphophonemic alternations. Since this is precisely the step criticised by Lass (1977), it is worth emphasising that this follows from the adoption of a somewhat different perspective from that adopted by Lass. His perspective is to test the justifiability of particular reconstructions, including those made against the background of attested cross-linguistic typological variation, and on this basis he concludes that such a reconstruction violates general constraints on language as we know it. He does note, however, that there might be some other domain of enquiry, beyond the limits of the constraints on conventional historical linguistics, in which one might investigate such questions (Lass 1977: 12). He even proposes the name 'palaeolinguistics' for this domain of enquiry, a suggestion that I would have been happy to accept had the term not unfortunately been pre-empted for another domain of linguistic enquiry, namely the attempt to correlate the reconstructed lexicon of a proto-language with the culture in which that language might have been spoken. And just as we strip away morphophonemic alternations, likewise we can strip away bound morphemes, on the assumption that bound morphemes always have some origin other than as bound morphemes, most typically as separate lexical items that eventually become reduced to bound morphemes. (This does not exclude the possibility that in particular cases a morpheme may have some other origin. For instance, Russian has a morpheme *n-* prefixed to third-person pronouns to indicate that they are governed by a preposition, so that the instrumental singular masculine *im* appears as *s n-im, pod n-im* after the prepositions *s* 'with' and *pod* 'under' which govern the instrumental case. Historically, this *n* arises by metanalysis of the final nasal of the earlier form of a couple of frequent prepositions, including the earlier form *sun* (cf. Latin *cum*) of the preposition *s* 'with', the *n-* prefix being subsequently generalised to occur after all prepositions. But note that even in this case, the bound morpheme does have an origin other than as a bound morpheme.)

One other possibility does, however, need to be considered. It might be the case that any currently attested complexity can be traced back to something less complex at an earlier stage, but that at this earlier stage there would be further complexities, perhaps lost in subsequent stages, that would have to be traced back to something less complex, and so on ad infinitum, i.e. the development of complexity would be part of a cyclic process that would be traceable, in principle, indefinitely far back in time, with some sort of 'conservation of complexity' as we go back in time rather than a point at which lack of complexity would be reached. We can, of course, observe something like this in the study of the brief portion of human language history for which we have direct attestation. Germanic umlaut as a morphophonemic phenomenon can plausibly be stripped away to give an earlier stage at which there was no umlaut, and the later development of umlaut as a morphophonemic alternation can be explained on the basis of the regular operation of phonetic changes. But if we go back to an earlier stage of the Indo-European language family, we find plenty of evidence for another morphophonemic alternation, ablaut, which has been lost, at least as a productive device, in many of the descendant languages, but which was clearly abundantly operative in earlier stages. Although there are plausible explanations for some instances of some aspects of Indo-European ablaut – for instance, some instances of the so-called zero grade, with complete loss of the vowel, can plausibly be attributed to shift of the accent away from that vowel – there is no general explanation, so that ablaut remains a morphophonemic alternation for which we cannot reconstruct a plausible origin.

But there are two problems with this line of approach. First, the fact that we cannot, in a particular case, reduce morphophonemic alternation to being the historical outcome of something else does not mean that it is not the outcome of something else; at worst, we could accept a conclusion of agnosticism, but it would be at least as potentially misleading to conclude that ablaut must always have been there as to conclude that it must have arisen from something else. (If we did not have the evidence showing the earlier system that led to umlaut, we might by the same token conclude, counterfactually, that umlaut had always been there.) Second, the cyclic approach fails to address the question of the origin of complexity in language, and thus fails to provide any insight into the central question addressed in this section. To take an analogy from another field concerned with history: from the fact that my parents were humans, and that their parents were humans, and that their parents were humans, etc., one cannot logically conclude that there have been humans around from the beginning of time.

In general, then, the methodology outlined in this section leads to positing an earlier stage of language, lacking at least many of the complexities of at least many present-day languages, but providing an explicit account of how these complexities could have arisen, by means of historically well-attested processes applied to this less complex earlier state. I return in section 4 to further consideration of the validity of this methodology against the background of general principles of philosophy of science.

Before concluding the discussion of this section, I want to consider briefly an alternative approach to the origin of complexity in human language, one that has been developed in recent years in particular by Alison Wray – see for instance Wray (1998). This alternative agrees with the approach outlined in the earlier part of the present section in that it assumes no complexity of the kind engendered by morphophonemic alternations, bound morphology, etc. at early stages of the development of human language. Rather, it assumes that at the early stage of the development of human language, all messages involved a global relation between form and content, without any possibility of breaking up the form and relating parts of the form to parts of the content. In other words, the signal for 'beware of the lion' would bear no relation either to that for 'beware of the snake' or to that for 'I've killed the lion', the latter indeed bearing no relation to 'I'm going to kill the lion'. (The particular examples are chosen purely as illustrative, and are not necessarily meant to be even plausible utterances from the relevant period of human history.) From the viewpoint of present-day languages, every sentence of this early language would be fully suppletive.

I am not going to argue for or against this particular hypothesis as an early stage of human communication, perhaps even as one that fed into the development of human language as we know it today, rather I would only point out that such a system cannot be the sole origin for human language as we know it today. For such a system to change into a system where there are links between parts of the form and parts of the meaning of a signal, it would be necessary for there to be chance similarities between the parts of two signal forms happening to correlate with similarities between the parts of two signal meanings, like a kind of folk etymology run wild. While one can readily imagine a few chance similarities of this kind, perhaps even occasional examples where the parts of the meaning could be exhaustively matched against the parts of the form of the signal and vice versa, the laws of chance would suggest that such instances would be extremely rare. In other words, at some point such a system would have to be replaced, or almost completely replaced (say, bar certain signals such as greetings or expressions of pain), by a system in which there is a systematic pairing between parts of the form and parts of the meaning of a signal. And it is the origin of this stage of human language that the body of this section has been designed to account for.

4   The uniformitarian hypothesis revisited

An objection that is often made to the kind of approach outlined in section 3 is that it violates uniformitarian assumptions; indeed this point is explicitly noted by Lass (1977: 12). It is therefore necessary to examine in more detail the extent to which this is a valid objection.

The approach presented in section 3 necessarily leads, in the case of languages with complexities such as complex morphology, to the reconstruction of an earlier stage where these complexities were absent. This can be seen as a violation of at least one version of the uniformitarian hypothesis in at least two ways. First, it concludes that for the languages in question, their ancestors were simpler in the relevant respects, and thus assigns them to a different language type than the attested languages. For instance, if we have a set of languages that are all agglutinating or fusional, such as the Dravidian languages, then this would suggest that even if a classical reconstruction of Proto-Dravidian using the comparative method would reconstruct an agglutinating or fusional system, then one can go beyond this to hypothesise an earlier stage at which there was no bound morphology at all. (Of course, it is conceivable that this earlier stage might include the common ancestor not only of Dravidian but also of other languages and language families, so that it would not properly be called Proto-Dravidian.) In other words, it would be the case that a particular language or language family would be able to change its morphological or other type over the course of history, a conclusion specifically referred to by Lass (1977: 10). However, even in attested language change, it is not the case that the morphological or other typology of a language remains constant, indeed we know of several instances of languages that have radically changed their typology, for instance, from a complex fusional type as in the older Germanic languages to a by-and-large isolating type with a small amount of agglutination and only relics of fusion in English, or from a word order that is predominantly verb-initial with some verb-medial alternants to one that is overwhelmingly verb-final in Semitic languages of Ethiopia. And even in the many instances where one would have to rely on a reconstruction for earlier historical states, we find variation among genealogically related languages which means that their common ancestor, whichever system it had, must have had one that is at odds with at least some of the descendant languages. Sino-Tibetan languages, for instance, range from near-isolating languages like Chinese and Burmese to languages with complex verb morphologies like some languages spoken in the Himalayas. Thus, typological consistency is not even an observed constraint in the histories of those few languages for which we have actual documentation, nor in the comparison of languages that are known to be genealogically related.

But the question is somewhat different when we turn to the reconstruction attempted in section 3 of an earlier stage of language that lacked many of the complexities that are universal or widespread in contemporary languages. Of course, if a complexity is widespread but not universal, then reconstructing language at an earlier stage as lacking the complexity in question should not, on these grounds alone, be problematic. If there are attested languages that have property X, e.g. lack of bound morphology (as in isolating languages), then there is no typological reason why a reconstructed language should not have this property. But let us suppose that our reconstruction leads us back to a stage where the reconstructed language lacks some property that is found in all attested languages. A plausible instance in question would be morphophonemic alternations. Let us suppose, at least for the sake of argument, that it is the case that all currently spoken languages have morphophonemic alternations – and note that even in the case of isolating languages like the Chinese languages that lack or virtually lack segmental morphophonemic alternations, there are nonetheless often quite complex phenomena of tone sandhi, i.e. morphophonemic alternations involving tone and therefore at the prosodic level. And let us suppose, as was indeed suggested in section 3, that our reconstruction techniques lead us to posit an earlier stage of language at which there were no morphophonemic alternations (other than perhaps minimal accommodations resulting from the phonetic environment). Under this scenario, we would clearly have reconstructed an earlier language type that is fundamentally different from the type of any attested language, and would thus in one sense have violated the uniformitarian hypothesis. What does this mean for the evaluation of the reconstruction against general principles of the philosophy of science?

To answer this question, it is necessary to look more closely at what is meant by the uniformitarian hypothesis in other sciences. The hypothesis was apparently first proposed, in relation to geology, by James Hutton in the late eighteenth century, and the term was not created until the mid-nineteenth century by George Whewell, but what is usually considered to be the first explicit characterisation of the concept is its use by Lyell (1830–3); all of these relate to the field of geology. In geology, certain processes can be observed as ongoing during recorded history, such as the formation of mountains and their subsequent erosion by wind and rain. The uniformitarian hypothesis, which did so much to raise geology to its present scientific level, assumes that these same processes also characterised the Earth's prehistory. In other words, in order to explain earlier geological formations, we are not permitted to appeal to processes other than those that have characterised the more recent period. But it is important to realise that what is constrained by the uniformitarian hypothesis is the set of processes that have formed the earth, not the set of states that are separated by these processes. Thus, one could imagine starting from a state that is radically different from the present state of the Earth, say a perfectly smooth spherical or near-spherical object, and then initiate operation of the processes of mountain formation and erosion to produce something like the present-day Earth. In other words, the typological consistency implied by the uniformitarian hypothesis in geology is a typological consistency of processes, not a typological consistency of states. And indeed one can adhere to this version of the uniformitarian hypothesis while reconstructing earlier states that are radically different from the present appearance of the Earth, provided only that one maintains consistency with respect to the processes that are needed to get from the posited earlier state to the currently observed state. And note further that in geology it is not literally possible to go back in time to check whether a particular reconstruction of an earlier period is correct or not; at best, such a reconstruction is our currently most plausible hypothesis, given known kinds of geological processes, of how a currently observed state got to be the way it is, not much different in principle from the kind of linguistic reconstruction suggested in section 3.

We may now apply this historically more appropriate concept of uniformitarianism, from the viewpoint of the philosophy of science, to the kind of linguistic reconstruction that we proposed in section 3. It now becomes clear that our reconstruction is indeed compatible with this conception of the uniformitarian hypothesis. We propose no processes that are not attested in the historical period. In particular, the narrower conception of internal reconstruction, which 'reconstructs away' morphophonemic alternations, relies on the observed possibility for phonetic change to destroy environments for allophony, thus leading to the phonemicisation and in appropriate instances the morphologisation of allophonic alternations. No new types of processes are proposed. However, the operation of these processes can take us from an earlier stage that is typologically different from attested languages to a later stage that is compatible with our knowledge of attested language states. The proposal outlined in section 3 is therefore fully compatible with the uniformitarian hypothesis as it is usually understood in the philosophy of science, and as it needs to be understood in such sciences as geology.

Of course, there is no guarantee that the particular version of a hypothesis, such as the uniformitarian hypothesis, that is valid in one science is necessarily valid in another. (To take a trivial example, the concept of 'exception' is so useful in linguistics that it would be difficult to do away with it, yet it is not clear what analogue there is to this concept in, for instance, physics.) But what this does mean is that there is no a priori reason for rejecting proposals that are in fact consistent with a particular principle of the general philosophy of science on the grounds that they violate some stricter version of that principle. Indeed, the history of linguistics shows that the field has often come unstuck precisely through assuming that linguistics can adopt stricter versions of the general philosophy of science in order to validate its credentials as a science: the attempt to construct algorithms ('discovery procedures') for reconstructing history or for synchronic analysis being a case in point, as rightly noted by Lass (1977). In other words, if there are good reasons for adopting a stricter stance in linguistics, then this stricter stance must be justified, not assumed a priori. And certainly uniformitarianism as a general scientific principle cannot be appealed to as a reason for rejecting reconstructions of the kind proposed in section 3.

5   Conclusions

In this chapter, I have come to conclusions apparently very different from those espoused by Lass (1977; 1993), arguing that it is a valid exercise to reconstruct stages in the development of human language typologically different from, in particular less complex than, attested human languages. But let it also be noted that there are substantial points of agreement, in particular that methods of linguistic reconstruction cannot be interpreted as algorithms guaranteeing correct reconstructions. Moreover, the difference in conclusions stems largely from a difference in perspective. I am asking a different question, namely: how might the complexity that is found in present-day languages have come about? And once one asks this question, with the main constraint being the plausibility of the reconstructed simplicity given current knowledge about language change, then the conclusions can be maintained without in any way rejecting the methodological warnings, salutary as always, that are given by Lass.

REFERENCES

Comrie, Bernard. 1992. 'Before complexity', in John A. Hawkins and Murray Gell-Mann (eds.), *The Evolution of Human Languages* (Santa Fe Institute Studies in the Sciences of Complexity 11), Redwood City, CA: Addison-Wesley, 193–211.
Comrie, Bernard. 2000. 'From potential to realization: an episode in the origin of language', in Jacques Arends (ed.), *Creoles, Pidgins, and Sundry Languages: Essays in Honor of Pieter Seuren (= Linguistics 38.5)*, Berlin: Mouton de Gruyter, 989–1004.
Heine, Bernd, Ulrike Claudi and Friederike Hünnemeyer. 1991. *Grammaticalization*. Chicago: University of Chicago Press.
Lass, Roger. 1977. 'Internal reconstruction and generative phonology', *Transactions of the Philological Society* 1975: 1–26.
Lass, Roger. 1993. 'How real(ist) are reconstructions', in Charles Jones (ed.), *Historical Linguistics: Problems and Perspectives*, London: Longman, 156–89.
Lyell, Charles. 1830–3. *Principles of Geology*. 3 volumes. London: Murray. (Reprinted 1990–1. Chicago: University of Chicago Press).
McWhorter, John. 2001. 'The world's simplest grammars are creole grammars', *Linguistic Typology*, 125–66.
Renfrew, Colin and Paul Bahn. 2000. *Archaeology: Theories, Methods and Practice*. 3rd edition. London: Thames & Hudson.
Wray, Alison. 1998. 'Protolanguage as a holistic system for social interaction', *Language and Communication* 18: 47–67.

15   Reanalysis and typological change

Raymond Hickey

1   Introduction

The concern of the present chapter is to examine the typological change in morphology which took place in Irish and which sets it off both from members of related Indo-European subgroups and partly from other Celtic languages, i.e. the P-Celtic languages.[1] This typological change resulted in the rise of a system of initial mutations (a common Insular Celtic development) and the rise of functional palatalisation in Irish, in all probability due to reanalysis by language learners triggered by the demise of inherited inflections from earlier stages of Celtic. This kind of typological change is quite unique among the Indo-European languages which generally have used other devices to accommodate the shift from synthetic to analytic type. The uniqueness of the Irish solution makes it worthwhile examining it as an instance of what constitutes a possible language change and so match the tenor of the other contributions to the present volume. The framework I am adopting is a broadly typological perspective which attempts to give a unified interpretation of several apparently disparate phenomena which appear in the earliest history of Irish. The period at which the changes would seem to have begun is the immediately pre-Old Irish period (before 600) and the typological adjustment continued throughout the remainder of the recorded history of Irish, albeit with disturbances due to developments on linguistic levels other than that of morphology.

I will proceed by looking at groups of phonetic/phonological changes between Ogam (the inscriptional language used in the pre-Old Irish period) and the earliest stages of Irish to see to what extent these are responsible for the typological reorientation of the language over a span of several centuries. Viewed from a high vantage point, the developments can be summarised as phonetic attrition and loss at an early stage, followed by a basic realignment of the morphology of Irish with several readjustments in the period after the re-orientation had taken place, roughly in the course of the attested stages of Irish (from about 600 onwards). Importantly, this realignment can be viewed as the result

---

[1] The terms Q-Celtic and P-Celtic refer to the differential treatment of Indo-European /kʷ/ in the Celtic languages; see note 5 below for more detail.

of first-language learners reanalysing the phonetic blurring which occurred at the beginnings of words (the product of phrase-level sandhi, Ó Cuív 1986) as being of systemic significance, in this case as the exponence of key grammatical categories, such as number, case, tense, etc.

The term *reanalysis* can be understood in different ways. In a syntactic sense, there is an interpretation which involves only surface structures, e.g. 'Reanalysis is a mechanism which changes the underlying structure of a syntactic pattern and which does not involve any modification of its surface manifestation' (Harris and Campbell 1995, ch. 4 'Reanalysis', p. 61). But for the present discussion, reanalysis is understood as the switch from one surface feature to another in the realisation of a *grammatical* category. In this scenario one has two features which appear together in one grammatical context, for instance in an oblique case like the genitive or in the plural. Of these two features one is historically prior and is the inherited exponent of the category in question. The second is an attendant, noncentral feature, usually derived from some allophonic process like secondary articulation, for instance the fronting of vowels before *j* and *i* in following syllables, i.e. umlaut in North and West Germanic, or external sandhi, i.e. the initial mutations in Celtic. The shift is one of status. The low-level, secondary feature attains systemic status, normally because of the demise of the older feature, frequently through phonetic attrition, hence the functionalisation of umlaut in Germanic and of the initial mutations in Celtic on the decline of the inherited Indo-European inflections. In the terminology employed by Croft the shift is from an interpretation of features from 'contextual' to 'inherent', a case of 'hypoanalysis' (see his discussion of umlaut, Croft 2000: 126–9).

This scenario for reanalysis implies that the switchover must last for a period of time because both the former systemic features – inflections in Germanic and Celtic – and the newer subsystemic features – umlaut in Germanic and initial mutation in Celtic – must be present for language learners to reanalyse the newer features as the exponence of the grammatical category with which they co-occur in speech. The duration of overlap between the old and new systems is difficult to determine and remnants of the earlier grammatical exponents – inflections in Indo-European – may never be completely removed.

The beneficial effect of reanalysis, the maintenance of grammatical distinctions under threat of being lost, is an epiphenomenon of the renanalyis. The language learners in no way attempt to rescue the language system, rather they reinterpret distinctions in form. At some stage in the development of Celtic the initial mutations were reinterpreted as having systemic significance. The particular interpretation made depends on the grammatical contexts in which the mutations occurred, e.g. as the exponence of the genitive singular or the plural or the preterite. The *goal* was not to rescue a grammatical system but this was the *effect* of reanalysis.

In the following the details of this reanalysis are outlined. To grasp its work-ings it is necessary to start with Continental Celtic before the first remains of Irish appear and offer a brief characterisation of it.

1.1   Stress type and placement in Celtic

In common with Germanic and (pre-Latin) Italic, Celtic has initial stress accent (Salmons 1992: 146ff.). This is a feature which was already effective on the continent before the formation of Insular Celtic. There are no indications of a period of variable stress at some earlier stage as there are in the workings of Verner's Law in Germanic for example. The placement of stress is on the first syllable which in Celtic is the root. In cases of prefixation the root maintains the stress. Initial stress among languages with stress accent often leads to a reduction and blurring in later syllables, in the case of Indo-European daughter languages in the inflectional endings (Lehmann 1992: 214). This reduction does not necessarily hold for languages which broadly show pitch accent, such as Finnish, because the contrast between accented and nonaccented syllables is re-alised by a contrast in frequency pitch and not primarily by loudness and length as with stress-accent systems. With the latter the nonaccented syllables are gen-erally shorter, something which contributes over time to their indistinctiveness and eventual loss.[2]

1.2   Developing alternative strategies

Given that language is an adaptive evolutionary phenomenon (Croft 1995: 137), it is understandable that if changes occur which are detrimental to the function-ing of the system then language learners will undertake reinterpretations which are likely to counterbalance such effects. This would appear to be true irrespec-tive of whether the disruption occurs because of a force within the language itself or for external reasons. In the specific case of Irish, one has a rapid blurring and subsequent loss of inflectional syllables due to the natural phenomenon of phonetic weakening.[3] The process in the prehistory of Irish moved quickly and homophony in such central areas as case marking or pronominal distinctions may well have existed. The following chart illustrates briefly how phonetic sub-stance was lost in words from the very earliest attestations through Old Irish to

---

[2] The distinction here is a rough and ready one. Among so-called stress-accent languages one can note considerable differences; just recall the reduction of short unstressed vowels in English to shwa and their retention in German as an example (Hickey 1995).

[3] I am not addressing the question here as to whether this propensity for weakening was a contact phenomenon as there is no reliable means for establishing this at such great time depth. The situation is different with the co-existence of Celtic and English in the Old English period where one can make a case for a low-level influence of the former on the latter (Hickey 1995).

Modern Irish. The second half of the chart shows instances of morphologically conditioned lenition as manifested in Modern Irish (essentially similar to Old Irish).

(1)   Ogam   Old Irish   Modern Irish
        senobena   →   *senben* → *seanbhean*   'old
                                                                       woman'
        inigena   →   *ingen*   → *iníon*   'daughter'
        maqqos   →   *maqq*   → *mac* /kk /→ /k/   'son'
        Modern Irish
        cáin   /kaːn/   'tax'
                                        (feminine
                                          noun)
        an cháin   /ə xaːnʲ/   'the tax'
        beag   /bʲag/   'small'
        an-bheag   /anʲvʲag/   'very
                                         small'
        ró-bheag   /roːvʲag/   'too
                                         small'
        brisim   /bʲrʲIsʲImʲ/   'I break'
        bhris mé   /vʲrʲIsʲ mʲeː/   'I broke'

In the transition stage from Continental Celtic to pre-Old Irish a reaction appeared to the attrition caused by phonetic weakening, that is the phenomenon came, through reanalysis, to be interpreted as systemic. The phonetic weakening in Irish was both word-internal (no further consequences for the morphology) and, due to sandhi, word-external. Grammatical elements such as determiners could induce lenition (shift of stop to fricative) at the beginning of the following noun or verb. Any such preceding element which originally ended in a nasal (such as the numerals 7, 9 and 10, cf. Latin *septem, novem, decem*) causes nasalisation (shift of voiced stop to nasal or voicing of a voiceless obstruent, see below) at the beginning of the following word.

1.3   Functionalisation of phonetic weakening

During the immediately pre-Old Irish period this phonetic effect was reanalysed and hence functionalised so that the contrast between lenition, nasalisation or no change was exploited for grammatical purposes. For instance, no phonetic change was typical of the masculine nominative and lenition was indicative of the feminine nominative as the original article in Celtic (and ultimately Indo-European) ended in an obstruent /-s/ in the first case and in a vowel /-a/ in the second. The sandhi between article and noun triggered lenition with the feminine article as the initial consonant was intervocalic in this instance.

The phenomena of lenition and nasalisation are conventionally referred to in combination as *initial mutations*.[4] Basically, an initial mutation is a segmental change at the beginning of a word induced by another word which precedes it. The words affected are usually lexical stems: nouns, adjectives, verbs, etc. The words causing the mutation are usually grammatical words: articles, pronouns, particles of various types. The mutation involved usually only affects consonants and leads in the main to a change in the manner of articulation, changes in place may also be concomitant on the mutation, though less rarely so.

1.3.1   Release from phonetic motivation

Functionalisation of a low-level phenomenon such as phonetic weakening has a number of consequences. One is that the original phonetic triggering is no longer necessary, that is, the phenomenon can occur in environments in which it would not have done so originally. For instance, nasalisation in Irish would not have been triggered by the number 8 as this did not end in a nasal (cf. Latin *octō*), but in Irish it came to nasalise and so fit into the series of numerals which induce nasalisation of a following noun.

1.3.2   Blocking of further developments

Another consequence of functionalisation is that, after it is initiated, phonetic developments are then arrested. Thus /ɣ/, resulting from the lenition of /g/, does not disappear initially as it does word-internally in Irish (though it has disappeared in Welsh). /s/ does not lenite beyond /h/ as opposed to Andalusian Spanish, for example, which has /s/ → /h/ → Ø, e.g. *las casas*, [lah kasah], [la kasa]. With regard to palatalisation (see next section), /k/ does not assibilate to /ʃ/ via /t/ as it has done in French, for instance, but remains a palatal stop /kʲ/, phonetically [c] (IPA).

The external sandhi which resulted in the Celtic mutations went hand in hand with a decrease in the lexical status of the mutating particles as these lost stress and phonetic distinctiveness. Given the phonological bond with the following mutated lexical word, one would expect movement on the following morphologisation cline (Hopper and Traugott 1993: 132) with the particles ending up as prefixes or being lost completely.

(2)   lexical item > clitic > affix

---

[4] These mutations are common to all the Celtic languages (Hickey 1996). In my opinion they can hardly represent a shared innovation in each individual language as the probability of this occurring, given the statistical rarity of the phenomenon across the world's languages, is very slight indeed. The only other plausible explanation is that the seeds of the later functionalisation were present in Continental Celtic (as subphonemic phenomena) before part of it branched off into Insular Celtic. Furthermore, the beginnings of the mutations must be postulated as common to both P- and Q-Celtic.

But while the mutating particles in Celtic share many of the characteristics of clitics (low phonetic profile, for instance), they do not undergo affixation. If they were absorbed by the following word this would lead to severe loss of grammatical function, to homophony and ambiguity of the kind which initiated the system of mutation in the first place. Such a development would have forced – within a comparatively short period of time – another typological reorientation to compensate for this new kind of grammatical syncretism.

1.4   The development of palatalisation

A prominent feature of the phonology of Q-Celtic[5] is the existence of two series of consonants, one palatal and the other nonpalatal (phonetically velarised). The origin of these is quite straightforward: a high front vowel, typically an inflection in Indo-European, had the effect of palatalising the preceding consonant (usually the coda of the root) by articulatory assimilation. These endings were lost with palatalised consonants remaining as their reflex in later forms of Q-Celtic. After this stage there was a phonemic contrast between palatalised and nonpalatalised consonants. As with umlaut in Germanic, an attendant phonetic effect of an inflection became reanalysed as the marker of a certain grammatical category, for instance of genitive singular or nominative plural in Irish, like the plural or comparative in Germanic. Just as with the initial changes, there was a spread of palatalisation into domains not affected by the original phonetic palatalisation. This can be viewed as analogical regularisation after grammatical functionalisation.

1.5   Inherent deficiencies in the system

It is important to view the initial mutations as a reaction to a disturbance in the morphology of late Continental Celtic, indeed as a functionalisation of just this disturbance, phonetic weakening and external sandhi. It obviously was not a planned reaction and is in no way an artifact of speakers of Celtic at any particular stage. Hence one should not be surprised to find that the new

---

[5] The two major divisions of Celtic are conventionally labelled *P-Celtic* and *Q-Celtic*. These designations derive from the treatment of original /kʷ/ in Brythonic and Goidelic, very roughly the British and the Irish-Scottish forms of Celtic respectively. In Goidelic (and in Celtiberian) the inherited labialised velar is retained whereas in Brythonic and Gaulish /p/, a consonant originally lost in all Celtic languages, was regained by the shift of /kʷ/ to /p/ as seen in Old Welsh *map* (> Modern Welsh *mab*) and Irish *mac* /-k/ 'son'; Modern Welsh *penn* /pen/ and Modern Irish *ceann* /kʲaːn/ 'head': Irish later reintroduced the bilabial stop via Latin loans like *pian* 'pain' or *póg* 'kiss' (< *pacis*) and still later via Anglo-Norman loanwords like *píosa* 'piece' or *pláta* 'plate'. Note that the closing of a labial element to a stop had a precedent in the shifting of IE g^w to /b/ in Celtic, cf. Old Irish *ben* 'woman' < IEg^w*ena*; compare Old Irish *béo* 'alive' and Latin *vivos* (Thurneysen 1946: 117).

grammatical system in Celtic had certain deficiencies. The most severe of these were evident in those words which started with segments which could not be fricativised, i.e. with sonorants. This is a source of ambiguity to this very day, where it is not possible to tell if lenition has applied to a sonorant-initial form.[6] And of course nasalisation can only apply vacuously to words with an initial nasal. For instance in Modern Irish *a neart* can mean 'his, her, their strength' and the correct interpretation rests entirely on context.

Another deficiency in the mutation system is that there are instances of overlap, for example the result of leniting /p/ is /f/ which exists as an independent, nonmutated segment to begin with, thus *a phian* 'his pain' and *a fíon* 'her wine' are both phonetically /ə fiən/.

The point to note here is that the new system of initial mutation combined with the distinction between palatals and nonpalatals at the end of word forms was nonetheless communicatively adequate.

1.6   Later disturbances of the system

Typological changes in languages move at different paces. If one neglects the extreme case of abrupt creolisation and the immediate establishment of SVO and nominal pre-specification for the moment, then one sees that syntactic typology moves fairly slowly (measured in centuries) and that morphological typology changes very slowly (measured in several centuries if not in millennia). Thus Nichols (1992) notes that clause alignment (nominative–accusative vs. ergative–absolute) is something which shows great stability over time whereas word order changes at a relatively quicker pace but shows areal stability. This would seem to indicate that word order is a phenomenon which diffuses areally between languages.[7] One reason for this could be that a language has many word-order types at any one time: a basic one and others used for topicalisation purposes. There may occur a shift in status from topicalised to basic especially under the influence of another language which already has the order in question as basic. But with clause alignment a language has either the one order or the other (unless it is a case of 'split ergativity').

---

[6] In Old Irish there was a distinction of phonemic length among sonorants and *phonological* lenition, i.e. the grammatical principle, may well have had as its phonetic exponence the degemination of long sonorants, e.g. /ll, nn, mm/+ Lenition → /l, n, m/, for a fuller discussion of this see Hickey (1996).

[7] In the realm of syntactic typology Irish poses an interesting problem: the development of VSO and nominal post-modification may well have been the result of substratum influence from a language of ultimately Afro-Asiatic origin already in Ireland before the arrival of the Celts. Various older authors such as Pokorny and Wagner have supported this view and it has received recent attention from Theo Vennemann who adheres to it (see Vennemann 1997 for example). The standard language-internal interpretation is outlined in Watkins (1963). Ahlqvist (1980) sees cleft sentences as providing the model for a generalised VSO word order.

The upshot of the relative stability of morphological typology is that once it establishes itself it has considerable momentum and a reorientation requires a 'life-threatening situation' so to speak such as the collapse of pronominal distinctions or the syncretism of case marking for subjects and objects. In Irish the shift away from the original suffixal inflection strategy inherited from Indo-European towards the new system of grammatically relevant alterations at the margins of words (initial mutation at the beginning and palatalisation vs. nonpalatalisation at the end) has shown remarkable stability throughout the entire period of attested Irish (roughly from 600 to the present day).

This stability has been threatened on a number of occasions. Despite the gravity of changes which impaired Irish morphological typology the system has survived and adjusted itself to the altered circumstances.

The first disruption of the system was the loss of phonological length during the Middle Irish period. Exact dating is difficult here. In the present context it suffices to point out that in Old Irish there existed long consonants, in particular long sonorants, and that a potential contrast (Feuth 1983; Greene 1956) existed between long and short sonorants which could have been interpreted morphologically as the difference between a nonlenited and a lenited segment. After the Middle Irish period this option no longer existed.[8]

The second disruption was initiated by the shift, again in the Middle Irish period – this time probably towards the end (O'Rahilly 1926) – of the ambidental fricatives /θ/ and /ð/. Note that these segments were the result of leniting /t/ and /d/ respectively in Old Irish. The shift was to /h/ in the case of the voiceless dental fricative and to /ɣ/ in the case of the voiced one. The shifts resulted in homophony as the output of leniting /s/ was /h/ and of /g/ was /ɣ/ already.

(3)   a. *a thuí*   /ə hiː/   'his straw'
           a shuí   /ə hiː/   'his sitting'
       b. *a dhaol*   /ə ɣiːl/   'his beetle'
           a ghaol   /ə ɣiːl/   'his relationship'

One can speculate on why these shifts should have occurred. Cross-linguistically (at least in Indo-European) there is more of a tendency for languages to lose ambidental fricatives than to develop them. The continental Germanic languages (bar Danish) are a good example of this. Here the original fricative input – ultimately deriving from Grimm's Law – was strengthened to a stop (German, Dutch, Swedish, Norwegian). Equally the Romance languages (bar Spanish and central Italian dialects) have lost ambidental fricatives which

---

[8] An exception is the dialect of the northwest, that roughly comprising the county of Donegal today, which according to many scholars (Wagner 1979 and Ó Baoill 1979) still retains a length contrast for sonorants.

had resulted from lenition stages[9] in their development from the regional forms of Latin which provided their various starting-points.

The Irish case is a good example of competing motivation. A natural phonetic development, the demise of segments with low acoustic prominence – compare the slight phonetic salience of /θ/ with that of /s/ or /x/ which is much higher – disturbs the morphology of the language (a different linguistic level) which then adjusts accordingly.

The central question here is just how much homophony a language subsystem like morphology can tolerate before a major reorientation becomes imperative. The wholescale loss or blurring of grammatical suffixes would seem to be criterion enough: witness the development of the Irish mutational system from a Continental Celtic starting point in the first place. The historical phases of Irish, however, show that considerable homophony can be accommodated in a language, more than is frequently assumed by linguists. For instance the reshuffling of the pronominal system in late Old English was largely motivated by a threatened or actual homophony of pronouns for the third-person singular and plural. This is probably the degree of homophony which triggers a remedial response from speakers (promotion of dialect *she* and borrowing of northern forms with initial *th-*). However one should be careful not to assume that homophony anywhere in the morphology will initiate a therapeutic reaction. The Irish case shows that complete homophony for the third person possessive pronouns with sonorant-initial nouns (recall the example of *a neart* 'his, her, their strength') was not enough to provoke such a reaction. It is probably only when exhaustive contextualisation is insufficient that a closed-class subsystem like morphology will be forced into a major reorientation. Furthermore, one should note that language contact such as that of English with Scandinavian and French is not necessary to trigger widespread typological reorientation. In the case of Celtic there is no direct evidence that the system of mutation and, in Q-Celtic, that of palatalisation/de-palatalisation is the result of any kind of substratal transfer.[10]

2   A morphological typology of Irish

This section is concerned with describing in principle how the morphology of Modern Irish works, especially in view of the developments which have been

---

[9] One view sees the lenition in Celtic and in western Romance as being linked, cf. Martinet (1952) and Ternes (1977).

[10] This matter may not be quite as simple as I am presenting it here. If one accepts that the pre-Celtic language(s) of Ireland was/were of an ultimately Afro-Asiatic origin then one could see in the functionalisation of secondary articulation, leading to the grammaticalisation of palatalisation /de-palatalisation, a parallel to that of the distinction between pharyngealised and nonpharyngealised consonants – and their functional exploitation – in Afro-Asiatic languages like Arabic. This could mean that the functionalisation in Irish was influenced by the model of a precursor language or languages in Ireland.

discussed so far. It should be emphasised that this system is essentially the same as that for Old Irish. Both the mutations and palatalisation/de-palatalisation existed in the older form of the language. The former were not indicated consistently, or at all, in the orthography and other aspects of Old Irish morphology, such as its complex verbal system, cloud the picture. In addition much regularisation has taken place so that Modern Irish is a more consistent and symmetrical language from the point of view of its morphology. One important reason for this is that the phonetic attrition which represented the initial momentum for the typological reorientation continued and eliminated virtually all instances of suffix inflection in the nominal area – except for productive endings, such as /-əx/, which now can be interpreted as root extensions rather than inflections in their own right. Case endings were blurred and lost, for instance there is no dative ending in Modern Irish, and in the verbal area very considerable simplification of forms occurred reducing productive morphology in this area and leading to an attendant increase in lexicalisation.

When describing Modern Irish one finds that the categories of conventional morphological typology, inflecting, agglutinating, etc., are not entirely adequate as they do not capture the central features which characterise the organisation of Irish morphology. Instead of trying to adapt traditional terms I offer an alternative method of characterising the inflecting morphology of Irish which is based on an analysis of the means which it uses for signalling grammatical categories such as singular and plural, various cases, conjugational forms of verbs and the like.

The outset for any consideration of Irish morphology is the phonetic attrition which set in at the earliest stages of the attested language, between Primitive Old Irish and the Old Irish period proper as outlined above, this attrition leading to a loss of profile with inherited Indo-European inflections.

For the new typological principle which arose in Irish I use the term *base-margin alteration*, which involved the functionalisation of phenomena at the beginning and end of words, hence the qualifier 'margin': to talk of 'words' in this connection is too inaccurate. The alterations which became the central part of the language's grammar affected the base form in any paradigm.

2.1 Base and root

Base. Taking the first major category, nouns, one can state that the base is the unaltered form of the noun, in the nominative case, singular person, citation form for a dictionary, i.e. it can stand alone. It may consist of one or two syllables (in rare cases three). If two or more syllables, then the second (and third) is a *root extension*. The latter does not usually carry any lexical information and only has a few manifestations, typically /əx/.

Root. This is a base minus its extension, if present. The lexical part is the root and is identical with the base in monosyllabic forms.

Transparent root extensions. /əx/ → /iː/+ palatalisation, historically /ɪç /-> /ɪj/ -> /ɪː/:

marcach : *marcaigh*	'rider'-NOM : 'rider'-GEN
báisteach : *báistigh*	'rain'-NOM : 'rain'-GEN

Opaque root extensions. Examples are *eolas* 'knowledge', *samhraidh* 'sommer', *amadán* 'fool'. Some of these may be old Latin loans as in *peaca* 'sin' (from *peccatum*), *airgead* 'silver' (from *argentus*), *anam* 'soul' (from *anima*).

Others are Anglo-Norman loans from the Middle English period: *séipéil* 'church' (from *chapel*), *seomra* 'room' (from *chambre*).

Depalatalisation can include the adding of a root extension as with fifth declension nouns: *riail* : *briseadh na rialach* 'rule': 'breaking of the rule'.

2.2   Type of alteration

The base form of any paradigm can undergo various alterations when indicating different grammatical categories. In this connection one should note that at the beginning of a base a *mutation* can occur. At the end of a base a change in *consonantal quality* may appear. By the latter term is meant a change from palatal to nonpalatal or vice versa with any consonant.

Changes in consonantal quality. A prominent feature of Irish phonology is that all consonants, except /h/, occur in palatal and nonpalatal pairs. There are no affricates. Voiceless fricatives are primary, voiced ones are derived by mutation, i.e. /f/, /s/ and /x/ are primary and occur in lexical forms, whereas /v/ and /ɣ/ (and /x/ in initial position) are secondary and only arise due to mutation. /s/ alternates with /h/; there are no voiced sibilants in Irish.

The distinction between long and short vowels is phonemic. With short vowels the system is basically threefold /ɪ/ : /a/ : /ʊ/. The distinction between /ɪ/ and /ɛ/ is weak. [ʌ] and [ʊ] do not contrast but vary according to ambient consonantal quality. A final unstressed short syllable always has /ə/ as its vowel.

Long vowels have a five-way distinction: /iː/ - /eː/ -/aː/ -/oː/ -/uː/. Diphthongs (/ai/ and /au/) have arisen (i) through absorption of lenited consonants into the nucleus of a syllable or (ii) because of on-glides to palatal or nonpalatal (velarised) consonants.

Now the changes in consonantal quality involve a consonant which is nonpalatal becoming palatal or one which is palatal being de-palatalised. Phonetically nonpalatal sounds are velarised to improve phonetic contrast. Palatalisation in Irish only involves a change in the feature [palatal]. There is no assibilation or affrication with palatalisation as in Slavic languages. Note that as the language has palatalisation as a grammatical phenomenon, e.g. when forming the genitive or plural, nonpalatal consonant quality is systemically significant (on the right margin of words) and should not be considered as somehow 'neutral'. In the following simple examples the final consonant in the singular is nonpalatal, /k/ and /x/ respectively. In the plural this changes to /kj/ [c] for the first word but to /iː/ (see remarks under 'Root' above) for the second so that with many words in present-day Irish, grammatical palatalisation is no longer phonetic palatalisation due to various historical changes (here: vocalisation of a final palatal fricative).[11]

(4)   Sg (nonpalatal)   Pl (palatal)
   a. *cnoc*   'hill'   *cnoic*   'hills'
   b. *marcach*   'rider   *marcaigh*   'riders'

2.3   Initial mutations

By initial mutation is meant a change in the manner and possibly place of articulation of a consonant at the beginning of a word. As mentioned above such changes were originally sandhi phenomena, i.e. the intervocalic voicing of voiceless segments or the fricativisation of voiced ones. This is paralleled by the nasalisation of words preceded by nasals. Inflections play a secondary role and are phonetically reduced. In Modern Irish the phonological parameters which vary are (1) voiced, fricative or nasal quality for syllable onsets and (2) palatal versus nonpalatal quality for syllable codas. This leads to Irish becoming a type in which morphological categories are indicated by a change in the margins of root syllables. This principle functionally links initial mutation and changes in consonant quality (palatal versus nonpalatal) at the ends of bases. Suffixal inflection, typically /-ə/ or /-iː/, is only retained for those cases where there is no change in the value for [palatal] in the coda of a base syllable, for instance with the plurals of many nouns, e.g. *lámh* 'hand' : *lámha* 'hands'.

2.3.1   Lenition

Lenition in Irish essentially involves the change of stops to fricatives; this is both a diachronic phonological process and part of the synchronic morphological process which is the concern in the present section. All stops in the language can become fricatives in an environment for lenition. In addition, /f/ lenites to zero and /s/ lenites to /h/. The only sonorant which is affected by this change is /m/, which can lenite as the language has a homorganic (voiced) fricative,

---

[11] Similar information on the morphology of Modern Irish can be gleaned from existing grammars. In English the best practical grammar is that of the Christian Brothers (1977) while the best descriptive grammar of a living dialect is de Bhaldraithe (1953) which, however, is in Irish.

namely /v/. Alveolar sonorants do not lenite. The velar nasal does not occur in base forms word-initially so the question of lenition does not arise.

2.3.2   Nasalisation

This is a process which affects consonants and not vowels to which the term usually refers in other languages. What is meant by nasalisation is that a voiced stop is changed to its nasal equivalent under certain grammatical circumstances, i.e. the feature [nasal] is set to a positive value. Consider a case like the following:

(5)   *seacht ndún* 'seven castles'

If one compares *seacht* with Latin *septem* one sees that there was originally a nasal at the end of this word which caused the following consonant of a noun to change to a homorganic nasal. With voiceless segments only the first stage of nasalisation takes place, i.e. these are voiced; contrast the items under (a) and (b) below.

(6)   a. *capall: a gcapaill* 'horse': 'their horses'
       b. *gúna: a ngúnaí* 'dress': 'their dresses'

Synchronically the rule is as follows: alter one feature in a segment. This leads to nasalisation of voiced segments, /b/ → /m/ for instance, but to voicing of voiceless segments as voice is a precondition of nasalisation. It stops here as only one change is legal. Needless to say if a word begins with a nasal anyway the nasalisation mutation has no effect.

(7)   Nasalisation

voiceless		*voiced*	*nasal*
p	→	b	
		b	→	m

Nasalisation only applies to stops; fricatives and nasals are unaffected with the exception of /f/ which nasalises to /v/ for example:

(8)   a. *fir: caint na* [v-] *bhfear* 'men': 'talk of the men'
      b. *focal: a* [v-] *bhfocail* 'word': 'their words'

/s/ to /z/ is not an option, given the absolute prohibition on voiced sibilants in Irish both in its history and its contemporary form. /x/ to /ɣ/ does not occur because word-initially /x/ is itself the result of lenition and cannot therefore form the input to a further mutation.

   Note that as certain consonants occur both independently and as the result of mutation there are instances of primary and derived segments in Irish.

(9)   a. Primary nasal   *maith*   /ma/   'good'
      b. Derived by mutation   *a mba*   /ə ma/   'their cows'

2.4   Manifestation of the initial mutations

Lenition and nasalisation are general phonological processes. Whether they are implemented depends on the segments they are applied to. The result must always be a legal segment in the language. Of course appropriate segments could have developed over time. But Irish phonology is quite conservative (it has lost dental fricatives and has no voiced sibilants and no affricates), cf. Welsh which has developed voiceless liquids. Only obstruents and the bilabial nasal /m/ are affected by lenition and nasalisation. Of the two mutations, the latter is phonetically more regular.

(10)   *Lenition*   *Nasalisation*

p, b	→	f, v	p, b	→	b, m
t, d	→	h, ɣ	t, d	→	d, n
k, g	→	x, ɣ	k, g	→	g, ŋ
f	→	0	f	→	v
s	→	h			
m	→	v			

2.4.1   Anomalies in the mutation system

Sonorants These segments undergo neither lenition nor nasalisation and so morphological categories must be recognised from the context.

(11)   a. *a rún* 'his, her, their secret'
         b. *a lámha* 'his, her, their hands'

While it is true that lenition does not affect words (i) beginning with a vowel or (ii) beginning with a cluster with an initial /s/, the pressure of morphological distinctiveness would seem to have led to the establishment of a prefix /t/ before certain noun forms. The rules are approximately as follows. /t/ is prefixed to vowel-initial nouns after the article when lenition would *not* have applied.

(12)   a.   *an t-arán* /ə taraːn/ 'the bread' (MASC, NOM)
         b. but: *an áit* /ən aːtⱼ/ 'the place' (FEM, NOM)

Certain prepositions cause this rule to be waived.

(13)   a. *an t-am*   'time',   but   *ag an am*   'at the time'
         b. *an t-im*   'butter',   but   *leis an im*   'with the butter'

Prefixation to a noun with an /s/-initial cluster only applies where there would be lenition. Note that prefix /t/ overrides lenition in cases of /s/ + V.

(14)   a. *an tsláinte*   'health'   (FEM, NOM)
         b. *an tslí*   'the way'   (FEM, NOM)
         c. *in aice an tsiopa*   'beside the shop'   (MASC, GEN)
         d. *an tseachtain*   not: *an sheachtain* 'the week'   (FEM, NOM)

Nasalisation is realised before vowels as a prefix /n/. Here it contrasts with lenition, which has no manifestation before vowels. However, the lack of lenition before a vowel-initial word is realised as *h* in the genitive of nouns and with the possessive pronoun 'her'; compare the following contrasting forms.[12]

(15)   *a aois* 'his age' : *a h-aois* 'her age' : *a n-aois* 'their age'

2.5   Base-margin alteration

Left margin alteration	(1) Lenition	(2) Nasalisation
Right margin alteration	(1) Palatalisation	(2) De-palatalisation

Base onset	*Base nucleus*	*Base coda*
C-	**-V-**	**-C**
voiceless stop	palatal	(affects any type
voiced stop	non-palatal	of consonant)
fricative		
nasal		
initial mutation with		final mutation where
manner of		consonant quality alters;
articulation affected		pairs exist for all
(rarely place)		consonants (except /h/)

The changes in the quality of the base coda do not affect the quality of preceding long vowels but do affect short vowels. These shift from a front to a back articulation or vice versa depending on the nature of the quality change of the final consonant or cluster. Furthermore, short front vowels may diphthongise to /ai/ and back short vowels to /au/ on a change of consonant quality.

(16)

Base:	*bás* 'death'	*Onset*	*Coda*
a bhás	'his death'	Lenited	Non-palatal
a bás	'her death'	Neutral	Non-palatal
a mbás	'their death'	Nasalised	Non-palatal
am a bháis	'the time of his death'	Lenited	Palatal
am a báis	'the time of her death'	Neutral	Palatal
am a mbáis	'the time of their death'	Nasalised	Palatal

---

[12] The third-person possessive pronouns represent one of the clearest cases of the original phonetic conditioning which led to the mutations. It will be remembered that the possessive pronouns have their origin in Indo-European in the genitive of personal pronouns which was used for this purpose. The reconstructed forms are as follows (Szemerényi 1989: 219): *esjo* sing masc, *esjas* sing fem, *eisom* plural. Reflexes of these can be seen for the singular in Sanskrit *asya, asyâs* and in Greek in the nonreflexive personal pronouns. In Irish for the oldest stage of the language these forms had all already been reduced to a single sound *a* /a/ (Thurneysen, 1946: 278) with lenition as a reflex of the final vowel of the masculine, prefixed *h* as a reflex of the final *-s* of the feminine and nasalisation in the plural as that of the final nasal in the original Indo-European forms.

Older loans in the language always undergo base-margin alteration as if they were native words.

(17) a. *páipéar* : *dath an pháipeír*   'paper' : 'colour of the paper'
      b. *peann* : *barr an phinn*   'pen' : 'tip of the pen'

2.5.1   Root extension and remnants of older patterns

If root extension for an inflected form of a word coincides with base-margin alteration compared with the uninflected lexical form, then this always involves a transparent extension, in effect /əx/ in Modern Irish as in the following examples:

(18) a. *cáin* : *méid na cánach*   'tax' : 'the amount of tax'
      b. *beoir* : *blas na beorach*   'beer' : 'the taste of the beer'
      c. *traein* : *uimhir na traenach*   'train' : 'the number of the train'

Base extension may trigger syncope if the phonotactic conditions are right, e.g. when an obstruent and sonorant come together.

(19)   *eochair* : *cuma na h-eochrach*   'key' : 'shape of the key'

There are remnants of a consonantal inflection (*n* or *d*) for a few nouns as in:

(20) a. *comharsa* : *iníon na*   'neighbour' : 'the neighbour's daughter'
         comharsan
      b. *cara* : *ainm an charad*   'friend' : 'name of the friend'

2.5.2   Scope of base-margin alteration

Base-margin alteration applies above all to the area of nouns and adjectives. With verbs one still has inflections, but these are often uniform for a tense and furthermore all consonant-initial verbs show lenition in the past.

The principle of base-margin alteration applies to those categories which involve a binary distinction such as nominative versus genitive. An inflectional short vowel is often retained for a third category, usually the plural.

With verbs, base-margin alteration is used to indicate the difference between present and past as the latter has lenition as its distinctive inflection. The future is irregular, very often with suppletive forms or an ending /hə/ which is added to the root. In a system where lenition is a marker of a certain tense, here the past, the absence of lenition becomes significant. Thus the lack of lenition in the present and future in Irish contrasts with the situation for past forms.

Initial mutation or the lack of it applies to all persons and both numbers in verbal paradigms. It also applies to the two main conjugational types which exist in Modern Irish. These differ in the inflections they show, but agree in the use of initial mutations. Finally note that nasalisation does not occur with independent verb forms but is frequently triggered by pre-verbal particles such as clause relativisers or a variety of adverbial forms.

(21) a. *Lenition*   Past, Imperfect, Conditional
     b. *No lenition*   Present, Future, Subjunctive

A consquence of this system of base-margin alteration is that consonants have been foregrounded in Irish phonology and vowels downplayed accordingly. For the present-day language one can say that the vowel-length difference is still systemically relevant, but among short vowels there is really only a binary difference between a front vowel [ɪ] or [ɛ] governed by a following palatal consonant and a low-back vowel [a] or [ʊ] governed by a following nonpalatal (velarised) consonant.

(22) a. *fliuch* [fʲlʲʌx]   'wet'   *níos fliche* [fʲlʲɪçə] 'wetter'
     b. *muc*   [mʌk]   'pig'   *muice*   [mɪkʲə]   'pig'-GEN

3   Irish developments in a broader perspective

When viewed cross-linguistically one sees that the morphology of Irish is unique in its combination of features. While palatalisation/de-palatalisation is a common axis along which to differentiate sounds (Bhat 1978), the initial changes are very seldom found with a grammatical function (Andersen 1986).

Palatalisation is a natural assimilation phenomenon whereby the feature of highness spreads from a vowel to a consonant, usually a preceding one. It establishes itself most easily with coronal sonorants and fricatives, probably because the secondary articulation is most easily perceived with these segments: witness the many palatal sonorants in Romance languages and the common distinction between /s/ and /ʃ/ in many languages. The functionalisation of palatalisation is not that uncommon: within Indo-European it is found on a wide scale in Celtic, Slavic and Indo-Iranian. With those languages in which it attains a grammatical function it is usual to find a secondary palatalisation of labials with tense lips and a brief [j] on release of the labial as the phonetic correlates of phonological palatalisation, cf. Irish and Russian (Jones and Ward 1969).

The initial mutations are cross-linguistically much rarer. Those languages which are known to have alterations of word-initial segments that have attained a grammatical function are few and far between. Apart from Celtic, there is Fula (possibly with Serer), both West Atlantic languages spoken mostly in Nigeria and Ghana (Sapir 1971; Anderson 1976), and there is Nivkh (formerly called Gilyak), a language isolate in the Paleosiberian group spoken along the lower reaches of the Amur river and on part of Sakhalin Island (Panfilov 1962–5; Jakobson 1971b). Berber is a language (or group, depending on the interpretation of internal differences) in which there is an alternation at the beginning of nouns depending on syntactic contexts (what is called *free* and *annexed* in the relevant literature, see Basset 1952). There are also instances of initial mutation recorded for Burmese and several Oceanic languages (Terry Crowley, personal communication).

The functionalisation of initial mutation implies that it has taken over from other grammatical devices which have been lost or at least defunctionalised in a language. The pre-stage to this state can be seen in several dialects/languages. For instance, the so-called *gorgia toscana* in Tuscan Italian comprises fricativisation and gemination of initial segments of a noun depending on the original form of a preceding grammatical word. Thus the feminine article *la* causes fricativisation (*la casa* /la xasa/) and the preposition *a* (< Latin *ad*) triggers gemination (*a porta* /a pporta/< Latin *ad portam*) (Lepschy and Lepschy 1986). Here one can see what a mutational system looks like embryonically. In order for the functionalisation of initial mutation to be grammatically adequate at least three distinctions must be possible.

(23)   *Irish*   *Tuscan Italian*
    a. zero mutation
    b. mutation 1   lenition   lenition
    c. mutation 2   nasalisation   gemination

A language may have more than three distinctions, for instance Welsh divides lenition into (i) fricativisation and (ii) stop voicing and has nasalisation anyway, this resulting in three mutations, that is, with zero mutation, a four-way system of distinctions.

For initial mutations to become the dominant means of indicating grammatical categories in a language a minimum of three distinctions is necessary, which is probably why systems with only two distinctions, say no change and initial fricativisation, simply do not qualify as candidates for typological reorientation. Of course a three-way distinction is a necessary, but by no means a sufficient, condition for functionalisation. Here a look at the phenomenon of consonant gradation in Finnish is fruitful. There are four types, divided into two groups: gradation proper and assimilation. These consist of the following processes: (1) simplification, (2) voicing and fricativisation, (3) vocalisation. But the gradation occurs word-internally in Finnish. It is triggered by a closed short syllable which leads to the phonetic reduction of the consonants preceding it. Such a short syllable is typically represented by an inflection, such as the genitive, cf.

(24)   *jalka* 'foot' : *jalan* 'foot'-GEN

Now the agglutinative suffixes of Finnish are of course still present as opposed to Estonian which, due to the loss of final inflections, has opacified gradation as a sychronic process. The upshot of this is that there is no immediate motivation to functionalise gradation in Finnish and hence its application is not exceptionless. For instance, not all loanwords undergo gradation, cf.

(25)   *auto* 'car' : *auton* 'car'-GEN and not **audon*

Finnish consonant gradation is not word-initial and depends on syllable structure rather than on external sandhi, as does Celtic mutation. But it has enough
distinctions for functionalisation to be effective if there was decay of the inflectional suffixes. The great imponderable of whether a language would go down
that path remains, even if it had the requisite means to do so.

Lastly, a few remarks on the relationship of morphological to syntactic typology are called for. The realignment of morphology which has been the topic
of this chapter took place at roughly the same time (during the immediately
pre-Old Irish period) when the syntax of Irish moved from an inherited SOV
basic word order with pre-specification (as is largely attested in Continental
Celtic) to the reverse of this, namely VSO and consistent post-specification for
nominal dyads (noun plus genitive, noun plus adjective, etc.). There are various
views on this (Hickey 2002a), from a language-internal one which depends
on topicalisation, the operation of Wackernagel's Law and the drag of second-
place clitics on verbs to the front of the sentence, to an external account which
appeals to a pre-Celtic substrate which was already VSO and post-specifying
(the Afro-Asiatic substratum hypothesis). The relative merits of these views
are in the opinion of the present author irrelevant to the morphology of Irish.
The changes in the latter were effected to deal with gender, case and number
marking with nouns and tense marking with verbs and so were independent of
any forces operative in the repositioning of clause constituents, the domain of
syntactic typology.

4   Conclusion

The rise of a system of initial mutation for the indication of grammatical categories is statistically unusual across the world's languages. However, within
the context of developments in early Celtic, it can be seen as something which
is fairly natural. The phonetic blurring, which led to the demise of inherited inflections, was something which not only affected the ends of words but also led
to a reduction of the beginning of words. This originally subphonemic process
came to be interpreted by language learners as systemic so that the indication
of grammatical categories switched from suffixal inflection to initial mutation.
This is a good case of reanalysis during first-language acquisition which, when
viewed externally, might be interpreted as a case of typological repair, but
which, from the speaker perspective, shows how language learners can come
to interpret cues about the system of the language they are acquiring, leading
to a set of principles different from those determined by previous generations.
There are a number of theoretical issues which result from this scenario, the

most important of which concerns whether there was a period of overlap during which one or more generations had both systems in parallel favouring the new one of initial mutation and backgrounding the older one of suffixal inflection.

REFERENCES

Ahlqvist, Anders. 1980. 'On word in Irish', in Traugott et al. (eds.), 107–13.
Andersen, Henning. 1986. *Sandhi phenomena in the languages of Europe*. Berlin: de Gruyter.
Anderson, Stephen. 1976. 'On the description of consonant gradation in Fula', *Studies in African Linguistics* 7: 93–136.
Basset, André. 1952. *La langue berbère*. Oxford.
Bhat, D. N. S. 1978. 'A general study of palatalization', in Greenberg (ed.), 47–92.
Christian Brothers. 1977. *New Irish grammar*. Dublin: Fallons.
Croft, William. 1995. 'Modern syntactic typology', in Shibatani and Bynon (eds.), 85–144.
Croft, William. 2000. *Explaining language change: an evolutionary approach*. London: Longman.
De Bhaldraithe, Tomás. 1953. *Gaeilge Chois Fhairrge. An deilbhíocht* [The Irish of Cois Fhairrge (Co. Galway). The morphology]. Dublin: Dublin Institute for Advanced Studies.
Feuth, Els. 1983. 'Gemination: an Old Irish mutation rule?', *Ériu* 34: 143–56.
Fisiak, Jacek (ed.). 1996. *Linguistic typology and reconstruction*. Berlin: Mouton de Gruyter.
Greenberg, Joseph. 1978. *Universals of human language*. 4 vols. Stanford University Press.
Greene, David. 1956. 'Gemination', *Celtica* 3: 284–9.
Harris, Alice C. and Lyle Campbell. 1995. *Historical syntax in cross-linguistic perspective*. Cambridge University Press.
Hickey, Raymond. 1995. 'Early contact and parallels between English and Celtic', *Vienna English Working Papers* 4.2: 87–119.
Hickey, Raymond. 1996. 'Sound change and typological shift: initial mutation in Celtic', in Fisiak (ed.), 133–82.
Hickey, Raymond. 2002a. 'Internal and external forces again: changes in word order in Old English and Old Irish', in Hickey (ed.), 261–83.
Hickey, Raymond (ed.). 2002b. *Collecting views on language change: a donation to Roger Lass on his 65th birthday*. (Special issue of *Language Sciences*, 2002:1).
Hickey, Raymond and Stanisław Puppel (eds.). 1997. *Language history and linguistic modelling: a festschrift for Jacek Fisiak on his 60th birthday*. Berlin: Mouton de Gruyter.
Hopper, Paul and Elizabeth Closs Traugott. 1993. *Grammaticalization*. Cambridge University Press.
Jackson, Kenneth H. 1953. *Language and history in early Britain*. Edinburgh University Press.
Jakobson, Roman. 1971a. *Selected writings*, vol. 2: *Word and language*. The Hague: Mouton.

Jakobson, Roman. 1971b. 'Notes on Gilyak', in Jakobson, 72–97.

Jones, Daniel and Denis Ward. 1969. *The phonetics of Russian.* Cambridge University Press.

Karlsson, Fred. 1979. *Finsk grammatik,* 2nd edition. Helsinki: Suomalaisen Kirjallisuuden Seura.

Lehmann, Winfred P. 1992. *Historical linguistics,* 3rd edition. London: Routledge.

Lepschy, Giulio and Anna Lepschy. 1986. *Die italienische Sprache.* German translation. Tübingen: Narr.

Lewis, Henry and Holger Pedersen. 1937. *A concise comparative Celtic grammar.* Göttingen: Vandenhoeck und Ruprecht.

Martinet, André. 1952. 'Celtic lenition and Western Romance consonants', *Language* 28: 192–217.

Nichols, Johanna. 1992. *Language diversity through space and time.* Chicago University Press.

Ó Baoill, Dónall (ed.). 1979. *Papers in Celtic phonology.* Coleraine: New University of Ulster.

Ó Cuív, Brian. 1986. 'Sandhi phenomena in Irish', in Andersen (ed.), 395–414.

O'Rahilly, Thomas F. 1926. 'Notes on Middle Irish pronunciation', *Hermathena* 44: 152–95.

Panfilov, V. Z. 1962–5. *Grammatika nivxskogo jazyka* [A grammar of the Nivkh language]. 2 vols. Moscow.

Pedersen, Holger. 1897. *Aspirationen i irsk* [Aspiration (lenition) in Irish]. Copenhagen: Spirgatis.

Pedersen, Holger. 1909–13. *Vergleichende Grammatik der keltischen Sprachen.* Göttingen: Vandenhoeck und Ruprecht.

Salmons, Josephs C. 1992. *Accentual change and language contact: comparative survey and a case study of early Northern Europe.* Stanford University Press.

Sapir, J. David. 1971. 'West Atlantic: an inventory of the languages, their noun class systems, and consonant alternations', in Sebeok (ed.), 45–112.

Sebeok, Thomas A. (ed.). 1971. *Current trends in linguistics,* vol. 7: *Linguistics in Sub-Saharan Africa.* The Hague: Mouton.

Shibatani, Masayoshi and Theodora Bynon (eds.). 1995. *Approaches to language typology.* Oxford: Clarendon Press.

Szemerényi, Oswald. 1989. *Einführung in die vergleichende Sprachwissenschaft,* 3rd edition. Darmstadt: Wissenschaftliche Buchgesellschaft.

Ternes, Elmar. 1977. 'Konsonantische Anlautveränderungen in den keltischen und romanischen Sprachen', *Romanistisches Jahrbuch* 28: 19–53.

Thurneysen, Rudolf. 1946. *A grammar of Old Irish.* Dublin: Dublin Institute for Advanced Studies.

Traugott, Elizabeth et al. (eds.). 1980. *Papers from the 4th International Conference on Historical Linguistics.* Amsterdam: John Benjamins.

Vennemann, gen. Nierfeld, Theo. 1997. 'Some West Indo-European words of uncertain origin', in Hickey and Puppel (eds.), 879–910.

Wagner, Heinrich. 1979 [1959]. *Gaeilge Theilinn* [The Irish of Teilinn (Co. Donegal)], 2nd edition. Dublin: Dublin Institute for Advanced Studies.

Watkins, Calvert. 1963. 'Preliminaries to a historical and comparative reconstruction of the Old Irish verb', *Celtica* 6: 1–49.

Index

This index contains references to scholars, languages and subjects related to the theme of the present book. Where a subject is essentially that of an entire chapter, no references are included here. For instance, the occurrences of 'metaphor' in the chapter by Jean Aitchison have not been entered into this index as the entire chapter deals with this subject. References to subjects which do not form the central theme of a chapter, as reflected in the title, are of course included.